The Practice of Writing

SECOND EDITION

The Practice of Writing

SECOND EDITION

ROBERT SCHOLES
Brown University

NANCY R. COMLEY
Queens College, CUNY

ST. MARTIN'S PRESS   NEW YORK

For information, write St. Martin's Press, Inc.
175 Fifth Avenue
New York, NY 10010

cover design: Melissa Tardiff
cover art: Jean-Pierre Desclozeaux

ISBN: 0-312-63546-X

ACKNOWLEDGMENTS

Bertrand Russell, "Forms of Power" from POWER. Copyright 1975 by
George Allen & Unwin (Publishers) Ltd. By permission of George Allen
& Unwin (Publishers) Ltd.
C. G. Hanzlicek, "Elegy for Samuel Herrera, My Student Killed in a Tac-
tical Squad Stakeout" from CALLING THE DEAD © 1982. By per-
mission of Carnegie-Mellon Press.
Mary Ellen Reilly and Leon F. Bouvier, "Tables on Women—Education,
Employment, Income," reprinted with permission from "Women in
American Society," by Mary Ellen Reilly and Leon F. Bouvier. From
Population Profiles. Unit is copyrighted by the Center for Information on
America, Washington, CT.
Erwin D. Canham, "Mayor Daley's Troops," and Saville R. Davis, "A
Night of Raging Protest," reprinted by permission of *The Christian Science
Monitor*.

Acknowledgments and copyrights continue at the back of the book on pages
353–355, which constitute an extension of the copyright page.

TO OUR STUDENTS,
who have taught us so much

Only where love and need are one,
And the work is play for mortal stakes,
Is the deed ever really done
For Heaven and the future's sakes.

ROBERT FROST

Give a man a mask and he will tell you the truth.

OSCAR WILDE

First question: who is speaking? Who, among the totality of speaking individuals, is accorded the right to use this sort of language? Who is qualified to do so? Who derives from it his own special quality, his prestige, and from whom, in return, does he receive if not the assurance, at least the presumption that what he says is true? What is the status of the individuals who—alone—have the right, sanctioned by law or tradition, juridically defined or spontaneously accepted, to proffer such a discourse?

MICHEL FOUCAULT

In our society, and probably in all others, capacity to bring off an activity as one wants to—ordinarily defined as the possession of skills—is very often developed through a kind of utilitarian make-believe. The purpose of this practicing is to give the neophyte experience in performing under conditions in which (it is felt) no actual engagement with the world is allowed, events having been "decoupled" from their usual embedment in consequentiality. Presumably muffing or failure can occur both economically and instructively. What one has here are dry runs, trial sessions, run-throughs—in short, "practicings."

ERVING GOFFMAN

A man knowing little or nothing of medical science could not be a good surgeon, but excellence at surgery is not the same thing as knowledge of medical science; nor is it a simple product of it. The surgeon must indeed have learned from instruction, or by his own inductions and observations, a great number of truths; but he must also have learned by practice a great number of aptitudes. Even where efficient practice is the deliberate application of considered prescriptions, the intelligence involved in putting the prescriptions into practice is not identical with that involved in intellectually grasping the prescriptions. There is no contradiction, or even paradox, in describing someone as bad at practising what he is good at preaching. There have been thoughtful and original literary critics who have formulated admirable canons of prose style in execrable prose. There have been others who have employed brilliant English in the expression of the silliest theories of what constitutes good writing.

GILBERT RYLE

Practice, practice. Put your hope in that.

W. S. MERWIN

PREFACE

The way to write better is to write more—but not alone, not aimlessly, not without guidance and encouragement. This text is designed to facilitate the tasks of those engaged in learning and teaching about writing. It has been composed by two teachers who are themselves committed to writing as both a field of study and an occupation.

Our philosophy of composition is implicit in the epigraphs we have chosen for our book. As Frost says about all deeds, writing must be work *and* play, both serious *and* joyful, if it is to be done well. Any text in writing, then, must preserve the joy of composition for those who use it, even while providing the work that needs to be done.

We also believe, with Wilde, in the usefulness of masks. Nowhere in all their work are students so vulnerable as in their writing classes. Nowhere do they feel their personalities, their very selves, so open to criticism of a very painful sort. If the style is the person, to criticize the style is to wound the individual behind it. Many of our assignments are designed to free students from the burden of self by offering them personae, voices, and roles already chosen for their suitability to a given form of writing. The true self of a writer must be given space to grow in and should be protected while growing.

There is a public dimension to writing, as well. As Michel Foucault reminds us, certain forms of writing accompany certain social, economic, and political roles. In a society that encourages self-development and economic mobility, the skills of language—and foremost among them, writing—are the major path to advancement, whether personal, professional, or social. The language games and writing exercises presented here must be undertaken with the awareness that each individual's ability to develop and function socially will depend partly on the compositional skills of that individual. Our play at writing is for "mortal stakes" indeed.

Yet it is still play—what Goffman calls "utilitarian make-believe." In writing classes students are "neophytes" engaged in "dry runs, trial sessions . . . 'practicings'." As Gilbert Ryle points out, we learn some things by instruction, but the actual doing of anything must be learned by practice. For that reason we have provided models for analysis and discussion, short exercises for the classroom, and a range of longer assignments for homework papers. We take our motto from W. S. Merwin: "Practice, practice. Put your hope in that."

In preparing this second edition, we consulted a hundred teachers who had used the first edition, to see what they had used and what they had omitted, what had worked well and what had been less successful. We accepted their advice and cut ruthlessly all but the most effective material from the first edition before starting to compose the second. We also made a number of changes to produce a stronger and more useful text.

We increased the number of readings, so that virtually every writing assignment is based on a text that is to be used either as a model or as a point of departure for the student's own writing. We took steps throughout the book to draw attention to the process of writing and to show how certain forms of writing are related to particular aspects of the writing process: the form of reflection to revision, for instance. We also reflected on our own writing and, as a result, revised our first two chapters to make them into a single more readable chapter—and to devote more attention to the writing process.

The most important changes to the chapters on the various forms of writing are as follows. We have greatly strengthened the chapter on argumentation at every point: a longer introduction, some excellent new readings, and more varied writing assignments. We have also rearranged the chapters on topic-oriented forms in order to put argumentation directly before analysis and synthesis. In the analysis chapter we have emphasized the analysis of texts, and to the synthesis chapter we have added extensive new materials for synthetic projects.

Because of their success in the first edition, we have added further material based on advertising, art, photography, and literature, as well as the more expository and argumentative kinds of writing. These readings are intended to provide interesting texts for class discussions as well as to function as bases for written assignments. (There is, in fact, enough reading material here so that a separate collection of readings is unnecessary.) We have frequently provided questions to help organize class discussions of the readings. In the questions we have tried to treat the readings as a writing instructor (as opposed to a literature instructor) must; that is, to emphasize *how* the text has been composed rather than *what* it means. You will find here variety, interest, and a clear progression from the more personal and subjective to the more impersonal and objective forms of writing.

In our preface to the first edition, we thanked those who field-tested the book and who, along with our reviewers, gave us the invaluable advice and criticism that helped to shape *The Practice of Writing*. We would like to thank them again and to add to that group all those instructors who used *Practice* and sent us their comments and suggestions for the second edition: Susan McDermott (Junior College of Albany); Ann Parrish, Dennis Radford (Atlantic Union College); Pamela Hardman (Baldwin-Wallace College); Janice Broder (Brandeis University); Frederick Lang (Brooklyn College, CUNY); Rosemary Hake (California State University—Los Angeles); Clark Mayo (California State University—San Bernardino); William Seibenschuh (Case Western Reserve University); Ann K. Jordan (Clermont College); Michele Barale, Lynn L. Merrill, Gloria Rittenhouse (University of Colorado—Boulder); John Bethune, R. T. Farrell, Michael Grillo, Judith May, Beth Schwartz (Cornell University); Ann Amsler, Susan Jenkins, Ian Johns, George Miller (University of Delaware); Jonathan Cross (Emerson College); John Leavey, Gregory Ulmer (University of Florida); Walter Blue (Hamline University); Earl P. Murphy (Harris-Stowe State College); Roger Ferrand (Hobart and William Smith College); Gary Williams (University of Idaho—Moscow); Diane M. Calhoun-French, Alice A. Cleveland (Jefferson Community College); Irving Warner (Kodiak Community College); Susan L. Blake (Lafayette College); E. A. James (Lehigh University); Joyce Freundlich (Livingston College); Gwen Snodgrass, Julie Sosnin (University of Louisville); Catherine Blair (Lycoming College); Joseph Popson (Macon Junior College); Patricia Burnes, Alison Gooding, Paul M. Puccio (University of Maine—Orono); John McKernan (Marshall University); Robert E. Hosmer, Jr. (University of Massachusetts); John G. Parks (Miami University); A. C. Goodson (Michigan State University); Edward Cooper (Mira Costa College); Leslie Jean Campbell, Michael P. Dean, Natalie Schroeder, Ronald A. Schroeder (University of Mississippi); Sharon Kelly (University of Nebraska); Rick A. Eden (University of New Mexico—Albuquerque); Ronald A. Bosco, Donald Stauffer (State University of New York—Albany); Janice Doan (State University of New York—Buffalo); James Olney (North Carolina Central University); E. Guiney Sandvick (North Hennepin Community College); Antoinette Azar, Renu Bhargava, Susan Crowl, Gary Davis, Jane Denbow, David Fritts, Naton D. Leslie, Mark Rollins, John D. Tatter, Curtis A. Yehnert, Joan E. Zook, John Zubrickey (Ohio University—Athens); Rebecca Martin (Pace University—Pleasantville); Jeffrey A. Kuvnit (Pace University—White Plains); Arlen J. Hansen (University of the Pacific); Sansa Kalt, Beverley Moore, Carol A. Nowotny-Young, Stanley P. Witt (Pima County Community College); Mary Hall (University of Pittsburgh); Ellen Summers (C. W. Post Center—Long Island University); Judith Mitchell, Michele Moragne, Elaine Palm, John Roche (Rhode Island College); Cheryl Barnes (Russell Sage College); Neal Tolchin (Rutgers University); Lois Greene Stone (St. John Fisher College); Tonita H. Rowden, Yovanne S. Terpening (San Diego State University); Linda Cravens, Rhonda Hanisch, Craig Volk, Nancy T. Zuercher (University of South Dakota); Catherine Calloway, Kathryn Kersker, Mark G. Newton, Gianna Russo (University of South Florida); Mimi Schwartz (Stockton State College); Bonnie Dickinson, Thora Thurn (Texas Christian College); Jean E. Jost (Virginia Commonwealth University); Elizabeth S. Byers, Constance Gefvert, Robert Siegle, Jane Bryan Vance (Virginia Polytechnic Institute and State University); Ruth Ray (Wayne State University); Stephen Sossaman (Westfield State College); Michael North (College of William and Mary); Frank Hubbard (University of Wisconsin—Milwaukee); James Ayer (Worcester State College); Norman Finkelstein (Xavier University). Special thanks go to our colleagues and students at Brown University, the University of Oklahoma, and Queens College of the City University of New York.

We continue to be grateful for our creative and diligent editors: Thomas Broadbent, who "discovered" us and whose encouragement sustained us; and Nancy Perry, Mark Gallaher, and the tireless and enthusiastic staff of St. Martin's Press who made the work of revision a pleasure.

R.S./N.R.C.

A NOTE ON THE USE OF THIS TEXT

This book is devoted to the *practice* of writing. It presents more opportunities for writing—"practices," as we call them—than anything else. The book also contains numerous "readings." This is so because we believe that, just as talking is based on listening, and drawing is based on looking, writing is based on reading. The readings in this book are not meant to be put upon pedestals and admired, however admirable they may be. They are there to be worked with and responded to—in writing. They are there to be transformed, imitated, analyzed, argued with, and incorporated into new writing by the students who use this book.

Actually, there is more material here than anyone could possibly use in a single quarter or semester. The reason for this abundance is to provide instructors with options, choices, flexibility. After the first chapter, which is introductory, the writing opportunities move from the personal to the more impersonal and academic. The weight of the book, however, falls upon the more academic or scholastic kinds of writings, the forms and processes required for college courses. Thus, the last four chapters move from classification and argument to the kinds of analytic and synthetic writing required in research papers.

Obviously, we think that work in all the forms of writing is useful, or we would not have included them all in the book. But we understand also that there are many reasons why an instructor may wish to touch only lightly on the materials in Parts Two and Three, in order to concentrate heavily on Part Four. The book is designed to allow for this emphasis. There is, in fact, more material in every part than would be needed if all the parts were emphasized equally. The instructor will find that this text will support any emphasis that he or she chooses to make, though we have anticipated an emphasis on argument, analysis, and synthesis, providing the greatest depth in those chapters.

Within each chapter we present a particular form of writing, beginning with the most basic kinds of practice and moving toward more extended and demanding assignments. Using the chapter introduction, the first reading/practice set, and one further set will allow an instructor to treat a particular chapter without lingering over it for too long; there is enough variety so that the second assignment can be chosen to suit the interests and capabilities of a given class.

Although we think the order in which we present the forms of writing in this book makes sense, we have tried not to be dogmatic. The forms of writing may in fact be covered in any order, so long as the arrangement leads to synthesis at the end. In the chapter on synthesis, we have provided sufficient material so that library research is not necessary, but many of the suggested assignments there can be expanded and enriched by library work if the instructor desires it.

It is our conviction that writing is a form of thought and that thinking is a pleasurable activity. Have fun.

CONTENTS

PART ONE   WRITING AS A HUMAN ACT

1   Practicing Writing: Situation, Form, Process   *2*

Communication and Language   *2*
Speaking and Writing   *3*
Practice:
    An Experience in Your Life   *4*
Practice:
    An Experience in Someone Else's Life   *5*
The Writing Situation   *6*
The Forms of Writing   *8*
Reading and Practice   *12*
Practice and Confidence   *14*
The Act of Writing: Prewriting, Drafting, Revising   *15*
The Writer as Role-Player   *20*
Practice:
    Bad Situation at School   *21*
Practice:
    You Met Somebody . . .   *23*

PART TWO   WRITER-ORIENTED FORMS

2   Expression: Your Self as Subject   *26*

Reading:
    The Open-Ended Writing Process   *27*
        Peter Elbow, from *Writing With Power*   *27*
Practice:
    Open-Ended Writing   *28*
Reading:
    Expression as Transformation   *28*
        Peter Handke, from ''Self-Accusations''   *29*

Practice:
    Transformations *29*
Reading:
    Expression Through Association *30*
        W. H. Gass, from *On Being Blue* *30*
Practice:
    On Being _____ *31*
Reading:
    Expression of Mood *32*
        "Mid-August at Sourdough Mountain
          Lookout"—Gary Snyder *32*
        Sylvia Plath, from *The Bell Jar* *33*
Practice:
    Mood in a Place *34*
Reading:
    Ideas about the Telephone *34*
        Federico Fellini, from *Fellini on Fellini* *34*
        Roland Barthes, from *A Lover's Discourse* *35*
Practice:
    Ideas about a Common Object *36*
Reading:
    Interpreting Character *37*
        Ernest Hemingway, "Cat in the Rain" *37*
Practice:
    Expression Through Role-Playing *40*

3   Reflection: Your Self as Object *41*

Reading:
    Your Own Expressive Writing *42*
Practice:
    Reflection as Revision *43*
Reading:
    School Days Revisited *43*
        Margaret Mead, from *Blackberry Winter* *43*
        Russell Baker, from *Growing Up* *45*
Practice:
    Reflection on Your School Days *47*
Reading:
    An Unreflective Poem? *48*
        "We Real Cool"—Gwendolyn Brooks *48*
Practice:
    Reflecting on the Golden Shovel *49*

Reading:
   Looking at Pictures   *49*
       ''Looking At Pictures To Be Put Away''—
          Gary Snyder   *50*
       Roland Barthes, ''Looking For My Mother''   *50*
Practice:
   Reflecting on a Photograph   *51*
Reading:
   From Thing to Thought   *53*
       Isak Dinesen, ''The Iguana''   *53*
Practice:
   Reflecting on Experience   *54*

PART THREE   READER-ORIENTED FORMS

4   Direction: Guiding Your Reader   *58*

Reading:
   Direction Through the Ages   *60*
       Theophilus, ''On Carving Crystal''   *60*
       Benjamin Franklin, ''How to Make a Lightning
          Rod''   *61*
       Diana Nyad and Candace Lyle Hogan, ''The Ninety
          Second Test''   *61*
Practice:
   How to Make or Do Something   *63*
Reading:
   The Art of Eating Spaghetti   *64*
Practice:
   The Art of Eating _____   *64*
Reading:
   The Absent-Minded Writer   *65*
       Ashley Moonstone, from ''How I Write''   *65*
Practice:
   Directing the Absent-Minded Lecturer   *65*
Reading:
   The Unassembled Kiddy-Car   *66*
Practice:
   Assembling Arnold's Kiddy-Car   *67*
Reading:
   Pseudodirection   *67*
       W. S. Merwin, ''Unchopping a Tree''   *68*

Practice:
  Reversing the Irreversible   *70*

5   Persuasion: Moving Your Reader   *71*

Reading:
  Persuasion in Advertising   *72*
    Fly-Tox Advertisement, 1926   *72*
Practice:
  The Ghastly Resort Hotel   *75*
Reading:
  Reaching a Different Audience   *77*
    The Marlboro Man, 1954   *78*
Practice:
  Changing the Persuasive Pattern   *79*
Reading:
  Hemingway on Ballantine Ale   *79*
Practice:
  Your Favorite Celebrity on _____   *81*
Reading:
  Political Persuasion   *81*
    Franklin D. Roosevelt, ''First Inaugural Address''   *82*
Practice:
  The Enemy of the People   *87*
Practice:
  The Difficult Campaign Speech   *88*
Reading:
  The Job Letter and Résumé   *89*
    The Résumé   *89*
    The Letter   *91*
Practice:
  The Serious Job Letter   *93*
Practice:
  The Not-So-Serious Job Letter   *97*

PART FOUR   TOPIC-ORIENTED FORMS

6   Narration: Organizing Time   *100*

Reading:
  Cartoon as Narrative   *101*
    George Booth, ''Ip Gissa Gul''   *102*
Practice:
  From Cartoon to Written Narrative   *102*

Reading:
   Time and Tense   *103*
         Ambrose Bierce, from ''An Occurrence at Owl Creek
         Bridge''   *103*
Practice:
   The Management of Tense   *104*
Reading:
   A Familiar Process   *104*
         E. B. White, from ''Farewell, My Lovely''   *105*
Practice:
   Narrating a Familiar Process   *105*
Reading:
   Natural Process   *106*
         George Stewart, ''The Abandoned City'' and
         ''The Empty Park'' (from *Earth Abides*)   *106*
Practice:
   Narrating a Natural Process   *107*
Reading:
   The Process of a Day   *108*
         Margaret Mead, ''A Day in Samoa''   *108*
Practice:
   Process Narrative: A Day in _____   *112*
Reading:
   Narrating an Event   *112*
         Julio Cortázar, ''Simulacra''   *112*
Practice:
   Suppose Your Family Built a _____   *116*
Reading and Practice:
   The Life of Stephen Crane   *117*
Practice:
   The Life of Yourself   *124*

7 Description: Organizing Space   *125*

Reading:
   Hogarth's ''Noon'' Described   *126*
Practice:
   Describing a Hogarth Street Scene   *129*
Reading:
   Point of View in Description   *129*
         George Orwell, ''A Room'' (from *The Road to Wigan
         Pier*)   *131*
         James Joyce, ''A Restaurant'' (from *Ulysses*)   *131*
         Charles Dickens, ''A Town'' (from *Hard Times*)   *132*
         Willa Cather, ''Fields'' (from *O Pioneers!*)   *132*

Practice:
    Organizing a Space   *133*
Reading:
    A Place with a History   *134*
        Eudora Welty, ''The Natchez Trace''   *134*
Practice:
    Describing a Place with a History   *137*
Reading:
    A Critic Describes a Face   *138*
        James Agee, ''Buster Keaton''   *138*
Practice:
    Describing a Famous Face   *140*
Reading:
    ''La Gioconda''   *140*
        Walter Pater, from *The Renaissance*   *141*
Practice:
    ''Il Giocondo''   *142*

8   Classification: Organizing Data   *144*

Reading:
    Social Groups in a Town   *146*
        Vance Packard, from *A Nation of Strangers*   *147*
Practice:
    Social Groups in a Place That You Know   *148*
Reading:
    Classifying Commercials   *148*
        John W. Wright, from ''TV Commercials That Move the
           Merchandise''   *148*
Practice:
    The Class of Full-Page Ads   *153*
Reading:
    The Student Body   *154*
        Robert and Helen Lynd, from *Middletown*   *154*
Practice:
    Your Student Body   *157*
Practice:
    People in a Particular Place   *158*
Reading:
    Classifying Forms of Power   *158*
        Bertrand Russell, from *Power*   *159*
Practice:
    From Abstract to Concrete   *160*
Practice:
    Power in an Institution You Know   *160*

9 Argumentation: Presenting a Thesis *162*

Reading:
> An Argument About Persuasion   *165*
>> Plato, from "Gorgias"   *165*

Practice:
> A Dialogue on Advertising   *168*

Reading:
> A Paleontologist Responds to Creation Science   *169*
>> Stephen Jay Gould, "Evolution as Fact and Theory"   *170*

Practice:
> Reconstructing Gould's Argument   *177*

Reading:
> A Feminist Discusses Women and Names   *178*
>> Dale Spender, from *Man-Made Language*   *178*

Practice:
> Arguing About Men and Women   *183*

Reading:
> A Politician Argues About Slavery   *184*
>> Abraham Lincoln, from "Speech at Cooper Union, New York"   *184*

Practice:
> Reconstructing Lincoln's Argument   *190*

Practice:
> Arguing from Statistics—Baseball   *191*

Practice:
> Women—Education, Employment, Income   *200*

Reading:
> Two Essays on Punishment of Crimes   *206*
>> Karl Menninger, "The Crime of Punishment"   *206*
>> C. S. Lewis, "The Humanitarian Theory of Punishment"   *213*

Practice:
> Arguing a Hypothetical Case of Punishment or Treatment of a Convicted Criminal   *220*

10 Analysis: Taking Things Apart *222*

Reading:
> Comparison and Contrast   *223*
>> Stephen Crane, "The Last of the Mohicans"   *223*

Practice:
> Analysis of an Analysis   *225*

Practice:
  Myth and Reality *226*
Reading and Practice:
  · Two Poets Look at a Painting *226*
      ''Musée des Beaux Arts''—W. H. Auden *228*
      ''Landscape with the Fall of Icarus''—
        William Carlos Wiliams *230*
Reading:
  Analyzing an Advertisement *231*
      Monica Weimersheimer, ''Analysis of a Manhattan Shirt
        Advertisement'' *231*
Practice:
  Analyzing a Full-Page Advertisement *234*
Reading:
  A Critic Looks at Advertising *234*
      John Berger, from *Ways of Seeing* *234*
Practice:
  Images of Women in Advertising *236*

11   Synthesis: Putting Things Together   *245*

Reading and Practice:
  On the Relationship Between Pictures and Captions *246*
Reading and Practice:
  Working People *255*
      Research: The Interview *255*
      Studs Terkel, from *Working* *256*
      Suzanne Seed, from *Saturday's Child* *258*
      Colin Henfrey, from *Manscapes* *259*
      Barbara Ehrenreich, from ''Is Success Dangerous to
        Your Health?'' *259*
      From interviews by students at the University of
        Oklahoma *260*
Reading:
  Objective Journalism *264*
      Tom Wicker, from *On Press* *264*
Practice:
  Objective and Subjective Reporting *267*
      Erwin D. Canham, from *The Christian Science Monitor* *268*
      Lewis Chester, Godfrey Hodgson, Bruce Page, from
        An American Melodrama *270*
      Norman Mailer, from *Miami and the Siege of Chicago* *271*
      J. Anthony Lukas, from *The New York Times* *278*
      Saville R. Davis, from *The Christian Science Monitor* *283*
      Jack Gould, from *The New York Times* *289*

R. W. Apple, Jr., from *The New York Times*   290

Reading:

The Western: Theory and Practice   *292*

John Cawelti, from *The Six-Gun Mystique*   *293*

Stephen Crane, ''The Bride Comes to Yellow Sky''   *307*

Stephen Crane, ''The Blue Hotel''   *317*

Practice:

Stephen Crane and the Western Formula   *341*

Practice:

Crane: The Man and the Stories   *342*

Reading and Practice:

The Elegy   *342*

''On My First Son''—Ben Jonson   *343*

''In Memory of My Grandchild Elizabeth Bradstreet . . .''
—Anne Bradstreet   *344*

From ''*In Memoriam* A. H. H.''—Alfred, Lord
Tennyson   *344*

''To an Athlete Dying Young''—A. E. Housman   *345*

''Bells for John Whiteside's Daughter''—John Crowe
Ransom   *346*

''A Refusal to Mourn the Death, by Fire, of a Child
in London''—Dylan Thomas   *346*

''Elegy for Jane''—Theodore Roethke   *348*

''Ricky''—Philip Levine   *348*

''Elegy for Samuel Herrera, . . .''—
C. G. Hanzlicek   *351*

Index   *356*

PART ONE

WRITING AS A HUMAN ACT

1 Practicing Writing: Situation, Form, Process

Communication and Language

Hand most human beings a baby and they will make faces at it. Why do they do that? Why do human beings talk to cats and dogs and even to babies in language far more complicated than an animal or a human infant could possibly understand? The answer is simple. Human beings need to communicate, and they will speak to any creature that appears to listen. To communicate with a baby, an adult will often make a face that imitates the face the baby is making. Baby sticks tongue out—adult sticks tongue out. Adults mimic babies all the time. In this way (and others) babies learn to mimic adults. And from the first simple sentences children hear, they develop a grammar—they acquire a language.

An extraordinary thing, language, yet every human being can learn one. In learning a language we learn not only the language itself, but also two ways of using it. One way is public. We call it "speech." The other way is private. We call it "thought." With language we gain control over our environment. Words let us name the things we experience, as well as describe these things in relation to each other and to ourselves. They also help us to remember things we no longer have before us, and even to think of things we have never seen: unicorns, the universe, God, woman, man. We see men and women of course, and this man and that woman, but we do not see "man" or "woman." Those words name classes or categories, what the philosophers call *universals*. Language gives them to us and we use them to think with. "All humans are mortal," we think, along with other things that do not trouble the minds of cats, dogs, or babies.

Learning a language gives us the power to think and to express our thoughts in speech. But human development does not end here, because, at a certain point in the history of human culture, speaking is inevitably extended to include writing. Anthropologists have found isolated tribes that are still on the other side of that great linguistic divide, but even these "primitives" are moving toward written language, making signs of some sort, being driven by evolutionary pressures toward what we call civilization. And civilization, as Sigmund Freud reminded us, has its discontents. For many people, writing is one of them.

Speaking and Writing

What is writing? It is not simply frozen speech. If you tape record a message, it can be played when you are gone and the message will still be supported by your voice, your accents, your emphasis. But if you write the same message for others to receive, they will have to read it, which means they will have to speak it to themselves in their own voices though not in their own words. Will it really be the same message under these circumstances? Can you see how problems might arise?

You have perhaps heard of the experiment involving a circle of people in a room. One person writes down a message and holds it, whispering the message to the person to the left. That person then repeats it to the next person, and so on around the room. When the message returns to the sender, it is compared to the written text. If the message is long enough and the number of people large enough, the message returned never coincides with the message sent. If, on the other hand, the written message itself were passed around the circle, it would obviously remain the same, although it would probably not mean exactly the same thing to each person who read it. The importance of this will become apparent if we take that circle of people in the room and imagine it stretched out over time, spanning many generations.

Imagine a document written down hundreds of years ago and carefully preserved because its message was felt to be of great

4 importance. Imagine, as well, a story, equally important, but instead of being written down, passed on from parent to child over many generations. Most scholars would agree about the fate of these two messages as they moved through the generations to the present. The written document would remain the same in its form, but because the language in which it had been written was itself changing over the years, the document would become more and more difficult to understand. It would require interpretation, commentary—perhaps even translation, such as texts written in Old English now receive. The oral text, however, the story transmitted from parent to child, would be thought of as the same story—''My mother told me this when I was little, and now, my child, I am telling you the same story.'' But actually, little changes would have crept in with every telling because one must always use the language as it is at a given moment. In face-to-face communication, the speaker always wants to be understood and will make any changes that are necessary to ensure that the listener understands.

In face-to-face communication, we have the luxury of a present audience, a listener we can see and who encourages us to make our message immediately understandable. Written communication doesn't offer this luxury. Every writer is always writing for a reader who is some distance away in space and time. For the writer there are no friendly smiles, nods, ''uh-huhs''—nor any helpful questions like, ''Hey, wait a minute, I don't get that.'' Writers must always imagine their audience and try to predict how a future reader will respond to the words being set down on a page.

PRACTICE

An Experience in Your Life

A. Assume that you are in a small group of people that you have just gotten to know and like. There are only three or four of you sitting around, relaxed. Maybe it is late at night. Because you are all getting to know one another, you have been taking turns telling about a memorable experience in your life—one you remember because you felt some strong emotion at the time, such as joy, sadness, anger, fear, contentment, or excitement.

Set this down on paper exactly as you would tell it to the group. Try to capture your ordinary conversational style as well as you can. If you have access to a tape recorder, you might try speaking this narrative first and then writing down what you have recorded. If not, try to write it the way it *would* come out if you had recorded it.

B. After you complete the first part of this assignment, exchange stories with one of your classmates. As you read your classmate's story, make notes of those parts that are unclear to you, or of people or events in the story that you'd like to know more about. For example, is it clear how the writer felt about the experience? If you had been present during the telling of the story, you could have asked, or you could have read his or her facial expressions and known something of what the speaker felt at the time.

You should then exchange these notes and discuss each other's stories, making more notes of what needs more development in your story, and of what might be cut out. You should then revise your story, making sure that your written words will show your reader why this experience was memorable for you.

PRACTICE

An Experience in Someone Else's Life

A. We all know people who are good storytellers: older relatives who reminisce about events from the family's past; clever friends who can take almost any experience and turn it into a suspenseful or hilarious monologue; public speakers (like teachers or ministers) who can move an audience to sympathy or understanding by bringing an incident to life.

Try to remember such a story told by one of these people. Even better, observe the storyteller in the act of telling, and tape record the story or make careful notes in which you capture the flavor of the speaker's voice. Then write the story out as it was told, creating as close an approximation as possible of the way the speaker sounds. Finally, have other members of your class read the story and tell you what impression they get of the storyteller from the way you have set the story down.

B. Now revise this story for an audience who does not know the speaker by providing a narrative frame. Start with an introduction in which you describe the speaker, and if relevant, the circumstances in which the story is told, how often, and under what conditions. Then provide a conclusion in which you consider how the speaker takes account of his or her listeners and in which you describe your reaction to the story and the storyteller.

The Writing Situation

Every act of communication involves a sender who initiates a message and a receiver who interprets it: an adult making faces and a baby watching, a speaker telling a story and a listener paying attention, a writer explaining communication and a reader deciphering symbols on a page. But the elements that make up the situation in which communication takes place can be specified even further. All writing situations, for example, may be described by a simple diagram:

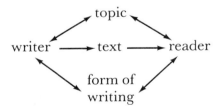

The central level of the diagram (writer ⟶ text ⟶ reader) describes the basic process of written communication. As the arrows indicate, the writer produces a written message (the *text*) that is transmitted to the reader. The reader reads it, interprets it, and understand it, thus completing the process. In order for this to happen, however, the writer and reader must share two kinds of knowledge, indicated on the diagram by the upper and lower terms (*topic* and *form of writing*). Both of these terms are connected to the writer and reader by double-ended arrows, indicating that this knowledge is shared by writer and reader from the beginning.

First of all, writer and reader must share some knowledge of the topic under discussion—the subject of the text—in order to communicate about it. A student's response to an essay question will be meaningless if the student has no familiarity with the subject of the question. A simple report of a football game will be incomprehensible to someone who has had absolutely no experience of football, who has never heard of a quarterback or a tackle or a scrimmage. Some knowledge of the topic—and of what has been communicated about that topic in the past—is essential if writer and reader are to complete the communication process.

Also essential is a shared knowledge of what we are calling a *form of writing*. At a fundamental level this means that reader and writer must be literate in the same language. If we write in Greek, you must read Greek to understand us. If we use a period, you must understand what such a symbolic marking may indicate.

At another level, a shared understanding of conventional forms means something more immediately relevant to the practice of writing. Every writing job is done within a framework of expectations about the kind of words that will be used, kinds of sentence structures that are appropriate, and the sort of organization that will make communication most effective. In other words, given a particular relationship between a writer and the intended reader and a particular topic with a history of its own, of which the participants inevitably have some awareness, the communication that results is likely to take a certain form—to have features in common with other communications occurring in similar circumstances. This helps to explain why, say, a letter from a seller to a prospective buyer sounds so unlike a funeral oration or an opinion of the Supreme Court, while a news article differs greatly from all three—and why we are able to make predictions about how any of these will sound before we have read them. Understanding the requirements of a writing situation allows us to choose a form appropriate to the particular writing task. In this book, our purpose is to help you gain such an understanding as well as to provide instruction and practice in the forms of writing that are most important for success in college and for participation in a modern industrial society.

The Forms of Writing

Although the number of possible writing situations is potentially infinite, they can, in fact, be reduced to a relatively small number that students of writing should actually practice. Let's look again at our diagram of the writing situation:

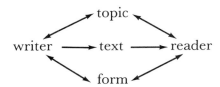

There are five units or elements in the diagram. The *text*, of course, is what the writer is going to produce. It is the thing all the fuss is about: the writing itself. The *form* is the set of rules and conventions that will guide the writer in writing and the reader in reading the text. In this book we are suggesting the study of ten basic forms of writing. These ten forms fall into three categories, oriented to the other three elements of the writing situation, giving us three types of form: those oriented to the writer, those oriented to the reader, and those oriented to the topic.

In actuality these ten forms are frequently mixed, but, for purposes of understanding and practice, it helps to isolate them. In this way we can concentrate on the prominent features of each form. It is our belief that a well-rounded writer should be capable of working in a range of forms, and that often a skill which is central in one form will prove useful in a form that emphasizes an entirely different aspect of writing.

Writer-Oriented Forms

By *writer-oriented forms* we mean forms of writing in which the writer is the center of attention. These personal forms are the furthest removed from the kind of writing most often required in academic situations. They need feeling and thought, but they do not require research, documentation, or a structure of logical argument. If your most urgent need is to learn how to produce an acceptable term paper, it is quite proper to put most of your energy into mastering other forms. But writing is not a mechanical process and you are not a machine. Writing is a way of thinking as well as a means of communication, and one of the things it can be used to think about is yourself. Some writing must be impersonal. Certain forms of writing require that your personal feelings be restrained if not suppressed. This is easier to accomplish if you understand the personal forms of writing—and if you understand what your own feelings and values really are. To be fair, balanced, detached, and objective, you must understand your views *as views* and not confuse them with reality or truth.

We can readily recognize two main forms of writing that are writer-oriented: *expression* and *reflection*.

Expression. In this form the writer is most concerned with expressing certain feelings or thoughts for the sheer satisfaction of doing so. This is a primitive form, in a way, self-centered, an elaboration of such fundamental expressive gestures as a cry of rage or pain, a groan or sigh of depression, an ''mmm'' or ''ah'' of satisfaction. In writing expressively, we try to move from the basic feeling to some elaboration, some articulation of it in prose. Putting things into words can make us feel better and help us to understand ourselves. Practice in expressive writing can also give our thoughts a chance to grow and deepen. Much of our writing is for others. Expression is for ourselves.

Reflection. Reflection is very different from pure expression. If you stand in front of a mirror your image will be doubled. You will be present in the flesh and your reflected image will be present also. In reflective writing, the writer's self is doubled. We don't simply write subjectively *from* ourselves, as in expression; we write objectively *about* ourselves as well. To do this we must get some distance on ourselves, some perspective. In reflection we look back—that is, our present, writing self looks back upon some previous self and measures, in some way, the distance between *then* and *now*. Reflection allows us to discover significance in the events of our own lives.

Reader-Oriented Forms

All writing must be concerned with its reader. For over two thousand years, teachers of rhetoric have been admonishing their students: "Know your audience; imagine how they will respond to your words." This lesson is still valuable. The forms of writing that are oriented to the reader give us a chance to practice the principle of paying attention to the reader. Once this becomes a habit, it can help us in any writing situation.

There are two major types of reader-oriented writing: *direction* and *persuasion*.

Direction. We are all familiar with directions. We find them in cookbooks, textbooks, exercise manuals, and all sorts of do-it-yourself pamphlets and instruction books.

Most directive writing must do two simple things: provide information, and arrange that information in the most useful and comprehensible order. The lessons learned from practicing directive writing are simple but powerful: how to be concerned for the reader, and how to organize a process in time so that the procedures presented—the directions—can be followed with a minimum of confusion and complaint.

Persuasion. In persuasion, too, the reader is the prime consideration, but instead of giving directions for something the reader is assumed to want already, persuasive writing is designed to create a want or motivate an action. The politician who wants your vote and the advertiser who wants your money are most likely to use persuasive techniques, but persuasion is not entirely absent from the writing of scientists and philosophers. Persuasion relies heavily on appeals to emotion. It often uses the same linguistic resources as poetry to achieve its end: vivid images, careful control of connotations, repetition, rhythm, even rhyme. In our society, highly persuasive writing is so frequently encountered and so skillfully deployed that every citizen should understand it thoroughly, if only to avoid being victimized by it.

Topic-Oriented Forms

Most academic situations call for topic-oriented forms of writing, where the personality of the writer is not a central concern and few direct appeals to the reader are made. Instead, the topic itself is examined and presented to the reader for the sake of informing or for thoughtful consideration. The careful reporting of observations, the reasoned examination of alternatives, the clear organization of a body of material are the virtues of topic-oriented writing, and skill in using these forms is one of the distinguishing marks of an educated person.

The six major types of topic-oriented writing are *narration, description, classification, argumentation, analysis*, and *synthesis*.

Narration. A narrative is a report on an event, a happening that unfolds in time. Narration is a form of writing shared by the creative writer, who invents the events to be narrated, and the reporter or researcher who seeks to record or recover some actual sequence of events. In this book we are not concerned with the art of writing fictional narratives, but with narration as a form of reporting observation or research. From practice in narration we learn to manage time—to organize language so as to capture events and display them clearly with the emphasis falling where we want it to. In actual writing, narration is often blended with other forms; for example, a story may be told to illustrate a point in an argument. But narration is sufficiently distinct as a form to be studied in itself.

Description. In description, we take a scene or an object and capture it in language. That is, we organize the details of the object or scene we wish to describe in the way that will most effectively convey the sensual image. Just as work in narration is practice in the organization of *time* in writing, work in description is practice in the organization of *space*. This is important not only because description is used in other forms of writing, but because what is being learned from practicing narration and description is organization itself. In the topic-oriented forms, organization is crucial. It is a skill that must be learned.

Classification. Classification is another form that puts a premium on organization. In classification we organize our material not by time or space, but by a principle of logic: all things with these features belong in this category, and this category is a subcategory of this larger class of things. In a form like classification we can see just how closely writing and thinking are related. Although we almost never encounter an entire piece of writing that consists of nothing but classification, we encounter very little writing in the academic disciplines that does not depend upon some system of classifying the material under discussion.

Argumentation. Argumentation differs from persuasion by being more rational. It is aimed at clarifying a topic rather than at moving a reader. Its function is to make the reader *see* things in a particular way rather than to make the reader *do* something. Argumentation is especially important to the student of writing because it offers the principles of organization that inform most academic prose. The basic structure of (1) a *thesis* to be argued, and (2) the evidence to support the thesis and certain very specific ways of reasoning from evidence—especially the logic of cause and effect—is at the heart of all research in the humanities, the social studies, and the sciences. In the major form of written research that we are calling *synthesis*, argumentation provides the skeletal structure that is fleshed out with features drawn from the other forms of writing.

Analysis. Analysis is both a way of observing and a way of writing about what we have observed. In particular, it involves taking things apart and seeing how the parts are related, so as to understand how the object of analysis *works*. This taking-apart, of course, is done mentally, not physically. The tools of analysis are comparing and contrasting, connecting and distinguishing, and the discovery of causes and effects. When the results of analysis are organized in the form of an argument, analysis moves toward synthesis.

Synthesis. Synthesis is the fullest and most complete form of academic writing. The word ''synthesis'' means ''putting together'' as the word ''analysis'' means ''taking apart.'' In synthesis the writer uses the structure of an argument, and the data provided by research and analysis, to develop a thesis about some body of material. The different academic subjects are concerned with the study of very different kinds of material, and they may present their results in different manners (using mathematical symbols, pictures, charts, graphs and other modes of presentation), but the ultimate goal of all academic research is the production of a synthesis of the materials that have been studied.

Reading and Practice

These, then, are the forms that one must master in order to become a successful writer. But how does one know when a particular form is appropriate and how does one achieve the necessary proficiency in these forms? The most effective way is through reading and practice.

Before every act of writing comes a reading. First, we must "read" the writing situation. (We are thinking here of the way a quarterback "reads" the opposing defense, or how a doctor "reads" a patient's symptoms.) Reading in this way is a means of diagnosing what will be required, of determining the course our writing should take: What will my reader know about the topic and what will be my reader's attitude? What can I, as a writer, discover about the topic? What form of writing will be suitable, given the topic itself, my particular concerns, and the expectations of my reader? Reading the writing situation will mean finding answers to questions like these.

As these questions suggest, reading the situation effectively will generally require other kinds of reading, as well. Of course, there is always the possibility of researching the topic in some way; as suggested earlier, you cannot write well on a subject you know nothing about. Just as important, though, is reading in order to become familiar with how people usually write about a topic, to discover the kind of writing a particular task requires, to understand the form that will be expected in the given situation.

Writing is like entering a conversation that is already going on before you start to speak. In order for readers to appreciate what you have to say, you must first assimilate several layers of rules and conventions, the framework of expectations, the appropriate forms necessary for a reader's understanding. Such conventions begin with matters like ending a sentence with a period, and move through the proper method of documenting sources for a term paper, or the differences between reporting on a sports event for a newspaper column and reporting on a similar event for a sociological study. How do you learn such forms? Babies learn the conventions of speech by observing and imitating the activities of adults; writers learn the conventions of a particular writing situation by reading and understanding how others have successfully approached the task.

Think for a moment about the many conventions of writing you have already assimilated. Even something as simple as a note to a friend involves a fairly complicated set of conventions, but such conventions more than likely come easily to you because you are familiar with the forms of writing such a situation requires—you have read many similar notes written by others, and have had many occasions to write notes yourself. But imagine being faced with writing a different kind of note: on your first day of a new job, your boss asks you to compose a memo to be circulated among the staff. Even if you've been given the topic and told fairly specifically what should be said, the task will pose significant problems until you have a sense of the conventions that you are expected to follow. The obvious solution to these problems will be to check the files for examples of how memos have been written in the past. Then, with the benefit of reading, imitation, and practice, writing a memo will begin to come as naturally to you as writing an informal note, so much so that you may soon find yourself modifying the received form, trying to discover a more effective means of communication for yourself.

In any field, we learn the conventions of particular forms of writing by reading and practicing those forms. This does not mean that all writing is imitation, but to achieve originality, we must read the work of our predecessors. Originality, then, begins as imitation and moves on to recombination, finally emerging as something new and different enough to be called original. Those who do not read and practice are condemned to repeat the work of those that they have not read, to reinvent the wheel when what is needed is the invention of the axle, the bearing, or the differential gear.

Practice and Confidence

In this book we will offer you some help in understanding what is required in different writing situations, we will provide examples of the various forms of writing for you to read, and, most important, we will give you a chance to practice these forms for yourself. But you must remember, practicing writing is not like football practice, where everybody goes out together with a lot of group support and encouragement. It is more like practicing tennis, where you bang a ball against a wall for hours, or practicing the guitar or the piano, where you make no progress from one lesson to the next if you don't put in time alone playing the instrument. Only you can do it. You should also remember that

in your writing class all your writing is practicing. You are trying things out, seeing where your strengths are, finding out
what you need to work on so that in time you can gain confidence in your writing skills.

Such confidence is essential, for every writing task brings
with it a certain amount of anxiety. Confronted with a blank
piece of paper and the prospect of setting down a part of oneself
for others to read, perhaps to reject, and certainly to judge, one
is bound to feel at least some slight nervousness. This is the
same kind of nervousness that every performer feels: the actress
before going on stage, the football player before the kickoff, the
politician before a speech. Even the best performers feel it, and
most of them say that they need it and use it. With the confidence that comes from understanding and practice, writers, like
performers, can convert their nervousness into excellence in the
performance itself.

As writers know, however, this nervousness can also cause
one to freeze up, to lose concentration, to go blank, particularly
when the audience one writes for is made up of strangers. Such
debilitating fear is really a fear of the end of writing, of being
read and evaluated, but it creeps back to inhibit the beginning.
Inexperienced writers sometimes assume that writing works this
way: first you have an idea; then you put it down on paper. But
this is not the case with good writing. Writing is not only a tool
for communication, for transmitting ideas or transcribing what
has already been thought: it is itself a way of thinking, of developing ideas, trying them out, arranging them, testing them. It
is a way of separating your thoughts from yourself—making
them take a visible form outside your mind—so that you can
think about them and improve them. It is, in fact, always practice, and realizing this can make you a stronger, more confident
writer.

The Act of Writing: Prewriting, Drafting, Revising

There is no one way to write, no magic process guaranteed to
produce a perfect piece of writing if followed step by step. Not
all writers work in the same way, and even an individual writer
approaches different taks in different ways, depending on his or

her writing habits and on the writing situation. But experienced writers can point to particular elements that generally occur in the act of writing, even though these elements may be combined in different ways. In addition to the basic psychomotor act of writing—the way the hand, eye, and brain work so that we can put words on paper—we can distinguish three phases in the practice of writing: prewriting, drafting, and revising. These phases are not isolated states in a strict sequence, since writing is a complex, interwoven process like a hooked rug, not a set of distinct compartments like a freight train. But each of these phases does represent a particular kind of work that writers do.

Prewriting

Your most productive way of beginning almost any writing task will be to collect your thoughts on paper without the pressure of structuring your expression into its final form. (Even a thank-you note to Aunt Bessie can be less difficult if you simply jot down various things you might say *before* you write "Dear Aunt Bessie.") If you consider your first words on paper as something tentative, as a way of starting to think rather than as a monument of perfected thought, you will be able to explore whatever subject you approach more deeply and fully and you will go a long way toward taking the initial nervousness out of writing. Such prewriting is your chance to practice what you have to say before you begin to worry about how your audience will judge the eventual form of your work.

This is not to say that prewriting doesn't involve some sense of form and audience. Indeed, all writers begin by considering these two elements of the writing situation along with their topic as they go about preparing to compose a text.

A writer must begin, of course, by choosing a subject to write about. Sometimes your choices will be fairly narrow, sometimes seemingly infinite; but in any case it will be important to give some thought to your possibilities. This may mean making a list of potential subjects, or experimenting with the sort of open-ended writing that will be discussed in Chapter 2. However you proceed, your purpose is to narrow your focus, to discover the limits that will allow you to work productively. Once you have determined your tentative topic, you may need to do some research—either by reading or by firsthand observation—and to take notes about what you learn; this may lead you to narrow your topic even further or to refine your initial approach. Only rarely will a fully realized topic come immediately to mind: you can only know what will work by trying things out, by testing your thoughts in writing.

During this process of testing a topic, you will need to give some attention to the possible forms your writing will take and what those forms will require. The practice you do throughout this course will help you learn more about the requirements of various forms of writing, and this understanding will, in turn, help you recognize the sort of prewriting that will be most useful for a particular assignment. If you're preparing to write a narrative, for example, your prewriting may involve a chronological outline of a sequence of actions: first this happened, then this happened, then this happened, etc. You may also give yourself a chance to discover and develop the significant details that will make your narration more than a shorthand reporting of events. Classification, on the other hand, will require that you spend some time describing the important features or characteristics of the objects you wish to classify. Then, by listing similarities and differences among these objects, you can begin to determine categories or classes into which the objects can be placed; writing out statements to see the kind of information you can squeeze from one set of classes may lead you to try another set of classes, then another, that will provide increasingly useful information about the objects themselves. For an argument you will want to define a tentative thesis—a position on a particular issue—and then, perhaps, to test your thesis by listing all the evidence you can come up with to support that thesis, as well as the evidence that might be used against it. Then you can go on to develop your evidence in more detail, to find the information that will make your evidence most convincing, maybe even to modify your thesis according to available evidence. Eventually, you will need to rank your evidence and to decide the most effective way of ordering that evidence as you structure your full argument.

As you test your topic within the conventions of particular forms, you will also need to take account of your eventual audience: What will they need to know? What are their likely preconceptions about this topic? Will they expect my writing to take a particular form? How can I interest them in what I have to say? Your answers to questions like these will be important in determining the choices you make during prewriting and drafting.

Prewriting, then, is essential to the practice of writing. Much of it will take place before drafting; but even as you write your first draft, you may find yourself jotting down ideas to use later or stopping to explore ways of working through a difficult section. And, of course, some prewriting may be done in your head. Allowing yourself to capture those thoughts on paper, however, gives you a sense of starting, rather than worrying about how to get started. It is natural to want to put off the anxiety of drafting; prewriting lets you do so productively.

Drafting

Drafting is the point at which you begin to put your ideas in some kind of order and to envision a potential shape for the work you will produce: a beginning, a middle, and an end. Before they begin drafting, some writers make an outline to remind themselves of how they wish to order their ideas. Such an outline is usually quite rough, and may be frequently rearranged and amended during the drafting process. Making an extensive formal outline before drafting is difficult because, as with prewriting, much of what you will say will be discovered during the act of writing and not beforehand. The process of putting words on paper is a process of thinking in which you should frequently look back at what you have written to see if what you are about to write will follow logically from what you wrote earlier. Pausing and rereading at frequent intervals will not cause you to forget the point you wanted to make; such pauses can spark new ideas for developing your point more effectively. Often, such ideas will not relate to the section you are working on, so you should jot them in the margin or on your outline to return to at the appropriate time. Remember that the first draft is still a process of exploration, and the greatest discoveries are those that are not on the map.

If you are writing a fairly long paper, you may, after a few pages of writing, want to pause and outline what you've written to see more clearly what points you have made and whether you have left anything out or are repeating yourself. Then continue on toward your proposed destination, and when you think you have finished your first draft, stop. You are now ready to begin revising.

19

Revising

Imagine a speaker halfway through a political talk stopping and saying, "Actually, I've begun this all wrong. Now I see what I really want to say. Forget what you've just heard. I'm going to start over." Ridiculous, is it not? Or imagine a football team watching movies of their last game and one of them saying, "I missed a block on that last play; run it again and I'll do it right this time." Impossible! But in writing this is exactly what we do all the time. We run the instant replay and correct our mistakes—not only the mistakes in execution, such as spelling or punctuation, but also the mistakes in conception. That is, if we see that one play isn't working, we can call another play entirely. Think what a tremendous advantage that would give a quarterback. It is an advantage we can all have if we *revise and rewrite before we present our work to the reader.* If you are the sort of writer who never revises, who never writes a second draft, who thinks of every word as a finished product, you are a prime candidate for writer's block. You are also doomed to remain at a superficial level of understanding about your subject. To refuse revision is to refuse thought itself.

The professional writer's secret is revision and revision and revision. Some of the greatest writers—poets, essayists, scholars—have begun their work with ordinary thoughts in sloppy language and refined it only through numerous revisions. Revision comes not only when a draft is complete, but at every stage of writing. Whenever you put the work down for a walk around the room or a trip down the hall, and especially when you are away from it for any length of time, you should reread it when you pick it up and make revisions where they are needed.

What guides you in revising? How can you tell when changes are necessary and what sort of changes must be made? This requires critical perspective. You must try to see your writing in terms of the form you are trying to achieve. If it is an argument, is it clear, honest, well reasoned? Does it need more evidence? Should you concede something or change your thesis? If it is a description, have you emphasized the right things, found the right words for them, put them in the right order?

You must also try to get outside of yourself and see things from another perspective, as you would in writing a reflective essay. Certain kinds of practice can help you achieve this critical distance. In some situations, particularly a writing class, you may very well have an opportunity to critique the drafts of other writers, as well as to consider revisions of your own drafts based on the comments you receive from your peers. You may also be given a chance to make revisions based on the comments of your instructor. You can learn a great deal from such opportunities. First, as a reader, you must articulate why you do or do not find certain elements of someone else's draft successful and to suggest possible improvements; if you take your role as a reader/critic seriously, you can develop critical powers that you can then transfer to your own work. In addition, the feedback you receive from other readers of your drafts can make you more aware of the needs of an audience of strangers. This awareness can lead you to imagine more clearly how those strangers, your readers, will react to a particular piece of writing. What will they find confusing or distracting in this work? If you can find the problems you can fix them.

The last act of rewriting must be proofreading, a check for mechanical errors in spelling and punctuation. Your reader can accept last minute corrections better than outright errors, and will be grateful to you for taking the trouble to correct the errors. Keep that stranger grateful if you can.

The Writer as Role-Player

As we have emphasized, confidence in yourself as a writer can come from thinking of your work as "practice": first, from using your writing class as an opportunity to practice different kinds of writing tasks, and second, from realizing that the act of writing always allows you the opportunity to practice what you have to say before you present it to an audience of strangers.

Finally, we must consider another aspect of the writing situation, one that especially pertains to confidence: the notion of the writer as an actor.

The existentialist philosopher Jean-Paul Sartre once observed that a waiter in a cafe was handling the most difficult part of his job—the strain of being shouted at, hurried, always referred to as *garçon* (''boy'')—by a simple but beautiful trick. He was *imagining* that he was a waiter in a cafe. Instead of presenting his real, vulnerable self to the abuse of customers and boss, he was acting out the role of waiter. He put the *role* of waiter between his actual self and his function as waiter. This enabled him to perform the job with a high degree of skill, without the anxiety of feeling that his real self was always on display.

Writers can learn a lesson from this. Even in writing tasks that involve our real selves—such as composing an application for a job we really desire—we may function better, may represent ourselves better if we accept the task as a role to play, rather than if we conceive of the situation as bringing our true selves forward for judgment and criticism.

You don't need any special training for role-playing, because you do it all the time. In a single day, you may play the role of attentive student in the classroom, irate driver in a traffic jam, affectionate child at home, romantic lover with a special friend. You move in and out of these roles almost unconsciously, and this skill you have in social situations can be transferred to writing situations.

When the idea of the writer as role-player is combined with the idea that the reader must be imagined by the writer, the stage is set for a certain kind of practice. By imagining yourself in a variety of situations, addressing a variety of readers, you can in fact increase the range of your imaginative skill. You can become a better actor as a writer. The final assignments in this chapter are designed to afford just this sort of practice.

PRACTICE

Bad Situation at School

A. You are asked here to write a series of three letters about the same subject. Each letter must have a different audience and must be written in a style suited to that audience. You should read the instructions for all three letters before starting to write the first one.

Letter 1

Imagine that you are a new student at your school and have encountered an annoying problem in your first week. It could be something to do with your living arrangements or your commuting situation or your food or your classes. It is painful but has its amusing side. Write a letter to a good friend or family member in which you describe the situation. Try to write the letter exactly as you would under the actual circumstances, with appropriate language, spelling, and punctuation.

Letter 2

A few days have passed since you wrote Letter 1. The situation has not improved. If anything, it is worse, and you are not amused. Write a letter to the appropriate authority to try to get the situation changed. You must state your case as clearly and sympathetically as possible. The situation must be one that the authority can do something about, and you must try to stay on the good side of the authority. You want help; you are asking, not threatening.

Letter 3

Despite your polite request for assistance—the clear and eloquent plea you developed in Letter 2—the situation remains the same. You must take your case to the public. In this case, a letter to the editor of your school paper is in order. In your letter, express all your anguish in such a way as to gain *public* sympathy and possibly put some pressure on the authorities to consider the situation in a new light. At the very least, this public expression of your anguish will make you feel better, so make it as expressive as you can. Write this letter exactly as it should appear in the paper.

B. Write appropriate replies to Letters 1 and 2 from the people to whom they were addressed. The style and the content of the letters should be suited to the writers. That is, your friend should answer you in a familiar style, and the authority should use a more formal, impersonal style.

You Met Somebody . . .

A. At a party or other social function you very briefly met somebody who seemed very attractive and interesting. You would really like to get to know this person better. However, at the last minute you found out that he or she was just visiting and actually lives some distance away at another school. You are broke and can't afford to telephone your new friend. You aren't even sure how well you will be remembered. Still, you decide to write a letter in which you will try to accomplish the following things:

1. Remind your new friend of how you met.
2. Impress him or her with your wit, charm, or other good qualities.
3. Find out if this person is equally interested in you.

Write the letter.

B. Now prepare to write an appropriate answer to the letter written for part A. Imagine yourself the person addressed in that letter, and write from his or her point of view a letter addressed to your real self, who wrote the first letter. Assume the following conditions:

1. You don't really remember the meeting referred to.
2. You don't really need another friend at this point.
3. You are curious, though, and want to see if you can get another letter from your new acquaintance without making any real commitment.
4. In any case you want this person to be favorably impressed with you.

Write the letter.

C. This is an alternative to part B. Assume that you remember your first meeting with the person who wrote you letter A, but that you found the meeting and the letter very unpleasant. Write a letter which will make this clear very directly and prevent this person from ever writing to you again.

PART TWO

WRITER-ORIENTED FORMS

2 Expression: Your Self as Subject

In a sense, all writing is expressive. At some level, we express ourselves in every act of writing, even if it is only by writing carelessly because we are not interested in the assigned topic. But in another sense, writing is never completely expressive, because its rules and practices are part of a social system over which we have little control. In writing, we can only say what the system of writing will let us say.

Whether or not you have thought about the problem in exactly this way, you have probably encountered it. Because modern life is so complicated, there are many barriers to full expression. We all feel a kind of censorship that prevents us from expressing things that might expose our weaknesses or show us to be different from our fellows, from leaving a durable record that may say more about ourselves than we had meant to say. We may also have trouble expressing ourselves because our language is full of ready-made expressions, clichés that can falsify and standardize whatever may be unique in our unshaped thoughts and feelings. This mixture of feelings—fear of being misunderstood and fear of being understood too well—is a major part of the anxiety about writing that most of us have.

Practice in expression is designed to ease both aspects of the writer's anxiety, and to provide opportunities for thoughts to grow and deepen. Freedom of expression is particularly important because it is what makes the activity of prewriting so productive, allowing writers to explore what is in their minds as elaborately or outrageously as they wish without holding back for fear something is "wrong" or not within acceptable social limits. Eventually, of course, the limits must be considered. Writers must become more self-critical and disciplined, and should work to refine the discoveries of expression within the constraints imposed by the writing situation. Such discipline, however, is not the first concern of expression.

Thus, the first writing opportunities that follow here are simply chances for you to write for yourself, to get started, to stretch your possibilities, before you think about presenting your thoughts and feelings to anyone else. The forms of practice presented later in this chapter will begin to ask for a more public kind of expression, in which you must consider the problem of expressing *your* self *to* some other self. The purpose of expression, after all, is to broaden your powers of communication.

READING

The Open-Ended Writing Process

Here is some good advice from an expert on how to get started in expressing yourself.

Peter Elbow, from Writing With Power

The open-ended writing process is ideal for the situation where you sense you have something to write but you don't quite know what. Just start writing about anything at all. If you have special trouble with that first moment of writing—that confrontation with a blank page—ask yourself what you *don't* want to write about and start writing about it before you have a chance to resist. First thoughts. They are very likely to lead you to what you are needing to write.

Keep writing for at least ten or twenty or thirty minutes, depending on how much material and energy you come up with. You have to write long enough to get tired and get past what's on the top of your mind. But not so long that you start pausing in the midst of your writing.

Then stop, sit back, be quiet, and bring all that writing to a point. That is, by reading back or just thinking back over it, find the center

1

2

3

or focus or point of those words and write it down in a sentence. This may mean different things: you can find the main idea that is there; or the new idea that is trying to be there; or the imaginative focus or center of gravity—an image or object or feeling; or perhaps some brand new thing occurs to you now as very important—it may even seem unrelated to what you wrote, but it comes to you now as a result of having done that burst of writing. Try to stand out of the way and let the center or focus itself decide to come forward. In any event don't worry about it. Choose or invent something for your focus. . . . The only requirement is that it be a single thing. Skip a few lines and write it down. Underline it or put a box around it so you can easily find it later. (Some people find it helpful to let themselves write down two or three focusing sentences.)

PRACTICE

Open-Ended Writing

Start writing, following Elbow's advice as closely as you can. That is, write as he suggests you do, read your writing, and find your point or focus. That's all you have to do. Save this material, however, for you may return to it later in the course.

READING

Expression as Transformation

Here are three paragraphs from a theater piece by a young German playwright, Peter Handke. The piece is called "Self-Accusation." As you can see, these paragraphs are about expression. They also present us with a model that can be imitated and adapted for other purposes. Read each paragraph and consider its method. Pay particular attention to three things: repetition, modification, and the introduction of new elements. In the first paragraph, for instance, the basic sentence is "I expressed myself through ideas." Then *ideas* is replaced by *expressions*. The sentences become more complicated after this, and each time a new element is added, it opens the way to modification: *before myself* becomes *before myself and others*. Then *others* is replaced by *impersonal power* and next *impersonal* is replaced by *personal*. The patterns of grammar and syntax are encouraging these extensions and substitutions.

There is something mechanical about this writing, as if a computer had been programmed to develop and modify a basic sentence. But if a human being experiments with language in this way, ideas and feelings that are below the surface of the mind will flow into the form. Handke's ideas grow more and more complex, ending with the introduction of the trapeze act in the penultimate sentence. Taken together, these paragraphs are *about* the limitations and possibilities of expression itself.

Peter Handke, from ''Self-Accusations''

I expressed myself. I expressed myself through ideas. I expressed myself through expressions. I expressed myself before myself. I expressed myself before myself and others. I expressed myself before the impersonal power of the law and of good conduct. I expressed myself before the personal power of God.   1

I expressed myself in movements. I expressed myself in actions. I expressed myself in motionlessness. I expressed myself in inaction.   2

I expressed approval in places where the expression of approval was prohibited. I expressed disapproval at times when the expression of disapproval was not desired. I expressed disapproval and approval in places and at times when the expression of disapproval and the expression of approval were intolerable. I failed to express approval at times when the expression of approval was called for. I expressed approval during a difficult trapeze act in the circus. I expressed approval inopportunely.   3

PRACTICE

Transformations

Write two or three short paragraphs in the manner of Handke. That is, begin with a verb in the first person and expand it in a formulaic way, like this: ''I watched. I watched others.'' ''I watched others watching. . . .'' Start with a basic action verb and go on from there. Refer back to Handke for examples of how to work these transformations. Save this exercise; you may be returning to it later.

READING

Expression Through Association

Here is the opening of a book on blueness and blue things by a philosopher who is also a fiction writer (or vice versa). You may find it difficult to follow every mention of blue as you read, but you can't help but get the idea. The piece is simply a list of things that are blue or that can have the word *blue* applied to them. You may be surprised by some, feel a shock of recognition at others, and find some just too tricky to decipher. As you read, just try to follow along, noting how the word *blue* goes with everything mentioned.

W. H. Gass, from On Being Blue

Blue pencils, blue noses, blue movies, laws, blue legs and stockings, the language of birds, bees, and flowers as sung by longshoremen, that lead-like look the skin has when affected by cold, contusion, sickness, fear; the rotten rum or gin they call blue ruin and the blue devils of its delirium; Russian cats and oysters, a withheld or imprisoned breath, the blue they say that diamonds have, deep holes in the ocean and the blazers which English athletes earn that gentlemen may wear; afflictions of the spirit—dumps, mopes, Mondays—all that's dismal—low-down gloomy music, Nova Scotians, cyanosis, hair rinse, bluing, bleach; the rare blue dahlia like that blue moon shrewd things happen only once in, or the call for trumps in whist (but who remembers whist or what the death of unplayed games is like?), and correspondingly the flag, Blue Peter, which is our signal for getting under way; a swift pitch, Confederate money, the shaded slopes of clouds and mountains, and so the constantly increasing absentness of Heaven (*ins Blaue hinein*, the Germans say), consequently the color of everything that's empty: blue bottles, bank accounts, and compliments, for instance, or, when the sky's turned turtle, the blue-green bleat of ocean (both the same), and, when in Hell, its neatly landscaped rows of concrete huts and gas-blue flames; social registers, examination booklets, blue bloods, balls, and bonnets, beards, coats, collars, chips, and cheese . . . the pedantic, indecent and censorious . . . watered twilight, sour sea: through a scrambling of accidents, blue has become their color, just as it's stood for fidelity. Blue laws took their hue from the paper they were printed on. Blue noses were named for a potato.

PRACTICE

On Being _____

Looking back at the passage by Gass, can you find examples of things in the world that are literally blue: things we perceive as having that color? Can you also find examples of things that are blue only in some figurative or metaphorical way? Gass is fascinated by the way language works, by the way that the name of a color is applied to all sorts of things that actually have no color at all. In the last two sentences he explains how two things that are not literally blue came to be called blue: laws and noses. Although many of his blue things are so-called for reasons lost in the history of language, Gass invents nothing here. In this passage he takes an inventory of the English language as he understands it, trying to summon up all the things that are regularly called blue. Their strange combinations, ordered by his own mind's patterns of association, make a kind of prose poem. By concentrating on the *word* "blue," in all its applications, he frees his mind to roam around, to make connections that are startling, to be creative, expressive.

It is important to note that Gass is not being merely personal and arbitrary here. He is not calling things blue just because he wants to (like the French poet who called oranges blue). This passage is a collaboration between Gass and his language. He is thus free to associate all things that have been called blue often enough to make their blueness part of the language.

Your job is simply to work as Gass has worked, but with another color. We suggest a primary color, one that has spread throughout the language, so that you can combine in your paragraph things that are literally that color with things that we only speak of figuratively as being that color. Save this exercise. You may be returning to it later.

READING

Expression of Mood

Consider the following poem. Reading it aloud once or twice would be a good idea. Then proceed to the questions.

Mid-August at Sourdough Mountain Lookout

Down valley a smoke haze   1
Three days heat after five days rain
Pitch glows on the fir-cones
Across rocks and meadows
Swarms of new flies.

I cannot remember things I once read   2
A few friends, but they are in cities.
Drinking cold snow-water from a tin cup
Looking down for miles
Through high still air.

GARY SNYDER

QUESTIONS

1. This poem consists of two stanzas of five lines each. In the first stanza each line introduces new details. Do the details themselves convey any consistent mood to you?
2. The second stanza introduces the speaker himself in the very first word and continues his actions (drinking, looking) for the rest of the poem. How would you describe the feeling conveyed by this stanza?
3. Reread the first stanza in the light of the second. Is there one consistent mood or feeling expressed throughout the poem? What are the links between a particular detail and the feeling expressed through it? In other words, *how* does Snyder express himself, without saying simply, "I feel _____"? If he were to fill in that blank, what word or words would he use?

In this passage a young woman is expressing the feelings and thoughts she experienced on a visit to a doctor's office, where she looked at a baby magazine and at a real mother and child. Read the passage and consider the questions that follow it.

I leafed nervously through an issue of *Baby Talk*. The fat, bright   1
faces of babies beamed up at me, page after page—bald babies,
chocolate-colored babies, Eisenhower-faced babies, babies rolling
over the the first time, babies reaching for rattles, babies eating
their first spoonful of solid food, babies doing all the little tricky
things it takes to grow up, step by step, into an anxious and unset-
tling world.

I smelt a mingling of Pablum and sour milk and salt-cod-stinky di-   2
apers and felt sorrowful and tender. How easy having babies seemed
to the women around me! Why was I so unmaternal and apart?
Why couldn't I dream of devoting myself to baby after fat puling
baby like Dodo Conway?

If I had to wait on a baby all day, I would go mad.   3

I looked at the baby in the lap of the woman opposite. I had   4
no idea how old it was, I never did, with babies—for all I knew it
could talk a blue streak and had twenty teeth behind its pursed,
pink lips. It held its little wobbly head up on its shoulders—it didn't
seem to have a neck—and observed me with a wise, Platonic
expression.

The baby's mother smiled and smiled, holding that baby as if it   5
were the first wonder of the world. I watched the mother and the
baby for some clue to their mutual satisfaction, but before I had discovered anything, the doctor called me in.

QUESTIONS

1. The voice in the passage belongs to Esther Greenwood. How would you
   describe the mood or moods she experiences in the doctor's office? What
   is the most appropriate word for her mood? What words in the passage
   are doing the most work in the expression of mood?
2. How would you describe Esther's personality as it is revealed in this passage? What details convey this most strongly?
3. Esther's mood is presented partly as a contrast to other possible responses to babies and motherhood. How are the other responses conveyed? How is an attitude toward them established?
4. Are ideas, as well as a mood or moods, expressed here? Make a sum-
   mary statement of what you take to be the main idea of the passage—if
   you feel that it does convey or imply any ideas.
5. At one point Esther says she "felt sorrowful and tender." Are these the
   words you would have chosen to describe her mood? Explain any discrepancy.
6. Consider the longest and shortest sentences in the passage. What does
   each contribute to the expressiveness of the text?

PRACTICE

Mood in a Place

You have just considered two examples of the expression of a mood or feeling inspired by being in a particular place at a particular time. In both cases, the things that are there to be experienced become the basis for the expression of a mood or feeling.

Your task in this exercise is to pick a place and use its details selectively to convey a mood or feeling of your own. Put yourself in a place where there are things to be seen and heard and even smelled that encourage your feelings to seek expression: a playground, for example, or an empty gymnasium or a noisy disco. You may come up with a subtle but unified feeling like Snyder or a flow of contradictory or contrary feelings like Plath. But remember to use your chosen place as the source of expressive details.

READING

Ideas about the Telephone

In these two passages, an Italian and a Frenchman speak of their personal feelings about the telephone. As you read each passage, follow the expression of ideas in it.

Federico Fellini, from **Fellini on Fellini**

Frankly, I don't see myself as the fanatical telephone user that   1
friends and colleagues have been calling me for years, with mischievous amusement. My work brings me into contact with a large number of people, which means I'm involved in an endless network of relationships, and so it's natural that a fair part of my day should be spent on the telephone. Like everyone else I consider and use the telephone as an indispensable, fast and practical means of communication. And yet this daily use of it hasn't yet managed to remove my astonishment at the fundamentally fantastic aspect of telephoning, that is, of communication at a distance. Apart from any hackneyed ideas about communication by telephone being the modern techni-

cal equivalent of ancient means of communication—telepathy, for instance—I want to make just a few odd, hurried remarks about it. I wonder, for instance, why it is easier to get out of an unexpected visit than to withstand the temptation to pick up the telephone when it keeps ringing? Just because the person speaking isn't physically present, communication on the telephone is more tenuous but more authentic, less real but more precise, more temporary but more spontaneous, more delicate but at the same time more intense. As a rule one pays more attention both to oneself and to the other person when talking on the telephone, one participates more. Feeling and impressions expand: good news becomes more exciting because right aways it is more privately taken in. A disaster become unbearable, because the imagination is fully stretched.

Terror is terror in its purest form: nothing is more chilling than a threat or a damning criticism pronounced on the telephone. Even the dullest, silliest joke on the telephone loses its dullness and pointlessness and takes on a disarming charm. For my part, I think solitude filled with voices is far preferable and far more joyful than the physical presence of others, when it has no meaning or point to it.   2

Roland Barthes, from **A Lover's Discourse**

My anxieties as to behavior are futile, ever more so, to infinity. If the other, incidentally or negligently, gives the telephone number of a place where he or she can be reached at certain times, I immediately grow baffled: should I telephone or shouldn't I? (It would do no good to tell me that *I can* telephone—that is the objective, reasonable meaning of the message—for it is precisely this *permission* I don't know how to handle.)   1

What is futile is what apparently has and will have no consequence. But for me, an amorous subject, everything which is new, everything which disturbs, is received not as a fact but in the aspect of a sign which must be interpreted. From the lover's point of view, the fact becomes consequential because it is immediately transformed into a sign: it is the sign, not the fact, which is consequential (by its *aura*). If the other has given me this new telephone number, what was that the sign of? Was it an invitation to telephone *right away*, for the pleasure of the call, or only *should the occasion arise*, out of necessity? My answer itself will be a sign which the other will inevitably interpret, thereby releasing, between us, a tumultuous maneuvering of images. *Everything signifies:* by this proposition, I entrap myself, I bind myself in calculations, I keep myself from enjoyment.   2

Sometimes, by dint of deliberating about "nothing" (as the world sees it), I exhaust myself; then I try, in reaction, to return—like a   3 drowning man who stamps on the floor of the sea—to a *spontaneous* decision (spontaneity: the great dream: paradise, power, delight): *go on, telephone, since you want to!* But such recourse is futile: amorous time does not permit the subject to align impulse and action, to make them coincide: I am not the man of mere "acting out"—my madness is tempered, it is not seen; it is *right away* that I fear consequences, any consequence: it is my fear—my deliberation—which is "spontaneous."

QUESTIONS

1. Try to describe the speaker suggested by each of the two voices. What kind of personality is suggested by each passage? What specific elements in each text are most expressive of the speaker's individuality? Which text is most revealing of its speaker's personality?
2. Consider the situation of each speaker in relation to the telephone. Does he consider himself mainly a caller, or a person likely to be called? Which passage develops the speaker's situation most elaborately?
3. Reduce each passage to its main idea or ideas about the telephone. Do the two passages express contradictory or complementary ideas? Which expresses views most compatible with your own?
4. Which passage is easiest to read? Why? Which one presents ideas that are least familiar to you? Which seems richest in ideas, most thoughtful? Which is most difficult? Why?
5. The telephone is a common subject in both passages—but are they *about* the telephone? If not, what are they about?

PRACTICE

Ideas about a Common Object

Using one of the two passages on telephones as an example, write a short expressive piece conveying your ideas about the telephone or about some other common piece of modern technology: the car, the airplane, the computer, the video game, the blaster (loud portable stereo). You might begin by writing the name of the object at the top of a page. Then jot down a list of thoughts about that object as they occur to you, or focus on the topic through the kind of open-ended writing described in the first reading of this chapter (p. 27). Based on these notes, write a draft that will clearly convey your thoughts to a reader.

Interpreting Character

Here is a complete short story by Ernest Hemingway. The story presents a brief, apparently trivial event in the life of a young American couple traveling in Italy in the period just after World War I. Read the story, paying particular attention to the relationship between husband and wife. Because Hemingway uses a very plain style, with little commentary on the meaning of events, the reader is forced to evaluate and interpret on the basis of the few details the author has chosen to present. The story, then, is not as simple as it seems, for it is you, the reader, who must complete it by making inferences and drawing conclusions.

Read!

Ernest Hemingway, "Cat in the Rain"

There were only two Americans stopping at the hotel. They did not 1
know any of the people they passed on the stairs on their way to and from their room. Their room was on the second floor facing the sea. It also faced the public garden and the war monument. There were big palms and green benches in the public garden. In the good weather there was always an artist with his easel. Artists liked the way the palms grew and the bright colors of the hotels facing the gardens and the sea. Italians came from a long way off to look up at the war monument. It was made of bronze and glistened in the rain. It was raining. The rain dripped from the palm trees. Water stood in pools on the gravel paths. The sea broke in a long line in the rain and slipped back down the beach to come up and break again in a long line in the rain. The motor cars were gone from the square by the war monument. Across the square in the doorway of the café a waiter stood looking out at the empty square.

The American wife stood at the window looking out. Outside 2
right under their window a cat was crouched under one of the dripping green tables. The cat was trying to make herself so compact that she would not be dripped on.

"I'm going down and get that kitty," the American wife said. 3

"I'll do it," her husband offered from the bed. 4

"No, I'll get it. The poor kitty out trying to keep dry under a 5
table."

38   The husband went on reading, lying propped up with the two pil-   6
lows at the foot of the bed.

"Don't get wet," he said.   7

The wife went downstairs and the hotel owner stood up and   8
bowed to her as she passed the office. His desk was at the far end of
the office. He was an old man and very tall.

"Il piove," the wife said. She liked the hotel-keeper.   9

"Si, si, Signora, brutto tempo. It's very bad weather."   10

He stood behind his desk in the far end of the dim room. The wife   11
liked him. She liked the deadly serious way he received any complaints. She liked his dignity. She liked the way he wanted to serve
her. She liked the way he felt about being a hotel-keeper. She liked
his old, heavy face and big hands.

Liking him she opened the door and looked out. It was rain-   12
ing harder. A man in a rubber cape was crossing the empty square
to the café. The cat would be around to the right. Perhaps she
could go along under the eaves. As she stood in the doorway an
umbrella opened behind her. It was the maid who looked after their
room.

"You must not get wet," she smiled, speaking Italian. Of course,   13
the hotel-keeper had sent her.

With the maid holding the umbrella over her, she walked along   14
the gravel path until she was under their window. The table was
there, washed bright green in the rain, but the cat was gone. She was
suddenly disappointed. The maid looked up at her.

"Ha perduto qualque cosa, Signora?"   15

"There was a cat," said the American girl.   16

"A cat?"   17

"Si, il gatto."   18

"A cat?" the maid laughed. "A cat in the rain?"   19

"Yes," she said, "under the table." Then, "Oh, I wanted it so   20
much. I wanted a kitty."

When she talked English the maid's face tightened.   21

"Come, Signora," she said. "We must get back inside. You will   22
be wet."

"I suppose so," said the American girl.   23

They went back along the gravel path and passed in the door. The   24
maid stayed outside to close the umbrella. As the American girl
passed the office, the padrone bowed from his desk. Something felt
very small and tight inside the girl. The padrone made her feel very
small and at the same time really important. She had a momentary
feeling of being of supreme importance. She went on up the stairs.
She opened the door of the room. George was on the bed, reading.

"Did you get the cat?" he asked, putting the book down.   25

"It was gone."

"Wonder where it went to," he said, resting his eyes from reading.   27

She sat down on the bed.   28

"I wanted it so much," she said. "I don't know why I wanted it   29
so much. I wanted that poor kitty. It isn't any fun to be a poor kitty
out in the rain."

George was reading again.   30

She went over and sat in front of the mirror of the dressing table   31
looking at herself with the hand glass. She studied her profile, first
one side and then the other. Then she studied the back of her head
and her neck.

"Don't you think it would be a good idea if I let my hair grow   32
out?" she asked, looking at her profile again.

George looked up and saw the back of her neck, clipped close like   33
a boy's.

"I like it the way it is."   34

"I get so tired of it," she said. "I get so tired of looking like a   35
boy."

George shifted his position in the bed. He hadn't looked away   36
from her since she started to speak.

"You look pretty darn nice," he said.   37

She laid the mirror down on the dresser and went over to the win-   38
dow and looked out. It was getting dark.

"I want to pull my hair back tight and smooth and make a big   39
knot at the back that I can feel," she said. "I want to have a kitty to
sit on my lap and purr when I stroke her."

"Yeah?" George said from the bed.   40

"And I want to eat at a table with my own silver and I want can-   41
dles. And I want it to be spring and I want to brush my hair out in
front of a mirror and I want a kitty and I want some new clothes."

"Oh, shut up and get something to read," George said. He was   42
reading again.

His wife was looking out of the window. It was quite dark now and   43
still raining in the palm trees.

"Anyway, I want a cat," she said, "I want a cat. I want a cat   44
now. If I can't have long hair or any fun, I can have a cat."

George was not listening. He was reading his book. His wife   45
looked out of the window where the light had come on in the square.

Someone knocked at the door.   46

"Avanti," George said. He looked up from his book.   47

In the doorway stood the maid. She held a big tortoise-shell cat   48
pressed tight against her and swung down against her body.

"Excuse me," she said, "the padrone asked me to bring this for   49
the Signora."

QUESTIONS

1. Consider everything the young husband says and does. What kind of man is he? What do you think of him?
2. Consider the young wife, especially what she thinks and feels about the padrone (the hotel manager) and what she says to her husband just before the maid knocks on the door at the end of the story. What kind of woman is she? What do you think of her?
3. Can you tell what the narrator or the author, Hemingway, thinks of the two main characters? Does he favor either the husband or the wife? How do *you* judge them? Are you more sympathetic to one or the other? What reasons do you have for your feelings?
4. Is the cat a symbol of something or just a cat?
5. What is the function of the padrone in the story? What would be missing if he weren't there?
6. What do you think will be the future of this couple? What things in the text support your view of their future?

PRACTICE

Expression Through Role-Playing

A. You are the American wife of the story. It is several hours later and you are seated at your dressing table, writing a letter to your old college roommate. You tell her a bit about the incident of the cat, but mostly you express your whole attitude toward your marriage and your life, what you have done and what you want to do.

B. You are the American husband of the story. It is several hours later and you are seated at a table inside the cafe, writing to your old college roommate. You tell him a bit about the incident of the cat, but mostly you express your whole attitude toward your marriage and your life, what you have done and what you want to do.

C. You are the padrone of the hotel. It is several hours later and you are seated in your office, writing a letter to your wife, who is visiting her sister in Firenze. You tell her about the incident of the cat, but mostly you express your whole attitude toward the American couple, including your predictions for their marriage.

Reflection: Your Self as Object

3

Reflection, like expression, is oriented to the writer. Unlike expression, however, it is not an immediate presentation of thought or feeling. It is mediated—by time, by distance, by experience and maturity. It is a *re*-flection, a looking-*back*. If expression is naturally a young person's form, reflection is the opposite: a form for those who have enough perspective to look back on things and see them differently from the way they seemed to be at the time. For a child, reflection is almost an impossibility. But as soon as we are old enough to remember childhood itself as a time when we were "different"—or are able to look across the gap of any great event, like a death in the family, the loss of a friend, or a danger experienced—we can begin to reflect on our experience. Being able to think reflectively is itself a sign of maturity.

Reflection usually depends on the difference between two moments: the time of the event or situation and the time of the writing—in other words, *then* and *now*. The writer of reflection must use this difference in time to express the feelings and thoughts of *now* by recalling or imagining the emotions and ideas present *then*. Reflection is not simply the telling of a tale or describing of a scene. These things may enter into it, but they are there for the sake of what they are only *now* seen to mean.

Reflection also has a crucial role to play in the writing process itself. Writing is not an instantaneous event. Not only does it take a certain amount of time to write even a single sentence, but any serious writing project may extend over a considerable period of time. During the time of writing there are many moments of reflection in which the writer examines the words already there on the page, sometimes thinking, "But that's not what I meant to say. I really meant. . . ." We feel the same way about deeds often enough ("I didn't mean to do *that*"), but deeds cannot be undone. Words, however, can be unwritten. We call this process *revision*, and it is an aspect of reflection that we can use in all the other forms of writing. Reflection is, above all, the move through writing toward a better understanding of the things we have already seen, done, and written.

READING

Your Own Expressive Writing

If you accepted our earlier invitation to follow Peter Elbow's advice and produce some open-ended writing—or to imitate Handke or Gass—you are eligible to participate in this exercise. The first step is to find the writing you did there and read it over. This kind of reflection on previous writing is crucial to every person's development of thought through the process of rewriting.

Read over your work, then, whether you did all three of the expressive exercises or only one or two. Try to read it with eyes that are both critical and creative. Don't be critical in a nit-picking way, looking for little errors. Read as a writer reads, looking for the expressions that are most revealing, most vigorous, that seem to capture something in language that is expressively equal to the idea or feeling that lies behind the language. Above all, look for patterns. If you have done all three exercises, look for any ideas or feelings or key words that appear in all three. If you only did the Elbow exercise, look for the "point" that Elbow suggested you would find.

It would be good to exchange your writing with a few others to find out what pattern or point they may find in your work. When you have discussed and considered your expressive writing thoroughly, you will be ready to use it as the basis for more practice in writing.

Reflection as Revision

The idea of this assignment is to use your earlier writing as raw material for a more finished, polished piece of work. In the expressive exercises, you allowed things to drift up into your consciousness without trying to pursue them and explore their implications. Reading over that work, you should now find one or more topics that are important to you, about which you have opinions, feelings, thoughts. Having located such a topic, you are now in a position to consider it more carefully, to reflect upon it, to develop your thoughts in a coherent way. That is exactly what we ask you to do. Beginning from your previous expressive writing, even using phrases from it where appropriate, *use* writing as a way of working toward your best answer to the question, "What do I really think about _____?" Keep on writing, reflecting, and revising until you are satisfied with your reflections.

READING

School Days Revisited

In the following selections from their autobiographies, the writers recall incidents from their school careers. Margaret Mead reflects upon her difficult freshman year at DePauw University, and Russell Baker reflects on a high school teacher who helped him make a career choice. (Mead became a well-known anthropologist and Baker became a well-known journalist.)

Margaret Mead, from Blackberry Winter

When I arrived at DePauw, I found that I had two roommates. One   1
was a girl who had come to college to join a sorority, and this had been arranged in advance; the other expected to be rushed by a sorority that had little prestige. I soon learned that no one belonging to a sorority could speak to an unpledged freshman. This, of course, explained why I heard nothing from the effusive girl who had writ-

ten me so many letters during the summer. When the invitations came out, I was invited to the Kappa rushing party. But when I arrived wearing my unusual and unfashionable dress that was designed to look like a wheat field with poppies blooming in it, my correspondent turned her back on me and never spoke to me again. I found the whole evening strangely confusing. I could not know, of course, that everyone had been given the signal that inviting me had been a mistake. Afterward, my two roommates got the bids they expected, but I did not get a bid.

It still took a little time for me to realize the full implications of what it meant to be an unpledged freshman in a college where everything was organized around the fraternities and sororities. For one thing, I had no dates; these were all arranged through commands to the freshman pledges of certain fraternities to date the freshman pledges of certain sororities. Although all freshmen had to live in dormitories, it meant also that there was a widening gulf between the pledges, who spent a lot of time at their sorority houses being disciplined and shaped up, and the unpledged freshmen and the few upperclassmen in the dormitories.

With a very few exceptions, these upperclassmen were pretty dismal. But there was Katharine Rothenberger, who became my lifelong friend; she had transferred from a college where she had turned down a sorority bid because it was too expensive. And there was an English girl, very tall and very serious, also a transfer, who in later life became a very well-known missionary. By and large, however, the girls who were, by sorority standards, ineligible were less attractive and less sparkling than their classmates who were among the chosen. Moreover, all those who still hoped had one characteristic in common—their fear of making friends with others of their own kind. Although I was experiencing the bitter injustice of being excluded, on grounds that I did not respect, I experienced also what I have come to regard as a principal reason for abolishing such exclusive institutions, that is, the damage done to the arbitrarily excluded who continue to believe that one day they still may enter the ranks of the chosen.

QUESTIONS

1. Reflection involves the manipulation of time. Look at the first paragraph and try to determine exactly how many different moments in time can be distinguished. Note especially all the words that help keep the reader clearly oriented in time. How many sentences in this paragraph are entirely lacking in markers that indicate some change or shift in time?

2. The essential feature of the management of time in reflective writing is a distinction between the time of the events being reflected upon and the moment of reflection itself. Read through these paragraphs noting every phrase that indicates a difference between time of events and the time of reflection. What has reflection added to this report that would have escaped a diary or journal that simply expressed what Mead felt at the time of the events themselves?

Russell Baker, from Growing Up

The notion of becoming a writer had flickered off and on in my head since the Belleville days, but it wasn't until my third year in high school that the possibility took hold. Until then I'd been bored by everything associated with English courses. I found English grammar dull and baffling. I hated the assignments to turn out "compositions," and went at them like heavy labor, turning out leaden, lackluster paragraphs that were agonies for teachers to read and for me to write. The classics thrust on me to read seemed as deadening as chloroform.

When our class was assigned to Mr. Fleagle for third-year English I anticipated another grim year in that dreariest of subjects. Mr. Fleagle was notorious among City students for dullness and inability to inspire. He was said to be stuffy, dull, and hopelessly out of date. To me he looked to be sixty or seventy and prim to a fault. He wore primly severe eyeglasses, his wavy hair was primly cut and primly combed. He wore prim vested suits with neckties blocked primly against the collar buttons of his primly starched white shirts. He had a primly pointed jaw, a primly straight nose, and a prim manner of speaking that was so correct, so gentlemanly, that he seemed a comic antique.

I anticipated a listless, unfruitful year with Mr. Fleagle and for a long time was not disappointed. We read *Macbeth*. Mr. Fleagle loved *Macbeth* and wanted us to love it too, but he lacked the gift of infecting others with his own passion. He tried to convey the murderous ferocity of Lady Macbeth one day by reading aloud the passage that concludes

> . . . I have given suck, and know
> How tender 'tis to love the babe that milks me.
> I would, while it was smiling in my face,
> Have plucked my nipple from his boneless gums. . . .

The idea of prim Mr. Fleagle plucking his nipple from boneless gums was too much for the class. We burst into gasps of irrepressible snickering. Mr. Fleagle stopped.

"There is nothing funny, boys, about giving suck to a babe. It is the—the very essence of motherhood, don't you see." 4

He constantly sprinkled his sentences with "don't you see." It wasn't a question but an exclamation of mild surprise at our ignorance. "Your pronoun needs an antecedent, don't you see," he would say, very primly. "The purpose of the Porter's scene, boys, is to provide comic relief from the horror, don't you see." 5

Late in the year we tackled the informal essay. "The essay, don't you see, is the. . . ." My mind went numb. Of all forms of writing, none seemed so boring as the essay. Naturally we would have to write informal essays. Mr. Fleagle distributed a homework sheet offering us a choice of topics. None was quite so simpleminded as "What I Did on My Summer Vacation," but most seemed to be almost as dull. I took the list home and dawdled until the night before the essay was due. Sprawled on the sofa, I finally faced up to the grim task, took the list out of my notebook, and scanned it. The topic on which my eye stopped was "The Art of Eating Spaghetti." 6

This title produced an extraordinary sequence of mental images. Surging up out of the depths of memory came a vivid recollection of a night in Belleville when all of us were seated around the supper table—Uncle Allen, my mother, Uncle Charlie, Doris, Uncle Hal—and Aunt Pat served spaghetti for supper. Spaghetti was an exotic treat in those days. Neither Doris nor I had ever eaten spaghetti, and none of the adults had enough experience to be good at it. All the good humor of Uncle Allen's house reawoke in my mind as I recalled the laughing arguments we had that night about the socially respectable method for moving spaghetti from plate to mouth. 7

Suddenly I wanted to write about that, about the warmth and good feeling of it, but I wanted to put it down simply for my own joy, not for Mr. Fleagle. It was a moment I wanted to recapture and hold for myself. I wanted to relive the pleasure of an evening at New Street. To write it as I wanted, however, would violate all the rules of formal composition I'd learned in school, and Mr. Fleagle would surely give it a failing grade. Never mind. I would write something else for Mr. Fleagle after I had written this thing for myself. 8

When I finished it the night was half gone and there was no time left to compose a proper, respectable essay for Mr. Fleagle. There was no choice next morning but to turn in my private reminiscence of Belleville. Two days passed before Mr. Fleagle returned the graded papers, and he returned everyone's but mine. I was bracing myself for a command to report to Mr. Fleagle immediately after school for discipline when I saw him lift my paper from his desk and rap for the class's attention. 9

"Now, boys," he said, "I want to read you an essay. This is titled 'The Art of Eating Spaghetti.'" 10

And he started to read. My words! He was reading *my words* out loud to the entire class. What's more, the entire class was listening. Listening attentively. Then somebody laughed, then the entire class was laughing, and not in contempt and ridicule, but with open-hearted enjoyment. Even Mr. Fleagle stopped two or three times to repress a small prim smile.

I did my best to avoid showing pleasure, but what I was feeling was pure ecstasy at this startling demonstration that my words had the power to make people laugh. In the eleventh grade, at the eleventh hour as it were, I had discovered a calling. It was the happiest moment of my entire school career. When Mr. Fleagle finished he put the final seal on my happiness by saying, "Now that, boys, is an essay, don't you see. It's—don't you see—it's of the very essence of the essay, don't you see. Congratulations, Mr. Baker."

For the first time, light shone on a possibility. It wasn't a very heartening possibility, to be sure. Writing couldn't lead to a job after high school, and it was hardly honest work, but Mr. Fleagle had opened a door for me. After that I ranked Mr. Fleagle among the finest teachers in the school.

QUESTIONS

1. What periods of time are being reflected upon in the first two paragraphs?
2. Mr. Fleagle is described and presented to us primarily through the eyes of the sixteen-year-old Baker. Why? What do you think of Mr. Fleagle?
3. What statement is being made about reflective writing in this reflective piece?

PRACTICE

Reflection on Your School Days

Choose an event or situation from your elementary or high school years. It may be an event similar to one of those in the Mead and Baker pieces concerning the difficulties (or pleasures) of making friends in a new school, or concerning a teacher you remember well. It may be an event of brief duration or a situation that extended over a period of time. You might list a number of events before you choose one to focus on.

Write out the event as you experienced it *then*, as if you were expressing your thoughts in a diary or in a letter to a close friend at the time the event took place. Read over what you have written, and reconsider the event from your present perspective. Then revise what you have written to emphasize this present perspective, being sure to provide a conclusion in which you reflect on what the event means to you *now*. Before you begin your draft, you might want to do some prewriting to see what particular details you can remember—about the people involved and what they did or said, about the place where the event occurred, about your expectations, and about what you learned.

READING

An Unreflective Poem?

We would like you to reflect on the following poem. Read it aloud a few times so that you can hear the rhythm of it.

We Real Cool
The Pool Players
Seven at the Golden Shovel

We real cool. We   1
Left school. We

Lurk late. We   2
Strike straight. We

Sing sin. We   3
Thin gin. We

Jazz June. We   4
Die soon.

GWENDOLYN BROOKS

QUESTIONS

1. Try writing the poem out in narrative form. What happens to the beat of the poem?

2. How does the poem define *cool*?

3. Who is the speaker in the poem? What does "We die soon" mean?
4. Note the tense of every verb in the poem. How do the past and future function in relation to the more frequently used present tense?

PRACTICE

Reflecting on the Golden Shovel

Imagine that you were one of the "Seven at the Golden Shovel." You have survived for twenty years since those days. Write a few reflective paragraphs about your youthful days from the point of view of your older self. Base your details of the past on the poem, but consider them from a more mature position. You may be either critical or indulgent looking back, but you should have some clear perspective that you develop by reflecting on the past and comparing it to your present situation. In writing, assume that you are writing for people like "yourself"—that is, like the imaginary person whose role you have assumed. If the person is successful in business, assume you are writing for other businesspeople who may or may not have spent their youths in places like the Golden Shovel. Make sure that you use the difference between the *now* of writing and the *then* of your past situation to develop your ideas and feelings.

READING

Looking at Pictures

We live in the age of mechanical reproduction of images: photographs, photoprinting, cinema, video, computer graphics. All of these, in their turn, may become the object of transformation into words. The following selections illustrate this process with two instances of writers looking at photographs and recording the moment with their own apparatus, the written word.

Looking at Pictures to Be Put Away

Who was this girl   1
In her white night gown
Clutching a pair of jeans

On a foggy redwood deck.   2
She looks up at me tender,
Calm, surprised,

What will we remember   3
Bodies thick with food and lovers
After twenty years.

GARY SNYDER

Roland Barthes, "Looking For My Mother"

There I was, alone in the apartment where she had died, looking at   1
these pictures of my mother, one by one, under the lamp, gradually
moving back in time with her, looking for the truth of the face I had
loved. And I found it.

The photograph was very old. The corners were blunted from   2
having been pasted into an album, the sepia print had faded, and the
picture just managed to show two children standing together at the
end of a little wooden bridge in a glassed-in conservatory, what was
called a Winter Garden in those days. My mother was five at the
time (1898), her brother seven. He was leaning against the bridge
railing, along which he had extended one arm; she, shorter than he,
was standing a little back, facing the camera; you could tell that the
photographer had said, "Step forward a little so we can see you";
she was holding one finger in the other hand, as children often do, in
an awkward gesture. The brother and sister, united, as I knew, by
the discord of their parents, who were soon to divorce, had posed
side by side, alone, under the palms of the Winter Garden (it was the
house where my mother was born, in Chennevières-sur-Marne).

I studied the little girl and at last rediscovered my mother. The   3
distinctness of her face, the naïve attitude of her hands, the place she
had docilely taken without either showing or hiding herself, and finally her expression, which distinguished her, like Good from Evil,
from the hysterical little girl, from the simpering doll who plays at
being a grownup—all this constituted the future of a sovereign *innocence* (if you will take this word according to its etymology, which is:
"I do no harm"), all this had transformed the photographic pose

into that untenable paradox which she had nonetheless maintained all her life: the assertion of a gentleness. In this little girl's image I saw the kindness which had formed her being immediately and forever, without her having inherited it from anyone; how could this kindness have proceeded from the imperfect parents who had loved her so badly—in short: from a family? Her kindness was specifically *out-of-play*, it belonged to no system, or at least it was located at the limits of a morality (evangelical, for instance); I could not define it better than by this feature (among others): that during the whole of our life together, she never made a single ''observation.'' This extreme and particular circumstance, so abstract in relation to an image, was nonetheless present in the face revealed in the photograph I had just discovered. ''Not a just image, just an image,'' Godard says. But my grief wanted a just image, an image which would be both justice and accuracy—*justesse*: just an image, but a just image. Such, for me, was the Winter Garden Photograph.

QUESTIONS

1. The camera is mechanical. What it records is fixed. But human memory is selective and changes as we move through time. Snyder's poem is about forgetting: ''Who?'' ''What?'' How are the poem's two questions related?
2. Why does Snyder use the present tense in line 5? How are past, present, and future considered in the nine lines of the poem?
3. What does ''thick with food and lovers'' mean? Why ''thick''?
4. Who are ''we''? Where are ''we''? When are ''we''? What are ''we'' doing?
5. Barthes says that his mother (even in her childhood picture) was characterized by ''the assertion of a gentleness.'' He calls this phrase a ''paradox.'' What does he mean by that?
6. In paragraph 3 what does Barthes mean by saying that his mother never made an ''observation,'' putting the word into quotation marks? What do you suppose he means by ''observation''?
7. What is a ''just'' image?

PRACTICE

Reflecting on a Photograph

Snyder shows us one way of writing about a photograph that preserves the image of someone no longer remembered by the writer—a way of reflecting on an image left behind by the process of mechanical reproduction. Barthes shows us one way of writing about a photograph of someone very close to the writer, someone remembered so well that the writer's reflections overwhelm the image, either filling it with the writer's feelings or noticing in it the absence of those qualities most important in the person whose image it is.

Both of these writers show how naturally photographs put us into a reflective mood. Because they freeze a moment of time, they force us to reflect in order to connect the flow of life to the frozen image reproduced by the camera. Taking these writers not as models but as inspiration, select a single photograph from your personal collection, and reflect upon it. Try to make your writing as serious and thoughtful as what you have just read. Here are some things to remember as you prepare to write:

A. The reader will *not* have the picture, so you will not be able to depend on the visual image to work for you. You will have to put into words whatever you want the reader to know about the image you are reflecting upon. You might begin prewriting by listing the important things that are in the picture, and those that are left out. Your essay may well turn upon the difference between these two lists.

B. Think of the image as unchanging while everything around it changes. How does the presence of the image before you as you prepare to write affect you? Where does the image direct your thoughts? Close your eyes and think about the image. Where do your thoughts want to go? What is *there*?

C. What do you remember, what have you forgotten, what will become of this image? If you have chosen a photograph of a person (as we suggest you do), try to determine what things about the person are important to you (you might list them), and compare these with what the camera has caught and what it has missed. Here is space for reflection.

D. Qualities caught and missed, time frozen and moving, the simplicities of mechanism and the complexities of life—these are your starting points.

From Thing to Thought

This is a complete reflection by the Danish writer Isak Dinesen, who lived in Africa for many years. She published her reminiscences in a book called *Out of Africa*, from which this selection has been taken. In reading the selection, we ask you to be especially alert to three things: (1) its management of time, (2) its use of descriptive and illustrative language, and (3) its organization.

Isak Dinesen, ''The Iguana''

In the Reserve I have sometimes come upon the Iguana, the big lizards, as they were sunning themselves upon a flat stone in a riverbed. They are not pretty in shape, but nothing can be imagined more beautiful than their coloring. They shine like a heap of precious stones or like a pane cut out of an old church window. When, as you approach, they swish away, there is a flash of azure, green and purple over the stones, the color seems to be standing behind them in the air, like a comet's luminous tail.

Once I shot an Iguana. I thought that I should be able to make some pretty things from his skin. A strange thing happened then, that I have never afterwards forgotten. As I went up to him, where he was lying dead upon his stone, and actually while I was walking the few steps, he faded and grew pale, all color died out of him as in one long sigh, and by the time that I touched him he was grey and dull like a lump of concrete. It was the live impetuous blood pulsating within the animal, which had radiated out all that glow and splendor. Now that the flame was put out, and the soul had flown, the Iguana was as dead as a sandbag.

Often since I have, in some sort, shot an Iguana, and I have remembered the one of the Reserve. Up at Meru I saw a young Native girl with a bracelet on, a leather strap two inches wide, and embroidered all over with very small turquoise-colored beads which varied a little in color and played in green, light blue and ultramarine. It was an extraordinarily live thing; it seemed to draw breath on her arm, so that I wanted it for myself, and made Farah buy it from her. No sooner had it come upon my own arm than it gave up the ghost. It was nothing now, a small, cheap, purchased article of finery. It had been the play of colors, the duet between the turquoise

1

2

3

and the "nègre"—that quick, sweet, brownish black, like peat and black pottery, of the Native's skin—that had created the life of the bracelet.

In the Zoological Museum of Pietermaritzburg, I have seen, in a stuffed deep-water fish in a showcase, the same combination of coloring, which there had survived death; it made me wonder what life can well be like, on the bottom of the sea, to send up something so live and airy. I stood in Meru and looked at my pale hand and at the dead bracelet, it was as if an injustice had been done to a noble thing, as if truth had been suppressed. So sad did it seem that I remembered the saying of the hero in a book that I had read as a child: "I have conquered them all, but I am standing amongst graves." 4

In a foreign country and with foreign species of life one should take measures to find out whether things will be keeping their value when dead. To the settlers of East Africa I give the advice: "For the sake of your own eyes and heart, shoot not the Iguana." 5

QUESTIONS

1. Make an outline of Dinesen's five-paragraph essay. What is covered in each paragraph?
2. Note all the major shifts in time of events or grammatical tense in the essay. How does the time structure compare to your organizational outline?
3. In this essay, reflection on individual experiences is brought to the point of generalization and advice. How is this accomplished? How does reflection turn into advice? How does the care for description contribute to the strength of the advice?

PRACTICE

Reflecting on Experience

Using Dinesen's essay as a model, reflect on two or three events you have experienced or observed that can be brought, under the pressure of reconsideration, to the point where a conclusion, a generalization, or some sort of advice can be drawn from your reflection upon them. This may well take some thought, some brainstorming, some free or open-ended writing to get you started. The idea, however, is to carry reflection as far as you can toward conclusions drawn from the events reflected upon through your writing.

You might begin by listing events or experiences in your life that were memorable for what you learned from them. For instance, have you ever been thoughtless, stupid, cruel, careless, or dishonest in a way that can serve as an example of mistaken behavior? (You must have had such experiences—we all do.) Try to describe one or more of these events so that your unique experience will come to represent a typical *kind* of experience.

Remember that Dinesen does not simply reach a conclusion for herself (''I shouldn't have done that,'' or ''I won't do that again''). She generalizes her experience as widely as she can. You may not manage to equal her range, but you can try to move in the direction she indicates, from herself to the world.

PART THREE

READER-ORIENTED FORMS

4 Direction: Guiding Your Reader

In writing directions, we assume that the reader wants to follow them. We do not have to engage in persuasion. All we have to do is make our verbal presentation so clear that the reader can get all the necessary information from our words. This is not as easy as it sounds. If you have ever tried to follow the directions that come with various unassembled products, you know something about how difficult it is. Inadequate directions are extremely frustrating and can almost always be traced to one problem: the writer's failure to imagine the reader clearly and to understand what the reader already knows and what new information must be provided.

The writer of directions has to imagine the reader out there somewhere, holding the directions in one hand and coming back to them every step of the way. How much explanation does the reader need? How much can be taken for granted? Cookbooks, for instance, often take a lot for granted. Here are some directions from *The New York Times Cook Book:*

BASIC PIE PASTRY   **Pastry for 9-inch pie or 6 tarts**

2 cups sifted all-purpose flour   ⅓ cup cold water,
1 teaspoon salt   approximately
⅔ cup shortening

1. Sift together the flour and salt.
2. Using a pastry blender or two knives, chop in the shortening until the mixture resembles coarse cornmeal.
3. Sprinkle water slowly over the top of the flour, while tossing the mixture up from the bottom of the bowl with a fork. After about three-quarters of the water has been added, press the dampened part of the dough into a ball and set aside. Add only enough water to dampen the remaining flour mixture. Press all the dough together and divide into two portions, one slightly larger than the other. If the kitchen is hot, chill the dough for one-half hour before rolling.
4. Place the larger ball of dough on a lightly floured pastry cloth or board, pat in all directions with a floured rolling pin and then roll from the center out in all directions, loosening the pastry and reflouring the cloth and rolling pin as necessary. Roll into a round one-eighth inch thick and two inches larger in diameter than the top of the pie pan.
5. Fold gently into quarters, place in the pan and unfold. Fit the dough into the pan loosely and press against the pan without stretching it. Trim the edge slightly larger than the outside rim of the pan. Add desired filling.
6. Stack the pastry trimmings on the remaining dough and roll until about one inch larger than the top of the pan. Fold gently into quarters and cut several small gashes to allow steam to escape.
7. Moisten the rim of the lower crust, place top crust on the filled pan and unfold. Do not stretch the pastry. Tuck the rim of the top beneath the edge of the undercrust and flute with the fingers, making a tight seal.
8. Bake as directed for the filling used.

For the uninitiated, there will be some mysteries here. How does one "chop in" shortening? What does coarse cornmeal look like? Why is the dough dampened in two steps, then pressed together, and then divided? What temperature must the kitchen be to be "hot"? Are the "pastry trimmings" the same thing as the dough cut off the edge of the pan? If so, when does "dough" become "pastry"? Moisten the rim with what? How do you "flute with the fingers"?

This cookbook is for those who don't need to ask such questions. Another book might proceed in a more elementary way. And someone just learning to cook might well prefer the more elementary book. All kinds of writing must be adjusted to the level of the potential reader, but directive writing is most sensitive to this because the reader has to do more than read it. He or she must act out the directions. Failures of communication that might go unnoticed in other kinds of writing will quickly become apparent when the reader tries to turn directions into deeds.

Here are a few rules (or directions) for you to follow when writing directions.

1. Always imagine the reader trying to perform your words, depending on them.
2. Give the reader as much information and explanation as is necessary—and no more.
3. Go step by step, following the order of procedure with your words so that the reader can follow the words with deeds.
4. Consider the morale of the reader, and offer encouragement when needed, as well as information.

READING

Direction Through the Ages

The following sets of directions are from three different centuries. The first is by Theophilus, a fifteenth-century craftsman, from his book *On Divers Arts*, translated from the Latin original. The second is by Benjamin Franklin, from a letter written in 1762 to David Hume, the Scottish philosopher. The last is from a recent book by an athlete, *Diana Nyad's Basic Training for Women*.

Theophilus, ''On Carving Crystal''

If you want to carve a piece of rock crystal, take a two- or three-year-old goat and bind its feet together and cut a hole between its breast and stomach, in the place where the heart is, and put the crystal in there, so that it lies in its blood until it is hot. At once take it out and engrave whatever you want on it, while this heat lasts. When it begins to cool and become hard, put it back in the goat's blood, take it out again when it is hot, and engrave it. Keep on doing so until you finish the carving. Finally, heat it again, take it out and rub it with a woolen cloth so that you may render it brilliant with the same blood.

Benjamin Franklin, "How to Make a Lightning Rod"

Prepare a steel rod about five or six feet long, about half an inch thick at its largest end, and tapering to a sharp point. This point should be gilded to prevent its rusting. Secure to the big end of the rod a strong eye or a ring half an inch in diameter. Fix the rod upright to the chimney or the highest part of a house. It should be fixed with some sort of staples or special nails to keep it steady. The pointed end should extend upward, and should rise three or four feet above the chimney or building to which the rod is fixed. Drive into the ground an iron rod about one inch in diameter, and ten or twelve feet long. This rod should also have an eye or ring fixed to its upper end. It is best to place the iron rod some distance from the foundation of the house. Ten feet away is a good distance, if the size of the property permits. Then take as much length of iron rod of a smaller diameter as will be necessary to reach from the eye on the rod above to the eye of the rod below. Fasten this securely to the fixed rods by passing it through the eyes and bending the ends to form rings too. Then close all the joints with lead. This is easily done by making a small bag of strong paper around the joints, tying it tight below, and then pouring in the molten lead. It is useful to have these joints treated in this way so that there will be a considerable area of contact between each piece. To prevent the wind from shaking this long rod, it may be fastened to the building by several staples. If the building is especially large or long, extending more than one hundred feet for example, it is wise to erect a rod at each end. If there is a well sufficiently near to the building to permit placing the iron rod in the water, this is even better than the use of the iron rod in the ground. It may also be wise to paint the iron to prevent it from rusting. A building so protected will not be damaged by lightning.

Diana Nyad and Candace Lyle Hogan, "The Ninety Second Test"

This is how you should look: feet placed flat on the floor making   1
your lower legs perpendicular to the floor so that they form 90-
degree angles with your thighs at the knees; toes pointed straight

ahead of you; feet about 12 inches apart; arms hanging loosely at your sides. Don't use your arms or hands in any way to support your weight.

The wall is your chair back; you look as if you are sitting in a chair but you have no chair. Now try to hold that position for 90 seconds—a terrific way to test your willpower. 2

This stationary exercise begins as soon as you've removed your supporting hand from the wall and are relying upon your quadriceps (the muscles along the tops of the thighs) to support your weight. Begin timing yourself. Remember: The goal is 90 seconds at one stretch. You probably won't be able to do it the first time out, but really try. Here is how you're going to feel at one time or another during this 90-second period. 3

Right away, after only about 10 seconds have passed, you're starting to feel a warm sensation in your thighs. You notice how the long muscle at the top of each thigh is flexed, feeling firm to the touch. Breathe—rhythmically, calmly. 4

As the seconds tick by, you're passing through different phases of one single sensation. It may feel like dozens of various sensations, but in fact what you are feeling is the quadriceps resisting gravity. When you are standing up, your skeleton more than your muscles is supporting your weight. But when you are bent like this in 90/90's, your position of resistance against gravity is far different. This position calls upon your quadriceps (and to a lesser degree the muscles of the back of the thigh, the buttocks and the calves) to prevent you from slipping down to the floor with the pull of gravity. To do this work the quadriceps are in an isometric (stationary) contraction, a position that never hurt Charles Atlas, and is not going to hurt you. 5

QUESTIONS

1. Although subject matter changes through the ages, the form of directive writing stays remarkably the same. What features of direction do you find in all three selections?
2. Note the features of each sample that seem aimed specifically at the reader. Which sample seems most attentive to the reader? How is this attention expressed?
3. Can you find elements of one or more of these samples that seem aimed more at the reader's morale or spirit than at information or instruction? How important is this? It is equally important in each case?

How to Make or Do Something

This exercise has three stages: writing, testing, and revising.

A. *Writing.* Think of something that you know more about than the average person. It can't simply be "knowledge of" in this case; it must be "knowing how to" make something or do something. It must also be something that another person might conceivably want to learn how to do. It can be anything from how a football guard should pull out of the line and block the opposing linebacker or safety on a sweep, to how to bake a cake or tune a guitar.

The first part of your task is to describe clearly the person or the sort of person you are writing this for. How familiar or unfamiliar is he or she with the background? In choosing your audience try not to make your task either too hard or too easy. Choose some type of person who knows something about the subject but doesn't know how this particular thing is done. Remember to write a description of this person first. Then name your project: How to _____. Make a list of all the steps required to complete the task. Next, consider this list in terms of the audience you have described: Will any further explanation be necessary? Can any explanations be simplified? Are there places where you will need to consider your reader's morale? Finally, produce the best set of directions you can for the task you have chosen.

B. *Testing.* Exchange your set of directions with another person in your class. Then, each of you should mark every point at which you feel in doubt about the writer's intentions or feel that you could not follow the directions. Do this, imagining that each of you is exactly the type of person named as audience. Ideally, you should give your paper to the person in the class who fits your audience profile the most closely, but do the best you can in any case. Your reader should provide you with a set of written directions for the revision of your directions.

C. *Revising.* Follow your reader's directions and revise your original directions as well as you can. Resubmit them to your reader for approval. If you ran into problems following your reader's directions for revision, just tell him or her about them. Don't write directions for revising the directions. Enough is enough.

READING

The Art of Eating Spaghetti

In an earlier selection, Russell Baker reflected on his first successful English composition, "The Art of Eating Spaghetti" (pages 45–47). Go back and read that section of the Baker selection and then return to the assignment below.

PRACTICE

The Art of Eating _____

We are told that Baker and his relatives discussed the "socially respectable method for moving spaghetti from plate to mouth," but we aren't told what that method is. Consider your experience with spaghetti and write up a socially respectable method for eating it. Or if you wish, you may write directions for eating another "difficult" food, such as a triple-decker ice cream cone, barbecued spare ribs, an artichoke, or a long hot dog with relish, onions, catsup, and sauerkraut on a short roll.

Whatever food you choose, remember that you are writing for an audience that is inexperienced in eating this particular food, does not have money to spare for dry-cleaning bills, and is easily embarrassed in public.

The Absent-Minded Writer

Ashley Moonstone, from "How I Write"

When I research the background for my novels, I literally lose my-   1
self in the locale. For *The Horror of Federal Hill*, I wandered the winding streets of Benevolence, drifting with its crowds, and dreaming of
its dark past, so redolent in its bleak, decaying squares (now, unfor-
tunately, undergoing restoration). So absorbed was I in imagining
the ancient terrors of its tunnels, the sinister secrets of its long-dead
slave traders, the restless bones beneath its dank bus station, that
when the police found me in a Woonsocket diner, I could not tell
them when or how I'd got there.

PRACTICE

Directing the Absent-Minded Lecturer

You have been appointed by your instructor to make arrangements to bring a speaker to your writing class. You have always
admired the novels and poetry of the well-known writer Ashley
Moonstone, so you wrote to Mr. Moonstone asking if he could
come and discuss the craft of writing with your class. He accepted your invitation and requested specific directions to your
classroom. He said he'd never been in your town before and
was afraid he'd get lost.

Given Mr. Moonstone's tendency to wander, you'll certainly
have to give him very explicit directions to your classroom. Decide which mode of transportation—bus, train, or plane—will
be most convenient for him so that you can write your careful
and explicit directions from the appropriate terminal, keeping
in mind one complicating factor: Ashley Moonstone is terrified
of taxis. (This terror stems from an experience of being wildly
driven in and out of New York City's St. Patrick's Day parade
by a drunken cab driver.) Mr. Moonstone prefers to walk, or if

the distance is very great he can be talked into taking a bus—but definitely *not* a taxi.

Write a letter in which you first direct Ashley Moonstone from the local airport or train or bus terminal to a point on or near your campus (a bus stop, subway stop, main intersection, etc.). Then tell him exactly how to proceed from this point to your classroom. He will not, of course, know the names of any buildings, so you must describe the landmarks he will need to find his way from his point of arrival to the door of your classroom. Do *not* plan to have anyone meet and guide him or to do so yourself. He would be insulted. Just tell him how to go as carefully and explicitly as you can, and hope for the best.

READING

The Unassembled Kiddy-Car

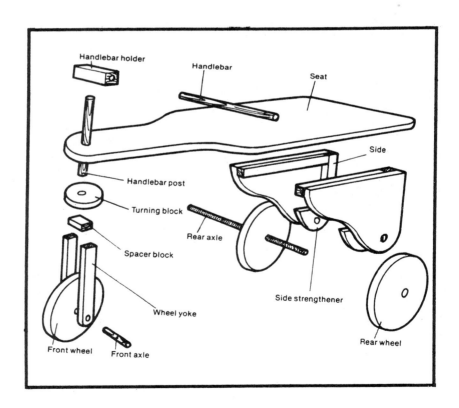

Assembling Arnold's Kiddy-Car

Your new mail order business, Natural Wooden Toys, has had a successful first year because of the quality of your products, their reasonable prices, and your attention to your customers. Your prices are low because you ship the toys unpainted and unassembled. The toys are easy to assemble with glue because of the very clear directions and the diagram you provide.

It is noon on Christmas eve. You've been out shopping and you return to your office for some last-minute business. Your secretary reports that a frantic customer, Mrs. Dilthey, has just called to say that the kiddy-car she ordered has arrived without the directions and the diagram. The kiddy-car must be ready for her three-year-old grandson Arnold on Christmas morning, but she has no idea how to assemble it. You try to call Mrs. Dilthey back, but she has apparently gone out for last-minute shopping. You must leave in 45 minutes to catch the last plane before Christmas to Bearpaw, Maine, where you intend to spend the holidays with your family at a remote ski lodge that has no phone.

You have never failed a customer, so you sit down to write out the directions so that your secretary can call Mrs. Dilthey later and read the directions to her. Remember that Mrs. Dilthey has no diagram to refer to, so you must help her to identify the parts by describing what they look like as well as how they go together and at what points they should be glued.

READING

Pseudodirection

In its grammar, W. S. Merwin's writing is typical of direction. He uses the imperative form of the verb for the most part, and he arranges his sentences in a sequence which corresponds to that of the actions to be performed: start with this; then do that; then the other; finish with this. It is only at the levels of meaning and action that Merwin's writing ceases to be directive. The task he describes is impossible; therefore, his text is only pseudodirective. It has a meaning different from its apparent meaning and is in fact a different kind of writing: persuasive. After you read the essay, consider the questions that follow it.

W. S. Merwin, "Unchopping a Tree"

Start with the leaves, the small twigs, and the nests that have been shaken, ripped, or broken off by the fall; these must be gathered and attached once again to their respective places. It is not arduous work, unless major limbs have been smashed or mutilated. If the fall was carefully and correctly planned, the chances of anything of the kind happening will have been reduced. Again, much depends upon the size, age, shape, and species of the tree. Still, you will be lucky if you can get through this stage without having to use machinery. Even in the best of circumstances it is a labor that will make you wish often that you had won the favor of the universe of ants, the empire of mice, or at least a local tribe of squirrels, and could enlist their labors and their talents. But no, they leave you to it. They have learned, with time. This is men's work. It goes without saying that if the tree was hollow in whole or in part, and contained old nests of bird or mammal or insect, or hoards of nuts or such structures as wasps or bees build for their survival, the contents will have to be repaired where necessary, and reassembled, insofar as possible, in their original order, including the shells of nuts already opened. With spiders' webs you must simply do the best you can. We do not have the spider's weaving equipment, nor any substitute for the leaf's living bond with its point of attachment and nourishment. It is even harder to simulate the latter when the leaves have once become dry—as they are bound to do, for this is not the labor of a moment. Also it hardly needs saying that this is the time for repairing any neighboring trees or bushes or other growth that may have been damaged by the fall. The same rules apply. Where neighboring trees were of the same species it is difficult not to waste time conveying a detached leaf back to the wrong tree. Practice, practice. Put your hope in that.

Now the tackle must be put into place, or the scaffolding, depending on the surroundings and the dimensions of the tree. It is ticklish work. Almost always it involves, in itself, further damage to the area, which will have to be corrected later. But as you've heard, it can't be helped. And care now is likely to save you considerable trouble later. Be careful to grind nothing into the ground.

At last the time comes for the erecting of the trunk. By now it will scarcely be necessary to remind you of the delicacy of this huge skeleton. Every motion of the tackle, every slight upward heave of the trunk, the branches, their elaborately reassembled panoply of leaves (now dead) will draw from you an involuntary gasp. You will watch for a leaf or a twig to be snapped off yet again. You will listen for the nuts to shift in the hollow limb and you will hear whether they are indeed falling into place or are spilling in disorder—in which case, or in the event of anything else of the kind—operations will have to cease, of course, while you correct the matter. The raising itself is no small enterprise, from the moment when the chains tighten around the old bandages until the bole hangs vertical above the stump, splinter above splinter. Now the final straightening of the splinters themselves can take place (the preliminary work is best done while the wood is still green and soft, but at times when the splinters are not badly twisted most of the straightening is left until now, when the torn ends are face to face with each other). When the splinters are perfectly complementary the appropriate fixative is applied. Again we have no duplicate of the original substance. Ours is extremely strong, but it is rigid. It is limited to surface, and there is no play in it. However the core is not the part of the trunk that conducted life from the roots up into the branches and back again. It was relatively inert. The fixative for this part is not the same as the one for the outer layers and the bark, and if either of these is involved in the splintered section they must receive applications of the appropriate adhesives. Apart from being incorrect and probably ineffective, the core fixative would leave a scar on the bark.

When all is ready the splintered trunk is lowered onto the splinters   4
of the stump. This, one might say, is only the skeleton of the resurrection. Now the chips must be gathered, and the sawdust, and returned to their former positions. The fixative for the wood layers will be applied to chips and sawdust consisting only of wood. Chips and sawdust consisting of several substances will receive applications of the correct adhesives. It is as well, where possible, to shelter the materials from the elements while working. Weathering makes it harder to identify the smaller fragments. Bark sawdust in particular the earth lays claim to very quickly. You must find your own ways of coping with this problem. There is a certain beauty, you will notice at moments, in the pattern of the chips as they are fitted back into place. You will wonder to what extent it should be described as natural, to what extent man-made. It will lead you on to speculations about the parentage of beauty itself, to which you will return.

The adhesive for the chips is translucent, and not so rigid as that   5
for the splinters. That for the bark and its subcutaneous layers is transparent and runs into the fibers on either side, partially dissolving them into each other. It does not set the sap flowing again but it does pay a kind of tribute to the preoccupations of the ancient thoroughfares. You could not roll an egg over the joints but some of the mine-shafts would still be passable, no doubt, for the first exploring insect who raises its head in the tight echoless passages. The day

DIRECTION: GUIDING YOUR READER

comes when it is all restored, even to the moss (now dead) over the wound. You will sleep badly, thinking of the removal of the scaffolding that must begin the next morning. How you will hope for sun and a still day!

The removal of the scaffolding or tackle is not so dangerous, perhaps, to the surroundings, as its installation, but it presents problems. It should be taken from the spot piece by piece as it is detached and stored at a distance. You have come to accept it there, around the tree. The sky begins to look naked as the chains and struts one by one vacate their positions. Finally the moment arrives when the last sustaining piece is removed and the tree stands again on its own. It is as though its weight for a moment stood on your heart. You listen for a thud of settlement, a warning creak deep in the intricate joinery. You cannot believe it will hold. How like something dreamed it is standing there all by itself. How long will it stand there now? The first breeze that touches its dead leaves all seems to flow into your mouth. You are afraid the motion of the clouds will be enough to push it over. What more can you do? What more can you do? 6

But there is nothing more you can do. 7

Others are waiting. 8

Everything is going to have to be put back. 9

QUESTIONS

1. Try to distinguish between the directive parts of the text (those cast in the form of directive writing) and any other parts. What is the function of the nondirective parts of the text? In a genuinely directive essay, should there be sentences that do not give directions but function to explain, evaluate, reassure, exhort, amuse, and so on? Explain.
2. Single out several highly directive sentences. Do any seem to reveal the personality of the speaker? How important is voice in a directive essay?

PRACTICE

Reversing the Irreversible

Using W. S. Merwin's essay as an example, write a set of directions for some other impossible project, such as regaining your lost innocence, rebuilding a bombed-out school, unwriting an essay, reassembling the dinner you had last Thursday. The idea is to find some normally irreversible process and give directions for doing it in reverse. Remember, however impractical the content of your directive essay may be, it must be grammatically correct and orderly.

Persuasion: Moving Your Reader

5

In a democratic and capitalistic society, we depend upon persuasion to do what coercion does in a totalitarian society. Thus persuasion is used to move us to vote in certain ways and to spend in certain ways. We are, in fact, bombarded with persuasive texts, visual as well as verbal, by all the media of mass communication: newspapers, magazines, radio, and television. Written persuasion is also used in more personal ways: to seek employment, to redress grievances, to make changes in an organization or group. In public life, persuasion dominates our law courts as well as our halls of government.

Although many political speeches and some advertising do, in fact, mix rational argument with the emotional appeal of persuasive language, we can make a clear distinction between argument and persuasion. Argument seeks to make a case for or against something; it tries to prove by logical connection that one view of a topic is right and another is wrong. It does not necessarily seek to motivate the reader to action. Persuasion, on the other hand, is always concerned with action and motivation: "buy this product," "vote for this candidate," "hire this applicant," "effect this change." At its most sophisticated, persuasion can even spur readers to action that is contrary to reason.

Every citizen needs to be able to deal with persuasion in two ways: to produce it when necessary and to defend oneself against it constantly. For purposes of defense, it is best to know how persuasion is put together from the inside. One who has written it knows firsthand how it works. These persuasive exercises, then, are designed with a double purpose: to improve your writing skills and to make you a more alert and critical reader of persuasive texts.

There are certain aspects of persuasion that are neither nice nor fair. Persuasion tries to subdue thought by appealing to emotion, and persuasive writing, in its most extreme forms, tries to ignore the alternatives to whatever cause it is pleading. Advertisers of cigarettes are not happy to include that little message from the Surgeon General in their ads. They would much prefer to ignore the dangerous side of their product. As it is, they will do everything they can to counter those ominous words about ill-health by projecting images of healthy outdoor life associated with the product.

In some of these assignments you will be asked to think in this same one-sided way, because this is the best way to learn how persuasive discourse works. These are language games we are playing here, to help develop your verbal abilities. We are not ''playing for keeps.'' So enter into them with good will, adopting the roles that are assigned. But be wary of learning these lessons too well. Persuasion is a dangerous toy.

READING

Persuasion in Advertising

The persuasive manner of the following ad may seem ludicrously obvious now, but its techniques are still used. Notice how the visual and verbal aspects of the ad reinforce one another. Few contemporary ads would rely so heavily on verbal copy. (Because the verbal print is so small in our reduced copy, we have reproduced the language of the fine print from the ad.) After you have examined the pictures and text, consider the questions that follow them.

Fly-Tox Advertisement, 1926

In many finely appointed homes spraying every room with Fly-Tox   1
is a daily summertime accomplishment. This is not just an excep-

What is your baby worth?

Priceless! A great gift that can never be replaced! Innocent and defenseless. Its comfort and health, even life itself, depend on little duties that constitute vigilant care and loving thoughtfulness.

In the summertime no greater service can be rendered than to shield the child and its food from the perilous contact with flies and mosquitoes.

The fly is the filthiest insect known. Literally hundreds—some scientists say, thousands—of deadly bacteria swarm in the putrescent ooze of a fly's spongy foot. It contaminates everything it touches. Sows the germs of disease on the very delicacies a child likes to eat.

The mosquito is no less an assassin. Whole epidemics have been traced by its ravages. Penetrating a child's tender skin, the bite is bitterly painful. And with the germ of fever firing their blood, little bodies writhe in the burning torture of flaming torment. The end—sometimes is tragic.

Flies and mosquitoes transmit typhoid fever, dysentery, infantile paralysis. Safety is only possible when these insects are killed. That is why devoted parents in millions of homes use Fly-Tox. It destroys flies and mosquitoes. It safeguards the health and comfort of our most precious possession—little children.

Wherever there are flies, use Fly-Tox

In many finely appointed homes spraying every room with Fly-Tox is a daily summertime accomplishment. This is not just an exceptional refinement. Indeed, it is considered a requisite to good housekeeping.

Spraying the entire room with Fly-Tox reaches and kills offensive household insects even in their places of hiding. That insures unmolested summer comfort. Musty, flytainted odors are displaced by an atmosphere of cleanliness. The draperies are unsoiled, spotless, beautiful. The upholstery fresh and bright, radiant with cleanliness. In the absence of unclean household insects, every room in the house glows with a refreshing, cleanly charm—a charm in which every housewife enjoys a rightful pride.

The Modern Safeguard to Health and Comfort

Fly-Tox is an established, efficient household insecticide. It was developed at Mellon Institute of Industrial Research. Stainless. Harmless to humans. Yet when its cleanly fragrant spray touches them these insect enemies to man's health and comfort crumple up and die. Fly-Tox has brought to millions of homes a new summer comfort—a house without flies or mosquitoes. Most people prefer the hand sprayer. It gives better satisfaction. However, a trial sprayer is given free with every small bottle.

HALF PINT · 50C   PINT · 75C   QUART · $1.25   GALLON · $4.00

Gallons in glass jugs are especially suitable for hotels, restaurants, summer camps, institutions

FLY-TOX
KILLS FLIES
MOSQUITOES
MOTHS, ROACHES, ANTS, FLEAS

PERSUASION: MOVING YOUR READER

tional refinement. Indeed, it is considered a requisite to good house-keeping.

Spraying the entire room with Fly-Tox reaches and kills offensive household insects even in their places of hiding. That insures unmolested summer comfort. Musty, fly-tainted odors are displaced by an atmosphere of cleanliness. The draperies are unsoiled, spotless, beautiful. The upholstery fresh and bright, radiant with cleanliness. In the absence of unclean household insects, every room in the house glows with a refreshing, cleanly charm—a charm in which every housewife enjoys a rightful pride.

Fly-Tox is an established, efficient household insecticide. It was developed at Mellon Institute of Industrial Research. Stainless. Harmless to humans. Yet when its cleanly fragrant spray touches them these insect enemies to man's health and comfort crumple up and die. Fly-Tox has brought to millions of homes a new summer comfort—a house without flies or mosquitoes.

Most people prefer the hand sprayer. It gives better satisfaction. However, a trial sprayer is given free with every small bottle.

In the summertime no greater service can be rendered than to shield the child and its food from the perilous contact with flies and mosquitoes. The fly is the filthiest insect known. Literally hundreds—some scientists say, thousands—of deadly bacteria swarm in the putrescent ooze of a fly's spongy foot. It contaminates everything it touches. Sows the germs of disease on the very delicacies a child likes to eat.

The mosquito is no less an assassin. Whole epidemics have been traced by its ravages. Penetrating a child's tender skin, the bite is bitterly painful. And with the germ of fever firing their blood, little bodies writhe in the burning torture of flaming torment. The end—sometimes is tragic.

Flies and mosquitoes transmit typhoid fever, dysentery, infantile paralysis. Safety is only possible when these insects are killed. That is why devoted parents in millions of homes use Fly-Tox. It destroys flies and mosquitoes. It safeguards the health and comfort of our most precious possession—little children.

2

3

4

5

6

7

QUESTIONS

1. Advertising is usually aimed at a specific audience. How would you describe the target group for this ad? What details in the ad indicate the audience the copywriter had in mind?
2. Persuasion often appeals to "absolutes" or accepted standards of value or behavior. How many different appeals of this sort can you detect in the Fly-Tox ad? What emotions are most directly evoked by the text?
3. Consider the use of connotative language in the text of the ad. What connotations are most frequently and powerfully evoked? How are con-

trasting connotations used to motivate the prospective buyer? How
much information about the composition of the product is actually
given? Where do you suspect the ad to be farthest from the truth?
Where is it most accurate?

4. How do the visual images work to persuade? What is the function of
each of the five separate pictures presented? Can you link certain images
with specific words in the text?

PRACTICE

The Ghastly Resort Hotel

You have just landed a job writing advertising copy for a resort
hotel on a small island off the coast of the United States. The
hotel management has brought you to the island for a few days
of exploration, during which you have noted the following features:

1. The hotel seems made of plastic. It features shiny, new,
   bright, loud colors and wildly patterned wallpaper.
2. The rooms are very small, the walls are thin, and music
   from the hotel bar can be heard all night long.
3. Hot water for bathing is seldom available.
4. The hotel band, a group of local kids playing on garbage
   can lids and harmonicas, seems to know only three
   songs.
5. The island is run by a dictator whose soldiers are everywhere. You saw three of them savagely beat a ragged
   child who tried to steal a loaf of bread.
6. The one town on the island is really a small village full of
   battered shacks with outdoor plumbing facilities.
7. The beach consists of a small amount of imported white
   sand spread over the local mud.
8. A swimmer at the beach was recently attacked and badly
   wounded by a barracuda.
9. At two minutes after sunset, hordes of large, vicious mosquitoes come out.
10. It is blazing hot while the sun is out but damp and cold at
    night.
11. The hotel owns one large motor launch. Every few days,
    when the launch is in good repair, it takes a crowded

group of tourists to a small sand bar where they look for shells but mostly find cans and bottles left by other tourists.

 12. The food in the hotel, prepared by native cooks, is highly flavored with some mysterious local herb that lingers in your taste buds for days. The most frequently featured dish is a local specialty: octopus.

All in all, this is not a place you would choose for yourself or recommend to a friend. But the job is important to you, and you have already run up a large bill that you cannot pay until you receive your fee for writing the copy. You decide that you will not leave out any of the material from the above list (to satisfy your conscience), but you will try to put everything in the most favorable light possible (to appease your employer). You sit down in your room to write the most attractive copy you can. You can hear the band playing one of their three tunes. You begin to write . . .

But before you begin, let us give you some technical advice. You have several problems to contend with here. One is organizational. The twelve items you have to cover must be grouped in paragraphs according to some system. You must look for natural groupings and then organize your writing accordingly, with an appropriate introduction and conclusion. Another problem is connotation. Nothing in your copy must have an unpleasant connotation. The word *barracuda*, for instance, would be as out of place as the word *cancer* in a cigarette ad. This problem, in turn, leads to a denotative problem. To satisfy what is left of your conscience, you must use some word or phrase that points to the barracuda you happen to know about, although this reference must be disguised or prettied-up in some way. And so it is for every detail. To inspire you, we provide here an actual advertisement of a similar place. This is the tone you must catch:

Vacation in **ARUBA**
—the friendship is free!

When you pay for a Caribbean island vacation, you *expect* sunny beaches, beautiful water, excellent hotels, superb food—the "usuals." And you get them in Aruba. But there's something else, that money can't buy—the friendship of the people who live there. And that's *free* in Aruba!

Ask anyone who's been to Aruba. Ask what was most unusual, most out- 2 standing about the island. Ask why they return so often. The answer is always the same—the *people* in Aruba!

Sure, the usual features are here. You'll enjoy the sun and water, and every- 3 thing you do under and in it. Sunbathing, fishing, swimming, snorkeling, sailing, tennis, hiking—they're all yours. When the sun goes down (it does, for a short while, every 24 hours) there are casinos, supper clubs, gourmet restaurants, nite clubs and discos. Plus sunset sailing and walks along the beach.

Even during the day, you're bound to take some time from the beach to visit 4 our shopping center or hotel boutiques. They abound with bargains from Holland (to whom we're related) and other far reaches of the globe.

Stay at a large resort complex or a secluded beach hotel at water's edge—ei- 5 ther way, you'll enjoy everything Aruba has to offer, virtually at your doorstep. You'll even enjoy the low excursion rates via KLM and American Airlines.

And you'll certainly enjoy the friendship. Remember—it's free! 6

READING

Reaching a Different Audience

The following advertisement appeared in 1954, in a campaign designed to change the image of Marlboro cigarettes. Marlboro cigarettes were identified as a "feminine high-style cigarette" when the company decided to go masculine. This is the way that marketing researcher Pierre Martineau described that campaign in *Motivation in Advertising* (1957): "1. No women were shown in the advertising. 2. All models were very virile men. . . . 3. The models were also chosen as successful, forceful personalities to inspire emulation, identification with an admirable figure. . . . 4. To reinforce the notion of virility and also to hint of a romantic past, each man had a plainly visible tattoo on his hand. . . . This symbol gave richness to the product image, bringing it all into focus."

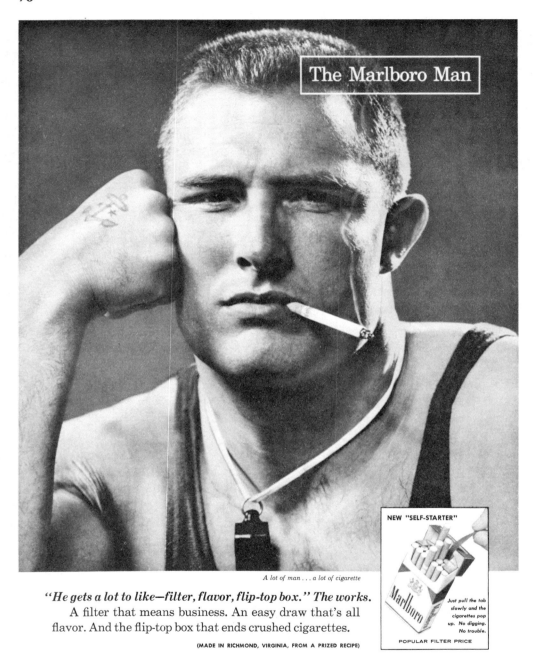

The Marlboro Man

A lot of man . . . a lot of cigarette

"He gets a lot to like—filter, flavor, flip-top box." The works.
A filter that means business. An easy draw that's all
flavor. And the flip-top box that ends crushed cigarettes.

(MADE IN RICHMOND, VIRGINIA, FROM A PRIZED RECIPE)

NEW "SELF-STARTER"

Just pull the tab
slowly and the
cigarettes pop
up. No digging.
No trouble.

POPULAR FILTER PRICE

Changing the Persuasive Pattern

Pierre Martineau's analysis makes clear the motivation behind the Marlboro Man ad. Your job in this assignment is to produce an ad for a different but similar advertising campaign.

First find a product that is clearly associated with one particular type of person (a certain sex, age, class, race, profession). Then construct an ad designed to make that same product appeal to a very different type of person. Make an entire full-page ad, with visual and verbal material laid out in the most effective way. (This is a cut-and-paste job.)

Along with the ad, submit a paragraph in which you explain what you have done. Describe the association pattern you are trying to change, and the sort of consumer you are trying to persuade to buy your product.

READING

Hemingway on Ballantine Ale

In 1952, Ballantine ran a two-page spread featuring Ernest Hemingway. On the left sat Ernest himself, outdoors in a garden, wearing shorts and reading a book. Under the picture ran the following caption in very tiny print: "Ernest Hemingway, who has been called the greatest living American writer, is also internationally famous as a deep-sea fisherman. Since publication of *The Sun Also Rises* in 1926, his novels and short stories have enriched the literature of the English language, year after year. His latest best seller is *Across the River and Into the Trees*." On the right-hand page appeared the material we have reproduced below. The advertising agency insists that Hemingway actually wrote the copy that is attributed to him.

Read the ad closely. How would you describe Hemingway's life style? What audience did Ballantine wish to appeal to by using the Hemingway name and life style?

HOW WOULD YOU put a glass of Ballantine Ale into words?

Here—Ernest Hemingway turns his famous hand to it...

Ernest Hemingway

FINCA VIGIA, SAN FRANCISCO DE PAULA, CUBA

Bob Benchley first introduced me to Ballantine Ale. It has been a good companion ever since.

You have to work hard to deserve to drink it. But I would rather have a bottle of Ballantine Ale than any other drink after fighting a really big fish.

We keep it iced in the bait box with chunks of ice packed around it. And you ought to taste it on a hot day when you have worked a big marlin fast because there were sharks after him.

You are tired all the way through. The fish is landed untouched by sharks and you have a bottle of Ballantine cold in your hand and drink it cool, light, and full-bodied, so it tastes good long after you have swallowed it. That's the test of an ale with me: whether it tastes as good afterwards as when it's going down. Ballantine does.

Ernest Hemingway

More people like it...   More people buy it...   than any other ale...   ...by Four to One!

BALLANTINE ALE

Since 1840

PURITY · BODY · FLAVOR

P. Ballantine & Sons, Newark, N.J.

1951
This advertisement appeared in LIFE — September 8, 1952

READER-ORIENTED FORMS

Your Favorite Celebrity on _____

Using the Ballantine ad as a model, think of a product that would be appropriate for your favorite writer (or any other well-known personality whose style you are familiar with) to endorse. Then write the endorsement, following the pattern of the Hemingway endorsement as closely as is appropriate.

Remember, your text should reflect the life style and personality of the writer or celebrity. In other words, don't follow the style of Hemingway's letter, but the style of the person you have chosen. A writer or celebrity with a pronounced image of his or her own will obviously be a good choice.

You had best read (or look or listen) a bit until you get the feel of your person's image. Then determine the audience the person would appeal to and the kind of product he or she could be expected to use. (The product may be something actually on the market or something that you make up.) Take some time to discover how you can best suggest the celebrity's style of expression: the language, the attitude, the image. Then give some attention to what should be emphasized about the product itself. Remember, your purpose is to persuade a particular group of readers to buy the product.

READING

Political Persuasion

The speech reprinted here was given by Franklin D. Roosevelt on his inauguration as President of the United States on March 4, 1933. Roosevelt had been elected President in 1932, after the country had been shaken by the stock market crash of 1929 and the various farm and business failures related to it.

When this speech was delivered, hundreds of the nation's banks were closed, unemployment was widespread and rising, business and industry were working well below capacity, and many people felt helpless and desperate. As you read the speech (which was carried on radio), try to imagine how it would have struck its first audience.

In Roosevelt's speech, you will see an excellent example of the way a skilled persuasive writer can set about gaining the confidence of an audience, enlisting their support for certain difficult and perhaps unpleasant actions he will soon propose to them. The two practices that follow the speech are occasions for you to attempt a similar task. The first is adapted from a century-old play by Henrik Ibsen, and the other has been invented for this occasion, but each offers you the opportunity to practice one of the most important features of persuasive writing: getting the audience on your side.

Franklin D. Roosevelt, ''First Inaugural Address''

I am certain that my fellow Americans expect that on my induction into the Presidency I will address them with a candor and a decision which the present situation of our Nation impels. This is preeminently the time to speak the truth, the whole truth, frankly and boldly. Nor need we shrink from honestly facing conditions in our country today. This great Nation will endure as it has endured, will revive and will prosper. So, first of all, let me assert my firm belief that the only thing we have to fear is fear itself—nameless, unreasoning, unjustified terror which paralyzes needed efforts to convert retreat into advance. In every dark hour of our national life a leadership of frankness and vigor has met with the understanding and support of the people themselves which is essential to victory. I am convinced that you will again give that support to leadership in these critical days.

In such a spirit on my part and on yours we face our common difficulties. They concern, thank God, only material things. Values have shrunken to fantastic levels; taxes have risen; our ability to pay has fallen; government of all kinds is faced by serious curtailment of income; the means of exchange are frozen in the currents of trade; the withered leaves of industrial enterprise lie on every side; farmers find no markets for their produce; the savings of many years in thousands of families are gone.

More important, a host of unemployed citizens face the grim problem of existence, and an equally great number toil with little return. Only a foolish optimist can deny the dark realities of the moment.

Yet our distress comes from no failure of substance. We are stricken by no plague of locusts. Compared with the perils which our forefathers conquered because they believed and were not afraid, we have still much to be thankful for. Nature still offers her bounty and human efforts have multiplied it. Plenty is at our doorstep, but a generous use of it languishes in the very sight of the supply. Primarily this is because rulers of the exchange of mankind's goods have failed through their own stubbornness and their own incompetence, have admitted their failure, and have abdicated. Practices of the unscrupulous money changers stand indicted in the court of public opinion, rejected by the hearts and minds of men.

True they have tried, but their efforts have been cast in the pattern of an outworn tradition. Faced by failure of credit they have proposed only the lending of more money. Stripped of the lure of profit by which to induce our people to follow their false leadership, they have resorted to exhortations, pleading tearfully for restored confidence. They know only the rules of a generation of self-seekers. They have no vision, and when there is no vision the people perish.

The money changers have fled from their high seats in the temple of our civilization. We may now restore that temple to the ancient truths. The measure of the restoration lies in the extent to which we apply social values more noble than mere monetary profit.

Happiness lies not in the mere possession of money; it lies in the joy of achievement, in the thrill of creative effort. The joy and moral stimulation of work no longer must be forgotten in the mad chase of evanescent profits. These dark days will be worth all they cost us if they teach us that our true destiny is not to be ministered unto but to minister to ourselves and to our fellow men.

Recognition of the falsity of material wealth as the standard of success goes hand in hand with the abandonment of the false belief that public office and high political position are to be valued only by the standards of pride of place and personal profit; and there must be an end to a conduct in banking and in business which too often has given to a sacred trust the likeness of callous and selfish wrongdoing. Small wonder that confidence languishes, for it thrives only on honesty, on honor, on the sacredness of obligations, on faithful protection, on unselfish performance; without them it cannot live.

Restoration calls, however, not for changes in ethics alone. This Nation asks for action, and action now.

Our greatest primary task is to put people to work. This is no unsolvable problem if we face it wisely and courageously. It can be accomplished in part by direct recruiting by the Government itself, treating the task as we would treat the emergency of a war, but at the same time, through this employment, accomplishing greatly needed projects to stimulate and reorganize the use of our natural resources.

Hand in hand with this we must frankly recognize the overbalance 11 of population in our industrial centers and, by engaging on a national scale in a redistribution, endeavor to provide a better use of the land for those best fitted for the land. The task can be helped by definite efforts to raise the values of agricultural products and with this the power to purchase the output of our cities. It can be helped by preventing realistically the tragedy of the growing loss through foreclosure of our small homes and our farms. It can be helped by insistence that the Federal, State, and local governments act forthwith on the demand that their cost be drastically reduced. It can be helped by the unifying of relief activities which today are often scattered, uneconomical, and unequal. It can be helped by national planning for and supervision of all forms of transportation and of communications and other utilities which have a definitely public character. There are many ways in which it can be helped, but it can never be helped merely by talking about it. We must act and act quickly.

Finally, in our progress toward a resumption of work we require 12 two safeguards against a return of the evils of the old order; there must be a strict supervision of all banking and credits and investments, so that there will be an end to speculation with other people's money; and there must be provision for an adequate but sound currency.

These are the lines of attack. I shall presently urge upon a new 13 Congress, in special session, detailed measures for their fulfillment, and I shall seek the immediate assistance of the several States.

Through this program of action we address ourselves to putting 14 our own national house in order and making income balance outgo. Our international trade relations, though vastly important, are in point of time and necessity secondary to the establishment of a sound national economy. I favor as a practical policy the putting of first things first. I shall spare no effort to restore world trade by international economic readjustment, but the emergency at home cannot wait on that accomplishment.

The basic thought that guides these specific means of national re- 15 covery is not narrowly nationalistic. It is the insistence, as a first consideration, upon the interdependence of the various elements in and parts of the United States—a recognition of the old and permanently important manifestation of the American spirit of the pioneer. It is the way to recovery. It is the immediate way. It is the strongest assurance that the recovery will endure.

In the field of world policy I would dedicate this Nation to the policy of the good neighbor—the neighbor who resolutely respects himself and, because he does so, respects the rights of others—the neighbor who respects his obligations and respects the sanctity of his agreements in and with a world of neighbors. 16

If I read the temper of our people correctly, we now realize as we have never realized before our interdependence on each other; that we cannot merely take but we must give as well; that if we are to go forward, we must move as a trained and loyal army willing to sacrifice for the good of a common discipline, because without such discipline no progress is made, no leadership becomes effective. We are, I know, ready and willing to submit our lives and property to such discipline, because it makes possible a leadership which aims at a larger good. This I propose to offer, pledging that the larger purposes will bind upon us all as a sacred obligation with a unity of duty hitherto evoked only in time of armed strife. 17

With this pledge taken, I assume unhesitatingly the leadership of this great army of our people dedicated to a disciplined attack upon our common problems. 18

Action in this image and to this end is feasible under the form of government which we have inherited from our ancestors. Our Constitution is so simple and practical that it is possible always to meet extraordinary needs by changes in emphasis and arrangement without loss of essential form. That is why our constitutional system has proved itself the most superbly enduring political mechanism the modern world has produced. It has met every stress of vast expansion of territory, of foreign wars, of bitter internal strife, of world relations. 19

It is to be hoped that the normal balance of Executive and legislative authority may be wholly adequate to meet the unprecedented task before us. But it may be that an unprecedented demand and need for undelayed action may call for temporary departure from that normal balance of public procedure. 20

I am prepared under my constitutional duty to recommend the measures that a stricken Nation in the midst of a stricken world may require. These measures, or such other measures as the Congress may build out of its experience and wisdom, I shall seek, within my constitutional authority, to bring to speedy adoption. 21

But in the event that the Congress shall fail to take one of these two courses, and in the event that the national emergency is still critical, I shall not evade the clear course of duty that will then confront me. I shall ask the Congress for the one remaining instrument to meet the crisis—broad Executive power to wage a war against the 22 emergency, as great as the power that would be given to me if we were in fact invaded by a foreign foe.

For the trust reposed in me I will return the courage and the devotion that befit the time. I can do no less. 23

We face the arduous days that lie before us in the warm courage of national unity; with the clear consciousness of seeking old and precious moral values; with the clean satisfaction that comes from the stern performance of duty by old and young alike. We aim at the assurance of a rounded and permanent national life. 24

We do not distrust the future of essential democracy. The people of the United States have not failed. In their need they have registered a mandate that they want direct, vigorous action. They have asked for discipline and direction under leadership. They have made me the present instrument of their wishes. In the spirit of the gift I take it. 25

In this dedication of a Nation we humbly ask the blessing of God. May He protect each and every one of us. May He guide me in the days to come. 26

QUESTIONS

1. This is not so much a case of persuasion to action—to buy something or vote for someone—as it is persuasion to believe in something and someone. What, exactly, is the audience being asked to believe?
2. Consider the ways in which the speaker establishes a positive relationship with the audience. How often does he say ''I'' or ''me''? How often does he say ''you''? How often does he say ''we'' or ''us''?
3. The rhetorician James L. Kinneavy (whose analysis of this speech in his book *A Theory of Discourse* has put us and many others in his debt) has observed that many of the confident maxims and assertions made by Roosevelt (such as ''the only thing we have to fear is fear itself'' in paragraph 1) are in fact questionable. Can you find other maxims, generalizations, assertions that you think are dubious or incorrect?
4. Kinneavy argues that ''the art of Roosevelt . . . has consisted in making something *appear* very plausible when in fact its probability is really, by objective standards, much lower'' (page 235). He attributes Roosevelt's success in accomplishing this to the air of self-confidence that he established and maintained throughout the speech. Can you find particular words and phrases that convey this attitude? Start with the opening three words.
5. Roosevelt came into office with a program of legislation he wished to enact. In his inaugural address, he set out to win the emotional support of the people for the program he was proposing. Among the emotional qualities Kinneavy finds in this speech are appeals to hope, religion, morality, and nationalism. It is especially instructive to trace the patri-

otic and religious appeals. What quotations or allusions to the Bible can you find in this speech? Does Roosevelt suggest at any point an analogy between his own situation and that of Jesus Christ? How does he use patriotic feeling to persuade the public to support his program?

PRACTICE

The Enemy of the People

Assume that you are a doctor at a small resort town. The economy of the town depends heavily on the seasonal business of tourists who come to swim in clean waters and enjoy cool breezes. You have just made some tests and discovered that sewage from the town has begun to pollute the beach water, posing a danger to the health of bathers. In your judgment, the town must either close the beach to swimming or put in expensive equipment to treat the sewage before it is pumped into the water.

News of your discovery has leaked out, some of it in wildly exaggerated form. Since closing the beach would hurt many people financially, you are rapidly becoming an unpopular person. You have been getting obscene phone calls, and garbage has been dumped on your doorstep. Your children say they don't want to go to school but won't say why—though they never were reluctant to go to school in the past.

Some of the owners of small hotels along the shore have found another doctor who will swear that the beach is perfectly healthy. Someone is spreading a rumor that you have been trying to scare people and drive real estate prices down so that you can make a profit for yourself. This is complicated by the fact that you *have* been looking for a larger house to buy, closer to the beach.

The situation is very ugly. At this point the mayor calls a town meeting to discuss the water and sewage problem. You know the other doctor will be there. You have received a threatening letter telling you to stay away. But you have resolved to take your case to the people. You know that you will have to be very persuasive to get a fair hearing. You sit down to write your speech . . .

PERSUASION: MOVING YOUR READER

PRACTICE

The Difficult Campaign Speech

Persuasive discourse is important in all elections for public office, from dogcatcher to President of the United States. The following assignment is designed to let you try your hand at writing a political speech under certain specific conditions.

You are running for the office of mayor (or some other office in local government) in your hometown. Your opponent is one of the richest and most influential members of the community. His family has been prominent for generations. He attended private school and graduated from Harvard College with highest honors and then from Yale Law School. He is now the senior partner in your community's most prestigious law firm.

You are a member of a minority group (ethnic, religious, or sexual). You went to the local public schools and the state or city college, where your record was undistinguished. Since graduation, you have held a number of jobs and have been arrested once for possession of marijuana, but released without trial for lack of evidence. At present you have become well-to-do through part ownership of a used-car lot and a chain of hairdressing establishments. Your opponent has just told the public about your police record. He has also questioned your business experience as preparation for the office of mayor. You are making a campaign speech at a local community college. The audience will be composed largely of students who live in your town and are eligible to vote. They are mostly, but not all, in or near their twenties.

In writing your speech, you must decide how to deal with your own record, with your opponent, and with your audience. You may choose to ignore some things, but remember that it might be better to deal with them than to leave them undiscussed. In particular, you must work to leave this audience feeling good about you—not merely sympathetic, but convinced that you have qualities that will make you the better official from the point of view of their attitudes and interests. You may promise things, as all politicians do, but if you promise too much you may lose credibility. Above all, you must leave the audience with faith in your ability and integrity. In an actual situation, your clothing, posture, voice, gestures, gaze, and other things would help or hinder you. Here, you have only words to work with. Make them work for you.

READING

The Job Letter and Résumé

When you apply for a job, most business and professional organizations require you to submit a letter of application and a résumé of your educational and work experience. On the basis of these two documents, they decide whether or not to grant you an interview, so it's important that your letter of application be direct, sincere, persuasive, and well written, and that your résumé be factual and neat in appearance.

The Résumé

Following is a sample résumé presenting the facts about Jennifer Hazard, who is seeking a position in a bank. Her résumé follows one of the standard formats. In drawing up your own résumé, you may want to check with the job placement office at your school for suggestions or consult one of the many books on writing résumés that are now available.

```
                              Résumé


                          JENNIFER HAZARD

65 Bridge Road
Warlock, Rhode Island   02885
Phone:   401-247-8694


Education:

    1976-1980       Warlock High School, Warlock, Rhode Island

    1980-1982       Ocean State Junior College, Cranberry, Rhode
                    Island
                    Major:  Accounting

    1982-1984       Pawtuxet College, Providence, Rhode Island;
                    will graduate May 21, 1984 with a B.A. degree.
                    Major:  Economics
                    Minor:  Sociology


Extracurricular Activities:

    1982-1984       Pawtuxet College Women's Swim Team

    1983-1984       Business Manager, Pawtuxet College Clarion


Experience:

    1979-1980       Cashier, Joe's Family Drive-In, Warlock, Rhode
                    Island

        1980        Counselor, Swimming Instructor, Stone Hill Camp,
                    Rumstick, Rhode Island

    1982-1983       Bookkeeper, Mercury Hardware Store, Warlock,
                    Rhode Island

    1983-present    Teller, Warlock Town Bank, Warlock, Rhode
                    Island


References:

    Professor John McNulty, Department of Economics,
    Pawtuxet College, Providence, Rhode Island 02903

    Professor Marilyn Vargas, Department of Sociology,
    Pawtuxet College, Providence, Rhode Island 02903

    Mr. Joseph DiSano, Manager, Warlock Town Bank,
    Warlock, Rhode Island 02885
```

READER-ORIENTED FORMS

Your letter of application should elaborate on the information in your résumé that is most pertinent to the job for which you are applying. Letters of application also follow a fairly standard format:

Paragraph 1: State the job for which you are applying. Explain where you saw the advertisement or who told you about the job.

Paragraph 2: Describe your college training, stressing those courses and activities most relevant to the job for which you are applying.

Paragraph 3: Describe your previous work experience and how it relates to the position you want.

Paragraph 4: Tell why you'd like to work for the particular company or organization.

Paragraph 5: State that your résumé is enclosed (and any other material requested, such as letters of recommendation), and that you are available for an interview.

Following are a sample job advertisement and a letter from Jennifer Hazard.

BRANCH MANAGER TRAINEES

Friendly National Bank seeks recent college graduates interested in a challenging career as Branch Managers in our rapidly expanding bank. If you are hard-working, self-starting, enjoy responsibility, and love working with people, you will be right for our training program. Some experience in banking, or training in economics, management, or accounting preferred.

Send letter and résumé to:
Harold O'Brien
Personnel Department
Friendly National Bank
Providence, Rhode Island 02905

65 Bridge Road
Warlock, Rhode Island 02885
May 1, 1984

Mr. Harold O'Brien
Personnel Department
Friendly National Bank
Providence, Rhode Island 02905

Dear Mr. O'Brien:

I wish to apply for the position as Branch Manager Trainee which was advertised in the <u>Providence Daily Bugle</u> on April 30.

This month I shall be graduating from Pawtuxet College, where I've been majoring in economics. Because I've been interested in a career in banking, I decided to research the functions of the two banks in my hometown of Warlock for my economics honors thesis. I wanted to know what services were most used by the customers of these banks and how the banks were working with small businesses to help them expand or to improve their facilities. Warlock, like so many older towns, has had to revitalize its downtown business area in order to compete with the new malls outside town. Such renewal has been possible because of the cooperation of the banks, the town planning committee, and the businesspeople. Writing this thesis showed me how important a part of a community a bank can be when it takes an active interest in the growth of that community.

I've had practical experience in financial affairs as Business Manager of the college newspaper and in my summer and part-time work as a bookkeeper and as a teller. In fact, doing the books for a small hardware store which wanted to expand gave me a good picture of small business problems. It was this experience that started my thesis research.

I'd especially enjoy working for Friendly National Bank because of the innovations in banking you've introduced and because I am looking for a challenging position in a bank that gives the same attention to the small businessperson as to a large corporation.

I have enclosed my résumé, and if my credentials interest you, I am available for an interview at your convenience.

Sincerely yours,

Jennifer Hazard

JENNIFER HAZARD

The Serious Job Letter

We have provided six job advertisements adapted from advertisements that appeared in various newspapers. Choose one of these advertisers as a prospective employer, or if you prefer, find an advertisement in your local newspaper for a job you would like.

First, you should draw up a résumé following the model in this book or another standard format. You can list your own qualifications or imagine you are someone else and invent some suitable qualifications for the job you're interested in.

Second, write a letter applying for the job. Remember, be direct and sincere, and be sure to read the job advertisement very carefully. For example, look at the Byron Badway advertisement for video game designers. This company stresses its "creative design group" and development of electronic games, so you should show in your letter that you have held creative, developmental positions either at work or at school. Also, this company produces "sensational" games. Therefore they want to hire people with a strong background in their field ("avid and experienced game-player") and related areas ("computers, animation, technical drawing"). In other words, you'll have to convince them that you're knowledgeable, creative, ambitious, deeply interested in what they manufacture, and that you work well with others.

Choose your job, and start writing.

VIDEO GAME DESIGNER

The Byron Badway Company has an opening for a Video Game Designer. Join our creative design group and help us develop new games as sensational as our latest hit, VENUSIAN VELCRO WARS. In addition, you will participate in the developing of electronic games and toys and traditional board and 3-D games.

The person we seek should have a BSID degree or the equivalent, and experience in such related fields as computers, film animation, or technical drawing. He or she should also be an avid and experienced game-player.

Send your letter and résumé to:
Personnel Manager
Byron Badway Co.
615 Circuit Drive
North Melba, New Jersey 05697

Fragrance Evaluator

Lucretia Borgia Cosmetics, maker of Spring Mist, Ravishing, and Ariel fragrances, offers an excellent opportunity for a qualified individual to function as an in-house expert in the evaluation of Lucretia Borgia Fragrances, as well as our health and beauty products.

Two years of fragrance evaluation experience, coupled with an extensive knowledge and appreciation of fine fragrances and fragrance products, is required. The individual we seek should also possess well-developed communication and interpersonal skills in order to deal with all types of personnel.

We offer a highly competitive salary, and excellent benefits including major medical, life insurance, pension plan, and paid relocation expenses.

Qualified individuals should send letter and résumé to: Personnel Department,

Lucretia Borgia Cosmetics, Inc.
Ripley Industrial Park
Ripley, New York 10612

READER-ORIENTED FORMS

PERSUASION: MOVING YOUR READER

The Not-So-Serious Job Letter

The previous assignment called for a serious presentation of yourself as a candidate for a job. Here you are asked to be more playful, to let your imagination go for a bit on a similar topic. The point of this is that by trying a flight of fancy, you may discover an ease and liveliness of expression that will enhance every other qualification you have.

You are job hunting and have just seen the following two advertisements in the "Help Wanted" column of your local newspaper:

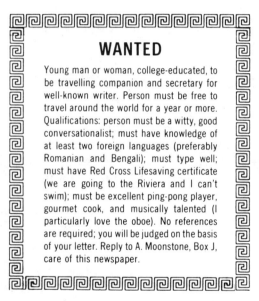

WANTED

Young man or woman, college-educated, to be travelling companion and secretary for well-known writer. Person must be free to travel around the world for a year or more. Qualifications: person must be a witty, good conversationalist; must have knowledge of at least two foreign languages (preferably Romanian and Bengali); must type well; must have Red Cross Lifesaving certificate (we are going to the Riviera and I can't swim); must be excellent ping-pong player, gourmet cook, and musically talented (I particularly love the oboe). No references are required; you will be judged on the basis of your letter. Reply to A. Moonstone, Box J, care of this newspaper.

Now put yourself in *one* of the following situations:

A. You want one of these jobs very badly, and you have *all but two* of the qualifications. You are sure that many others will apply for the job, so your letter must be very persuasive. Write the letter.

B. You want the job offered by A. Moonstone very badly, but you have *very few* of the qualifications. For example, you've had only one year of college; the two languages you know are English and Lithuanian; you can type about twenty words per minute with two fingers; you can't swim well, but you can tread water and float on your back; you know plenty of traveling salesman jokes; you were ping-pong champion at your day camp when you were nine; you've been a hamburger cook at Burger King; and you play the harmonica very well. Write a persuasive letter in which you play down your weak points and emphasize the qualifications you *do* have.

C. You want the job offered by C. Earnshaw very badly, but you have *very few* of the qualifications. You do remember how to roast hot dogs and marshmallows from your campfire days that summer at Camp Sunshine; you have always found your way home in fogs, and you have never got lost in a library. You are a devoted reader of historical romances, and you are adventurous. Write a letter in which you play down your weak points and emphasize the qualifications you *do* have.

PART FOUR

TOPIC-ORIENTED FORMS

6 Narration: Organizing Time

To narrate is to tell the story of a sequence of events, whether long or short, great or small, real or fictional. The most important element of narration is time. The writer must establish the chronological order of events being presented in a way that the reader can follow. The simplest method for accomplishing this is to let the order of things in the narration correspond to the order of things being narrated: to begin at the beginning and continue to the end. The more complex way is to begin by plunging into the middle of things (*in medias res*, as the Roman critics called it) and then tell the story with flashbacks into the past and returns to the present.

In the art of fiction, narration is developed in the direction of emotional intensity. Whether comic or serious, fiction is designed to make us feel concern for the characters and interest in the events. But narration is also common in speech and thought. We tend to see our lives as narratives. We use narration to report on interesting events and to preserve the memory of things that have happened to people. At night we narrate the events of our day to friends or family. Newspaper journalists also narrate events, but they don't attempt to create suspense or to involve the reader deeply in the events.

There is also a kind of technical narration that is sometimes called "description of a process." In writing of this sort, a sequence of events must be recorded in chronological order. Because it is organized by time rather than space, we prefer to call this type of writing "narration" rather than "description." But the events are not unique—events that occur only one time to one particular person. A process is typical. Many processes are repeated again and again. Others, like biological evolution, may happen only once in this world but could, in principle, be duplicated on others.

Process narration is related to directive writing as well. Narrating how a thing happens is not very different from instructing someone in how to make it happen. But directive writing is aimed at the reader and uses the imperative form of the verb (*do* this; *fix* that; *put* the cat out) while narration of a process uses the present indicative either in the active (she *does* this; she *fixes* that; she *puts* the cat out) or in the passive (this *is done*; that *is fixed*; the cat *is put* out). A narration of events would normally use the past tense (he *did* this; he *fixed* that; he *put* the cat out).

In the reading and practice in writing that we present in this chapter, you will have a chance to study the ways in which narrative writing organizes time. We are not trying to prepare you for a career in creative writing—only to help you develop control over the use of tense in language as a way of organizing time in the world. All writing consists of the imposition of order on phenomena. Control of time and tense is important in many other types of writing. In studying narrative we simply put that dimension of writing in the foreground.

READING

Cartoon as Narrative

George Booth's cartoon sequence, "Ip Gissa Gul," consists of eleven frames that must be read in sequence across the page. Your first job is to tell what is happening in each of the frames, and we suggest you translate the speeches of Ip and the other creatures into English before proceeding to the writing assignments.

Drawing by Booth; ©1975 The New Yorker Magazine, I

PRACTICE

From Cartoon to Written Narrative

This cartoon, like most cartoons, does not "tell" or "narrate" the story it presents. Each frame is a little scene or dramatic episode. This practice is designed to provide the basic experience of translating cartoon scenes into a prose narrative. As you write, take particular care to use the proper tense for each verb that describes a scene or narrates an event. The normal tense for all narrative is the simple past: "Once there was a creature. . . ." We offer the following suggestions for the points of view you might take in your translation.

A. Write a narrative version for your five-year-old niece. You might begin, "Once upon a time there was a creature named. . . ."

B. Write a narrative version from the point of view of one of the following:

1. Ip
2. Gul
3. one of Ip's four friends (we assume you've noted that they do not all share the same point of view).

C. Write a narrative interpreting the action from the point of view of one of the following:

1. an anthropologist (for an example, see Margaret Mead's "A Day in Samoa").
2. a sociologist (for an example, see the excerpt from *Middletown* by Robert and Helen Lynd).

READING

Time and Tense

The following passage from Ambrose Bierce's short story describes the thoughts and feelings of a man about to be hanged. You are asked to read it, thinking not of hanging but of time and tense.

Ambrose Bierce, from "An Occurrence at Owl Creek Bridge"

He closed his eyes in order to fix his last thoughts upon his wife and children. The water, touched to gold by the early sun, the brooding mists under the banks at some distance down the stream, the fort, the soldiers, the piece of drift—all had distracted him. And now he became conscious of a new disturbance. Striking through the thought of his dear ones was a sound which he could neither ignore nor understand, a sharp, distinct, metallic percussion like the stroke of a blacksmith's hammer upon the anvil; it had the same ringing quality. He wondered what it was, and whether immeasurably distant or near by—it seemed both. Its recurrence was regular, but as slow as the tolling of a death knell. He awaited each stroke with impatience and—he knew not why—apprehension. The intervals of silence grew progressively longer; the delays became maddening. With their greater infrequency the sounds increased in strength and sharpness. They hurt his ear like the thrust of a knife; he feared he would shriek. What he heard was the ticking of his watch.

PRACTICE

The Management of Tense

Here are a couple of simple exercises, designed to give you a check on your ability to manage different tenses and to keep their relations clear and consistent.

A. Rewrite the paragraph from Bierce in the present tense, making all your verb forms consistent with this change and grammatically correct, beginning with ''He closes his eyes'' or ''He is closing his eyes.''

B. Now rewrite it in the future, beginning ''He will close his eyes. . . .''

C. If you need more work on these matters, try it in the first person (''I closed my éyes . . .'') or second person (''You closed your eyes . . .''). If you want a real challenge, try the future perfect (''He will have closed . . .''), the conditional (''He would close . . .''), or the past conditional (''He would have closed . . .'').

READING

A Familiar Process

This paragraph is from E. B. White's loving description of life with a Model T Ford in the 1930s.

During my association with Model T's, self-starters were not a prevalent accessory. They were expensive and under suspicion. Your car came equipped with a serviceable crank, and the first thing you learned was how to Get Results. It was a special trick, and until you learned it (usually from another Ford owner, but sometimes by a period of appalling experimentation) you might as well have been winding up an awning. The trick was to leave the ignition switch off, proceed to the animal's head, pull the choke (which was a little wire protruding through the radiator) and give the crank two or three nonchalant upward lifts. Then, whistling as though thinking about something else, you would saunter back to the driver's cabin, turn the ignition on, return to the crank, and this time, catching it on the downstroke, give it a quick spin with plenty of That. If this procedure was followed, the engine almost always responded—first with a few scattered explosions, then with a tumultuous gunfire, which you checked by racing around to the driver's seat and retarding the throttle. Often, if the emergency brake hadn't been pulled all the way back, the car advanced on you the instant the first explosion occurred and you would hold it back by leaning your weight against it. I can still feel my old Ford nuzzling me at the curb, as though looking for an apple in my pocket.

QUESTIONS

1. How does this process narrative differ in form from the story of some particular sequence of events? Look at the verbs in particular as you answer this question.
2. Which features of this writing are purely narrative, which are descriptive, and which convey the narrator's feelings about the process he is narrating? Try to make these distinctions as precisely as you can, and note especially anything that resists such classification. What functions do extra-narrative elements have in a process narrative?

PRACTICE

Narrating a Familiar Process

Taking White's process narrative as your guide, write a short narrative describing some process familiar to you, about which you have some strong feelings of affection or aversion, such as getting packed for the annual vacation trip; preparing for an ordeal like exams or a trip to the dentist; repairing, maintaining, or using some old, familiar object—for example, car, bike, computer, or lacrosse stick. Present a clear narrative of how the process works, using your feelings about it as a way of lending interest to the process. The trick here is not to clutter your narrative with irrelevancies, but not to detach yourself from it either; just to keep the reader interested by allowing your own feelings to color your narrative.

Remember, also, that you are narrating a process, not telling a story—not ''once upon a time,'' but often, ''many's the time. . . .''

READING

Natural Process

The following two selections are taken from a science fiction novel in which George Stewart imagined the world almost completely depopulated by an epidemic, leaving natural things to resume their seasonal existences. In these two passages, he presents the process of renaturalization taking place in New York City and Central Park.

In reading these, notice particularly the management of time and tense that distinguishes this process narrative from the narration of specific human events. It is as if, without human beings to personalize and singularize time into history and story, there is only process left, a generalized unfolding of seasons and predictable occurrences.

George Stewart, ''The Abandoned City'' and ''The Empty Park'' (from Earth Abides)

Stretched out between its rivers, the city will remain for a long time. Stone and brick, concrete and asphalt, glass—time deals gently with them. Water leaves black stains, moss shows green, a little grass springs up in the cracks. (That is only the surface.) A window-pane grows loose, vibrates, breaks in a gusty wind. Lightning strikes, loosening the tiles of a cornice. A wall leans, as footings yield in the long rains; after years have passed, it falls, scattering bricks across the street. Frost works, and in the March thaw some flakes of stone scale off. (It is all very slow.) The rain washes quietly through the gutters into the storm-drains, and if the storm-drains clog, the rain runs still through the gutters into the rivers. The snow piles deep in the long canyons, drifting at the street corners; no one disturbs it. In the spring, it too runs off through the gutters. As in the desert, a year is like an hour in the night; a century, like a day.

Indeed the city is much like the desert. From the asphalt and concrete-coated soil the rain runs off both ways into the rivers. Here and there in a crack the subtle grass and the hardy weeds grow up a little, but no tree or vine or tall grass takes root. The very shade trees by the avenues, lacking man's care, die in their shallow pockets. The deer and the rabbits shun the empty streets; after a while even the rats go away. Only the flying creatures find there a refuge—the birds nest on the high ledges, and at morning and evening the bats fly out and in through the few broken windows. It will remain a long time, a very long time.

An island within an island, the green oblong of the Park will remain. It has open soil where the rain penetrates. The sun shines upon it. In the first season the grass grows tall; the seeds fall from the trees and bushes, the birds bring in more seeds. Give it two seasons, three seasons, and the eager saplings are sprouting. Give it twenty years, and it is a jungle of second growth with each tree straining upward to gain light above its fellows, and the hardy natives, fast-growing ash and maple, crowding out the soft exotics which man once planted there. You hardly see the bridle path any more; leaf-litter lies thick on the narrow roads. Give it a hundred years, and you walk in full-grown forest, scarcely knowing that man was ever there except where the stone arch still spans the under-pass, making a strange cave. The doe walks in the woods, and the wild-cat leaps upon the rabbit, and the bass jumps in the lake.

PRACTICE

Narrating a Natural Process

A. Taking Stewart's narratives as your model, imagine some portion of your own world as it would be if you and all the other people in it suddenly disappeared forever. Think of your house, your room, your pet, your garden—or whatever. How would they be transformed by time? Don't simply think of a day after you are gone. Think of time *passing*. Think of time as a force. Think in seasons, years, decades. You can learn how to do this by paying close attention to Stewart's writing. In a paragraph or so, narrate what you imagine taking place.

B. Narrate any process that might take place outside of human life: the life cycle of a stone, a field, a mountain; or a prehistoric age. Remember *not* to turn it into something personal or specific, with a unique history, but keep it on the level of the typical—not what happened *once* but what *always* happens or always will happen.

READING

The Process of a Day

In the following passage, an anthropologist narrates the process of a typical day in a Samoan village during the 1920s. As you read it, pay particular attention to the management of time by the narrator.

Margaret Mead, "A Day in Samoa"

The life of the day begins at dawn, or if the moon has shown until daylight, the shouts of the young men may be heard before dawn from the hillside. Uneasy in the night, populous with ghosts, they shout lustily to one another as they hasten with their work. As the dawn begins to fall among the soft brown roofs and the slender palm trees stand out against a colorless, gleaming sea, lovers slip home from trysts beneath the palm trees or in the shadow of beached canoes, that the light may find each sleeper in his appointed place. Cocks crow, negligently, and a shrill-voiced bird cries from the breadfruit trees. The insistent roar of the reef seems muted to an undertone for the sounds of waking village. Babies cry, a few short wails·before sleepy mothers give them the breast. Restless little children roll out of their sheets and wander drowsily down to the beach to freshen their faces in the sea. Boys, bent upon an early fishing, start collecting their tackle and go to rouse their more laggard companions. Fires are lit, here and there, the white smoke hardly visible against the paleness of the dawn. The whole village, sheeted and frowsy, stirs, rubs its eyes, and stumbles towards the beach. "Talofa!" "Talofa!" "Will the journey start to-day?" "Is it bonito fishing your lordship is going?" Girls stop to giggle over some young ne'er-do-well who escaped during the night from an angry father's pursuit and to venture a shrewd guess that the daughter knew more about his presence than she told. The boy who is taunted by another, who has succeeded him in his sweetheart's favour, grapples with his rival, his foot slipping in the wet sand. From the other end of the village comes a long drawn-out, piercing wail. A messenger has just brought word of the death of some relative in another village. Half-clad, unhurried women, with babies at their breasts, or astride their hips, pause in their tale of Losa's outraged departure from her father's house to the greater kindness in the home of her uncle, to wonder who is dead. Poor relatives whisper their requests to rich relatives, men make plans to set a fish trap together, a woman begs a bit of yellow dye from a kinswoman, and through the village sounds the rhythmic tattoo which calls the young men together. They gather from all parts of the village, digging sticks in hand, ready to start inland to the plantation. The older men set off upon their more lonely occupations, and each household, reassembled under its peaked roof, settles down to the routine of the morning. Little children, too hungry to wait for the late breakfast, beg lumps of cold taro which they munch greedily. Women carry piles of washing to the sea or to the spring at the far end of the village, or set off inland after weaving materials. The older girls go fishing on the reef, or perhaps set themselves to weaving a new set of Venetian blinds.

In the houses, where the pebbly floors have been swept bare with a 2 stiff long-handled broom, the women great with child and the nursing mothers, sit and gossip with one another. Old men sit apart, unceasingly twisting palm husk on their bare thighs and muttering old tales under their breath. The carpenters begin work on the new house, while the owner bustles about trying to keep them in a good humor. Families who will cook today are hard at work; the taro, yams and bananas have already been brought from inland; the children are scuttling back and forth, fetching sea water, or leaves to stuff the pig. As the sun rises higher in the sky, the shadows deepen under the thatched roofs, the sand is burning to the touch, the hibiscus flowers wilt on the hedges, and little children bid the smaller ones, "Come out of the sun." Those whose excursions have been short return to the village, the women with strings of crimson jellyfish, or baskets of shellfish, the men with coconuts, carried in baskets

NARRATION: ORGANIZING TIME

slung on a shoulder pole. The women and children eat their break-fasts, just hot from the oven, if this is cook day, and the young men work swiftly in the midday heat, preparing the noon feast for their elders.

It is high noon. The sand burns the feet of the little children, who 3 leave their palm leaf balls and their pinwheels of frangipani blossoms to wither in the sun, as they creep into the shade of the houses. The women who must go abroad carry great banana leaves as sunshades or wind wet cloths about their heads. Lowering a few blinds against the slanting sun, all who are left in the village wrap their heads in sheets and go to sleep. Only a few adventurous children may slip away for a swim in the shadow of a high rock, some industrious woman continue with her weaving, or a close little group of women bend anxiously over a woman in labor. The village is dazzling and dead; any sound seems oddly loud and out of place. Words have to cut through the solid heat slowly. And then the sun gradually sinks over the sea.

A second time, the sleeping people stir, roused perhaps by the cry 4 of "a boat," resounding through the village. The fishermen beach their canoes, weary and spent from the heat, in spite of the slaked lime on their heads, with which they have sought to cool their brains and redden their hair. The brightly colored fishes are spread out on the floor, or piled in front of the houses until the women pour water over them to free them from taboo. Regretfully, the young fisher-men separate out the "Taboo fish," which must be sent to the chief, or proudly they pack the little palm leaf baskets with offerings of fish to take to their sweethearts. Men come home from the bush, grimy and heavy laden, shouting as they come, greeted in a sonorous rising cadence by those who have remained at home. They gather in the guest house for their evening kava drinking. The soft clapping of hands, the high-pitched intoning of the talking chief who serves the kava echoes through the village. Girls gather flowers to weave into necklaces; children, lusty from their naps and bound to no particular task, play circular games in the half shade of the late afternoon. Fi-nally the sun sets, in a flame which stretches from the mountain be-hind to the horizon on the sea, the last bather comes up from the beach, children straggle home, dark little figures etched against the sky; lights shine in the houses, and each household gathers for its evening meal. The suitor humbly presents his offering, the children have been summoned from their noisy play, perhaps there is an hon-ored guest who must be served first, after the soft, barbaric singing of Christian hymns and the brief and graceful evening prayer. In front of a house at the end of the village, a father cries out the birth of a son. In some family circles a face is missing, in others little run-aways have found a haven! Again quiet settles upon the village, as first the head of the household, then the women and children, and last of all the patient boys, eat their supper.

After supper the old people and the little children are bundled off 5 to bed. If the young people have guests the front of the house is yielded to them. For day is the time for the councils of old men and the labors of youth, and night is the time for lighter things. Two kinsmen, or a chief and his councillor, sit and gossip over the day's events or make plans for the morrow. Outside a crier goes through the village announcing that the communal breadfruit pit will be opened in the morning, or that the village will make a great fish trap. If it is moonlight, groups of young men, women by twos and threes, wander through the village, and crowds of children hunt for land crabs or chase each other among the breadfruit trees. Half the village may go fishing by torchlight and the curving reef will gleam with wavering lights and echo with shouts of triumph or disappoint-ment, teasing words or smothered cries of outraged modesty. Or a group of youths may dance for the pleasure of some visiting maiden. Many of those who have retired to sleep, drawn by the merry music, will wrap their sheets about them and set out to find the dancing. A white-clad, ghostly throng will gather in a circle about the gaily lit house, a circle from which every now and then a few will detach themselves and wander away among the trees. Sometimes sleep will not descend upon the village until long past midnight; then at last there is only the mellow thunder of the reef and the whisper of lov-ers, as the village rests until dawn.

QUESTIONS

1. How do you know this is a process narrative and not a story?
2. Which features of this text seem to suggest it is *not* a process narrative, but the story of a single, unique day? How are these features blended in with the others that establish this as a typical day, a hypothetical day, no single day at all?
3. How is this narrative organized? Consider each paragraph as a unit in a larger order. What governs their arrangement? Consider a single para-graph as a unit in itself. What governs the order of the sentences within the paragraph? Consider a single sentence, like the last sentence of the fourth paragraph or of the final paragraph. What governs the ordering of the elements within the sentence? How is the last sentence of this nar-rative connected to the first?

PRACTICE

Process Narrative: A Day in _____

Taking "A Day in Samoa" as a good example, write the narrative of a typical day in some place you know. It can be a particular work place or living place or a larger unit like a school or a town. But don't bite off more than you can tell.

We suggest you begin by making a list of the typical events that might take place in your chosen spot. Don't be afraid to list more events for your *typical* day than might occur in an *average* day, which could, after all, be dull and uneventful. When you have a good list, arrange the units into the order in which they would occur on a typical day. This chronological list will make a good working outline. In writing, you will have to decide which events are most important and deserve the most space, and you will need to consider how to divide your day into paragraphs.

Careful discussion of Mead's organization of material should help you to organize your own narrative.

READING

Narrating an Event

Here is a complete work of fiction by the Argentine writer Julio Cortázar. It may be some sort of parable about the state of contemporary art, but we won't worry about that. We will take it as a simple narrative that might give somebody an idea for some writing of their own. Please read it and then consider the questions that follow the story.

Julio Cortázar, "Simulacra"

We are an uncommon family. In this country where things are done   1
only to boast of them or from a sense of obligation, we like independent occupations, jobs that exist just because, simulacra which are completely useless.

We have one failing: we lack originality. Nearly everything we decide to do is inspired by—let's speak frankly, is copied from—celebrated examples. If we manage to contribute any innovation whatsoever, it always proves to have been inevitable: anachronisms, or surprises, or scandals. My elder uncle says that we're like carbon copies, identical with the original except another color, another paper, another end product. My third-youngest sister compares herself to Andersen's mechanical nightingale. Her romanticizing is disgusting.

There are a lot of us and we live in Humboldt Street.   3

We do things, but it's difficult to tell about it because the most   4
important elements are missing: the anxiety and the expectation of doing the things, the surprises so much more important than the results, the calamities and abortive undertakings where the whole family collapses like a card castle and for whole days you don't hear anything but wailing and peals of laughter. Telling what we do is hardly a way of filling in the inevitable gaps, because sometimes we're poor or in jail or sick, sometimes somebody dies or (it hurts me to mention it) someone goes straight, finks out, renounces us, or heads in the UNPOSITIVE DIRECTION. But there's no reason to conclude from this that things are terrible with us or that we're incurably unhappy. We live in this lower-middle-class neighborhood called the barrio Pacífico, and we do things every chance we get. There are a lot of us who come up with ideas and manage to put them into action. The gallows for instance: up till now, no one's agreed on how the idea got started; my fifth sister asserts that it was one of my first cousins, who are very much philosophers, but my elder uncle insists that it occurred to him after reading a cloak-and-dagger novel. Basically, it's not very important to us, the only thing that counts is to do things, and that's why I tell it, unwillingly almost, only so as not to feel so close the emptiness of this rainy afternoon.

The house has a garden in front of it, an uncommon thing in   5
Humboldt Street. It's not much bigger than a patio, but it's three steps higher than the sidewalk, which gives it the fine aspect of a platform, the ideal site for a gallows. As it has a high railing of ironwork and masonry, one can work without the passers-by being, as one might say, installed in the house itself; they can station themselves at the railings and hang around there for hours, which doesn't bother us. "We shall begin at the full moon," my father ruled. By day we went to find lengths of wood and iron in the warehouses in the Avenida Juan B. Justo, but my sisters stayed home in the parlor practicing the wolf howl, after my youngest aunt maintained that

gallows trees draw wolves and move them to howl at the moon. The responsibility of acquiring a supply of nails and other hardware fell to my cousins; my elder uncle made a sketch of the plans, and discussed with my mother and my other uncle the variety and quality of the various instruments of torture. I remember the end of that discussion: they decided austerely on a reasonably high platform upon which would be constructed the gibbet and a rack and wheel, with an open space which could be used for torture or beheading, depending upon the case. It seemed to my elder uncle a rather poor and meeching construction compared with his original idea, but the size of the front garden and the cost of construction materials are always restricting the family's ambitions.

We began the construction work on a Sunday afternoon after the 6 raviolis. Although we had never concerned ourselves with what the neighbors might think, it was clear that the few onlookers thought we were adding one or two floors to enlarge the house. The first to be astonished was Don Cresta, the little old man in the house across from us, and he came over to inquire why we were putting up a platform like that. My sisters were gathered in one corner of the garden and were letting loose with a few wolf howls. A goodly group of people gathered, but we went on working until nightfall and got the platform finished and the two little sets of stairs (for the priest and the condemned man, who ought not to go up together). Monday one part of the family went to its respective employments and occupations, after all, you have to live somehow, and the rest of us began to put up the gibbet while my elder uncle consulted ancient engravings to find a model for the rack and wheel. His idea was to set the wheel as high as possible upon a slightly irregular pole, for example a well-trimmed poplar trunk. To humor him, my second-oldest brother and my first cousins went off with the pickup truck to find a poplar; my elder uncle and my mother, meanwhile, were fitting the spokes of the wheel into the hub and I was getting an iron collar ready. In those moments we amused ourselves enormously because you could hear hammering on all sides, my sisters howling in the parlor, the neighbors crowding against the iron railings exchanging impressions, and the silhouette of the gibbet rose between the rosaniline bed and the evening mallows and you could see my younger uncle astride the crosspiece driving in the hook and fixing the running knot for the noose.

At this stage of things the people in the street could not help real- 7 izing what it was we were building, and a chorus of threats and protests was an agreeable encouragement to put the final stroke to the day's labor by erecting the wheel. Several disorderly types had made an effort to keep my second-oldest brother and my cousins from conveying into the house the magnificent poplar trunk which they'd fetched in the pickup truck. An attempt at harassment in the form of a tug of war was won easily by the family in full force tugging at the trunk in a disciplined way, and we set it down in the garden along with a very young child trapped in the roots. My father personally returned the child to its exasperated parents, putting it genteelly through the railings, and while attention was concentrated on these sentimental alternatives, my elder uncle aided by my first cousins fitted the wheel onto one end of the trunk and proceeded to raise it. The family was congregated on the platform at the moment the police arrived and commented favorably on how well the gallows looked. My third sister had stationed herself alone by the gate, so the dialogue with the deputy commissioner himself was left up to her; it was not difficult for her to persuade him that we were laboring within the precincts of our own property upon a project only the use of which could vest it with an illegal character, and that the complaints of the neighborhood were the products of animosity and the result of envy. Nightfall saved us from losing any more time.

We took supper on the platform by the light of a carbide lamp, 8 spied upon by a crowd of around a hundred spiteful neighbors; never had the roast suckling pig tasted more exquisite, or the chianti been blacker and sweeter. A breeze from the north swung the gallows rope gently back and forth; the wheel of the rack creaked once or twice, as though the crows had already come to rest there and eat. The spectators began to go off, muttering vague threats; some twenty or thirty stayed on, hanging around the iron railing— they seemed to be waiting for something. After coffee we put out the lamp so that we could see the moon, which was rising over the balustrades of the terrace, my sisters howled, and my cousins and uncles loped slowly back and forth across the platform, their steps making the foundation shake underfoot. In the subsequent silence the moonlight came to fall at the height of the noose, and a cloud with silver borders seemed to stretch across the wheel. We looked at it all, so happy it was a pleasure, but the neighbors were murmuring at the railings as if they were disappointed or something. They were lighting cigarettes or were wandering off, some in pajamas and others more slowly. Only the street remained, the sound of the cop's nightstick on pavement in the distance, and the 108 bus which passed every once in a while; as for us, we had already gone to sleep, and were dreaming of fiestas, elephants, and silk suits.

QUESTIONS

1. Our dictionary defines "simulacrum" ("simulacra" is the plural) in the following way:
   a. an image; something that is formed in the likeness of a being or thing.
   b. a semblance having the form without the substance.
   c. a phantom or shadowy likeness of something; especially a vague, unreal semblance; a mock appearance; a sham.

   A resemblence of something

   Restate the definition in your own words. Is a character in a story a simulacrum? Is everything named or described in writing a simulacrum of something real? *Yes*

2. In the story, why do people try to interfere with the building of the simulacrum? What, exactly, does it simulate?

3. In the end the neighbors seem disappointed. Is this because the gallows is only a simulacrum? What do you suppose they expected?

4. Is this story itself a simulacrum? What is the use of simulacra? Are there works of art that are *not* simulacra? Can something be real and a simulacrum at the same time?

5. Suppose someone was executed on the simulacrum of the gallows. Would it then become real? What do we mean by "execute"—it's not just killing, is it?

6. Why is the story called "simulacra" rather than "The Simulacrum"? That is, why do you suppose the author used the plural form of the word? There is only one gallows. Are there other simulacra in the story?

PRACTICE

Suppose Your Family Built a _____

In Cortázar's story, you have seen how the building of a replica or simulacrum of a gallows affects the "real" world around the fake gallows. Of course the "real" world is a fiction, too, invented by Cortázar, even if it names real places like Humboldt Street.

We suggest you use "Simulacra" as the inspiration for a narrative of your own. Suppose your family, or your sorority, or your gang, or any group that you are in should build something that looks like it might have some real and disturbing use (such as a rocket, a bomb, an "adult" book store, a dog pound, a fertilizer factory, an all-night discotheque, etc.). What would happen? How would people react? How would you feel about it?

Imagine it. Report on it as if it has already happened. Narrate it.

The Life of Stephen Crane

The year is 1900. After a long search for employment, you've traveled to the Oklahoma Territory and found a job as the reporter for the Panhandle *Gazette*, a weekly newspaper. Your editor has just received news of the death of Stephen Crane, the well-known writer, and he asks you to write Crane's obituary. You don't know very much about Crane; you haven't read any of his fiction, poetry, or newspaper articles. There's no library in Panhandle, and you haven't time to send for any of Crane's books. You search desperately through the newspaper's files and find a chronology of Crane's life, some reviews of his work, one of his articles on the Spanish-American War, and some comments about him, all of which have been reprinted below.

Your editor wants a vivid account of Crane's life. He reminds you that your readers know less than you do about Crane, so you must give them an idea of what Crane's accomplishments were, what sort of person he was, what motivated him, and finally, an assessment of Crane's brief and active life. You can't cover all the events in the chronology because you don't have enough information. Rather, you must analyze what data you do have, looking for patterns of events in Crane's history that will help you create the story of his life.

Read through all the material several times, making notes to yourself about what information seems most significant and where you see important connections. Then, compose an obituary that will satisfy your editor's demands.

Stephen Crane: A Chronology

1871 Birth of Stephen Crane on November 11 at 14 Mulberry Place, Newark, New Jersey. The fourteenth and last child of Reverend Jonathan Townley Crane, graduate of the College of New Jersey (later Princeton University) and presiding elder for the Newark district of Methodism; and his wife Mary Helen, daughter of a well-known Methodist minister, George Peck.

1876 Family moves to Paterson, New Jersey, where Dr. Crane is appointed to Cross Street Church.

NARRATION: ORGANIZING TIME

1878 Dr. Crane is appointed pastor at Port Jervis, New York. In 3
September, Stephen begins his public school education here,
the locale of his later *Whilomville Stories* and "The Monster."

1880 Death of Dr. Crane in Port Jervis on February 16. Mrs. 4
Crane supports family by writing for Methodist papers and
the New York *Tribune* and the Philadelphia *Press*.

1883 Mrs. Crane moves to Asbury Park, New Jersey, where 5
Stephen attends school.

1885 Stephen writes his first story, "Uncle Jake and the Bell Han- 6
dle," never published during his lifetime. Enrolls at Pennington Seminary, Pennington, New Jersey.

1888 In January, Stephen enrolls at Hudson River Institute 7
(Claverack College) in Claverack, New York, and remains
here until 1890. Publishes his first sketch, "Henry M. Stanley," in school magazine *Vidette* (February 1890), and is promoted to captain in military drill. Probably hears Civil War
tales from history teacher, retired General Van Petten. During the summer months (1888–92), Stephen assists his
brother Townley who operates a news bureau at Asbury
Park.

1890 Stephen enters Lafayette College in September as mining en- 8
gineering student. Poor class attendance.

1891 Transfers to Syracuse University in January. Correspondent 9
for the New York *Tribune* in Syracuse. Presumably sells
sketches to the Detroit *Free Press*; publishes his first story,
"The King's Favor," in May issue of the Syracuse *University
Herald*; and begins writing *Maggie*. Spends little time in the
classroom; ends college career in June. During the summer,
he meets Hamlin Garland at Avon-by-the-Sea and reports his
lecture on William Dean Howells (August 18). In love with
Helen Trent. Mother dies in Paterson on December 7.

1892 First substantial publication of his short fiction; five of his *Sul-* 10
livan County Sketches appear in the New York *Tribune* (July 3,
10, 17, 24, 31). First of his New York City sketches published,
"The Broken-Down Van" (July 10). Fired as reporter by
Tribune for writing sardonic article on parading Junior Order
of United American Mechanics at Asbury Park (August 21).
In love with Lily Brandon Munroe.

1893 *Maggie: A Girl of the Streets* is rejected by various publishers; 11
Crane publishes it at his own cost under pseudonym Johnston
Smith. Receives encouragement from Garland and Howells.
Begins writing *The Red Badge of Courage*.

1894 Sells abridged version (18,000 words) of *The Red Badge* to 12
Bacheller-Johnson Syndicate for ninety dollars; it appears

first in the Philadelphia *Press* (December 3–8). Short stories and sketches on social issues appear in *The Arena* and New York *Press*.

1895   In January, meets and falls in love with Nellie Crouse. This   13
same month he begins his trip to the American West and Mexico, writing special features for the Bacheller-Johnson Syndicate. Meets Willa Cather in Lincoln, Nebraska. Publishes volume of free verse in March, *The Black Riders.* . . . The complete version (50,000 words) of *The Red Badge* is published by Appleton in October and becomes a best seller and wins a large following in England.

1896   *George's Mother* and revised version of *Maggie* published in May   14
and June, respectively. In September, Crane defends Dora Clark, arrested for "soliciting"; this incident makes him continual target of New York City police. Publishes his first collection of stories, *The Little Regiment and Other Episodes of the American Civil War*, in November, his "last thing dealing with battle." Meets Cora Taylor (Howorth) in November in Jacksonville, Florida, at her establishment, Hotel de Dream.

1897   Shipwrecked off Florida coast on January 2 on *Commodore*,   15
carrying contraband to Cuban insurgents; this incident is source of "The Open Boat," which appears in June. With Cora Taylor he covers short-lived Greco-Turkish War (April–May) as war correspondent for New York *Journal* and *Westminister Gazette*. Publishes *The Third Violet* in May (serialized the previous year). Resides at Ravensbrook House (Oxted, Surrey) in England with Cora; no evidence that they were ever legally married. Friendships with Joseph Conrad, Henry James, Ford Madox Ford, Harold Frederic, and others. Travels to Ireland in September.

1898   To Cuba and the Spanish-American War as correspondent   16
for Pulitzer's New York *World* and later Hearst's New York *Journal*; first dispatches in April, and last in November. Richard Harding Davis names him the best of the war correspondents in Cuba. Publishes *The Open Boat and Other Tales of Adventure* (April). At the peak of his short story craft, with the appearance of "The Bride Comes to Yellow Sky" (February), "Death and the Child" (March), "The Monster" (August), and "The Blue Hotel" (November–December).

1899   Crane returns to England and to Cora in January; resides at   17
Brede Place (Sussex), legend-filled castle. Publishes second book of poems, *War Is Kind; The Monster and Other Stories*; and *Active Service*, a novel based on his Greek experiences. Writes at feverish pace to pay off many debts; plans a novel on the

American Revolution, never finished; and starts *The O'Ruddy*, his last novel.

1900 Recurrence of earlier tubercular attacks in January and peri-   18
odically until his death on June 5 in a sanitorium at Baden-
weiler, Germany. Buried at Hillside, New Jersey. Appearance of *Whilomville Stories* and Cuban war stories, *Wounds in the
Rain.*

—THOMAS GULLASON

1891   Crane at Syracuse University

Clarence Loomis Peaslee, a classmate of Crane's:

He has a deep regard for true learning, but not for the rubbish that   19
often passes under that name, and if he has not burned the midnight
oil in search of "school" knowledge, he has worked as but few men
have in the field of observation and the study of mankind. In college
Crane was an omnivorous reader and sat up late at night, diligently
poring over the masterpieces of literature or trying to put upon paper his own peculiar views of man and life . . . He wanted to produce something that would make men think, that would make men
feel as he felt, and to do this he early realized that for him it must
come through hard work.

Another classmate:

He gloried in talking with shambling figures who lurked in the dark   20
doorways on deserted slum streeets, and his love for adventure constantly kept his feet on ill-lighted thoroughfares honeycombing the
city.

1895   Reviews of Crane's novel *The Red Badge of Courage*

From the Boston Transcript:

It is a tremendous grasping of the glory and carnage of all war; it is   21
the rendering, in phrases that reveal like lightning flashes, of the raw
fighter's emotions, the blind magnificent courage and the cowardice
equally blind of a youth first possessed by the red sickness of battle.

From Outlook *magazine (December 21, 1895):*

The story is not pleasant by any means, but the author seems to lay   22
bare the very nerves of his character; practically, the book is a minute study of one man's mind in the environment of war in all its horrible detail.

A note from Stephen Crane: "I have never been in a battle, of   23
course, and I believe that I got my sense of the rage of conflict on the
football field. The psychology is the same. The opposing team is an
enemy tribe."

1896   Publication of *Maggie: A Girl of the Streets*

From a note from Crane written on the cover of Hamlin Garland's copy of
Maggie:

It is inevitable that you will be greatly shocked by this book, but con-   24
tinue please with all possible courage to the end. For it tries to show
that environment is a tremendous thing in the world and frequently
shapes lives regardless. If one proves that theory one makes room in
heaven for all sorts of souls (notably an occasional street girl) who
are not confidently expected to be there by many excellent people. It
is probable that the reader of this small thing may consider the author to be a bad man; but obviously that is a matter of small consequence.

From an English review:

Maggie is a study of life in the slums of New York, and of the hopeless   25
struggle of a girl against the horrible conditions of her environment;
and so bitter is the struggle, so black the environment, so inevitable
the end, that the reader feels a chill at his heart, and dislikes the book
even while he admires it. Mr. Crane's realism is merciless and un-
sparing; in these chapters are set before us in cold blood hideous
phases of misery, brutality, drunkenness, vice; while oaths and blasphemies form the habitual speech of the men and women who live
and move in this atmosphere of vileness. Yet every scene is alive and
has the unmistakable stamp of truth upon it. The reader does not
feel that he is reading about these horrors; he feels as if the outer
walls of some tenement houses in the slums had been taken away
and he could see—and see with comprehension—the doings of the
teeming inmates. Over the whole grimly powerful tragedy is the redeeming grace of the author's implied compassion; but he never
mars the effect of the story by speaking this compassion or by pointing a moral. He has drawn a vivid picture of life at its lowest and
worst; he has shown us the characters as they would be, with no false
glamor of an impossible romance about them; and the moral may
confidently be left to look after itself, since it stares from every page.
Maggie herself is a wonderfully well-drawn character, and the book,
repellent though it is, is in its way a triumph.

1897   The *Commodore* disaster

From the New York Press, *January 5, 1897:*

CRANE'S SPLENDID GRIT

"That man Crane is the spunkiest fellow out," said Captain Mur-   26
phy tonight to The Press correspondent, in speaking of the wreck
and incidents pertaining to it. "The sea was so rough that even old
sailors got seasick when we struck the open sea after leaving the bar,
but Crane behaved like a born sailor. He and I were about the only
ones not affected by the big seas which tossed us about. As we went
south he sat in the pilot house with me, smoking and telling yarns.
When the leak was discovered he was the first man to volunteer aid.

JOKES AMID DANGER

"His shoes, new ones, were slippery on the deck, and he took them   27
off and tossed them overboard, saying, with a laugh: 'Well, captain,
I guess I won't need them if we have to swim.' He stood on deck
with me all the while, smoking his cigarette, and aided me greatly
while the boats were getting off. When in the dinghy he suggested
putting up the overcoat for a sail, and he took his turn at the oars or
holding up the oar mast.

TRIES TO SAVE HIGGINS

"When we went over I called to him to see that his life preserver was   28
on all right and he replied in his usual tones, saying that he would
obey orders. He was under the boat once, but got out in some way.
He held up Higgins when the latter got so terribly tired and endeav-
ored to bring him in, but the sailor was so far gone that he could
hardly help himself. When we were thrown up by the waves, Crane
was the first man to stagger up the beach looking for houses. He's a
thoroughbred," concluded the captain, "and a brave man, too,
with plenty of grit."

**1898   Crane as correspondent in the Spanish-American
       War**

From Langdon Smith in Cosmopolitan *magazine, September 1898:*

Crane was standing under a tree calmly rolling a cigarette; some   29
leaves dropped from the trees, cut away by the bullets; two or three
men dropped within a few feet. Crane is as thin as a lathe. If he had
been two or three inches wider or thicker through, he would undoubtedly have been shot. But he calmly finished rolling his ciga-

rette and smoked it without moving away from the spot where the bullets had suddenly become so thick.

From Crane's report of the battle of San Juan in the New York World, *July 14, 1898:*

The road from El Paso to San Juan was now a terrible road. It 30 should have a tragic fame like the sunken road at Waterloo. Why we did not later hang some of the gentry who contributed from the trees to the terror of this road is not known.

The wounded were stringing back from the front, hundreds of 31 them. Some walked unaided, an arm or shoulder having been dressed at a field station. They stopped often enough to answer the universal hail "How is it going?" Others hobbled or clung to a friend's shoulders. Their slit trousers exposed red bandages. A few were shot horribly in the face and were led, bleeding and blind by their mates.

And then there were the slow pacing stretcher-bearers with the 32 dead or the insensible, the badly wounded, still figures with blood often drying brick color on their hot bandages.

Prostrate at the roadside were many others who had made their 33 way thus far and were waiting for strength. Everywhere moved the sure-handed, invaluable Red Cross men.

Over this scene was a sort of haze of bullets. They were of two 34 kinds. First, the Spanish lines were firing just a trifle high. Their bullets swept over our firing lines and poured into this devoted roadway, the single exit, even as it had been the single approach. The second fire was from guerillas concealed in the trees and thickets along the trail. They had come in under the very wings of our strong advance, taken good positions on either side of the road and were peppering our line of communication whenever they got a good target, no matter, apparently, what the target might be.

Red Cross men, wounded men, sick men, correspondents and at- 35 taches were all one to the guerilla. The move of sending an irregular force around the flanks of the enemy as he is making his front attack is so legitimate that some of us could not believe at first that the men hidden in the forest were really blazing away at the non-combatants or the wounded. Viewed simply as a bit of tactics, the scheme was admirable. But there is no doubt now that they intentionally fired at anybody they thought they could kill.

You can't mistake an ambulance driver when he is driving his am- 36 bulance. You can't mistake a wounded man when he is lying down and being bandaged. And when you see a field hospital you don't mistake it for a squadron of cavalry or a brigade of infantry.

NARRATION: ORGANIZING TIME

PRACTICE

The Life of Yourself

Following the example of the biographical material presented for Stephen Crane in the previous assignment, draw up a chronology of ten to fifteen important events in your life from your birth to the present. Also provide five short paragraphs elaborating on those events you consider the most important. For example, your first day in kindergarten may have been an exciting or terrifying experience, and you should briefly describe that event. You should bring this material to class and exchange it with a student you don't know very well. You and this student will then write each other's biographies.

In analyzing the other student's material, remember that you are writing the *story* of a person's life. In arranging this story, you don't have to begin with the person's birth (unless something extraordinary occurred). You might start with what you consider the most outstanding event and trace it back. To do this, you should look for related events in the material. For example, if the person is a football player, can you trace this competitive interest back to elementary school days? Or if the person is majoring in pre-med or nursing, look for a reason—perhaps volunteer work in a hospital or a death or illness in the family has been influential.

Now write a short biography of this other student. Your instructor can decide whether or not this material should be presented anonymously.

Description: Organizing Space

7

In a sense, narration is easy because events unfolding in time have a linear shape or structure. When someone is having difficulty in reporting an event to us, we say, "Just begin at the beginning." We can do this because both events and narratives have beginnings. Descriptions have beginnings, too. The problem is that the things being described often do not. We may describe what we hear, taste, smell, or feel, but because human beings are sight-dominated creatures, we most often describe what we see. That is, we translate our perceptions of space-bound objects with no perceivable beginning or end into a time-bound, linear form: writing.

For the writer, description of a visual object poses a number of problems: where to begin? what to include next? where to end? All these problems can be reduced to one: the problem of order. How should description be arranged? There is, however, another problem hiding behind this one: what information should be selected for inclusion in a written description? Even a blank wall presents a nearly infinite amount of information for anyone who inspects it closely enough. Selection and arrangement, the twin problems of descriptive writing, can be solved in the same way. The writer must have a *point of view* about the object being described. That is, as a writer you must see something in the object that will enable you to make a statement about it—which will in turn help you to organize the impressions you are receiving from the object. Once you have a point of view, you will know what to look for, what to record; and you will have the option of moving from one item to another according to the way the objects relate to your point of view.

A scientist describing a specimen will leave out certain irrelevant details. A poet or essayist describing the same object might include much that the scientist would consider irrelevant and exclude the data of most concern to the scientist. The purpose shapes the presentation and helps to generate the point of view required for good description. Some of the following assignments are designed to develop your awareness of the way in which point of view shapes description. In others we have posed problems in translation from a visual text to a verbal one or even more complicated problems in the imitation of a verbal style and description of a visual object simultaneously.

READING

Hogarth's "Noon" Described

William Hogarth was England's leading caricaturist and visual satirist in the eighteenth century. He is famous for his series of engravings depicting male and female degeneration and disaster, called *The Rake's Progress* and *The Harlot's Progress*. The engraving we are reprinting here is from a much milder series, called *The Four Times of Day*. This one is "Noon," first printed in 1738. Along with the engraving we are providing a sample description of it, to give you some ideas on how to write your own description.

This is a picture of a street scene in a bustling city, full of people in eighteenth-century clothing. The street itself is made of cobblestones, and has an open sewer or gutter running down the middle of it. A dead cat lies in the gutter near some broken stones.

The right side of the picture is dominated by a large brick building with windows of leaded glass. A crowd is emerging from a small door in the building, half of them coming closer to our viewpoint, the other half walking away with their backs turned. Some of this crowd have severe expressions on their

faces and carry black books. They may be coming from a rather puritanical church after service.

In the right foreground, among this crowd, are a man, woman, and child dressed in what must have been the height of fashion. The man is wearing shoes with buckles, stockings, knee-britches, an immense bowtie and a long coat with frills and over twenty buttons. He is making elegant gestures with his hands, pointing his feet like a dancer, with a cane dangling by a ribbon from his ruffled wrist, and a sword hanging from his other side.

This elegant fop is speaking to a richly dressed lady, while in front of them is a creature like a midget, but probably a small boy, dressed like a miniature of the man, complete with a cane, a wig, and a toy sword. He has a hand inside his long vest as he gazes downward, smiling, possibly at the dead cat. These three seem to be a family group.

On the other side of the gutter there is a group of people who have obviously not been to church. They stand in front of a sign that says "Good Eating" between two very large teeth topped with a picture of a man's head on a platter. From a window above a woman is throwing an old piece of meat from a platter toward the gutter, while a man grabs for it from behind her, and misses. Near the window hangs a sign with a picture of a woman standing so that the top of the sign is at the level of her neck, leaving her headless.

Down below in the street a boy is scratching his bushy head and bellowing over a huge pie he has apparently just dropped, while a poorly dressed girl scrambles at his feet for the broken pieces, stuffing them into her mouth. Just behind these two stand another couple, a woman holding a hot pie with her apron, while a black man reaches around her from behind to fondle her breasts and kiss her cheek. She seems to be encouraging this but her pie is tilting, dripping its liquid center towards the cobblestones. The whole pie may soon be headed that way.

The gutter seems to divide the well-do-do from the less affluent, the pious from the boisterous. This division gives a sense of the diversity of city life. But it is a very unflattering picture. There are no attractive people in the picture, except the young woman who is losing her pie and perhaps more than that. Even a building in the background has a huge crack, parallel to the gutter, running down its side.

Describing a Hogarth Street Scene

On page 130 is a London street scene done by Hogarth a few years after the one just presented and discussed. Your assignment is to write a description of this scene that is about as complete and accurate as our description of the other engraving by Hogarth.

You should not try to follow the other description. That one was organized partly by the gutter that Hogarth used to divide his picture. (Such gutters were called ''kennels'' in Hogarth's day.) You must find an organizing principle in this engraving that will guide you in making your description of it.

This one seems to tell a bit more of a story than the first. Certainly it offers a thematic way of organizing the material. There is no single correct way of doing this, but rather several possible ways. Your job is to find one and use it here.

READING

Point of View in Description

Here are examples of four notable writers at work describing things. The four selections serve to illustrate how a writer can organize an interior space like a bedroom or a restaurant, an exterior urban space such as a city, and finally, an exterior rural space, such as cultivated fields.

In reading each selection you should consider in particular each writer's point of view. How has the writer actually organized the space to get it on paper? What has been included? What has been excluded? For instance, every room has a floor, a ceiling, and four walls. Which of these has Orwell included and excluded? Of the things that the writer has chosen to include, which are mentioned first? What pattern can you find in the movement from one object to the next? Can you tell how the writer has decided upon a particular order? If you were going to make a film based on the description of the place, could you do it with a single location? Could your camera capture everything in one steady movement, or would it have to hop around, fre-

TOPIC-ORIENTED FORMS

quently changing position, distance, and angle? You might also ask what aspects of the written description a camera could not capture.

The writer's point of view requires some consistent feeling or attitude toward the scene being described. You should try to reduce the attitude in each of the following descriptions to the shortest possible expression—a single word if you can—that expresses the dominant feeling conveyed by the description. Which of the following words best suits the Orwell selection: pleasure, displeasure, fascination, disgust, disapproval, sympathy? Can you find words or phrases that sum up the point of view that is used to unify each of the other three examples?

After reading and discussing all four examples, you should try to articulate the general principles of descriptive writing. What features do all four of these different writers employ in their descriptions? What is unique to each one?

George Orwell, "A Room" (from The Road to Wigan Pier)

Hanging from the ceiling there was a heavy glass chandelier on which the dust was so thick that it was like fur. And covering most of one wall there was a huge hideous piece of junk, something between a sideboard and a hall-stand, with lots of carving and little drawers and strips of looking-glass, and there was a once-gaudy carpet ringed by the slop-pails of years, and two gilt chairs with burst seats, and one of those old-fashioned horsehair armchairs which you slide off when you try to sit on them. The room had been turned into a bedroom by thrusting four squalid beds in among this wreckage.

James Joyce, "A Restaurant" (from Ulysses)

His heart astir he pushed in the door of the Burton restaurant. Stink   1
gripped his trembling breath: pungent meatjuice, slop of greens. See the animals feed.

Men, men, men.   2

Perched on high stools by the bar, hats shoved back, at the tables   3
calling for more bread no charge, swilling, wolfing gobfuls of sloppy food, their eyes bulging, wiping wetted moustaches. A pallid suet-faced young man polished his tumbler knife fork and spoon with his napkin. New set of microbes. A man with an infant's saucestained napkin tucked round him shovelled gurgling soup down his gullet. A

man spitting back on his plate: halfmasticated gristle: no teeth to chewchewchew it. Chump chop from the grill. Bolting to get it over. Sad booser's eyes. Bitten off more than he can chew. Am I like that? See ourselves as others see us. Hungry man is an angry man. Working tooth and jaw. Don't! O! A bone! That last pagan king of Ireland Cormac in the schoolpoem choked himself at Sletty southward of the Boyne. Wonder what he was eating. Something galoptious. Saint Patrick converted him to Christianity. Couldn't swallow it all however.

—Roast beef and cabbage.   4

—One stew.   5

Smells of men. His gorge rose. Spaton sawdust, sweetish warmish   6 cigarette smoke, reek of plug, spilt beer, men's beery piss, the stale of ferment.

Couldn't eat a morsel here. Fellow sharpening knife and fork, to   7 eat all before him, old chap picking his tootles. Slight spasm, full, chewing the cud. Before and after. Grace after meals. Look on this picture then on that. Scoffing up stewgravy with sopping sippets of bread. Lick it off the plate, man! Get out of this.

Charles Dickens, "A Town" (from **Hard Times***)*

It was a town of red brick, or of brick that would have been red if the smoke and ashes would have allowed it; but as matters stood it was a town of unnatural red and black like the painted face of a savage. It was a town of machinery and tall chimneys, out of which interminable serpents of smoke trailed themselves for ever and ever, and never got uncoiled. It had a black canal in it, and a river that ran purple with ill-smelling dye, and vast piles of building full of windows where there was a rattling and a trembling all day long, and where the piston of the steam engine worked monotonously up and down, like the head of an elephant in a state of melancholy madness. It contained several large streets all very like one another, and many small streets still more like one another, inhabited by people equally like one another, who all went in and out at the same hours, with the same sound upon the same pavements, to do the same work, and to whom every day was the same as yesterday and tomorrow, and every year the counterpart of the last and the next.

Willa Cather, "Fields" (from **O Pioneers!***)*

From the Norwegian graveyard one looks out over a vast checker-   1 board, marked off in squares of wheat and corn; light and dark, dark and light. Telephone wires hum along the white roads, which always run at right angles. From the graveyard gate one can count a dozen gaily painted farmhouses; the gilded weathervanes on the big red barns wink at each other across the green and brown and yellow fields. The light steel windmills tremble throughout their frames and tug at their moorings, as they vibrate in the wind that often blows from one week's end to another across that high, active, resolute stretch of country.

The Divide is now thickly populated. The rich soil yields heavy harvests; the dry, bracing climate and the smoothness of the land make labor easy for men and beasts. There are few scenes more gratifying than a spring plowing in that country, where the furrows of a single field often lie a mile in length, and the brown earth, with such a strong, clean smell, and such a power of growth and fertility in it, yields itself eagerly to the plow; rolls away from the shear, not even dimming the brightness of the metal, with a soft, deep sigh of happiness. The wheat-cutting sometimes goes on all night as well as all day, and in good seasons there are scarcely men and horses enough to do the harvesting. The grain is so heavy that it bends toward the blade and cuts like velvet.

There is something frank and joyous and young in the open face of the country. It gives itself ungrudgingly to the moods of the season holding nothing back. Like the plains of Lombardy, it seems to rise a little to meet the sun. The air and the earth are curiously mated and intermingled, as if the one were the breath of the other. You feel in the atmosphere the same tonic, puissant quality that is in the tilth, the same strength and resoluteness.

PRACTICE

Organizing a Space

A. Describe a place that you know. Choose a place you can look at as you write or a place so strong in your memory that you don't need to look at it. Begin by just jotting down details of the scene or words that capture your feeling about it. Don't hurry yourself, but take some time accumulating bits of language that serve to capture some aspect of the place for you.

When you have enough material, read it over and then begin drafting your written description. As you write, ask yourself if you are making the right choices for selection and arrangement of details. Are you leaving out something important? Are you mentioning things that are not necessary to convey the impression you want to convey? What impression *do* you want to convey?

B. Let another person or a group read your description, and, without any coaching from you, tell you the impression they received from your writing. If they seem to be missing something, getting a confused impression, or getting an impression different from what you wished to convey, you should undertake a revision of your description that will eliminate as many of these problems as possible.

READING

A Place with a History

In the following selection from "Some Notes on River Country," Eudora Welty gives us an excellent example of how knowledge of the history of a place can make that place interesting. She also gives us a good example of how to write a description in which historical information is integrated with physical details. As you read her essay, be thinking about some place of historical interest that you might describe and pay particular attention to the ways she has found to include the past—what is *not* there now—with what is actually present.

Eudora Welty, "The Natchez Trace"

A place that ever was lived in is like a fire that never goes out. It flares up, it smolders for a time, it is fanned or smothered by circumstance, but its being is intact, forever fluttering within it, the result of some original ignition. Sometimes it gives out glory, sometimes its little light must be sought out to be seen, small and tender as a candle flame, but as certain.

I have never seen, in this small section of old Mississippi River country and its little chain of lost towns between Vicksburg and Natchez, anything so mundane as ghosts, but I have felt many times there a sense of place as powerful as if it were visible and walking and could touch me.

The clatter of hoofs and the bellow of boats have gone, all old communications. The Old Natchez Trace has sunk out of use; it is deep in leaves. The river has gone away and left the landings. Boats from Liverpool do not dock at these empty crags. The old deeds are done, old evil and old good have been made into stories, as plows turn up the river bottom, and the wild birds fly now at the level where people on boat deck once were strolling and talking of great expanding things, and of chance and money. Much beauty has gone, many little things of life. To light up the nights there are no mansions, no celebrations. Just as, when there were mansions and celebrations, there were no more festivals of an Indian tribe there; before the music, there were drums.

But life does not forsake any place. People live still in Rodney's Landing; flood drives them out and they return to it. Children are born there and find the day as inexhaustible and as abundant as they run and wander in their little hills as they, in innocence and rightness, would find it anywhere on earth. The seasons come as truly, and give gratefulness, though they bring little fruit. There is a sense of place there, to keep life from being extinguished, like a cup of the hands to hold a flame.

To go there, you start west from Port Gibson. This was the frontier of the Natchez country. Postmen would arrive here blowing their tin horns like Gabriel where the Old Natchez Trace crosses the Bayou Pierre, after riding three hundred wilderness miles from Tennessee, and would run in where the tavern used to be to deliver their mail, change their ponies, and warm their souls with grog. And up this now sand-barred bayou trading vessels would ply from the river. Port Gibson is on a highway and a railroad today, and lives on without its river life, though it is half diminished. It is still rather smug because General Grant said it was "too pretty to burn." Perhaps it was too pretty for any harsh fate, with its great mossy trees and old camellias, its exquisite little churches, and galleried houses back in the hills overlooking the cotton fields. It has escaped what happened to Grand Gulf and Bruinsburg and Rodney's Landing.

A narrow gravel road goes into the West. You have entered the loess country, and a gate might have been shut behind you for the difference in the world. All about are hills and chasms of cane, forests of cedar trees, and magnolia. Falling away from your road, at times merging with it, an old trail crosses and recrosses, like a tunnel through the dense brakes, under arches of branches, a narrow, cedar-smelling trace the width of a horseman. This road joined the Natchez Trace to the river. It, too, was made by buffaloes, then used by man, trodden lower and lower, a few inches every hundred years.

Loess has the beautiful definition of aeolian—wind-borne. The loess soil is like a mantle; the ridge was laid down here by the wind, the bottom land by the water. Deep under them both is solid blue clay, embalming the fossil horse and the fossil ox and the great mastodon, the same preserving blue clay that was dug up to wrap the head of the Big Harp in bandit days, no less a monstrous thing when it was carried in for reward. 7

Loess exists also in China, that land whose plants are so congenial to the South; there the bluffs rise vertically for five hundred feet in some places and contain cave dwellings without number. The Mississippi bluffs once served the same purpose; when Vicksburg was being shelled from the river during the year's siege there in the War Between the States, it was the daily habit of the three thousand women, children and old men who made up the wartime population to go on their all-fours into shelters they had tunneled into the loess bluffs. Mark Twain reports how the Federal soldiers would shout from the river in grim humor, "Rats, to your holes!" 8

Winding through this land unwarned, rounding to a valley, you will come on a startling thing. Set back in an old gray field, with horses grazing like small fairy animals beside it, is a vast ruin—twenty-two Corinthian columns in an empty oblong and an L. Almost seeming to float like lace, bits of wrought-iron balcony connect them here and there. Live cedar trees are growing from the iron black acanthus leaves, high in the empty air. This is the ruin of Windsor, long since burned. It used to have five stories and an observation tower—Mark Twain used the tower as a sight when he was pilot on the river. 9

Immediately the cane and the cedars become more impenetrable, the road ascends and descends, and rather slowly, because of the trees and shadows, you realize a little village is before you. Grand Gulf today looks like a scene in Haiti. Under enormous dense trees where the moss hangs long as ladders, there are hutlike buildings and pale whitewashed sheds; most of the faces under the straw hats are black, and only narrow jungly paths lead toward the river. Of course this is not Grand Gulf in the original, for the river undermined that and pulled it whole into the river—the opposite of what it did to Rodney's Landing. A little corner was left, which the Federals burned, all but a wall, on their way to Vicksburg. After the war the population built it back—and the river moved away. Grand Gulf was a British settlement before the Revolution and had close connection with England, whose ships traded here. It handled more cotton than any other port in Mississippi for about twenty years. The old cemetery is there still, like a roof of marble and moss overhanging the town and about to tip into it. Many names of British gentry stare 10 their kingdom in that dark-green tangle.

Two miles beyond, at the end of a dim jungle track where you can   11
walk, is the river, immensely wide and vacant, its bluff occupied
sometimes by a casual camp of fishermen under the willow trees,
where dirty children playing about and nets drying have a look of
timeless roaming and poverty and sameness . . . By boat you can
reach a permanent fishing camp, inaccessible now by land. Go till
you find the hazy shore where the Bayou Pierre, dividing in two,
reaches around the swamp to meet the river. It is a gray-green land,
softly flowered, hung with stillness. Houseboats will be tied there
among the cypresses under falls of the long moss, all of a color.
Aaron Burr's "flotilla" tied up there, too, for this is Bruinsburg
Landing, where the boats were seized one wild day of apprehension.
Bruinsburg grew to be a rich, gay place in cotton days. It is almost
as if a wand had turned a noisy cotton port into a handful of shanty
boats. Yet Bruinsburg Landing has not vanished: it is this.

Wonderful things have come down the current of this river, and   12
more spectacular things were on the water than could ever have
sprung up on shores then. Every kind of treasure, every kind of
bearer of treasure has come down, and armadas and flotillas, and
the most frivolous of things, too, and the most pleasure-giving of
people.

PRACTICE

Describing a Place with a History

Provide a description, long or short as your instructor prefers,
of a place that is interesting partly because of its history. Ideally,
there should be some visible remains of that past, but also some
things that would be quite unperceivable without historical
knowledge. You should not select a place that is simply a monument to the past, like Colonial Williamsburg or Mt. Rushmore,
but rather a place where history lies buried under new growth
or construction, like a battlefield that has become a shopping
mall or a working farm.

Your job is to integrate what *is* there with what *was* there, to
describe both the present and the absent, the present and the
past. Before you write, take another look at the way Eudora

Welty solved the problem of integrating past and present in her essay. For instance, you might examine her third paragraph. Notice the way she uses negative constructions to put into her text what is no longer *there* in the place she is describing. "Boats . . . do not dock . . . no mansions, no celebrations." Notice also how she makes connections between what *is* there now and what *was* there then: "wild birds fly now at the level where people . . . once were strolling. . . ." What other ways has she found of describing the absent features of the past?

READING

A Critic Describes a Face

Here is a short excerpt from James Agee's description of the great silent film comedian, Buster Keaton. In these two paragraphs Agee concentrates on Keaton's face, mentioning his body and movements, but always returning to his face. As you read, try to analyze the way Agee gets his effects. Does he dwell on specific features? How does he use adjectives? (You might make a list of them.) How does he convey what the face signifies? How does he use comparisons to specify the qualities of Keaton's facial expression and body movement? We have provided a picture to give you some sense of what Agee is trying to capture.

James Agee, "Buster Keaton"

Keaton's face ranked almost with Lincoln's as an early American archetype; it was haunting, handsome, almost beautiful, yet it was irreducibly funny; he improved matters by topping it off with a deadly horizontal hat, as flat and thin as a phonograph record. One can never forget Keaton wearing it, standing erect at the prow as his little boat is being launched. The boat goes grandly down the skids and, just as grandly, straight on to the bottom. Keaton never budges. The last you see of him, the water lifts the hat off the stoic head and it floats away. 1

No other comedian could do as much with the dead pan. He used this great, sad, motionless face to suggest various related things: a 2 one-track mind near the track's end of pure insanity; mulish imperturbability under the wildest of circumstances; how dead a human being can get and still be alive; an awe-inspiring sort of patience and power to endure, proper to granite but uncanny in flesh and blood. Everything that he was and did bore out this rigid face and played laughs against it. When he moved his eyes, it was like seeing them move in a statue. His short-legged body was all sudden, machinelike angles, governed by a daft aplomb. When he swept a semaphorelike arm to point, you could almost hear the electrical impulse in the signal block. When he ran from a cop his transitions from accelerating walk to easy jogtrot to brisk canter to headlong gallop to flogged-piston sprint—always floating, above this frenzy, the untroubled, untouchable face—were as distinct and as soberly in order as an automatic gearshift.

Buster Keaton, with Virginia Fox, in one of his early movies (*Culver Pictures, Inc.*)

PRACTICE

Describing a Famous Face

Using what you have learned from studying Agee's descriptive technique, try to match his description with a description of your own. Select a well-known figure who appears regularly in the media—a rock star, an actress, a former athlete, an anchorperson, a sportscaster, a politician—and try to capture the special qualities of his or her performance, particularly those that can be treated in terms of facial expressions and posture (rather than voice or language). The idea is to include the necessary minimum of physical details, but to go beyond such details to the impression they convey, using adjectives and comparisons in the way that Agee does. Make your description about as long as Agee's.

READING:

"La Gioconda"

"La Gioconda" ("The Smiling Woman"), better known as "Mona Lisa" ("Lady Lisa"), is perhaps the most famous painting in the world. Walter Pater's elaborate and impressionistic descriptive meditation on the painting (written a century ago) is also famous.

If you look closely at Pater's prose, you will see that it begins as a description and then moves away from the painting to a kind of meditation on what the painting symbolizes (in this case, the eternal feminine). Various meanings are "read into" the Mona Lisa by the writer. What he knows and what he imagines about the painting are all introduced to make this image bear a great symbolic burden.

The Mona Lisa
by Leonardo Da Vinci.
Louvre

Walter Pater, from **The Renaissance**

The presence that rose thus so strangely beside the waters, is expressive of what in the ways of a thousand years men had come to desire. Hers is the head upon which all "the ends of the world are come," and the eyelids are a little weary. It is a beauty wrought out from within upon the flesh, the deposit, little cell by cell, of strange thoughts and fantastic reveries and exquisite passions. Set it for a moment beside one of those white Greek goddesses or beautiful women of antiquity, and how would they be troubled by this beauty, into which the soul with all its maladies has passed! All the thoughts and experience of the world have etched and molded there, in that which they have of power to refine and make expressive the outward form, the animalism of Greece, the lust of Rome, the mysticism of the middle age with its spiritual ambition and imaginative loves, the return of the Pagan world, the sins of the Borgias. She is older than the rocks among which she sits; like the vampire, she has been dead many times, and learned the secrets of the grave; and has been a diver in deep seas, and keeps their fallen day about her; and trafficked for strange webs with Eastern merchants, and, as Leda, was the mother of Helen of Troy, and as Saint Anne, the mother of Mary; and all this has been to her but as the sound of lyres and flutes, and lives only in the delicacy with which it has molded the changing lineaments, and tinged the eyelids and the hands. The fancy of a perpetual life, sweeping together ten thousand experiences, is an old one; and modern philosophy has conceived the idea of humanity as wrought upon by, and summing up in itself, all modes of thought and life. Certainly Lady Lisa might stand as the embodiment of the old fancy, the symbol of the modern idea.

PRACTICE

"Il Giocondo"

Alfred E. Neuman
by Norman Mingo

J. R. Ewing
by Larry Hagman
(*Phototeque*)

In recent times we have come to know other smilers. We present two of them here for your consideration: *Mad* magazine's Alfred E. Neuman, who always says, "What, Me

Worry?''; and J. R. Ewing of the *Dallas* television drama. Your assignment is to provide a meditation on one of these two contemporary smilers, in the manner of Pater (whose writing, you will no doubt have noticed, is as strange and highly wrought as his ideas). While we would not like you to write this way as a regular habit, we encourage you to try it just this one time. Follow Pater's sentence structure as closely as you can, while letting your imagination go on the deep significance of your chosen face.

The purpose of this sort of exercise is twofold. The movement from description to symbolism is an important mental process, one well worth mastering. And the experience of matching your thoughts to an unfamiliar sentence structure will make you more aware of stylistic possibilities in your future writing. This is an exercise in the *form* of thought.

8 Classification: Organizing Data

Classification consists of organizing things according to categories. When we don't like it we call it pigeon-holing, implying that things are being stuffed into categories whether they fit or not. But this kind of organization is basic to language itself. Nouns like *sheep* and *goats* or adjectives like *red* and *green* are themselves categories that help us organize our world. What we are calling "classification" is simply a more systematic use of the power that language gives us to arrange and organize the flood of information or data that we encounter every day.

Classification is based on our ability to compare and contrast, to find common features that link all the members of one group of things, along with other features that distinguish all the members of *this* group from all the members of *that* group. This way of thinking is as old as Aristotle, but was developed extensively during the period when biology was becoming a science. Accurate classification enabled the modern theories of evolution and the origin of species to be generated. In other areas of study, especially the social sciences, a good classification system enables an investigator to perceive relationships that were not apparent earlier and, in fact, to give data meaning. Classification is especially important during the research and prewriting phase of a project.

If you look carefully, you will find classification used in all the readings included in our chapters on argument and analysis. Plato, for instance, classifies one kind of speech as persuasion and another as instruction, so that he can make his own argument against persuasion. Lincoln needs to define the category of "fathers of our country" in order to base his argument on what the "fathers" did. Gould needs the categories of "fact" and "theory" to make his case for the study of evolution as *both* fact and theory. We need categories to start composing an argument or analysis. The act of writing may then reveal that we haven't got the best categories for our argument. We then must revise our thinking so that we can revise our writing.

One of the skills we need in research is an ability to *play* with the data we are collecting. This is true of the most serious professional projects as well as of amateur practicing. But perhaps we should clarify what we mean by *play*. We are not suggesting fakery or carelessness, but rather that one should play as a child plays with blocks or tinker-toys, trying different arrangements to see what can be made of them. In academic research, *play* means trying out various systems of classification, and the basic move in classification is finding categories that enable you to bring together a group of things that would have been separated without these concepts (or categories) that unite them.

In biology, for example, the basic category is life itself, which brings all living things together and excludes stones, machines, and all those things that we call inorganic. The basic class is then refined and refined, yielding smaller groups at every level until the smallest biological group (the species) is reached. Thus, human beings are classified this way:

> Kingdom: Animalia
> Phylum: Chordata
> Subphylum: Vertebrata
> Class: Mammalia
> Subclass: Eutheria
> Order: Primates
> Family: Hominidae
> Genus: Homo
> Species: Sapiens

It is possible to continue breaking this down into smaller groups, but once we get below the level of species, we are moving into areas of less interest to biologists and more interest to anthropologists and other social scientists: races, nations, classes, tribes, occupational groups, kinship groups, and so on.

For any classifier, the first question is how many levels of classification are needed, and the second is how many categories at each level are required to cover all the material.

Let us look a little more closely at the way the biological classification system works. At the fourth level, *Class*, Mammals are distinguished from all the other creatures in the category above it—that is, all the other living things that have vertebrae or backbones (fish, birds, reptiles, and amphibia). Mammals, the Class mammalia, are defined in biology books as "warm-blooded animals whose skin is covered with hair; the females have mammary glands that secrete milk for the nourishment of the young." Within the class of mammals there are three subclasses that are distinguished by the ways they give birth: eggs, like the platypus; pouches, like the possum; or a womb or uterus, like the rat, bat, whale, human, and many others. This third subclass, *Eutheria*, is then broken down into twelve orders, so that even-toed mammals with hooves (cows and hippopotamuses, for instance) can be distinguished from odd-toed mammals with hooves (horses and rhinoceroses, for instance). One of these twelve orders is distinguished as the first, the highest, and is therefore called *Primate*. This order includes humans, who devised the whole system, and there is a moral in this: those who write, rank. The "highest" order, primate, is distinguished by having hands and large brains, both of which may be used to "grasp" things. The human brain grasps powerfully by naming and classifying things. The "highest" primate—Genus, Homo; Species, Sapiens—is the classifying primate.

Classification can be used in many ways on many topics, as you will see from the Readings and Practices that follow.

READING

Social Groups in a Town

This is a very short excerpt, but it illustrates the way in which a professional social scientist will try to make the casual classifications he encounters into more systematic and complete groupings.

A Darien businessman who has lived there all his life said: "The   1
town is divided between commuters and locals and they seldom cross
paths except in the stores; and there is a certain amount of resentment." The wife of a transferee who had lived in Darien two years
told me: "You feel you are not really accepted here because they expect you to move and so they don't care about getting acquainted."

A somewhat more precise picture of the divisions would show   2
three major groups, with little interaction between them:

1. The locals—people who were raised in Darien and make their   3
living there, as merchants, contractors, etc. Some are of old Irish-
Yankee stock, many are of Italian ancestry.

2. The Darien people—families from somewhere else who have   4
made it by living in Darien more than five years. They dominate the
town socially.

3. The transients—who will be moving on after one to four years   5
of residence.

QUESTIONS

1. What are the main differences between the classification suggested by
   the businessman and Packard's "more precise picture"?
2. Assume that Packard started with the genus of "all residents of Darien." On what basis has he distinguished the three species he finds
   within that genus?
3. Packard says of his first group that they "make their living" in Darien.
   How does this distinguish them from the others?
4. Packard's second group is said to "dominate the town socially." What
   does this mean? How does this relate to what the businessman and the
   transferee's wife told Packard? Are the businessman and the wife distinguishable in terms of Packard's categories?
5. One of the uses of classification is to prepare the way for interesting
   questions. For instance, if Packard's grouping is accurate and his information is correct, we are now in a position to ask *why* Group 2 dominates. We may not be able to answer on the basis of the information we
   have, but we now can formulate our need for more information—or we
   can speculate and suggest answers on the basis of what we already know.

   Two questions: What additional information would you like? Why do
   you suppose Group 2 dominates?

CLASSIFICATION: ORGANIZING DATA

PRACTICE

Social Groups in a Place That You Know

Using Packard's sample as a model, construct a brief social classification of the people in your own town, neighborhood, dormitory, or place of employment. This is meant to be more of a thought experiment than an occasion for polished prose. Try out different classification systems. If you can, discuss your classes with another person familiar with the place, revising until you have something that satisfies all concerned.

This process of making and testing classifications has elements of prewriting and revising in it. In fact, it is one of the basic ways of beginning a research paper. This is why learning how to generate and improve a set of classes is such an important part of producing academic writing.

Classifying is a skill that improves with study and practice. The improvements will be in direct proportion to the effort you put into practicing.

READING

Classifying Commercials

This is a fairly long example of the use of classification to organize a large body of material. As you read, look for the way the writer has organized the information into two major classes and several subclasses.

John W. Wright, from ''TV Commercials That Move the Merchandise''

Speaking in New York recently at one of a series of advertising seminars sponsored by *Advertising Age*, [Harry W.] McMahan railed against the malady of "Festivalitis," a disease of the ego which infected many advertising men during the sixties and drove them to seek creative awards for themselves rather than financial rewards for their clients. Inflation, unemployment, and a couple of energy shortages, however, combined to produce the no-nonsense atmosphere of the seventies in which sales results have been restored to their rightful place at the head of all other criteria. The once glamorous notion of the Mass Consumption Society working with well-oiled precision while elaborate and expensive TV commercials gently stroked the nation's collective subconscious has given way to the dull workaday task of discovering why some commercials actually succeed in establishing the end-all and be-all of contemporary American business, "brand preference."

Over the last ten years McMahan has examined literally tens of thousands of commercials, not in the simpleminded fashion of the dilettante, but in the manner of the structuralist who tries to reveal the essential but often hidden elements in a society, or a literary genre, or even an art form. Anthropologists have used the method for decades to delineate and codify the morals and mores of primitive tribes and this approach seems to work just as well when applied to successful television advertising. According to McMahan's tabulations, seventy-five percent of today's money-making commercials employ either one of two traditional advertising techniques: forty-two percent use a jingle, while thirty-three percent plant the face of a familiar personality on the screen in very close proximity to the product. (Occasionally there are commercials which use both, such as the one in which Petula Clark sings and dances for Burlington Mills.)

Jingles have been popular in broadcast advertising ever since the Ralston Straight Shooters sang the opening commercial to the *Tom Mix* radio program in 1933, the same year that the Wheaties Quartet introduced "Have You Tried Wheaties?" to the audience for *Jack Armstrong, the All-American Boy*. Everyone who grew up in the forties or fifties knows dozens of jingles, including "Pepsi-Cola Hits the Spot," "My Beer Is Rheingold, the Dry Beer," "You Get a Lot to Like with a Marlboro," "Winston Tastes Good Like a Cigarette Should." And they'll no doubt remember them till their dying day since each was constantly repeated for years on both radio and television. According to McMahan, the simple, melodic jingle has evolved into the sophisticated, fully orchestrated contemporary sound, which has become associated with the leading brands of consumer products such as Coke ("Coke Adds Life"), McDonald's ("We Do It All For You"), Budweiser ("Here Comes the King"), Cheerios ("You're Gonna Get a Powerful Start"), and Chevrolet ("Baseball, Hot Dogs, Apple Pie, and Chevrolet"). Most could be called hard-driving, foot-tapping, easy-to-hum, memorable tunes which, in ad-talk, help to define the product's "personality." Obviously some products have different requirements. Kodak, for example, uses the gentle, one might say bathetic, "Times of Your

Life"—a shameless exploitation of our deepest emotional relationships—to sell film and cameras to young parents or new grandparents. Pine-Sol, too, took the quiet route but still landed on top of its field. They all have, McMahan says, "the look of the leader."

But McMahan notes that the jingle can be a powerful tool in introducing new products as well. The stripteasing housewife singing "I've been sweet, and I've been good" helped to make Aviance the best selling new fragrance in less than six months. And in spectacular fashion the memorable production number for Leggs panty hose (featuring women dancing around a supermarket singing the slightly erotic "Our Leggs fit your legs, they'll hold you, they'll squeeze you, they'll never let you go") gave this Hanes brand name a thirty percent share of the panty hose market where just a few years before the leader had only four percent.

Not all advertisers find it necessary or even desirable to have a song written and arranged expressly for their product. As audience segmenting grows more sophisticated, the use of established popular songs can help to make the advertising relevant to the target group. For example a diet product called Figurines used the melody of *Tangerine*, a hit from the big band era, to sell to women over forty. (Some advertising people, said McMahan, believe the commercial was successful because women associated the song with their earliest romantic experiences.) On the other hand Clairol's Herbal Essence Shampoo recently used the Beach Boys' tune about California girls to reach the younger set, the increasingly important eighteen- to thirty-five-year-olds.

If good use of music can actually get consumers to sing about an advertiser's products, the use of a star or celebrity helps to catch the viewer's attention immediately and allows the advertiser to reinforce his arguments in magazines and at the point-of-purchase with posters and other pictorial material. Associating your product or service with a star enables you to stand out from the crowd, so celebrities are especially good in highly competitive markets such as airline travel (Robert Morley has made British Airways the leader in transatlantic flights so it comes as no surprise that Gene *An American in Paris* Kelly was hired by Air France), perfume (Catherine Deneuve for Chanel started a trend that now includes Margaux Hemingway for Babe and Candice Bergen for Cie), even automatic coffee makers (Joe DiMaggio's success for the number one Mr. Coffee must have induced Norelco to hire a coffee "expert" like Danny Thomas).

Several years ago the FTC foolishly tried to clamp down on the use of stars and celebrities but, as so often happens, the advertisers have been able to circumvent or ignore the regulations. The new rules failed, in part, because the FTC assumed that the American people were so naive they actually had to be told that celebrities were paid for giving endorsements. But the use of famous athletes, opera singers, prima ballerinas, writers, generals, admirals, socialites, and the stars of stage and screen dates back to the turn of the century when Sarah Bernhardt, Enrico Caruso, and the suffragette Elizabeth Cady Stanton lent their names and reputations to help sell manufactured goods. Even folk heroes such as Charles Lindbergh and Ernest Hemingway, or political heroes like General MacArthur or Lillian Hellman, found their way into the advertising pages of our leading magazines. During radio's heyday the biggest stars (including Benny, Vallee, Allen, Kate Smith) always took a big part in promoting the sponsor's product and this "tradition" carried over into early television. So, historically speaking, the public has been conditioned for a long time and through all of the media to accept the notion that in America, one of the perquisites due to a top flight athlete, artist, or popular performer is the money from endorsements.

McMahan claims that today twenty-one percent of all money-making TV commercials use stars and celebrities and chances are very good that the percentage will grow. Ironically, the FTC's increasingly stringent regulations on advertisers will help this to happen because, as McMahan says: "Stars are especially useful when there are limitations on what you can say about the product." That's one reason why Bobby *Baretta* Blake doesn't tell us what STP actually does he only guarantees that it works. And so potentially effective is his promise that he allegedly received twenty thousand dollars for one ten-second spot. This isn't much when compared to the multimillion dollar deals given to O. J. Simpson (Hertz, Tree-Sweet Orange Juice), Joe Namath (Brut, Hamilton Beach), and Bill Cosby (Ford, Jell-O, Del Monte), but it indicates that the cost factor can be a major drawback to any advertiser considering the endorsement technique. 8

Television is the one medium which allows advertisers to counteract this problem. Because so many Americans watch TV so frequently (it's on over six hours a day in the *average* home) advertisers have been able to create their very own thirty-second programs starring characters who are just as well known and just as one-dimensional as Kojak, Columbo, or John-Boy Walton. At a fraction of the cost of a star presenter, Madge the Manicurist, now in her twelfth year for Palmolive Dishwashing Liquid, or the longlasting, "lonely" Maytag Repairman bring with them that very important recognition factor necessary if consumers are to remember the brand name. It's known in the business as the "continuing central character," and McMahan estimates that twelve percent of the money makers have taken this route. 9

CLASSIFICATION: ORGANIZING DATA

The technique was first used on television more than twenty years 10
ago. At that time everyone involved with the fledgling medium was
obsessed with animation and trick photography so "Speedy" Alka-
Seltzer, Tony the Tiger, and Manners the Butler were typical as
well as famous and successful. Today commercial stars run the personality gamut from a finicky feline like Morris the Cat (who helped
9-Lives get twenty-five percent of the canned cat food market), to a
smart-ass company president such as Frank Perdue, whose brand-
name chickens clearly rule the roost. Of course animated characters
are still around and some, like the Keebler Elves, or the Pillsbury
Doughboy, are very effective. In fact, one of the biggest advertising
success stories of the last decade is the stork who talks like Groucho
Marx and delivers Vlasic pickles instead of babies. In just about five
years this small Detroit-based company has taken over twenty-four
percent of the pickle market, more than double that of the gigantic,
century-old Heinz corporation.

But if there's a trend, it's more toward true-to-life, trustworthy 11
characters like Pete the Butcher who does Shake 'n Bake, or Max-
well House's Cora (played by Margaret Hamilton, who earlier
achieved believability and immortality as the Wicked Witch in *The
Wizard of Oz*). It just may be, however, that these types seem pleasing only because of the constant presence of offensive characters, although this kind can also do the job of selling the goods. The continually revolting Mr. Whipple, for example, has made Charmin the
number-one "single-ply" toilet tissue, while the depressingly whole-
some Mr. Goodwin helps Crest maintain a staggering forty percent
of the toothpaste market. Meanwhile their female counterparts,
Aunt Bluebell and Rosie, lend particularly irksome vocal qualities to
the great paper-towel battle currently raging between Scott, the
leader, and Bounty, the challenger. Rosie, played by Nancy Walker
(who, as Rhoda's mother, could not be considered a star presenter),
has given Bounty over twenty percent of the paper towel market
even though the product is not yet distributed nationally. (Aunt
Bluebell, interestingly enough, is played by Mae Questel, who first
gained fame in the thirties doing the voices of Betty Boop and of
Popeye's girl friend, Olive Oyl.)

QUESTIONS

1. Wright uses only two main classes (music and personality), but introduces many more subdivisions to order his data. Make an outline of
   Wright's system, including all levels and subclasses, noting the refine-
   ments he uses to categorize types of commercials rather than simply
   naming the different ads.

2. How does Wright's classification system relate to the organization and paragraphing of his text?
3. Since Wright finished his essay (1979), many new commercials have appeared. Can you supply new data that will fit into his categories? How well have the categories themselves lasted? Can you improve them in any way?

PRACTICE

The Class of Full-Page Ads

A. You will need a magazine for this assignment. Choose one issue of a recent magazine with wide popular appeal, such as *People, Time, Ebony, Newsweek, Sports Illustrated,* or the *New Yorker.* Start with the back cover and work forward from there. Pick out the first thirty full-page advertisements. (If there aren't thirty, you don't have the right kind of magazine.)

Let your thirty samples represent the class of Full-Page Ads. Then find a method of dividing the ads into subclasses and orders. You may or may not need further subdivision into genus and species. Try not to make things too complicated for yourself. When you have finished making your classification, write a paragraph or two in which you discuss the reasons for your selection of categories and the problems you encountered in assigning the individual ads to them. Cut out and include the thirty ads with your paper.

In developing your categories, you may wish to emphasize formal qualities (color vs. black and white, amount of pictures vs. words, presence or absence of human figures, etc.), or you may prefer to emphasize subject matter (goods vs. services, food vs. beverages, luxury vs. necessity, etc.).

Remember, the point of this assignment is to test the possibilities of classification, not to achieve perfection. If you run into difficulties in classifying, then use these very difficulties in your discussion.

B. You and your classmates should break into small groups of three or four. Make sure each person in the group worked on a different magazine. Then, as a group, work out a classification system that will cover the ads from all three or four magazines, and produce a report on the different patterns of advertising you detect in each of the magazines. This report should be written, but suitable for oral presentation and discussion in class. The point is to *use* the classification system as a way of describing the differences in the magazines. You may wish, finally, to speculate on the reasons behind the differences.

READING

The Student Body

Here is a sample of classification done by a team of sociologists in the 1920s. We invite you to read it before you undertake your own essay in classification of a student body. Remember, this study was done over fifty years ago and was concerned with a high school population. You should not expect to follow it closely in your own work, but it may give you some ideas.

Robert and Helen Lynd, from Middletown

Less spectacular than athletics but bulking even larger in time demands is the network of organizations that serve to break the nearly two thousand individuals composing the high school microcosm into the more intimate groups human beings demand. These groups are mainly of three kinds: the purely social clubs, in the main a stepping down of the social system of adults; a long distance behind in point of prestige, clubs formed around curriculum activities; and, even farther behind, a few groups sponsored by the religious systems of the adults.

In 1894 the high school boasted one club, the "Turemethian Literary Society." According to the early school yearbook:

> The Turemethian Society makes every individual feel that practically he is free to choose between good and evil; that he is not a mere straw thrown upon the water to mark the direction of the current, but that he has within himself the power of a strong swimmer and is capable of striking out for himself, of buffeting the waves, and directing, to a certain extent, his own independent course. Socrates said, "Let him who would move the world move first himself." . . . A paper called The Zetetic

is prepared and read at each meeting. . . . Debates have created . . . a friendly rivalry. . . . Another very interesting feature of the Turemethian Society is the lectures delivered to us.
. . . All of these lectures help to make our High School one of
the first of its kind in the land. The Turemethian Society has
slowly progressed in the last year. What the future has in store
for it we can not tell, but must say as Mary Riley Smith said,
"God's plans, like lilies pure and white, unfold; we must not
tear the close-shut leaves apart; time will reveal the calyxes of
gold."

Six years later, at the turn of the century, clubs had increased to
the point of arousing protests in a press editorial entitled "Barriers
to Intellectual Progress." Today clubs and other extracurricular activities are more numerous than ever. Not only is the camel's head
inside the tent but his hump as well; the first period of the school
day, often running over into the next hour, has recently, at the request of the Mothers' Council, been set aside as a "convocation
hour" dedicated to club and committee meetings.

The backbone of the purely social clubs is the series of unofficial 3
branches of former high school fraternities and sororities; Middletown boasts four Alpha chapters. For a number of years a state law
has banned these high school organizations, but the interest of active
graduate chapters keeps them alive. The high school clubs have
harmless names such as the Glendale Club; a boy is given a long,
impressive initiation into his club but is not nominally a member of
the fraternity of which his club is the undergraduate section until after he graduates, when it is said that by the uttering of a few hitherto
unspoken words he comes into his heritage. Under this ambiguous
status dances have been given with the club name on the front of the
program and the fraternity name on the back. Two girls' clubs and
two boys' clubs which every one wants to make are the leaders.
Trailing down from them are a long list of lesser clubs. Informal
meetings are usually in homes of members but the formal fall,
spring, and Christmas functions are always elaborate hotel affairs.

Extracurricular clubs have canons not dictated by academic stan- 4
dards of the world of teachers and textbooks. Since the adult world
upon which the world of this intermediate generation is modeled
tends to be dominated primarily by getting a living and "getting
on" socially rather than by learning and "the things of the mind,"
the bifurcation of high school life is not surprising.

"When do you study?" some one asked a clever high school
Senior who had just finished recounting her week of club meetings, committee meetings, and dances, ending with three parties the night before. "Oh, in civics I know more or less about

politics, so it's easy to talk and I don't have to study that. In English we're reading plays and I can just look at the end of the play and know about that. Typewriting and chemistry I don't have to study outside anyway. Virgil is worst, but I've stuck out Latin four years for the Virgil banquet; I just sit next to———— and get it from her. Mother jumps on me for never studying, but I get A's all the time, so she can't say anything.''

The relative status of academic excellence and other qualities is fairly revealed in the candid rejoinder of one of the keenest and most popular girls in the school to the question, ''What makes a girl eligible for a leading high school club?''

''The chief thing is if the boys like you and you can get them for the dances,'' she replied. ''Then, if your mother belongs to a graduate chapter that's pretty sure to get you in. Good looks and clothes don't necessarily get you in, and being good in your studies doesn't necessarily keep you out unless you're a 'grind.' Same way with the boys—the big thing there is being on the basketball or football team. A fellow who's just a good student rates pretty low. Being good-looking, a good dancer, and your family owning a car all help.''

The clubs allied to curricular activities today include the Dramatic   5
Club—plays by sophomore, junior, and senior classes in a single spring have replaced the ''programs of recitations, selections, declamations, and essays'' of the old days; the Daubers, meeting weekly in school hours to sketch and in evening meetings with graduate members for special talks on art; the Science Club with its weekly talks by members and occasional lectures by well-known scientists; the Pickwick Club, open to members of English classes, meeting weekly for book reviews and one-act plays, with occasional social meetings; the Penmanship Club; and the Virgil Club, carrying with it some social prestige. Interest in the work of these clubs is keen among some students. All have their ''pledges,'' making their rituals conform roughly to those of the more popular fraternities and sororities.

On the periphery of this high school activity are the church and   6
Y.M.C.A. and Y.W.C.A. clubs. All these organizations frankly admit that the fifteen- to twenty-one-year person is their hardest problem. The Hi-Y club appears to be most successful. The Y.M.C.A. controls the extracurricular activities of the grade school boys more than any other single agency, but it maintains itself with only moderate success in the form of this Hi-Y Club among the older boys. A Hi-Y medal is awarded each commencement to the boy in the graduating class who shows the best all-round record, both in point of scholarship and of character. The Y.W.C.A. likewise maintains

clubs in the grades but has rough sledding when it comes to the busy, popular, influential group in high school. According to one representative senior girl:

> "High School girls pay little attention to the Y.W. and the Girl Reserves. The boys go to the Y.M. and Hi-Y club because it has a supper meeting once a month, and that is one excuse for getting away from home evenings. There aren't any supper meetings for the girls at the Y.W. It's not much good to belong to a Y.W. club; *any one* can belong to them."

All manner of other clubs, such as the Hiking Club and the Boys' and Girls' Booster Club and the Boys' and Girls' Pep Club, hover at the fringes or even occasionally take the center of the stage. [7]

PRACTICE

Your Student Body

You have been asked by *Squire* magazine to write a short article for their annual college issue. *Squire* wants to know what types of students attend your college. Your job is to devise a system of classification of the student body. You'll have to decide how this can best be done. For example, you might start with two large divisions, such as fraternity and nonfraternity groups or resident and commuter groups. However, within each large group there are bound to be a number of different types. Each fraternity, for example, is usually known for a special type of student, such as the prep school type, the athletic type, the studious type, and so on. There are a number of methods you can use, but you should choose a method of classification that will give the readers of *Squire* the clearest idea of what types of students they'd be likely to encounter on your campus.

The best way to proceed would be to make an outline of your classificatory system, including the distinguishing features of each group in your system. These features should include dress, social behavior, study habits, and so on.

Then you should take this outline and transform it into a brief article. And remember, if it's a good article, *Squire* might just offer you a permanent job.

CLASSIFICATION: ORGANIZING DATA

PRACTICE

People in a Particular Place

Having been impressed with the fine article you wrote for *Squire* magazine on the student body, your sociology professor suggests that you refine your powers of observation and classification still further. He asks you to observe, classify, and discuss one of the following:

1. the eating habits of people in a cafeteria, restaurant, or dining hall.
2. the shopping habits of people in supermarkets, discount department stores, or malls.
3. the spectatorial habits of football fans at a big game.
4. the sunbathing habits of people at a beach or park.

READING

Classifying Forms of Power

The following material first appeared as the opening to Chapter 3 of the philosopher Bertrand Russell's book *Power*. We present it to you as an excellent example of classification in action. In reading it, you should pay particular attention to the way it is organized. Russell is exceptionally careful to name the processes of thought he is using:

First Paragraph: ''Power may be defined . . . .''
Second: ''There are various ways of classifying . . . .''
Third: ''Power . . . may be classified . . . .''
Fifth: ''These forms of power are . . . displayed . . . .''
Sixth: ''All these forms . . . are exemplified . . . .''
Seventh–tenth: ''illustrates,'' ''typifies,'' ''show,'' ''are illustrative''
Eleventh: ''Let us apply these . . . analogies . . . .''
Twelfth: ''. . . organizations are . . . distinguishable . . . .''

Power may be defined as the production of intended effects. It is   1
thus a quantitative concept: given two men with similar desires, if
one achieves all the desires that the other achieves, and also others,
he has more power than the other. But there is no exact means of
comparing the power of two men of whom one can achieve one
group of desires, and another another; e.g., given two artists of
whom each wishes to paint good pictures and become rich, and of
whom one succeeds in painting good pictures and the other in becoming rich, there is no way of estimating which has the more
power. Nevertheless, it is easy to say, roughly, that A has more
power than B, if A achieves many intended effects and B only a few.

There are various ways of classifying the forms of power, each of   2
which has its utility. In the first place, there is power over human beings and power over dead matter or nonhuman forms of life. I shall
be concerned mainly with power over human beings, but it will be
necessary to remember that the chief cause of change in the modern
world is the increased power over matter that we owe to science.

Power over human beings may be classified by the manner of in-   3
fluencing individuals, or by the type of organization involved.

An individual may be influenced: A. By direct physical power   4
over his body, e.g., when he is imprisoned or killed; B. By rewards
and punishments as inducements, e.g., in giving or withholding employment; C. By influence on opinion, i.e., propaganda in its
broadest sense. Under this last head I should include the opportunity for creating desired habits in others, e.g., by military drill, the
only difference being that in such cases action follows without any
such mental intermediary as could be called opinion.

These forms of power are most nakedly and simply displayed in   5
our dealings with animals, where disguises and pretenses are not
thought necessary. When a pig with a rope round its middle is
hoisted squealing into a ship, it is subject to direct physical power
over its body. On the other hand, when the proverbial donkey follows the proverbial carrot, we induce him to act as we wish by per-
suading him that it is to his interest to do so. Intermediate between
these two cases is that of performing animals, in whom habits have
been formed by rewards and punishments; also, in a different way,
that of sheep induced to embark on a ship, when the leader has to be
dragged across the gangway by force, and the rest then follow will-
ingly.

All these forms of power are exemplified among human beings.   6
The case of the pig illustrates military and police power.   7
The donkey with the carrot typifies the power of propaganda.   8

Performing animals show the power of "education." 9

The sheep following their unwilling leader are illustrative of party 10 politics, whenever, as is usual, a revered leader is in bondage to a clique or to party bosses.

Let us apply these Aesopian analogies to the rise of Hitler. The 11 carrot was the Nazi program (involving, e.g., the abolition of interest); the donkey was the lower middle class. The sheep and their leader were the Social Democrats and Hindenburg. The pigs (only so far as their misfortunes are concerned) were the victims in concentration camps, and the performing animals are the millions who make the Nazi salute.

The most important organizations are approximately distinguish- 12 able by the kind of power that they exert. The army and the police exercise coercive power over the body; economic organizations, in the main, use rewards and punishments as incentives and deterrents; schools, churches, and political parties aim at influencing opinion. But these distinctions are not very clear-cut, since every organization uses other forms of power in addition to the one which is most characteristic.

PRACTICE

From Abstract to Concrete

Using Russell's very clear structure as a model (definition, classification, exemplification), produce a short essay in which you take some other large abstraction—love, faith, service, education, etc.—and produce your own discussion of it. To get started, brainstorm by writing down your definitions of the abstraction you have chosen. Compare your definitions with a dictionary's way of defining your chosen term. Then, work out the definition that will best suit your project. It is quite likely that you will want to revise your definition once you start the process of classifying the forms of the abstraction you have selected. You will, in fact, be testing the usefulness of your definition in the process of classification. Remember to follow the pattern of Russell's essay, in which the definition of power is followed by classification, and classification is supported by illustration and exemplification.

Title your essay "Forms of _____."

Power in an Institution You Know

Taking Russell's discussion of power as a point of departure, produce your own discussion of the forms of power encountered in some institution you have had dealings with: a school, a youth group, a military organization, a business or corporation, etc.

You should begin with Russell's categories as a working outline, but develop your own modifications of them as necessary to do justice to your subject. Make your organization as tight and clear as you can, balancing your examples against your categories.

9 Argumentation: Presenting a Thesis

Where persuasion seeks to put the mind to sleep, so that its appeal to emotion will be effective, argumentation aims at an unemotional appeal to reason. Persuasion is most at home in the rough and tumble worlds of advertising and politics. Argumentation is mainly an academic or scholastic use of language, requiring patience and detachment. In principle, an argument can always be reversed. New evidence or new reasoning can convince even the arguer that the matter under discussion should be seen in a different way. But you cannot convince an advertiser not to want your money or a politician to reject your vote.

For various reasons, persuasion and argumentation are often mixed in actual speech and writing, both in academic discourse and in the world of affairs, but in practicing we can isolate them in order to study and master the separate skills. The purest forms of argumentation appear in philosophy. Here, for instance, is Bertrand Russell reflecting (in *My Philosophical Development*, 1975) on one of his earlier books:

> In *The Analysis of Mind* I argued the thesis that the "stuff" of mental occurrences consists entirely of sensations and images. I do not know whether this thesis was sound. . . . (page 111)

As Russell indicates, a "thesis" is essential to argumentation. Although he is not arguing in this passage, but reflecting upon his earlier argument, he summarizes the thesis he had argued in the past, adding the interesting comment that he is no longer

certain that his thesis was sound. This kind of second thought is, as you know, typical of reflection, but it is also built into the processes of argumentation. The goal of argument is not persuasion but truth. Arguing a thesis is partly a way of testing it. A person writing advertising copy has a set goal: sell that product! The copywriter can revise to make the copy more persuasive, but cannot rethink the aim of the writing. A person writing an argument, on the other hand, begins with a tentative thesis that may be rethought during the writing, or even, as Russell indicates, after its publication in a book.

A thesis, then, is the point or organizing principle of an argument: "I argued the thesis," Russell says. But there is always something tentative about a thesis. The writers of arguments often consider counter-arguments against the theses they are supporting. Sometimes this is only a gesture, a persuasive trick, but in serious argumentation it is also a way of testing. If you do this scrupulously while writing, it may lead you to modify your thesis or qualify it in some important way.

Here is an example of a philosopher introducing a long and serious argument:

> Let me start with a confession.
>
> I wrote this paper in a fit of anger and self-righteousness caused by what I thought were certain disastrous developments in the sciences. The paper will therefore sound a little harsh, and it will perhaps also be a little unjust. Now while I think that self-righteousness has no positive function whatever and while I am convinced that it can only add to the fear and to the tensions that already exist, I also think that a little anger can on occasions be a good thing and can make us see our surroundings more clearly.
>
> I think very highly of science, but I think very little of experts, although experts form about 95 percent or more of science today. It is my belief that science was advanced, and is still being advanced, by *dilettantes* and that experts are liable to bring it to a standstill. I may be entirely wrong in this belief of mine, but the only way to find out is to tell you. Therefore, with my apologies, here is my paper. (Paul Feyerabend, "Experts in a Free Society," *The Critic* [November–December 1970])

This is unusually personal and informal for philosophical argument, but there are reasons for that. The author doesn't want to sound like an expert, so he makes a personal confession. He refers to his thesis as a "belief," but his attitude toward his belief is the attitude toward argumentation we have been describing. Even in his anger, his passionate concern, he does not want to carry the day by emotion. In fact, by confessing his own emotion he is putting the reader on guard against it. He has written in anger, but he will not appeal to anger in his readers. Above all, he does not want to bully readers into thinking that there are no alternatives to his own attitude. "I may be entirely wrong," he says, "but the only way to find out is to tell you." This is the true spirit of argumentation: make a case for your thesis as strongly as you can, but be prepared to rethink it on the basis of new evidence or an argument that you haven't foreseen.

Learning to argue well is a complex process, and there are no real short cuts. The study of formal logic may help, but this is a demanding discipline and gives no guarantee of effective writing. A little bit of it is likely to confuse more than it helps. It is our belief that the best way to learn every kind of writing is through close study of actual written texts and through disciplined practice, which is what we offer in the rest of this chapter.

The connection—and the gap—between the theory and practice of argument has been well described by the philosopher Gilbert Ryle, in his book *The Concept of Mind* (1949). Describing a man arguing a case before a court, Ryle says,

> He probably observes the rules of logic without thinking about them. He does not cite Aristotle's formulae to himself or to the court. He applies in his practice what Aristotle abstracted in his theory of such practices. He reasons with a correct method but without considering the prescriptions of a methodology. The rules that he observes have become his way of thinking, when he is taking care. (page 48)

All kinds of writing, including argumentation, are finally kinds of practice, not kinds of theory. As Ryle says elsewhere, "knowing how" is different from "knowing that." And he adds, a "surgeon must indeed have learned from instruction, or by his own inductions and observations, a great number of truths; but he must also have learned by practice a great number of aptitudes" (page 49).

Like surgery, writing must be learned by practice as well as by observation and instruction. There is no perfect method that will ensure the composition of a strong argument. But before you examine the practice of others and undertake some assignments of your own, we would like to offer you a brief reminder of the elements that are found in most good arguments: at least, it is our thesis that these elements will be found there. You can check for yourself and see if we are right.

1. The clear statement of a thesis or position to be argued
2. The orderly presentation of evidence to support this thesis
3. A convincing connection of the evidence to the argument
4. The fair consideration of evidence that runs counter to the thesis being argued
5. A conclusion that emphasizes the thesis

READING

An Argument About Persuasion

The following selection is adapted from a dialogue written by the Greek philosopher Plato around 400 BC. In this part of the dialogue, Plato's teacher, Socrates, is involved in a discussion with Gorgias, who taught persuasive speaking. The issue between them is the respective merits of their two disciplines, which correspond to what we have called *argument* (which Plato called "dialectic" and always presented in the form of dialogue or discussion) and what we have called *persuasion*.[1] Please read the dialogue and then consider the questions that follow it.

Plato, from "Gorgias"

GORGIAS: Ah, if only you knew all, Socrates, and realized that persuasion includes practically all other faculties under her control. And I will give you good proof of this. I have often, along with my brother and with other physicians, visited one of their patients who   1

[1]The translator of this selection, W. D. Woodhead, originally used the terms *rhetoric* and *rhetorician* to name Gorgias's profession, but, because current understanding of these two words is so ambiguous, we have chosen to substitute in each case *persuasion* or *persuasive speaker*. Other minor emendations have been made, as well, for the sake of consistency.

refused to drink his medicine or submit to the surgeon's knife or cautery, and when the doctor was unable to convince them, I did so, by no other art but persuasion. And I claim too that, if a persuasive speaker and a doctor visited any city you like to name and they had to contend in argument before the Assembly or any other gathering as to which of the two should be chosen as doctor, the doctor would be nowhere, but the man who could speak would be chosen, if he so wished. And if he should compete against any other craftsman whatever, the persuasive speaker rather than any other would convince the people to choose him, for there is no subject on which he would not speak more persuasively than any other craftsman, before a crowd.

Such then is the scope and character of persuasion, but it should be used, Socrates, like every other competitive art. We must not employ other competitive arts against one and all merely because we have learned boxing or mixed fighting or weapon combat, so that we are stronger than our friends and foes; we must not, I say, for this reason strike our friends or wound or kill them. No indeed, and if a man who is physically sound has attended the wrestling school and has become a good boxer, and then strikes his father or mother or any others of his kinsmen or friends, we must not for this reason detest or banish from our cities the physical trainers or drill instructors. For they imparted this instruction for just employment against enemies or wrongdoers, in self-defense not aggression, but such people perversely employ their strength and skill in the wrong way. And so the teachers are not guilty, and the craft is not for this reason evil or to blame, but rather, in my opinion, those who make improper use of it. And the same argument applies also to persuasion. The persuasive speaker is competent to speak against anybody on any subject, and to prove himself more convincing before a crowd on practically every topic he wishes, but he should not any the more rob the doctors—or any other craftsmen either—of their reputation, merely because he has this power. One should make proper use of persuasive skill as of athletic gifts. And if a man becomes a persuasive speaker and makes a wrongful use of this faculty and craft, you must not, in my opinion, detest and banish his teacher from the city. For he imparted it for a good use, but the pupil abuses it. And therefore it is the man who abuses it whom we should rightly detest and banish and put to death, not his instructor.

SOCRATES: I think, Gorgias, that, like myself, you have had much experience in discussions and must have observed that speakers can seldom define the topic of debate and after mutual instruction and enlightenment bring the meeting to a close, but if they are in dispute and one insists that the other's statements are incorrect or obscure, they grow angry and imagine their opponent speaks with malice toward them, being more anxious for verbal victory than to investigate the subject under discussion. And finally some of them part in the most disgraceful fashion, after uttering and listening to such abusive language that their audience are disgusted with themselves for having deigned to give ear to such fellows. Now why do I say this? Because, it seems to me, what you are now saying is not quite consistent or in tune with what you said at first about persuasion. But I am afraid to cross-examine you, for fear you might think my pertinacity is directed against you, and not to the clarification of the matter in question. Now, if you are the same kind of a man as I am, I should be glad to question you; if not, I will let you alone. And what kind of man am I? One of those who would gladly be refuted if anything I say is not true, and would gladly refute another who says what is not true, but would be no less happy to be refuted myself than to refute, for I consider that a greater benefit, inasmuch as it is a greater boon to be delivered from the worst of evils oneself than to deliver another. And I believe there is no worse evil for man than a false opinion about the subject of our present discussion. If you then are the same kind of man as I am, let us continue, but if you feel that we should drop the matter, then let us say good-by to the argument and dismiss it. . . .

GORGIAS: After all this, Socrates, it would be disgraceful of me to 4 refuse, when I personally volunteered to meet any question that might be put. But if those present agree, carry on the conversation and ask what you will.

SOCRATES: Then listen, Gorgias, to what surprises me in your 5 statement, for perhaps you were right and I misunderstood you. You claim you can make a persuasive speaker of any man who wishes to learn from you?

GORGIAS: Yes. 6

SOCRATES: With the result that he would be convincing about any 7 subject before a crowd, not through instruction but by persuasion?

GORGIAS: Certainly. 8

SOCRATES: Well, you said just now that such a speaker will be more 9 persuasive than a doctor regarding health.

GORGIAS: Yes, I said so, before a crowd. 10

SOCRATES: And before a crowd means among the ignorant, for 11 surely, among those who know, he will not be more convincing than the doctor.

GORGIAS: That is quite true. 12

SOCRATES: Then if he is more persuasive than the doctor, he is 13 more persuasive than the man who knows?

GORGIAS: Certainly. 14

SOCRATES: Though not himself a doctor. 15

GORGIAS: Yes. 16

SOCRATES: And he who is not a doctor is surely ignorant of what a   17
doctor knows.

GORGIAS: Obviously.   18

SOCRATES: Therefore when the persuasive speaker is more con-   19
vincing than the doctor, the ignorant is more convincing among the
ignorant than the expert. Is that our conclusion, or is something
else?

GORGIAS: That is the conclusion, in this instance.   20

SOCRATES: Is not the position of the persuasive speaker and of per-   21
suasion the same with respect to other arts also? He has no need to
know the truth about things but merely to discover a technique of
persuasion, so as to appear among the ignorant to have more knowledge than the expert?

GORGIAS: But is not this a great comfort, Socrates, to be able with-   22
out learning any other arts but this one to prove in no way inferior to
the specialists?

QUESTIONS

1. Summarize the argument of Gorgias (in his opening speech) in your
   own words. What is his thesis? What is his evidence?
2. Summarize the argument of Socrates in your own words. What is his
   thesis? What is his evidence?
3. All this was written by Plato. What do you suppose Plato's position to
   be? Does this whole conversation have a thesis?
4. Definition is important in argument. As precisely as you can, define the
   following words as they are used in the dialogue: *persuasion, argument, instruction, convincing, expert, ignorant.*
5. Consider the dialogue as a form of argument. What are its advantages
   and disadvantages, compared to our customary form of written argument? What traces of dialogue might you expect to find in modern written arguments?
6. Socrates says he is not "anxious for verbal victory." Do you believe
   him? Does he score one?

PRACTICE

A Dialogue on Advertising

Socrates and Gorgias have been reincarnated in the twentieth
century. Socrates is not surprised. He always taught that the
soul proceeds to heaven after death, where it is purified until it
can return to earth in a new body. In his new incarnation, So-

crates is an English teacher. He is hard-working, poor, but happy. One day an advertising executive visits his class. The soul of Socrates perceives the soul of Gorgias in this richly dressed representative of the advertising world.

The teacher challenges the advertising executive in much the same way that Socrates challenged Gorgias. Would the result be the same? Would it be different? Have things changed? What is *your* opinion about advertising? You will control this dialogue as Plato controlled the one you have just read. Give the speakers proper names. Imagine them debating before a class like your own. Write the dialogue. Don't just follow Plato. Produce your own arguments, suited to the present time.

This is your chance to express your opinions about advertising—pro and con. A dialogue is like a little drama, but a drama of thought rather than action. In writing a dialogue we can work out our ideas by allowing them to argue with one another until we know where we stand. Use the process of revision to make your own final position prevail in this argument. We suggest that you begin by jotting down the main arguments for and against advertising. Put them in two columns, and then number them for use in your dialogue.

READING

A Paleontologist Responds to Creation Science

The following essay is an argument by a paleontologist against the idea of "creation science." In reading it, be alert to the ways in which the author, Stephen Jay Gould, uses definitions like "fact" and "theory" to establish a framework for his evidence. You should also notice his attention to his opponents' arguments and his way of assembling a number of related arguments to support his major thesis. We will be asking you to make a sort of outline of the whole essay. You should read it straight through one time, then go directly to the Practice, which will tell you what to do on your second reading. This close observation of a well-structured argument will help you get a feel for the organization of your own argumentative writing.

Stephen Jay Gould, "Evolution as Fact and Theory"

Kirtley Mather, who died last year at age 89, was a pillar of both science and the Christian religion in America and one of my dearest friends. The difference of half a century in our ages evaporated before our common interests. The most curious thing we shared was a battle we each fought at the same age. For Kirtley had gone to Tennessee with Clarence Darrow to testify for evolution at the Scopes trial of 1925. When I think that we are enmeshed again in the same struggle for one of the best documented, most compelling and exciting concepts in all of science, I don't know whether to laugh or cry. 1

According to idealized principles of scientific discourse, the arousal of dormant issues should reflect fresh data that give renewed life to abandoned notions. Those outside the current debate may therefore be excused for suspecting that creationists have come up with something new, or that evolutionists have generated some serious internal trouble. But nothing has changed; the creationists have not a single new fact or argument. Darrow and Bryan were at least more entertaining than we lesser antagonists today. The rise of creationism is politics, pure and simple; it represents one issue (and by no means the major concern) of the resurgent evangelical right. Arguments that seemed kooky just a decade ago have re-entered the mainstream. 2

Creationism is Not Science

The basic attack of the creationists falls apart on two general counts before we even reach the supposed factual details of their complaints against evolution. First, they play upon a vernacular misunderstanding of the word *theory* to convey the false impression that we evolutionists are covering up the rotten core of our edifice. Second, they misuse a popular philosophy of science to argue that they are behaving scientifically in attacking evolution. Yet the same philosophy demonstrates that their own belief is not science, and that "scientific creationism" is therefore meaningless and self-contradictory, a superb example of what Orwell called "newspeak." 3

In the American vernacular, *theory* often means "imperfect fact"—part of a hierarchy of confidence running downhill from fact to theory to hypothesis to guess. Thus the power of the creationist argument: evolution is "only" a theory, and intense debate now rages about many aspects of the theory. If evolution is less than a fact, and scientists can't even make up their minds about the theory, then what confidence can we have in it? Indeed, President Reagan echoed this argument before an evangelical group in Dallas when he said (in what I devoutly hope was campaign rhetoric): "Well, it is a theory. It is a scientific theory only, and it has in recent years been 4 challenged in the world of science—that is, not believed in the scientific community to be as infallible as it once was.''

Well, evolution *is* a theory. It is also a fact. And facts and theories are different things, not rungs in a hierarchy of increasing certainty. Facts are the world's data. Theories are structures of ideas that explain and interpret facts. Facts do not go away when scientists debate rival theories to explain them. Einstein's theory of gravitation replaced Newton's, but apples did not suspend themselves in mid-air pending the outcome. And human beings evolved from apelike ancestors whether they did so by Darwin's proposed mechanism or by some other, yet to be discovered.

Moreover, *fact* does not mean "absolute certainty." The final proofs of logic and mathematics flow deductively from stated premises and achieve certainty only because they are *not* about the empirical world. Evolutionists make no claim for perpetual truth, though creationists often do (and then attack us for a style of argument that they themselves favor). In science, *fact* can only mean "confirmed to such a degree that it would be perverse to withhold provisional assent." I suppose that apples might start to rise tomorrow, but the possibility does not merit equal time in physics classrooms.

Evolutionists have been clear about this distinction between fact and theory from the very beginning, if only because we have always acknowledged how far we are from completely understanding the mechanisms (theory) by which evolution (fact) occurred. Darwin continually emphasized the difference between his two great and separate accomplishments: establishing the fact of evolution, and proposing a theory—natural selection—to explain the mechanism of evolution. He wrote in *The Descent of Man:* "I had two distinct objects in view; firstly, to show that species had not been separately created, and secondly, that natural selection had been the chief agent of change. . . . Hence if I have erred in . . . having exaggerated its [natural selection's] power . . . I have at least, as I hope, done good service in aiding to overthrow the dogma of separate creations.''

Thus Darwin acknowledged the provisional nature of natural selection while affirming the fact of evolution. The fruitful theoretical debate that Darwin initiated has never ceased. From the 1940s through the 1960s, Darwin's own theory of natural selection did achieve a temporary hegemony that it never enjoyed in his lifetime. But renewed debate characterizes our decade, and, while no biologist questions the importance of natural selection, many now doubt its ubiquity. In particular, many evolutionists argue that substantial amounts of genetic change may not be subject to natural selection and may spread through populations at random. Others are challenging Darwin's linking of natural selection with gradual, imperceptible change through all intermediary degrees; they are arguing that most evolutionary events may occur far more rapidly than Darwin envisioned.

Scientists regard debates on fundamental issues of theory as a sign of intellectual health and a source of excitement. Science is—and how else can I say it?—most fun when it plays with interesting ideas, examines their implications, and recognizes that old information may be explained in surprisingly new ways. Evolutionary theory is now enjoying this uncommon vigor. Yet amidst all this turmoil no biologist has been led to doubt the fact that evolution occurred; we are debating *how* it happened. We are all trying to explain the same thing: the tree of evolutionary descent linking all organisms by ties of genealogy. Creationists pervert and caricature this debate by conveniently neglecting the common conviction that underlies it, and by falsely suggesting that we now doubt the very phenomenon we are struggling to understand. — 9

Using another invalid argument, creationists claim that "the dogma of separate creations," as Darwin characterized it a century ago, is a scientific theory meriting equal time with evolution in high school biology curricula. But a prevailing viewpoint among philosophers of science belies this creationist argument. Philosopher Karl Popper has argued for decades that the primary criterion of science is the falsifiability of its theories. We can never prove absolutely, but we can falsify. A set of ideas that cannot, in principle, be falsified is not science. — 10

The entire creationist argument involves little more than a rhetorical attempt to falsify evolution by presenting supposed contradictions among its supporters. Their brand of creationism, they claim, is "scientific" because it follows the Popperian model in trying to demolish evolution. Yet Popper's argument must apply in both directions. One does not become a scientist by the simple act of trying to falsify another scientific system; one has to present an alternative system that also meets Popper's criterion—it too must be falsifiable in principle. — 11

"Scientific creationism" is a self-contradictory, nonsense phrase precisely because it cannot be falsified. I can envision observations and experiments that would disprove any evolutionary theory I know, but I cannot imagine what potential data could lead creationists to abandon their beliefs. Unbeatable systems are dogma, not science. Lest I seem harsh or rhetorical, I quote creationism's leading intellectual, Duane Gish, Ph.D., from his recent (1978) book *Evolution? The Fossils Say No!* "By creation we mean the bringing into being by a supernatural Creator of the basic kinds of plants and animals by the process of sudden, or fiat, creation. We do not know how the Creator created, what processes He used, *for He used processes* — 12

which are not now operating anywhere in the natural universe [Gish's italics.]
This is why we refer to creation as special creation. We cannot discover by scientific investigations anything about the creative processes used by the Creator." Pray tell, Dr. Gish, in the light of your
last sentence, what then is "scientific" creationism?

The Fact of Evolution

Our confidence that evolution occurred centers upon three general
arguments. First, we have abundant, direct, observational evidence
of evolution in action, from both the field and the laboratory. It
ranges from countless experiments on change in nearly everything
about fruit flies subjected to artificial selection in the laboratory to
the famous British moths that turned black when industrial soot
darkened the trees upon which they rest. (The moths gain protection
from sharp-sighted bird predators by blending into the background.) Creationists do not deny these observations; how could
they? Creationists have tightened their act. They now argue that
God only created "basic kinds," and allowed for limited evolutionary meandering within them. Thus toy poodles and Great Danes
come from the dog kind and moths can change color, but nature
cannot convert a dog to a cat or a monkey to a man.

13

The second and third arguments for evolution—the case for major
changes—do not involve direct observation of evolution in action.
They rest upon inference, but are no less secure for that reason. Major evolutionary change requires too much time for direct observation on the scale of recorded human history. All historical sciences
rest upon inference, and evolution is no different from geology, cos-
mology, or human history in this respect. In principle, we cannot
observe processes that operated in the past. We must infer them
from results that still survive: living and fossil organisms for evolution, documents and artifacts for human history, strata and topography for geology.

14

The second argument—that the imperfection of nature reveals
evolution—strikes many people as ironic, for they feel that evolution
should be most elegantly displayed in the nearly perfect adaptation
expressed by some organisms—the chamber of a gull's wing, or butterflies that cannot be seen in ground litter because they mimic
leaves so precisely. But perfection could be imposed by a wise creator or evolved by natural selection. Perfection covers the tracks of
past history. And past history—the evidence of descent—is our
mark of evolution.

15

Evolution lies exposed in the *imperfections* that record a history of
descent. Why should a rat run, a bat fly, a porpoise swim, and I type
this essay with structures built of the same bones unless we all inher-

16

ited them from a common ancestor? An engineer, starting from scratch, could design better limbs in each case. Why should all the large native mammals of Australia be marsupials, unless they descended from a common ancestor isolated on this island continent? Marsupials are not "better," or ideally suited for Australia; many have been wiped out by placental mammals imported by man from other continents. This principle of imperfection extends to all historical sciences. When we recognize the etymology of September, October, November, and December (seventh, eighth, ninth, and tenth, from the Latin), we know that two additional items (January and February) must have been added to an original calendar of ten months.

The third argument is more direct: transitions are often found in the fossil record. Preserved transitions are not common—and should not be, according to our understanding of evolution (see next section)—but they are not entirely wanting, as creationists often claim. The lower jaw of reptiles contains several bones, that of mammals only one. The non-mammalian jawbones are reduced, step by step, in mammalian ancestors until they become tiny nubbins located at the back of the jaw. The "hammer" and "anvil" bones of the mammalian ear are descendants of these nubbins. How could such a transition be accomplished? the creationists ask. Surely a bone is either entirely in the jaw or in the ear. Yet paleontologists have discovered two transitional lineages of therapsids (the so-called mammal-like reptiles) with a double jaw joint—one composed of the old quadrate and articular bones (soon to become the hammer and anvil), the other of the squamosal and dentary bones (as in modern mammals). For that matter, what better transitional form could we desire than the oldest human, *Australopithecus afarensis*, with its apelike palate, its human upright stance, and a cranial capacity larger than any ape's of the same body size but a full 1,000 cubic centimeters below ours? If God made each of the half dozen human species discovered in ancient rocks, why did he create in an unbroken temporal sequence of progressively more modern features—increasing cranial capacity, reduced face and teeth, larger body size? Did he create to mimic evolution and test our faith thereby?

An Example of Creationist Argument

Faced with these facts of evolution and the philosophical bankruptcy of their own position, creationists rely upon distortion and innuendo to buttress their rhetorical claim. If I sound sharp or bitter, indeed I am—for I have become a major target of these practices.

I count myself among the evolutionists who argue for a jerky, or episodic, rather than a smoothly gradual, pace of change. In 1972 my colleague Niles Eldredge and I developed the theory of punctuated equilibrium [*Discover*, October]. We argued that two outstanding facts of the fossil record—geologically "sudden" origin of new species and failure to change thereafter (stasis)—reflect the predictions of evolutionary theory, not the imperfections of the fossil record. In most theories, small isolated populations are the source of new species, and the process of speciation takes thousands or tens of thousands of years. This amount of time, so long when measured against our lives, is a geological microsecond. It represents much less than 1 percent of the average life span for a fossil invertebrate species—more than 10 million years. Large, widespread, and well-established species, on the other hand, are not expected to change very much. We believe that the inertia of large populations explains the stasis of most fossil species over millions of years.

We proposed the theory of punctuated equilibrium largely to provide a different explanation for pervasive trends in the fossil record. Trends, we argued, cannot be attributed to gradual transformation within lineages, but must arise from the differential success of certain kinds of species. A trend, we argued, is more like climbing a flight of stairs (punctuations and stasis) than rolling up an inclined plane.   20

Since we proposed punctuated equilibria to explain trends, it is infuriating to be quoted again and again by creationists—whether through design or stupidity, I do not know—as admitting that the fossil record includes no transitional forms. Transitional forms are generally lacking at the species level, but are abundant between larger groups. The evolution from reptiles to mammals, as mentioned earlier, is well documented. Yet a pamphlet entitled "Harvard Scientists Agree Evolution Is a Hoax" states: "The facts of punctuated equilibrium which Gould and Eldredge . . . are forcing Darwinists to swallow fit the picture that Bryan insisted on, and which God has revealed to us in the Bible."   21

Continuing the distortion, several creationists have equated the theory of punctuated equilibrium with a caricature of the beliefs of Richard Goldschmidt, a great early geneticist. Goldschmidt argued, in a famous book published in 1940, that new groups can arise all at once through major mutations. He referred to these suddenly transformed creatures as "hopeful monsters." (I am attracted to some aspects of the non-caricatured version, but Goldschmidt's theory still has nothing to do with punctuated equilibrium.) Creationist Luther Sunderland talks of the "punctuated equilibrium hopeful monster theory" and tells his hopeful readers that "it amounts to tacit admission that anti-evolutionists are correct in asserting there is no fossil evidence supporting the theory that all life is connected to a common ancestor." Duane Gish writes, "According to Goldschmidt, and   22 now apparently according to Gould, a reptile laid an egg from which the first bird, feathers and all, was produced.'' Any evolutionist who believed such nonsense would rightly be laughed off the intellectual stage; yet the only theory that could ever envision such a scenario for the evolution of birds is creationism—God acts in the egg.

Conclusion

I am both angry at and amused by the creationists; but mostly I am 23 deeply sad. Sad for many reasons. Sad because so many people who respond to creationist appeals are troubled for the right reason, but venting their anger at the wrong target. It is true that scientists have often been dogmatic and elitist. It is true that we have often allowed the white-coated, advertising image to represent us—''Scientists say that Brand X cures bunions ten times faster than. . . .'' We have not fought it adequately because we derive benefits from appearing as a new priesthood. It is also true that faceless bureaucratic state power intrudes more and more into our lives and removes choices that should belong to individuals and communities. I can understand that requiring that evolution be taught in the schools might be seen as one more insult on all these grounds. But the culprit is not, and cannot be, evolution or any other fact of the natural world. Identify and fight your legitimate enemies by all means, but we are not among them.

I am sad because the practical result of this brouhaha will not be 24 expanded coverage to include creationism (that would also make me sad), but the reduction or excision of evolution from high school curricula. Evolution is one of the half dozen ''great ideas'' developed by science. It speaks to the profound issues of genealogy that fascinate all of us—the ''roots'' phenomenon writ large. Where did we come from? Where did life arise? How did it develop? How are organisms related? It forces us to think, ponder, and wonder. Shall we deprive millions of this knowledge and once again teach biology as a set of dull and unconnected facts, without the thread that weaves diverse material into a supple unity?

But most of all I am saddened by a trend I am just beginning to 25 discern among my colleagues. I sense that some now wish to mute the healthy debate about theory that has brought new life to evolutionary biology. It provides grist for creationist mills, they say, even if only by distortion. Perhaps we should lie low and rally round the flag of strict Darwinism, at least for the moment—a kind of old-time religion on our part.

But we should borrow another metaphor and recognize that we 26 too have to tread a straight and narrow path, surrounded by roads to perdition. For if we ever begin to suppress our search to understand nature, to quench our own intellectual excitement in a misguided effort to present a united front where it does not and should not exist, then we are truly lost.

PRACTICE

Reconstructing Gould's Argument

This is not so much a writing assignment as a sort of outlining in reverse. The purpose of this kind of work is to see how a professional writer goes about putting together an argument on a controversial issue.

There are twenty-six paragraphs in Gould's essay. Your job is to try and reduce each paragraph to a simple declarative sentence, like this:

1. The reopening of the issues behind the 1925 Scopes trial makes me sad.
2. No new evidence or arguments have been presented to justify the creationist position.

Such reductions are obviously imperfect, but they can help us see the skeleton of an argument and the way the skeleton is articulated. In writing your twenty-six sentences you will need to read each paragraph carefully, more than once. You may find a sentence in the paragraph that seems to capture its main point, but beware of simply following the words of the original. Your job is to put the essence of each paragraph into your own words.

Leave some space between each numbered sentence for notes and questions or comments. You may want to remind yourself that a particular point is strongly or weakly made. You may wish to note, for instance, that paragraph 6 contains an important definition, and so on.

You should plan on comparing your finished reconstruction with others and discussing alternatives. Your final result should be an awareness of the strengths and weaknesses of Gould's argument.

A Feminist Discusses Women and Names

The following selection from Dale Spender's book *Man Made Language* is a straightforward argument for changing certain practices in the use of names and titles for women. In reading this, you should attempt to produce a clear paraphrase of the argument, and you should notice how the evidence supporting the argument is introduced. This is the sort of topic that often produces more emotion than reason. How many emotional appeals can you find in Spender's argument?

Dale Spender, from Man Made Language

One of the features of English language practices which is inherently   1
sexist is the use of names. In our society "only men have real names" in that their names are permanent and they have "accepted the permanency of their names as one of the rights of being male" (Miller and Swift, 1976:14). This has both practical and psychological ramifications for the construction—and maintenance—of male supremacy.

Practically it means that women's family names do not count and   2
that there is one more device for making women invisible. Fathers pass their names on to their sons and the existence of daughters can be denied when in the absence of a male heir it is said that a family "dies out." One other direct result of this practice of only taking cognizance of the male name has been to facilitate the development of history as the story of the male line, because it becomes almost impossible to trace the ancestry of women—particularly if they do not come into the male-defined categories of importance.

Very little is known about women, says Virginia Woolf (1972), for   3
"the history of England is the history of the male line" (p. 41); this point was brought home to Jill Liddington and Jill Norris (1978) when they undertook to document the story of women's suffrage in Lancashire for "this vital contribution had been largely neglected by historians" (p. 11). They had difficulty with sources, and one difficulty was not one which would be encountered in tracing men (1978:17):

> Sometimes we seemed to be forever chasing down blind alleys. For instance, one of the most active women, Helen Silcock, a weavers' union leader from Wigan, seemed to disappear after 1902. We couldn't think why, until we came across a notice of

"congratulations to Miss Silcock on her marriage to Mr. Fairhurst" in a little known labor journal, the *Women's Trade Union Review* . . . it was an object lesson for us in the difficulties of tracing women activists.

It is also an extremely useful device for eliminating women from history and for making it exceedingly difficult to perceive a continuum and develop a tradition.

When females have no right to "surnames," to family names of   4
their own, the concept of women as the property of men is subtly reinforced (and this is of course assisted by the title *Mrs*). Currently many women are changing their names and instead of taking the name of either their father or their husband they are coining new, autonomous names for themselves; for example, Cheris Kramer has become Cheris Kramarae, Julia Stanley has become Julia Penelope—there are almost countless examples of this change. A common practice has become that of taking the first name of a close female friend or relative—such as mother—as the new family name (for example, Janet Robyn, Elizabeth Sarah). When asked why she had legally dropped her surname and retained her first two given names, Margaret Sandra stated that a "surname" was intended as an indication of the "sire" and was so closely linked socially with the ownership of women that there was no "surname" that she found acceptable.

Although attempts have been made to trivialize these new naming   5
activities among women, such activities are serious and they do undermine patriarchal practices. At the very least they raise consciousness about the role men's names have played in the subordination of women, and at best they confound traditional patriarchal classification schemes which have not operated in women's interest. I have been told that it makes it very difficult to "pigeon-hole" women, to "place" them, if they persist with this neurotic practice of giving themselves new names. One male stated quite sincerely that it was becoming "jolly difficult to work out whether women were married these days because of the ridiculous practice of not taking their husband's names." In order to operate in the world, however, it has *never* been necessary to know from a name whether someone is married or single, as women can testify. Men have not thought that *not* changing their name upon marriage should present difficulties to women and once more the bias of language practices is revealed.

But many males are confused, and not without cause. The lan-   6
guage has helped to create the representation of females as sex objects; it has also helped to signal when a sex object is not available and is the property of another male. The patriarchal order has been maintained by such devices and when women consciously and inten-

tionally abolish them men have reason to feel insecure; they do not however have reason to protest.

There are also other "by-products" of this process of permitting the permanency of names only to males. Miller and Swift (1976) ask whether it is because of the unenduring nature of female family names that much more emphasis is placed on their first names. Whatever the reason, it is clear that males are more frequently addressed by their family name (and title) and women by their first name. Psychologically this can also work to produce sexual asymmetry. ₇

The use of first names can be evidence of intimacy or friendship but in such circumstances the practice, generally speaking, has to be reciprocal. When one party is referred to by the first name, and the other by the family name and title, it is usually evidence that one has more power than the other. So, for example, the employer may be Mr. Smith and the employees Bill and Mary. The practice of those "in power" referring to those "out of power" by their first names— while still retaining the use of their own title and family name—is widespread and applies to both sexes in a hierarchical society. But there are still instances where both sexes occupy comparable positions but where males are referred to by their family names and women referred to by their first names, indicating the operation of yet another hierarchy. ₈

This is frequently illustrated in the media. Even where there are both male and female contestants on some "quiz" shows, the women are more likely to be addressed by their first names. Interviewers are also more inclined to use women's first names. News items are more likely to make reference to women by their first name (and of course their coloring, for example, blond or brunette, and their age and marital status) and the usually male presenter of "talk-back" shows indicates a decided disposition to discriminate between the callers in this way. ₉

But it is not confined to the media. I have never heard a male complain that a medical practitioner addressed him (perhaps patronizingly) by his first name at the first consultation, yet this protest is often made by women. It would, however, break the social rules which govern subordination if women were to respond by addressing medical practitioners by their first names. This is precisely why I think they should do so. ₁₀

Regardless of the reason for the development of this practice of calling women by their first names in formal situations, it assists in making "visible" the subordination of the female. ₁₁

The practice of labelling women as married or single also serves supremely sexist ends. It conveniently signals who is "fair game" ₁₂

from the male point of view. There is tension between the representation of women as sex objects and the male ownership rights over women and this has been resolved by an explicit and most visible device of designating the married status of women. As women do not ''own'' men, and as men have many dimensions apart from their sexual ones in a patriarchal order, it has not been necessary to make male marital status visible. On the contrary, it could hinder rather than help male operations in the world so it has never appeared as a ''logical'' proposition.

Contrary to the belief of many people, the current usage of *Miss* and *Mrs.* is relatively recent, for until the beginning of the nineteenth century the title *Miss* was usually reserved for young females while *Mrs.* designated mature women. Marital status played no role in the use of these terms. How and why this usage changed is a matter of some speculation,[1] but there is nothing speculative about the ends that it serves.   13

It labels women for the convenience of men. It also labels those whom men do not want. To be over thirty and *Miss* Jones in times but recently passed was an advertisement of failure and an invitation for ridicule.   14

The question arises as to why more women have not objected to this offensive labelling in the past. Why was there not greater protest when in the late nineteenth century women were required to surrender even more of themselves and their identity and to become not just Mrs. *Jane* Smith, but Mrs. *John* Smith? (Casey Miller and   15

---

[1]Miller and Swift (1976) suggest that the use of *Miss* and *Mrs.* to designate marital status was a response to some of the pressures created by the industrial revolution, which disrupted the familiar patterns of small communities in which relationships were readily known. There was no need for this usage prior to the industrial revolution for a woman's marital status was already known in the community in which she lived, but with the migration of population that occurred at the onset of the revolution and with women's entry into the workforce outside the home or local community,

> a simple means of distinguishing married from unmarried women was needed [for men] and it served a double purpose: it supplied at least a modicum of information about women's sexual availability, and it applied not so subtle pressure toward marriage by lumping single women with the young and inexperienced. Attached to anyone over the age of eighteen, Miss came in time to suggest the unattractive or socially undesirable qualities associated with such labels as *old maid* and *spinster* or that dreadful word *barren*. So the needs of patriarchy were served when a woman's availability for her primary role as helper and sexual partner was made an integral part of her identity—in effect, a part of her name (p. 99).

Kate Swift point out that there would have been bewilderment if a letter had ever arrived addressed to Mrs. *George* Washington.)

It is I think a mark of the identity options open to women in a patriarchal order that so many women voluntarily and even enthusiastically seek to be labelled as the property of a male. The title *Mrs.* and the abandonment of their father's name (a name which required no effort on their part and could not be construed as an achievement) for their husband's name, appears to confirm their identity. In a patriarchal society it is not unrealistic to perceive that security lies in marriage—even if this is eventually revealed as a myth. That so many women continue to choose to be Mrs. Jack Smart and to become "invisible" is an indication of the success of patriarchal ideology. 16

This is why the refusal of some women to be designated *Mrs.* is significant. To insist on the title *Ms.* (if titles are unavoidable) does undermine some of the patriarchal practices. If the strength of the resistance is proportionate to the danger posed by the strategy then it is clear that some individuals are aware of the subversive influence of the use of *Ms.* 17

Numerous arguments other than the fundamental one have been advanced to substantiate the undesirability of the term *Ms.* and they share the common features of being inadequate and illogical—and even absurd. For example, one reason that has been given is that the pronunciation of *Ms.* cannot be determined by its spelling. This is a non-starter in English. If we were to find unacceptable all those words which do not reveal their pronunciation from their spelling we would have to dispense with a sizable number and we could begin with *Mr.* and *Mrs.* 18

The (unstated) reason for the undesirability of *Ms.* is that it is of no assistance in the maintenance of the patriarchal order and it can even be problematic for males. Again, this is why I think it extremely important that all women should make use of it as a title—if we are to persist with titles. 19

References

Liddington, Jill and Jill Norris, *One Hand Tied Behind Us: the Rise of the Women's Suffrage Movement*. Virago, 1978.

Miller, Casey and Kate Swift, *Words and Women: New Language in New Times*. New York: Anchor/Doubleday, 1976.

Woolf, Virginia, "Women and Fiction," in *Collected Essays: Virginia Woolf*, vol. 2 (ed. Leonard Woolf). Chatto & Windus, 1972.

1. What does Spender mean by saying in paragraph 1 that the English use of names is "inherently sexist"? What does "sexist" mean?
2. What do you think of the attempts of women to change their names (paragraphs 4 and 5)?
3. At the end of paragraph 6, Spender says "men have reason to feel insecure; they do not have reason to protest." Do you agree or disagree?
4. In paragraph 9 Spender speaks of the treatment of men and women on quiz shows and in newspapers. Are her statements still accurate?
5. What would happen if you called your doctor by his first name? What if the doctor were a woman?
6. Spender mentions the "patriarchal ideology" and the "patriarchal order." What does she mean by these terms? What have they to do with names?
7. Are you convinced by Spender's argument? Are some parts more convincing than others?

PRACTICE

Arguing About Men and Women

The air is full of debates about the roles of men and women. Take some issue that is current and produce a reasonable argument on one side or the other of the debate.

For example, you may wish to argue against Spender, who opposes the use of male surnames and favors the use of *Ms.* by all women. Before doing so, consider what assumptions, definitions, classes, and categories you will need to support your argument. Spender relies on such notions as "sexism" and "patriarchy." To argue with her you will have to either change the value signs attached to these notions (patriarchy is good, not bad) or change the categories in some way.

You may wish to take some other question, such as sexual segregation in sports or schools, and write an argument about that. The basic requirements are that you find a truly controversial issue in the area of male/female relationships and that you take a stand on a particular side of the controversy without losing your head. Concentrate on finding appropriate evidence to support your argument.

READING

A Politician Argues About Slavery

Abraham Lincoln's "Speech at Cooper Union," delivered to an audience of fifteen thousand New Yorkers in February, 1860, helped pave the way for his selection as the 1860 Republican Presidential candidate. We have not presented the whole speech, which is quite long, but the first part of it included here is an excellent illustration of how a complete argument is developed. As you read the opening paragraphs of the speech, notice how Lincoln clarifies the question to be argued, defines the terms of the argument, and presents evidence for one particular answer (his thesis) to the question he has raised, while considering evidence on the other side. The questions that follow the excerpt are designed to help you see how Lincoln used the five elements of argumentative composition in developing his speech.

Abraham Lincoln, from "Speech at Cooper Union, New York"

Mr. President and Fellow Citizens of New York:

The facts with which I shall deal this evening are mainly old and familiar; nor is there anything new in the general use I shall make of them. If there shall be any novelty, it will be in the mode of presenting the facts, and the inferences and observations following that presentation. In his speech last autumn at Columbus, Ohio, as reported in the New York *Times* Senator Douglas[1] said: 1

"Our fathers, when they framed the government under which we live, understood this question just as well, and even better, than we do now." 2

I fully endorse this, and I adopt it as a text for this discourse. I so adopt it because it furnishes a precise and an agreed starting-point for a discussion between Republicans and that wing of the Democracy headed by Senator Douglas. It simply leaves the inquiry: What was the understanding those fathers had of the question mentioned? 3

What is the frame of government under which we live? The answer must be, "The Constitution of the United States." That Con- 4

---

[1]Stephen A. Douglas, the Democratic senator from Illinois, had defeated Lincoln in the Illinois senatorial race in 1858. The Lincoln-Douglas debates helped Lincoln rise to national prominence.

stitution consists of the original, framed in 1787, and under which the present government first went into operation, and twelve subsequently framed amendments, the first ten of which were framed in 1789.

Who were our fathers that framed the Constitution? I suppose the "thirty-nine" who signed the original instrument may be fairly called our fathers who framed that part of the present government. It is almost exactly true to say they framed it, and it is altogether true to say they fairly represented the opinion and sentiment of the whole nation at that time. Their names, being familiar to nearly all, and accessible to quite all, need not now be repeated.   5

I take these "thirty-nine," for the present, as being "our fathers who framed the government under which we live." What is the question which, according to the text, those fathers understood "just as well, and even better, than we do now"?   6

It is this: Does the proper division of local from federal authority, or anything in the Constitution, forbid our federal government to control as to slavery in our federal territories?   7

Upon this Senator Douglas holds the affirmative, and Republicans the negative. This affirmation and denial form an issue; and this issue—this question—is precisely what the text declares our fathers understood "better than we." Let us now inquire whether the "thirty-nine," or any of them, ever acted upon this question; and if they did, how they acted upon it—how they expressed that better understanding. In 1784, three years before the Constitution, the United States then owning the Northwestern Territory, and no other, the Congress of the Confederation had before them the question of prohibiting slavery in that territory, and four of the "thirty-nine" who afterward framed the Constitution were in that Congress, and voted on that question. Of these, Roger Sherman, Thomas Mifflin, and Hugh Williamson voted for the prohibition, thus showing that, in their understanding, no line dividing local from federal authority, nor anything else, properly forbade the federal government to control as to slavery in federal territory. The other of the four, James McHenry, voted against the prohibition, showing that for some cause he thought it improper to vote for it.   8

In 1787, still before the Constitution, but while the convention was in session framing it, and while the Northwestern Territory still was the only territory owned by the United States, the same question of prohibiting slavery in the territory again came before the Congress of the Confederation; and two more of the "thirty-nine" who afterward signed the Constitution were in that Congress, and voted on the question. They were William Blount and William Few; and they both voted for the prohibition—thus showing that in their   9 understanding no line dividing local from federal authority, nor anything else, properly forbade the federal government to control as to slavery in federal territory. This time the prohibition became a law, being part of what is now well known as the Ordinance of '87.

The question of federal control of slavery in the territories seems not to have been directly before the convention which framed the original Constitution; and hence it is not recorded that the "thirty-nine," or any of them, while engaged on that instrument, expressed any opinion on that precise question. 10

In 1789, by the first Congress which sat under the Constitution, an act was passed to enforce the Ordinance of '87, including the pro-hibition of slavery in the Northwestern Territory. The bill for this act was reported by one of the "thirty-nine"—Thomas Fitzsim-mons, then a member of the House of Representatives from Penn-sylvania. It went through all its stages without a word of opposition, and finally passed both branches without ayes and nays, which is equivalent to a unanimous passage. In this Congress there were six-teen of the thirty-nine fathers who framed the original Constitution. They were John Langdon, Nicholas Gilman, William S. Johnson, Roger Sherman, Robert Morris, Thomas Fitzsimmons, William Few, Abraham Baldwin, Rufus King, William Paterson, George Clymer, Richard Bassett, George Read, Pierce Butler, Daniel Car-roll, and James Madison. 11

This shows that, in their understanding, no line dividing local from federal authority, nor anything in the Constitution, properly forbade Congress to prohibit slavery in the federal territory; else both their fidelity to correct principle, and their oath to support the Constitution would have constrained them to oppose the prohibi-tion. 12

Again, George Washington, another of the "thirty-nine," was then President of the United States, and as such approved and signed the bill, thus completing its validity as a law, and thus show-ing that, in his understanding, no line dividing local from federal au-thority, nor anything in the Constitution, forbade the federal gov-ernment to control as to slavery in federal territory. 13

No great while after the adoption of the original Constitution, North Carolina ceded to the federal government the country now constituting the state of Tennessee; and a few years later Georgia ceded that which constitutes the states of Mississippi and Alabama. In both deeds of cession it was made a condition by the ceding states that the federal government should not prohibit slavery in the ceded country. Besides this, slavery was then actually in the ceded coun-try. Under these circumstances, Congress, on taking charge of these countries, did not absolutely prohibit slavery within them. But they did interfere with it—take control of it—even there, to a certain ex- 14 tent. In 1798 Congress organized the territory of Mississippi. In the act of organization they prohibited the bringing of slaves into the territory from any place without the United States, by fine, and giving freedom to slaves so brought. This act passed both branches of Congress without yeas and nays. In that Congress were three of the "thirty-nine" who framed the original Constitution. They were John Langdon, George Read, and Abraham Baldwin. They all probably voted for it. Certainly they would have placed their opposition to it upon record if, in their understanding, any line dividing local from federal authority, or anything in the Constitution, properly forbade the federal government to control as to slavery in federal territory.

In 1803 the federal government purchased the Louisiana country.   15
Our former territorial acquisitions came from certain of our own states; but this Louisiana country was acquired from a foreign nation. In 1804 Congress gave a territorial organization to that part of it which now constitutes the state of Louisiana. New Orleans, lying within that part, was an old and comparatively large city. There were other considerable towns and settlements, and slavery was extensively and thoroughly intermingled with the people. Congress did not, in the Territorial Act, prohibit slavery; but they did interfere with it—take control of it—in a more marked and extensive way than they did in the case of Mississippi. The substance of the provision therein made in relation to slaves was:

1st. That no slave should be imported into the territory from foreign parts.

2d. That no slave should be carried into it who had been imported into the United States since the first day of May, 1798.

3d. That no slave should be carried into it, except by the owner, and for his own use as a settler; the penalty in all the cases being a fine upon the violator of the law, and freedom to the slave.

This act also was passed without ayes or nays. In the Congress   16
which passed it there were two of the "thirty-nine." They were Abraham Baldwin and Jonathan Dayton. As stated in the case of Mississippi, it is probable that both voted for it. They would not have allowed it to pass without recording their opposition to it, if, in their understanding, it violated either the line properly dividing local from federal authority, or any provision of the Constitution.

In 1819–20 came and passed the Missouri question. Many votes   17
were taken, by yeas and nays, in both branches of Congress, upon the various phases of the general question. Two of the "thirty-nine"—Rufus King and Charles Pinckney—were members of that Congress. Mr. King steadily voted for slavery prohibition and against all compromises, while Mr. Pinckney as steadily voted against slavery prohibition and against all compromises. By this,

Mr. King showed that, in his understanding, no line dividing local from federal authority, nor anything in the Constitution, was violated by Congress prohibiting slavery in federal territory; while Mr. Pinckney, by his votes, showed that, in his understanding, there was some sufficient reason for opposing such prohibition in that case.

The cases I have mentioned are the only acts of the "thirty-nine," or of any of them, upon the direct issue, which I have been able to discover.   18

To enumerate the persons who thus acted as being four in 1784, two in 1787, seventeen in 1789, three in 1798, two in 1804, and two in 1819–20, there would be thirty of them. But this would be counting John Langdon, Roger Sherman, William Few, Rufus King, and George Reed each twice, and Abraham Baldwin three times. The true number of those of the "thirty-nine" whom I have shown to have acted upon the question which, by the text, they understood better than we, is twenty-three, leaving sixteen not shown to have acted upon it in any way.   19

Here, then, we have twenty-three out of our thirty-nine fathers "who framed the government under which we live," who have, upon their official responsibility and their corporal oaths, acted upon the very question which the text affirms they "understood just as well, and even better than we do now"; and twenty-one of them—a clear majority of the whole "thirty-nine"—so acting upon it as to make them guilty of gross political impropriety and willful perjury if, in their understanding, any proper division between local and federal authority, or anything in the Constitution they had made themselves, and sworn to support, forbade the federal government to control as to slavery in the federal territories. Thus the twenty-one acted; and, as actions speak louder than words, so actions under such responsibility speak still louder.   20

Two of the twenty-three voted against congressional prohibition of slavery in the federal territories, in the instances in which they acted upon the question. But for what reasons they so voted is not known. They may have done so because they thought a proper division of local from federal authority, or some provision or principle of the Constitution, stood in the way; or they may, without any such question, have voted against the prohibition on what appeared to them to be sufficient grounds of expediency. No one who has sworn to support the Constitution can conscientiously vote for what he understands to be an unconstitutional measure, however expedient he may think it; but one may and ought to vote against a measure which he deems constitutional if, at the same time, he deems it inexpedient. It, therefore, would be unsafe to set down even the two who voted against the prohibition as having done so because, in their un-   21 derstanding, any proper division of local from federal authority, or anything in the Constitution, forbade the federal government to control as to slavery in federal territory.

The remaining sixteen of the "thirty-nine," so far as I have dis- 22 covered, have left no record of their understanding upon the direct question of federal control of slavery in the federal territories. But there is much reason to believe that their understanding upon that question would not have appeared different from that of their twenty-three compeers, had it been manifested at all.

For the purpose of adhering rigidly to the text, I have purposely 23 omitted whatever understanding may have been manifested by any person, however distinguished, other than the thirty-nine fathers who framed the original Constitution; and, for the same reason, I have also omitted whatever understanding may have been manifested by any of the "thirty-nine" even on any other phase of the general question of slavery. If we should look into their acts and declarations on those other phases, as the foreign slave-trade, and the morality and policy of slavery generally, it would appear to us that on the direct question of federal control of slavery in federal territories, the sixteen, if they had acted at all, would probably have acted just as the twenty-three did. Among that sixteen were several of the most noted anti-slavery men of those times—as Dr. Franklin, Alexander Hamilton, and Gouverneur Morris—while there was not one now known to have been otherwise, unless it may be John Rutledge, of South Carolina.

The sum of the whole is that of our thirty-nine fathers who framed 24 the original Constitution, twenty-one—a clear majority of the whole—certainly understood that no proper division of local from federal authority, nor any part of the Constitution, forbade the federal government to control slavery in the federal territories; while all the rest had probably the same understanding. Such, unquestionably, was the understanding of our fathers who framed the original Constitution; and the text affirms that they understood the question "better than we."

QUESTIONS

1. What is Lincoln's main point or thesis? How many times does he present it? In how many forms?
2. What minor points can you locate in the speech? How are they connected to the main point? How are they organized?
3. What sorts of evidence does Lincoln use to support his main point? How is the evidence related to the point being argued?
4. What counterevidence does Lincoln consider? How does he deal with it? Where does he locate it?

5. Locate the conclusion. Compare it to the earliest introduction of the main point. Has it been modified or qualified in the course of the essay, or has it simply been intensified?

6. Does Lincoln use emotional or purely persuasive language at any point in the essay?

7. Why does Lincoln use so much mathematical or statistical evidence here? Does he need all he uses?

8. What sort of impression does this speech convey of the speaker? Of the intended audience?

PRACTICE

Reconstructing Lincoln's Argument

The two Practices that follow this one ask you to construct arguments from statistics. To prepare for those assignments, we ask you to look closely at Lincoln's use of statistics by outlining his argument. You should summarize each paragraph in your own words, paying careful attention not only to what Lincoln said, but also to *how* he developed his argument. Each paragraph should be summarized in one sentence (two short paragraphs may be summarized in one sentence), although more complex paragraphs may require two sentences. Some examples follow:

1. Lincoln assures his audience that the facts he will deal with are "old and familiar," but that his treatment and discussion of those facts will be new.

2–3. He quotes Senator Douglas's statement, endorses it, adopts it as a starting point, and then proceeds to analyze it by questioning its meaning.

8. The question which our fathers "understood 'better than we'" is a current issue, answered affirmatively by Democrats and negatively by Republicans. In inquiring whether any of the thirty-nine fathers ever acted on this question, Lincoln cites that in 1784, three of them voted to prohibit slavery in the Northwestern Territory, and one voted against prohibition.

Compare your outline with those of your classmates. Do you all agree on the meaning of each paragraph? Consider the cumulative effect of Lincoln's use of statistics. Is he careful to discuss those he presents? Does he manipulate statistics in any way? If you were Senator Douglas, could you find a way to rebut Lincoln's argument?

PRACTICE

Arguing from Statistics—Baseball

It has been said that figures can't lie but liars can figure. At any rate, conclusions drawn from statistical evidence are an important part of contemporary thinking and decision-making. Our first example comes from baseball statistics because they are familiar to many people and are clear without being too simple. The material here consists of four charts giving batting leaders in the National and American leagues over a period of eighty-two years. Your assignment is to examine the four charts (batting champions, home run champions, runs batted-in leaders, and slugging average leaders) and to develop and present a thesis based on all four charts.[1]

The thesis may simply be an argument that "X was the greatest hitter in modern times." Evidence in such a case would be drawn from the four charts. You are not being asked to write a *persuasive* essay. You are supposed to weigh the evidence and base an argument on it, rather than an appeal to emotion. You could, for instance, qualify your statement: "X was the best all around hitter, although Y excelled him in home runs on average."

You can, of course, find other kinds of theses to argue. For instance, you might discover a particular year or decade that produced remarkable results and argue that it was the best (or

[1]To refresh your memory, batting average equals hits per time at bat, while home runs and runs batted in are simply totals for the year. Slugging average equals total bases per time at bat. For example, a home run counts as 4, a triple as 3, and so on. A hitter with ten singles for thirty times at bat will have the same slugging average as one with five doubles for the same thirty at-bats. A batter with one single, one double, one triple, and one home run in twenty at-bats will have a .200 batting average (four hits per twenty times at bat) and a slugging average of .500 (a total of ten bases for twenty at-bats). Slugging averages tend to be considerably higher than batting averages.

worst) year or decade for hitters during the period. Or you might argue that one league or the other had a better record in hitting for a particular period. But, whatever your thesis, you must present the evidence fairly and not ignore or distort anything that might weaken or contradict your thesis.

For this paper you are expected to confine yourself to the material presented here and not to consult other data.

Batting Champions—Major League Baseball

National League			American League		
1901	Jesse Burkett, Pittsburgh	.376	1901	Nap Lajoie, Philadelphia	.422
1902	Ginger Beaumont, St. Louis	.357	1902	Nap Lajoie, Philadelphia-Cleveland	.378
1903	Honus Wagner, Pittsburgh	.355	1903	Nap Lajoie, Cleveland	.355
1904	Honus Wagner, Pittsburgh	.349	1904	Nap Lajoie, Cleveland	.377
1905	Cy Seymour, Cincinnati	.377	1905	Elmer Flick, Cleveland	.306
1906	Honus Wagner, Pittsburgh	.339	1906	George Stone, St. Louis	.358
1907	Honus Wagner, Pittsburgh	.350	1907	Ty Cobb, Detroit	.350
1908	Honus Wagner, Pittsburgh	.354	1908	Ty Cobb, Detroit	.324
1909	Honus Wagner, Pittsburgh	.339	1909	Ty Cobb, Detroit	.377
1910	Sherry Magee, Philadelphia	.331	1910	Ty Cobb, Detroit	.385
1911	Honus Wagner, Pittsburgh	.334	1911	Ty Cobb, Detroit	.420
1912	Heinie Zimmerman, Chicago	.372	1912	Ty Cobb, Detroit	.410
1913	Jake Daubert, Brooklyn	.350	1913	Ty Cobb, Detroit	.390
1914	Jake Daubert, Brooklyn	.329	1914	Ty Cobb, Detroit	.368
1915	Larry Doyle, New York	.320	1915	Ty Cobb, Detroit	.369
1916	Hal Chase, Cincinnati	.339	1916	Tris Speaker, Cleveland	.388
1917	Edd Roush, Cincinnati	.321	1917	Ty Cobb, Detroit	.383
1918	Zack Wheat, Brooklyn	.335	1918	Ty Cobb, Detroit	.382
1919	Edd Roush, Cincinnati	.321	1919	Ty Cobb, Detroit	.384
1920	Rogers Hornsby, St. Louis	.370	1920	George Sisler, St. Louis	.407
1921	Rogers Hornsby, St. Louis	.397	1921	Harry Heilmann, Detroit	.394
1922	Rogers Hornsby, St. Louis	.401	1922	George Sisler, St. Louis	.420
1923	Rogers Hornsby, St. Louis	.384	1923	Harry Heilmann, Detroit	.403
1924	Rogers Hornsby, St. Louis	.424	1924	Babe Ruth, New York	.378
1925	Rogers Hornsby, St. Louis	.403	1925	Harry Heilmann, Detroit	.393
1926	Gene Hargrave, Cincinnati	.353	1926	Heinie Manush, Detroit	.378
1927	Paul Waner, Pittsburgh	.380	1927	Harry Heilmann, Detroit	.398
1928	Rogers Hornsby, Boston	.387	1928	Goose Goslin, Washington	.379
1929	Lefty O'Doul, Brooklyn	.396	1929	Lew Fonseca, Cleveland	.369
1930	Bill Terry, New York	.401	1930	Al Simmons, Philadelphia	.381
1931	Chuck Hafey, St. Louis	.349	1931	Al Simmons, Philadelphia	.390
1932	Lefty O'Doul, Brooklyn	.368	1932	Dale Alexander, Detroit-Boston	.367
1933	Chuck Klein, Philadelphia	.368	1933	Jimmy Foxx, Philadelphia	.356
1934	Paul Waner, Pittsburgh	.362	1934	Lou Gehrig, New York	.363
1935	Arky Vaughan, Pittsburgh	.385	1935	Buddy Myer, Washington	.349
1936	Paul Waner, Pittsburgh	.373	1936	Luke Appling, Chicago	.388

Batting Champions—Major League Baseball

National League			American League		
1937	Joe Medwick, St. Louis	.374	1937	Charley Gehringer, Detroit	.371
1938	Ernie Lombardi, Cincinnati	.342	1938	Jimmy Foxx, Boston	.349
1939	Johnny Mize, St. Louis	.349	1939	Joe DiMaggio, New York	.381
1940	Debs Garms, Pittsburgh	.355	1940	Joe DiMaggio, New York	.352
1941	Pete Reiser, Brooklyn	.343	1941	Ted Williams, Boston	.408
1942	Ernie Lombardi, Boston	.330	1942	Ted Williams, Boston	.356
1943	Stan Musial, St. Louis	.357	1943	Luke Appling, Chicago	.328
1944	Dixie Walker, Brooklyn	.357	1944	Lou Boudreau, Cleveland	.327
1945	Phil Cavarretta, Chicago	.355	1945	George Sternweiss, New York	.309
1946	Stan Musial, St. Louis	.365	1946	Mickey Vernon, Washington	.353
1947	Harry Walker, St. Louis-Philadelphia	.363	1947	Ted Williams, Boston	.343
1948	Stan Musial, St. Louis	.376	1948	Ted Williams, Boston	.369
1949	Jackie Robinson, Brooklyn	.342	1949	George Kell, Detroit	.343
1950	Stan Musial, St. Louis	.346	1950	Billy Goodman, Boston	.354
1951	Stan Musial, St. Louis	.355	1951	Ferris Fain, Philadelphia	.344
1952	Stan Musial, St. Louis	.336	1952	Ferris Fain, Philadelphia	.327
1953	Carl Furillo, Brooklyn	.344	1953	Mickey Vernon, Washington	.337
1954	Willie Mays, New York	.345	1954	Bobby Avila, Cleveland	.341
1955	Richie Ashburn, Philadelphia	.350	1955	Al Kaline, Detroit	.340
1956	Hank Aaron, Milwaukee	.328	1956	Mickey Mantle, New York	.353
1957	Stan Musial, St. Louis	.351	1957	Ted Williams, Boston	.388
1958	Richie Ashburn, Philadelphia	.350	1958	Ted Williams, Boston	.328
1959	Hank Aaron, Milwaukee	.355	1959	Harvey Kuenn, Detroit	.353
1960	Dick Groat, Pittsburgh	.325	1960	Pete Runnels, Boston	.320
1961	Roberto Clemente, Pittsburgh	.351	1961	Norm Cash, Detroit	.361
1962	Tommy Davis, Los Angeles	.346	1962	Pete Runnels, Boston	.326
1963	Tommy Davis, Los Angeles	.326	1963	Carl Yastrzemski, Boston	.321
1964	Roberto Clemente, Pittsburgh	.339	1964	Tony Oliva, Minnesota	.323
1965	Roberto Clemente, Pittsburgh	.329	1965	Tony Oliva, Minnesota	.321
1966	Matty Alou, Pittsburgh	.342	1966	Frank Robinson, Baltimore	.316
1967	Roberto Clemente, Pittsburgh	.357	1967	Carl Yastrzemski, Boston	.326
1968	Pete Rose, Cincinnati	.335	1968	Carl Yastrzemski, Boston	.301
1969	Pete Rose, Cincinnati	.348	1969	Rod Carew, Minnesota	.332
1970	Rico Carty, Atlanta	.366	1970	Alex Johnson, California	.329
1971	Joe Torre, St. Louis	.363	1971	Tony Oliva, Minnesota	.337
1972	Billy Williams, Chicago	.333	1972	Rod Carew, Minnesota	.318
1973	Pete Rose, Cincinnati	.338	1973	Rod Carew, Minnesota	.350
1974	Ralph Garr, Atlanta	.353	1974	Rod Carew, Minnesota	.364
1975	Bill Madlock, Chicago	.354	1975	Rod Carew, Minnesota	.359
1976	Bill Madlock, Chicago	.339	1976	George Brett, Kansas City	.333
1977	Dave Parker, Pittsburgh	.338	1977	Rod Carew, Minnesota	.388
1978	Dave Parker, Pittsburgh	.334	1978	Rod Carew, Minnesota	.333
1979	Keith Hernandez, St. Louis	.344	1979	Fred Lynn, Boston	.333
1980	Bill Buckner, Chicago	.324	1980	George Brett, Kansas City	.390
1981	Bill Madlock, Pittsburgh	.341	1981	Carney Landsford, Boston	.336
1982	Al Oliver, Montreal	.331	1982	Willie Wilson, Kansas City	.332

Home Run Champions—Major League Baseball

National League

1901	Sam Crawford, Cincinnati	16
1902	Tommy Leach, Pittsburgh	6
1903	Jimmy Sheckard, Brooklyn	9
1904	Harry Lumley, Brooklyn	9
1905	Fred Odwell, Cincinnati	9
1906	Tim Jordan, Brooklyn	12
1907	Dave Brain, Boston	10
1908	Tim Jordan, Brooklyn	12
1909	Red Murray, New York	7
1910	Fred Beck, Boston	10
	Wildfire Schulte, Chicago	10
1911	Wildfire Schulte, Chicago	21
1912	Heinie Zimmerman, Chicago	14
1913	Gavvy Cravath, Philadelphia	19
1914	Gavvy Cravath, Philadelphia	19
1915	Gavvy Cravath, Philadelphia	24
1916	Cy Williams, Chicago	12
	Dave Robertson, New York	12
1917	Dave Robertson, New York	12
	Gavvy Cravath, Philadelphia	12
1918	Gavvy Cravath, Philadelphia	8
1919	Gavvy Cravath, Philadelphia	12
1920	Fred Williams, Philadelphia	15
1921	George Kelly, New York	23
1922	Rogers Hornsby, St. Louis	42
1923	Fred Williams, Philadelphia	41
1924	Jacques Fournier, Brooklyn	27
1925	Rogers Hornsby, St. Louis	39
1926	Hack Wilson, Chicago	21
1927	H. Wilson, Chi., F. Williams, Philadelphia	30
1928	Hack Wilson, Chicago	31
	Jim Bottomley, St. Louis	31
1929	Chuck Klein, Philadelphia	43
1930	Hack Wilson, Chicago	56
1931	Chuck Klein, Philadelphia	31
1932	Chuck Klein, Philadelphia	38
	Mel Ott, New York	38
1933	Chuck Klein, Philadelphia	28
1934	Mel Ott, New York	35
	Rip Collins, St. Louis	35
1935	Wally Berger, Boston	34
1936	Mel Ott, New York	33
1937	Mel Ott, New York	31
	Joe Medwick, St. Louis	31

American League

1901	Nap Lajoie, Philadelphia	14
1902	Socks Seybold, Philadelphia	16
1903	Buck Freeman, Boston	13
1904	Harry Davis, Philadelphia	10
1905	Harry Davis, Philadelphia	8
1906	Harry Davis, Philadelphia	12
1907	Harry Davis, Philadelphia	8
1908	Sam Crawford, Detroit	7
1909	Ty Cobb, Detroit	9
1910	Jake Stahl, Boston	10
1911	Frank Baker, Philadelphia	9
1912	Frank Baker, Philedelphia	10
	Tris Speaker, Boston	10
1913	Frank Baker, Philadelphia	12
1914	Frank Baker, Philadelphia	8
	Sam Crawford, Detroit	8
1915	Braggo Roth, Chicago-Cleveland	7
1916	Wally Pipp, New York	12
1917	Wally Pipp, New York	9
1918	Babe Ruth, Boston	11
	Clarence Walker, Philadelphia	11
1919	Babe Ruth, Boston	29
1920	Babe Ruth, New York	54
1921	Babe Ruth, New York	59
1922	Ken Williams, St. Louis	39
1923	Babe Ruth, New York	41
1924	Babe Ruth, New York	46
1925	Bob Muesel, New York	33
1926	Babe Ruth, New York	47
1927	Babe Ruth, New York	60
1928	Babe Ruth, New York	54
1929	Babe Ruth, New York	46
1930	Babe Ruth, New York	49
1931	Babe Ruth, New York	46
	Lou Gehrig, New York	46
1932	Jimmy Foxx, Philadelphia	58
1933	Jimmy Foxx, Philadelphia	48
1934	Lou Gehrig, New York	49
1935	Jimmy Foxx, Philadelphia	36
	Hank Greenberg, Detroit	36
1936	Lou Gehrig, New York	49
1937	Joe DiMaggio, New York	46

Home Run Champions—Major League Baseball

National League			American League		
1938	Mel Ott, New York	36	1938	Hank Greenberg, Detroit	58
1939	Johnny Mize, St. Louis	28	1939	Jimmy Foxx, Boston	35
1940	Johnny Mize, St. Louis	43	1940	Hank Greenberg, Detroit	41
1941	Dolph Camilli, Brooklyn	34	1941	Ted Williams, Boston	37
1942	Mel Ott, New York	30	1942	Ted Williams, Boston	36
1943	Bill Nicholson, Chicago	29	1943	Rudy York, Detroit	34
1944	Bill Nicholson, Chicago	33	1944	Nick Etten, New York	22
1945	Tommy Holmes, Boston	28	1945	Vern Stephens, St. Louis	24
1946	Ralph Kiner, Pittsburgh	23	1946	Hank Greenberg, Detroit	44
1947	Ralph Kiner, Pittsburgh	51	1947	Ted Williams, Boston	32
	Johnny Mize, New York	51			
1948	Ralph Kiner, Pittsburgh	40	1948	Joe DiMaggio, New York	39
	Johnny Mize, New York	40			
1949	Ralph Kiner, Pittsburgh	54	1949	Ted Williams, Boston	43
1950	Ralph Kiner, Pittsburgh	47	1950	Al Rosen, Cleveland	37
1951	Ralph Kiner, Pittsburgh	42	1951	Gus Zernial, Chicago-Philadelphia	33
1952	Ralph Kiner, Pittsburgh	37	1952	Larry Doby, Cleveland	32
	Hank Sauer, Chicago	37			
1953	Eddie Mathews, Milwaukee	47	1953	Al Rosen, Cleveland	43
1954	Ted Kluszewski, Cincinnati	49	1954	Larry Doby, Cleveland	32
1955	Willie Mays, New York	51	1955	Mickey Mantle, New York	37
1956	Duke Snider, Brooklyn	43	1956	Mickey Mantle, New York	52
1957	Hank Aaron, Milwaukee	44	1957	Roy Sievers, Washington	42
1958	Ernie Banks, Chicago	47	1958	Mickey Mantle, New York	42
1959	Eddie Mathews, Milwaukee	48	1959	Rocky Colavito, Cleveland	42
				Harmon Killebrew, Washington	42
1960	Ernie Banks, Chicago	41	1960	Mickey Mantle, New York	40
1961	Orlando Cepeda, San Francisco	46	1961	Roger Maris, New York	61
1962	Willie Mays, San Francisco	49	1962	Harmon Killebrew, Minnesota	48
1963	Hank Aaron, Milwaukee	44	1963	Harmon Killebrew, Minnesota	45
	Willie McCovey, San Francisco	44			
1964	Willie Mays, San Francisco	47	1964	Harmon Killebrew, Minnesota	49
1965	Willie Mays, San Francisco	52	1965	Tony Conigliaro, Boston	32
1966	Hank Aaron, Atlanta	44	1966	Frank Robinson, Baltimore	49
1967	Hank Aaron, Atlanta	39	1967	Carl Yastrzemski, Boston	44
				Harmon Killebrew, Minnesota	44
1968	Willie McCovey, San Francisco	36	1968	Frank Howard, Washington	44
1969	Willie McCovey, San Francisco	45	1969	Harmon Killebrew, Minnesota	49
1970	Johnny Bench, Cincinnati	45	1970	Frank Howard, Washington	44
1971	Willie Stargell, Pittsburgh	48	1971	Bill Melton, Chicago	33
1972	Johnny Bench, Cincinnati	40	1972	Dick Allen, Chicago	37
1973	Willie Stargell, Pittsburgh	44	1973	Reggie Jackson, Oakland	32
1974	Mike Schmidt, Philadelphia	36	1974	Dick Allen, Chicago	32
1975	Mike Schmidt, Philadelphia	38	1975	Reggie Jackson, Oakland	36
				George Scott, Milwaukee	36
1976	Mike Schmidt, Philadelphia	38	1976	Graig Nettles, New York	32
1977	George Foster, Cincinnati	52	1977	Jim Rice, Boston	39
1978	George Foster, Cincinnati	40	1978	Jim Rice, Boston	46
1979	Dave Kingman, Chicago	48	1979	Gorman Thomas, Milwaukee	45

Home Run Champions—Major League Baseball

National League			American League		
1980	Mike Schmidt, Philadelphia	48	1980	Reggie Jackson, New York	41
				Ben Oglivie	41
1981	Mike Schmidt, Philadelphia	31	1981	Tony Armas, Oakland	22
				Dwight Evans, Boston	22
				Bobby Grich, California	22
				Eddie Murray, Baltimore	22
1982	Dave Kingman, New York	37	1982	Reggie Jackson, California	39
				Gorman Thomas, Milwaukee	39

Runs-Batted-In Leaders—Major League Baseball

National League			American League		
1901	Honus Wagner, Pittsburgh	126	1901	Nap Lajoie, Philadelphia	125
1902	Honus Wagner, Pittsburgh	91	1902	Buck Freeman, Boston	121
1903	Sam Mertes, New York	104	1903	Buck Freeman, Boston	104
1904	Bill Dahlen, New York	80	1904	Nap Lajoie, Cleveland	102
1905	Cy Seymour, Cincinnati	121	1905	Harry Davis, Philadelphia	83
1906	Harry Steinfeldt, Chicago	83	1906	Harry Davis, Philadelphia	96
	Jim Nealon, Pittsburgh	83			
1907	Sherry Magee, Philadelphia	85	1907	Ty Cobb, Detroit	116
1908	Honus Wagner, Pittsburgh	109	1908	Ty Cobb, Detroit	101
1909	Honus Wagner, Pittsburgh	100	1909	Ty Cobb, Detroit	115
1910	Sherry Magee, Philadelphia	123	1910	Sam Crawford, Detroit	120
1911	Wildfire Schulte, Chicago	121	1911	Ty Cobb, Detroit	144
1912	Heinie Zimmerman, Chicago	103	1912	Frank Baker, Philadelphia	133
1913	Gavvy Cravath, Philadelphia	128	1913	Frank Baker, Philadelphia	126
1914	Sherry Magee, Philadelphia	101	1914	Sam Crawford, Detroit	112
1915	Gavvy Cravath, Philadelphia	118	1915	Sam Crawford, Detroit	116
1916	Hal Chase, Cincinnati	84	1916	Wally Pipp, New York	99
1917	Heinie Zimmerman, New York	100	1917	Robert Veach, Detroit	115
1918	Fred Merkle, Chicago	71	1918	George Burns, Philadelphia	74
				Bobby Veach, Detroit	74
1919	Hy Myers, Brooklyn	72	1919	Babe Ruth, Boston	112
1920	George Kelly, New York	94	1920	Babe Ruth, New York	137
	Rogers Hornsby, St. Louis	94			
1921	Rogers Hornsby, St. Louis	126	1921	Babe Ruth, New York	170
1922	Rogers Hornsby, St. Louis	152	1922	Ken Williams, St. Louis	155
1923	Irish Meusel, New York	125	1923	Tris Speaker, Cleveland	130
				Babe Ruth, New York	130
1924	George Kelly, New York	136	1924	Goose Goslin, Washington	129
1925	Rogers Hornsby, St. Louis	143	1925	Bob Muesel, New York	138
1926	Jim Bottomley, St. Louis	120	1926	Babe Ruth, New York	145
1927	Paul Waner, Pittsburgh	131	1927	Lou Gehrig, New York	175
1928	Jim Bottomley, St. Louis	136	1928	Babe Ruth, New York	142
				Lou Gehrig, New York	142

Runs-Batted-In Leaders—Major League Baseball

	National League			American League	
1929	Hack Wilson, Chicago	159	1929	Al Simmons, Philadelphia	157
1930	Hack Wilson, Chicago	190	1930	Lou Gehrig, New York	174
1931	Chuck Klein, Philadelphia	121	1931	Lou Gehrig, New York	184
1932	Don Hurst, Philadelphia	143	1932	Jimmy Foxx, Philadelphia	169
1933	Chuck Klein, Philadelphia	120	1933	Jimmy Foxx, Philadelphia	163
1934	Mel Ott, New York	135	1934	Lou Gehrig, New York	165
1935	Wally Berger, Boston	130	1935	Hank Greenberg, Detroit	170
1936	Joe Medwick, St. Louis	138	1936	Hal Trosky, Cleveland	162
1937	Joe Medwick, St. Louis	154	1937	Hank Greenberg, Detroit	170
1938	Joe Medwick, St. Louis	122	1938	Jimmy Foxx, Boston	175
1939	Frank McCormick, Cincinnati	128	1939	Ted Williams, Boston	145
1940	Johnny Mize, St. Louis	137	1940	Hank Greenberg, Detroit	150
1941	Dolph Camilli, Brooklyn	120	1941	Joe DiMaggio, New York	125
1942	Johnny Mize, New York	110	1942	Ted Williams, Boston	137
1943	Bill Nicholson, Chicago	128	1943	Rudy York, Detroit	118
1944	Bill Nicholson, Chicago	122	1944	Vern Stephens, St. Louis	109
1945	Dixie Walker, Brooklyn	124	1945	Nick Etten, New York	111
1946	Enos Slaughter, St. Louis	130	1946	Hank Greenberg, Detroit	127
1947	Johnny Mize, New York	138	1947	Ted Williams, Boston	114
1948	Stan Musial, St. Louis	131	1948	Joe DiMaggio, New York	155
1949	Ralph Kiner, Pittsburgh	127	1949	Ted Williams, Boston	159
				Vern Stephens, Boston	159
1950	Del Ennis, Philadelphia	126	1950	Vern Stephens, Boston	144
				Walt Dropo, Boston	144
1951	Monte Irvin, New York	121	1951	Gus Zernial, Chicago-Philadelphia	129
1952	Hank Sauer, Chicago	121	1952	Al Rosen, Cleveland	105
1953	Roy Campanella, Brooklyn	142	1953	Al Rosen, Cleveland	145
1954	Ted Kluszewski, Cincinnati	141	1954	Larry Doby, Cleveland	126
1955	Duke Snider, Brooklyn	136	1955	Ray Boone, Detroit	116
				Jackie Jensen, Boston	116
1956	Stan Musial, St. Louis	109	1956	Mickey Mantle, New York	130
1957	Hank Aaron, Milwaukee	132	1957	Roy Sievers, Washington	114
1958	Ernie Banks, Chicago	129	1958	Jackie Jensen, Boston	122
1959	Ernie Banks, Chicago	143	1959	Jackie Jensen, Boston	112
1960	Hank Aaron, Milwaukee	126	1960	Roger Maris, New York	112
1961	Orlando Cepeda, San Francisco	142	1961	Roger Maris, New York	142
1962	Tommy Davis, Los Angeles	153	1962	Harmon Killebrew, Minnesota	126
1963	Hank Aaron, Milwaukee	130	1963	Dick Stuart, Boston	118
1964	Ken Boyer, St. Louis	119	1964	Brooks Robinson, Baltimore	118
1965	Deron Johnson, Cincinnati	130	1965	Rocky Colavito, Cleveland	108
1966	Hank Aaron, Atlanta	121	1966	Frank Robinson, Baltimore	122
1967	Orlando Cepeda, St. Louis	111	1967	Carl Yastrzemski, Boston	121
1968	Willie McCovey, San Francisco	105	1968	Ken Harrelson, Boston	109
1969	Willie McCovey, San Francisco	126	1969	Harmon Killebrew, Minnesota	140
1970	Johnny Bench, Cincinnati	148	1970	Frank Howard, Washington	126
1971	Joe Torre, St. Louis	137	1971	Harmon Killebrew, Minnesota	119
1972	Johnny Bench, Cincinnati	125	1972	Dick Allen, Chicago	113
1973	Willie Stargell, Pittsburgh	119	1973	Reggie Jackson, Oakland	117

Runs-Batted-In Leaders—Major League Baseball

National League			American League		
1974	Johnny Bench, Cincinnati	129	1974	Jeff Burroughs, Texas	118
1975	Greg Luzinski, Philadelphia	120	1975	George Scott, Milwaukee	109
1976	George Foster, Cincinnati	121	1976	Lee May, Baltimore	109
1977	George Foster, Cincinnati	149	1977	Larry Hisle, Minnesota	119
1978	George Foster, Cincinnati	120	1978	Jim Rice, Boston	139
1979	Dave Winfield, San Diego	118	1979	Don Baylor, California	139
1980	Mike Schmidt, Philadelphia	121	1980	Cecil Cooper, Milwaukee	122
1981	Mike Schmidt, Philadelphia	91	1981	Eddie Murray, Baltimore	78
1982	Dale Murphy, Atlanta	109	1982	Hal McRae, Kansas City	133
	Al Oliver, Montreal	109			

Slugging Average Leaders—Major League Baseball

National League			American League		
1901	Jimmy Sheckard, Brooklyn	.541	1901	Nap Lajoie, Philadelphia	.635
1902	Honus Wagner, Pittsburgh	.467	1902	Ed Delahanty, Washington	.589
1903	Fred Clarke, Pittsburgh	.532	1903	Nap Lajoie, Cleveland	.533
1904	Honus Wagner, Pittsburgh	.520	1904	Nap Lajoie, Cleveland	.549
1905	Cy Seymour, Cincinnati	.559	1905	Elmer Flick, Cleveland	.466
1906	Harry Lumley, Brooklyn	.477	1906	George Stone, St. Louis	.496
1907	Honus Wagner, Pittsburgh	.513	1907	Ty Cobb, Detroit	.473
1908	Honus Wagner, Pittsburgh	.542	1908	Ty Cobb, Detroit	.475
1909	Honus Wagner, Pittsburgh	.489	1909	Ty Cobb, Detroit	.517
1910	Sherry Magee, Philadelphia	.507	1910	Ty Cobb, Detroit	.554
1911	Frank Schulte, Chicago	.534	1911	Ty Cobb, Detroit	.621
1912	Heinie Zimmerman, Chicago	.571	1912	Ty Cobb, Detroit	.586
1913	Gavvy Cravath, Philadelphia	.568	1913	Joe Jackson, Cleveland	.551
1914	Sherry Magee, Philadelphia	.509	1914	Ty Cobb, Detroit	.513
1915	Gavvy Cravath, Philadelphia	.510	1915	Jacques Fournier, Chicago	.491
1916	Zack Wheat, Brooklyn	.461	1916	Tris Speaker, Cleveland	.502
1917	Rogers Hornsby, St. Louis	.484	1917	Ty Cobb, Detroit	.571
1918	Edd Roush, Cincinnati	.455	1918	Babe Ruth, Boston	.555
1919	Hy Myers, Brooklyn	.436	1919	Babe Ruth, Boston	.657
1920	Rogers Hornsby, St. Louis	.559	1920	Babe Ruth, New York	.847
1921	Rogers Hornsby, St. Louis	.659	1921	Babe Ruth, New York	.846
1922	Rogers Hornsby, St. Louis	.722	1922	Babe Ruth, New York	.672
1923	Rogers Hornsby, St. Louis	.627	1923	Babe Ruth, New York	.764
1924	Rogers Hornsby, St. Louis	.696	1924	Babe Ruth, New York	.739
1925	Rogers Hornsby, St. Louis	.756	1925	Ken Williams, St. Louis	.613
1926	Fred Williams, Philadelphia	.569	1926	Babe Ruth, New York	.737
1927	Chick Hafey, St. Louis	.590	1927	Babe Ruth, New York	.772
1928	Rogers Hornsby, Boston	.632	1928	Babe Ruth, New York	.709
1929	Rogers Hornsby, Chicago	.679	1929	Babe Ruth, New York	.697
1930	Hack Wilson, Chicago	.723	1930	Babe Ruth, New York	.732
1931	Chuck Klein, Philadelphia	.584	1931	Babe Ruth, New York	.700
1932	Chuck Klein, Philadelphia	.646	1932	Jimmy Foxx, Philadelphia	.749

Slugging Average Leaders—Major League Baseball

National League			American League		
1933	Chuck Klein, Philadelphia	.602	1933	Jimmy Foxx, Philadelphia	.703
1934	Rip Collins, St. Louis	.615	1934	Lou Gehrig, New York	.706
1935	Arky Vaughan, Pittsburgh	.607	1935	Jimmy Fox, Philadelphia	.636
1936	Mel Ott, New York	.588	1936	Lou Gehrig, New York	.696
1937	Joe Medwick, St. Louis	.641	1937	Joe DiMaggio, New York	.673
1938	Johnny Mize, St. Louis	.614	1938	Jimmy Foxx, Boston	.704
1939	Johnny Mize, St. Louis	.626	1939	Jimmy Foxx, Boston	.694
1940	Johnny Mize, St. Louis	.636	1940	Hank Greenberg, Detroit	.670
1941	Pete Reiser, Brooklyn	.558	1941	Ted Williams, Boston	.735
1942	Johnny Mize, New York	.521	1942	Ted Williams, Boston	.648
1943	Stan Musial, St. Louis	.562	1943	Rudy York, Detroit	.527
1944	Stan Musial, St. Louis	.549	1944	Bobby Doerr, Boston	.528
1945	Tommy Holmes, Boston	.577	1945	George Stirnweiss, New York	.476
1946	Stan Musial, St. Louis	.587	1946	Ted Williams, Boston	.667
1947	Ralph Kiner, Pittsburgh	.639	1947	Ted Williams, Boston	.634
1948	Stan Musial, St. Louis	.702	1948	Ted Williams, Boston	.615
1949	Ralph Kiner, Pittsburgh	.658	1949	Ted Williams, Boston	.650
1950	Stan Musial, St. Louis	.596	1950	Joe DiMaggio, New York	.585
1951	Ralph Kiner, Pittsburgh	.627	1951	Ted Williams, Boston	.556
1952	Stan Musial, St. Louis	.538	1952	Larry Doby, Cleveland	.541
1953	Duke Snider, Brooklyn	.627	1953	Al Rosen, Cleveland	.613
1954	Willie Mays, New York	.667	1954	Ted Williams, Boston	.635
1955	Willie Mays, New York	.659	1955	Mickey Mantle, New York	.611
1956	Duke Snider, Brooklyn	.598	1956	Mickey Mantle, New York	.705
1957	Willie Mays, New York	.626	1957	Ted Williams, Boston	.731
1958	Ernie Banks, Chicago	.614	1958	Rocky Colavito, Cleveland	.620
1959	Hank Aaron, Milwaukee	.636	1959	Al Kaline, Detroit	.530
1960	Frank Robinson, Cincinnati	.595	1960	Roger Maris, New York	.581
1961	Frank Robinson, Cincinnati	.611	1961	Mickey Mantle, New York	.687
1962	Frank Robinson, Cincinnati	.624	1962	Mickey Mantle, New York	.605
1963	Hank Aaron, Milwaukee	.586	1963	Harmon Killebrew, Minnesota	.555
1964	Willie Mays, San Francisco	.607	1964	Boog Powell, Baltimore	.606
1965	Willie Mays, San Francisco	.645	1965	Carl Yastrzemski, Boston	.536
1966	Dick Allen, Philadelphia	.632	1966	Frank Robinson, Baltimore	.637
1967	Hank Aaron, Atlanta	.573	1967	Carl Yastrzemski, Boston	.622
1968	Willie McCovey, San Francisco	.545	1968	Frank Howard, Washington	.552
1969	Willie McCovey, San Francisco	.656	1969	Reggie Jackson, Oakland	.608
1970	Willie McCovey, San Francisco	.612	1970	Carl Yastrzemski, Boston	.592
1971	Hank Aaron, Atlanta	.669	1971	Tony Oliva, Minnesota	.546
1972	Billy Williams, Chicago	.606	1972	Dick Allen, Chicago	.603
1973	Willie Stargell, Pittsburgh	.646	1973	Reggie Jackson, Oakland	.531
1974	Mike Schmidt, Philadelphia	.546	1974	Dick Allen, Chicago	.563
1975	Dave Parker, Pittsburgh	.541	1975	Fred Lynn, Boston	.566
1976	Joe Morgan, Cincinnati	.576	1976	Reggie Jackson, Baltimore	.502
1977	George Foster, Cincinnati	.631	1977	Jim Rice, Boston	.593
1978	Dave Parker, Pittsburgh	.585	1978	Jim Rice, Boston	.600
1979	Dave Kingman, Chicago	.613	1979	Fred Lynn, Boston	.637
1980	Mike Schmidt, Philadelphia	.624	1980	George Brett, Kansas City	.664
1981	Mike Schmidt, Philadelphia	.644	1981	Bobby Grich, California	.543
1982	Mike Schmidt, Philadelphia	.547	1982	Robin Yount, Milwaukee	.578

PRACTICE

Women—Education, Employment, Income

The following four tables give information on the education, employment, and income of women from 1960 to 1980. Your task is to use these materials as the basis for an argument. The thesis you present should involve the change or lack of change over this twenty-year period, and it should be supported by citations from the data provided.

First look at the data with some care, testing out possible theses as you check them through from table to table. The basic possibilities open to you with this relatively limited body of data are simple. The status of women has improved, deteriorated, or remained the same—these are the essential positions. A more complex thesis might argue yes and no; that is, the situation of women has changed with respect to one thing and remained the same with respect to another thing.

The more time you spend interpreting the statistics, the more complex and interesting your discussion will be. You should try to translate the statistics into human terms. For example, what advice would you give to a young woman about to graduate from high school who is interested in a clerical career, and is trying to decide whether to seek full-time clerical work or to enroll in a community college? Table 1 shows a continuing increase in the educational attainment of both men and women from 1960 to 1980. While a larger percentage of women (44.8%) completed high school than men (36.8%) in 1980, a larger percentage of men (20.5%) completed four years of college than women (15.5%). Table 2, which gives the educational attainment of men and women in various occupations, shows a larger percentage of male clerical workers with college education. In Table 3, we can see that from 1960 to 1981, women dominated the clerical sector of the labor force; in 1981, 80.5% of all clerical workers were women. Table 4 shows that in the same period, the earnings of women clerical workers *decreased* in proportion to the earnings of male clerical workers.

To advise the high school student, you might conjecture that the men's higher educational attainment is the reason for the discrepancy in salaries, and that the young woman would be better off if she furthered her education. But what if she asked you if the same disparities in pay and education exist in other occupations? Would she be better off in an occupation where the numerical proportions of male and female workers were more equal? You consult your tables. . . .

Remember, this is not the place for emotional persuasion. Nor should you need to bring additional data to bear on the question unless specifically invited to do so by your instructor. The best papers will make the richest possible use of this limited body of material to make an argument that is not obvious, but is nonetheless justified by the data being used.

TABLE 1 **Educational Attainment of the Population, 25 Years of Age and Over by Year and Sex (Percent)**

Educational Attainment	1960		1970		1979	
	M	**F**	**M**	**F**	**M**	**F**
No School	2.4	2.1	1.6	1.6	—	—
Elementary: 1–4 years	7.0	5.2	4.4	3.4	1.6	0.9
5–7 years	14.6	13.1	10.5	9.5	3.5	2.3
8 years	17.8	17.3	12.9	12.6	5.1	3.4
High School: 1–3 years	18.7	19.7	18.6	20.0	14.9	14.8
4 years	21.2	27.7	27.8	34.1	36.8	44.8
College: 1–3 years	8.6	9.0	10.6	10.7	17.6	18.2
4 years	9.6	5.8	13.5	8.1	20.5	15.5
Median Years Completed	10.3	10.9	12.1	12.1	12.7	12.6

Source: U.S. Bureau of the Census, 1960 Census, Subject Reports, *Educational Attainment,* Table 1, pp. 1, 3; 1970 Census, Subject Reports, *Educational Attainment,* Table 1, pp. 3, 6. For 1979: Bureau of Labor Statistics, Special Report 240.

TABLE 2 Educational Attainment of the Population, 16 Years of Age and Over by Sex in Selected Occupations, March, 1979

OCCUPATION AND SEX	TOTAL EMPLOYED (THOUSANDS)	TOTAL	ELEMENTARY			HIGH SCHOOL		COLLEGE			MEDIAN SCHOOL YEARS COMPLETED
			LESS THAN 5 YEARS[1]	5 TO 7	8	1 TO 3	4	1 TO 3	4	5 OR MORE	
BOTH SEXES											
ALL OCCUPATIONAL GROUPS	95,387	100.0	1.3	3.0	4.4	14.9	40.1	17.9	10.6	7.8	12.7
PROFESSIONAL, TECHNICAL, AND KINDRED WORKERS	15,310	100.0	0.1	0.1	0.3	1.8	13.7	19.3	30.4	34.3	16.5
MANAGERS AND ADMINISTRATORS, EXCEPT FARM	10,389	100.0	0.3	1.1	2.3	7.0	34.3	22.9	19.8	12.3	13.7
SALES WORKERS	6,022	100.0	0.2	1.0	2.3	12.8	38.7	24.7	15.8	4.4	12.9
CLERICAL AND KINDRED WORKERS	17,543	100.0	0.1	0.4	1.2	9.2	56.1	24.3	7.0	1.6	12.7
CRAFT AND KINDRED WORKERS	12,315	100.0	1.2	4.0	6.4	17.6	50.4	16.1	3.4	0.9	12.4
OPERATIVES, EXCEPT TRANSPORT	10,803	100.0	2.7	7.0	9.1	24.6	45.9	8.9	1.4	0.3	12.1
TRANSPORT EQUIPMENT OPERATIVES	3,488	100.0	1.5	5.5	8.4	24.4	45.2	12.2	2.0	0.8	12.2
LABORERS, EXCEPT FARM	4,169	100.0	4.5	6.1	7.4	28.2	40.8	11.0	1.4	0.5	12.1
PRIVATE HOUSEHOLD WORKERS	1,119	100.0	7.2	9.4	10.3	37.4	27.5	6.9	1.2	0.2	10.8
SERVICE WORKERS, EXCEPT PRIVATE HOUSEHOLD	11,767	100.0	2.3	4.8	6.5	25.9	40.8	15.5	3.3	0.9	12.3
FARM WORKERS	2,462	100.0	6.3	9.1	11.8	19.6	36.8	9.7	5.0	1.7	12.1
MEN											
ALL OCCUPATIONAL GROUPS	55,237	100.0	1.6	3.5	5.1	14.9	36.8	17.6	11.3	9.2	12.7
PROFESSIONAL, TECHNICAL, AND KINDRED WORKERS	8,679	100.0	0.1	0.1	0.3	1.7	11.9	18.3	28.0	39.6	16.6
ENGINEERS	1,367	100.0	—	0.1	0.3	1.5	10.6	18.1	44.0	25.4	16.4
MEDICAL AND OTHER HEALTH WORKERS	946	100.0	—	—	0.4	1.1	5.1	12.3	13.1	68.1	18.2
PHYSICIANS, DENTISTS AND RELATED PRACTITIONERS	666	100.0	—	—	—	—	1.2	1.5	8.4	89.0	18.4
HEALTH WORKERS, EXCEPT PRACTIONERS	281	100.0	—	—	1.2	3.8	14.3	37.9	24.4	18.4	18.4
TEACHERS, EXCEPT COLLEGE	980	100.0	0.2	—	0.7	0.7	3.1	4.0	35.9	55.4	17.3
ENGINEERING AND SCIENCE TECHNICIANS	850	100.0	—	0.2	0.7	4.1	33.0	44.9	10.7	6.5	13.9
OTHER PROFESSIONAL, TECHNICAL, AND KINDRED WORKERS	4,536	100.0	0.1	0.2	0.3	1.5	11.7	17.6	27.8	40.8	16.7
MANAGERS AND ADMINISTRATORS, EXCEPT FARM	7,886	100.0	0.3	1.2	2.4	7.0	31.3	23.0	21.5	13.2	14.1
SALARIED WORKERS	6,504	100.0	0.2	0.7	1.6	5.6	30.0	23.6	23.6	14.7	14.4
SELF-EMPLOYED WORKERS IN RETAIL TRADE	582	100.0	1.1	3.3	6.4	15.7	39.4	17.0	14.0	3.2	12.6
SELF-EMPLOYED WORKERS, EXCEPT RETAIL TRADE	801	100.0	1.0	3.7	6.3	11.9	36.5	22.1	10.5	8.0	12.7
SALES WORKERS	3,335	100.0	0.2	0.8	2.4	8.4	31.7	27.6	22.5	6.4	13.6
RETAIL TRADE	1,181	100.0	0.4	1.2	3.6	15.0	39.8	28.9	8.5	2.8	12.8
OTHER SALES WORKERS	2,154	100.0	0.1	0.6	1.7	4.7	27.3	26.9	30.1	8.5	14.5
CLERICAL AND KINDRED WORKERS	3,354	100.0	0.3	1.0	2.8	9.4	42.4	28.3	12.6	3.2	12.9
BOOKKEEPERS	160	100.0	—	—	—	5.0	34.0	31.0	21.1	5.4	13.7
OFFICE MACHINE OPERATORS	211	100.0	—	1.1	—	6.0	48.0	27.2	12.7	1.2	12.9
STENOGRAPHERS, TYPISTS, AND SECRETARIES	85	100.0	—	1.7	8.9	—	21.2	27.8	21.5	15.7	14.5
OTHER CLERICAL WORKERS	2,899	100.0	0.3	1.0	3.0	10.1	43.1	27.8	11.9	2.9	12.8
CRAFT AND KINDRED WORKERS	11,617	100.0	1.2	4.1	6.5	17.2	50.6	16.2	3.3	0.8	12.4
CARPENTERS	1,164	100.0	2.1	5.8	8.1	17.1	46.4	14.6	4.1	1.9	12.3
OTHER CONSTRUCTION CRAFTWORKERS	2,355	100.0	1.6	4.9	9.0	19.0	49.4	13.9	1.7	0.3	12.3
BLUE-COLLAR WORKER SUPERVISORS, NOT ELSEWHERE CLASSIFIED	1,457	100.0	0.8	4.0	4.6	15.8	48.8	17.9	7.3	0.8	12.5
METAL CRAFT WORKERS	1,221	100.0	0.6	2.7	6.5	16.2	57.6	14.0	1.8	0.7	12.4
MACHINISTS AND JOB-SETTERS	632	100.0	0.5	2.4	6.9	18.2	55.7	13.0	2.8	0.5	12.4
METAL CRAFT WORKERS EXCEPT MECHANICS, MACHINISTS, AND JOB-SETTERS	589	100.0	0.7	3.0	6.0	13.9	59.6	15.1	0.8	0.9	12.3
MECHANICS AND REPAIRERS	3,375	100.0	1.5	3.9	6.5	18.9	49.8	17.4	2.2	0.4	12.3
MECHANICS, AUTOMOBILE	1,264	100.0	4.0	4.4	6.3	24.7	49.2	20.7	1.7	0.3	12.3
MECHANICS, EXCEPT AUTOMOBILE	2,111	100.0	0.6	3.7	6.6	15.3	50.2	20.7	2.5	0.4	12.5

Occupation	Number (thousands)	Total	<5 yrs	5–7 yrs	8 yrs	HS 1–3	HS 4	Coll 1–3	Coll 4	Coll 5+	Median
MINE WORKERS	242	100.0	0.7	4.3	9.1	18.9	51.7	11.0	3.4	1.0	12.3
DURABLE GOODS MANUFACTURING	3,406	100.0	2.7	5.8	8.2	21.1	49.1	11.6	1.2	0.4	12.3
NONDURABLE GOODS MANUFACTURING	1,378	100.0	2.9	8.4	8.9	18.7	46.8	12.5	1.6	0.5	12.2
ALL OTHER	1,534	100.0	3.0	5.5	7.9	29.9	41.0	10.9	1.6	0.3	12.1
TRANSPORT EQUIPMENT OPERATIVES	3,230	100.0	1.6	5.6	8.9	24.7	44.7	11.7	2.0	0.8	12.2
DRIVERS AND DELIVERY WORKERS	2,708	100.0	1.6	5.4	6.0	24.4	44.4	12.1	2.1	–	12.2
ALL OTHER	521	100.0	1.5	6.6	7.6	26.1	46.1	12.1	1.7	0.6	12.1
LABORERS, EXCEPT FARM	3,691	100.0	4.9	6.5	7.6	28.3	39.6	11.4	1.1	0.6	12.1
PRIVATE HOUSEHOLD WORKERS	26	(²)	(²)	(²)	(²)	(²)	(²)	(²)	(²)	(²)	(²)
SERVICE WORKERS, EXCEPT PRIVATE HOUSEHOLD	4,779	100.0	3.4	5.5	6.5	25.3	35.8	17.3	4.6	1.6	12.3
CLEANING SERVICE	1,606	100.0	5.5	8.5	11.5	27.2	35.8	9.5	1.1	0.9	11.7
FOOD SERVICE	1,387	100.0	4.6	4.8	3.6	39.1	26.1	17.4	3.2	1.3	11.9
HEALTH SERVICE	175	100.0	0.5	5.0	2.5	18.6	36.3	26.1	10.7	3.2	12.6
PERSONAL SERVICE	396	100.0	0.6	5.7	6.4	15.1	46.4	17.1	5.7	3.0	12.5
PROTECTIVE SERVICE	1,214	100.0	–	2.3	3.7	11.3	43.5	26.5	9.6	2.6	12.7
FARM WORKERS	2,078	100.0	6.7	9.9	12.0	19.4	35.9	11.0	5.1	1.5	12.1
FARMERS AND FARM MANAGERS	1,254	100.0	2.7	5.9	12.8	15.2	43.3	11.9	6.1	2.1	12.3
FARM LABORERS AND SUPERVISORS	824	100.0	12.8	15.9	10.7	25.8	24.6	5.6	3.8	0.8	10.3
WOMEN											
ALL OCCUPATIONAL GROUPS	40,150	100.0	0.9	2.3	3.4	14.8	44.8	18.2	9.7	5.8	12.6
PROFESSIONAL, TECHNICAL, AND KINDRED WORKERS	6,631	100.0	–	0.1	0.2	2.1	16.1	20.7	33.6	27.2	16.3
MEDICAL AND OTHER HEALTH WORKERS	1,865	100.0	–	–	0.2	2.6	23.8	36.5	24.3	12.5	15.1
PHYSICIANS, DENTISTS AND RELATED PRACTITIONERS	91	100.0	–	–	1.4	0.7	10.5	3.7	7.2	76.6	(²)
HEALTH WORKERS, EXCEPT PRACTITIONERS	1,774	100.0	–	–	0.1	2.7	24.5	38.2	25.7	9.3	15.0
TEACHERS, EXCEPT COLLEGE	2,340	100.0	–	–	0.2	1.0	5.6	7.2	47.7	38.3	15.8
ENGINEERING AND SCIENCE TECHNICIANS	164	100.0	–	0.2	1.0	4.8	43.4	33.9	12.9	4.1	13.1
OTHER PROFESSIONAL, TECHNICAL, AND KINDRED WORKERS	2,262	100.0	0.2	–	0.3	2.6	18.6	20.5	28.1	29.7	16.3
MANAGERS AND ADMINISTRATORS, EXCEPT FARM	2,503	100.0	0.2	1.1	1.7	7.1	43.7	22.7	14.3	9.4	12.9
SALARIED WORKERS	2,148	100.0	–	0.5	1.2	5.6	44.3	23.5	15.0	9.9	13.0
SELF-EMPLOYED WORKERS	355	100.0	1.1	4.2	4.9	15.9	40.0	18.2	9.7	6.1	12.6
SALES WORKERS	2,687	100.0	0.3	1.7	2.3	18.2	47.3	21.1	7.5	1.9	12.6
RETAIL TRADE	1,941	100.0	0.3	3.7	2.9	21.9	48.7	19.1	4.4	4.4	12.5
OTHER SALES WORKERS	746	100.0	0.1	0.5	0.7	8.5	43.7	26.4	15.8	4.3	12.9
CLERICAL AND KINDRED WORKERS	14,189	100.0	0.1	0.3	0.9	9.2	59.3	23.4	5.7	1.2	12.7
BOOKKEEPERS	1,784	100.0	–	0.2	0.5	5.9	64.8	22.7	4.7	1.3	12.7
OFFICE MACHINE OPERATORS	694	100.0	–	0.2	0.3	7.4	65.6	21.0	4.5	1.0	12.6
STENOGRAPHERS, TYPISTS, AND SECRETARIES	4,873	100.0	0.3	–	0.3	5.1	60.3	27.0	6.0	1.1	12.6
OTHER CLERICAL WORKERS	6,837	100.0	0.1	0.5	1.4	13.2	56.6	21.2	5.8	1.1	12.6
CRAFT AND KINDRED WORKERS	699	100.0	1.3	2.0	5.1	23.5	46.4	15.0	4.8	1.9	12.4
OPERATIVES, EXCEPT TRANSPORT	4,242	100.0	2.9	8.4	10.2	27.8	44.6	4.8	1.2	0.2	12.0
DURABLE GOODS MANUFACTURING	1,760	100.0	2.3	5.0	8.0	27.6	49.1	5.3	1.2	0.3	12.1
NONDURABLE GOODS MANUFACTURING	1,836	100.0	2.8	11.4	12.4	26.5	42.1	6.4	1.0	–	11.7
ALL OTHER	646	100.0	4.8	8.9	10.4	28.1	39.7	6.4	1.4	0.3	11.8
TRANSPORT EQUIPMENT OPERATIVES	258	100.0	0.2	4.6	1.9	20.3	51.9	15.0	2.2	0.7	12.4
LABORERS, EXCEPT FARM	477	100.0	1.7	3.4	6.1	26.9	50.1	8.1	3.6	0.1	12.2
PRIVATE HOUSEHOLD WORKERS	1,093	100.0	7.3	9.6	10.4	36.7	27.6	7.0	1.2	0.2	10.8
SERVICE WORKERS, EXCEPT PRIVATE HOUSEHOLD	6,988	100.0	1.5	4.3	6.5	26.3	44.2	14.2	2.4	0.5	12.3
CLEANING SERVICE	885	100.0	5.9	8.9	12.2	29.0	37.3	5.5	0.9	0.2	12.5
FOOD SERVICE	3,015	100.0	1.1	3.8	5.9	34.9	41.0	11.1	2.6	0.4	12.1
HEALTH SERVICE	1,615	100.0	0.3	2.8	4.2	16.2	44.0	22.4	5.9	0.4	12.4
PERSONAL SERVICE	1,343	100.0	1.2	4.4	7.9	19.3	49.7	15.6	2.6	0.6	12.4
PROTECTIVE SERVICE	130	100.0	–	0.9	6.6	10.1	43.7	28.1	4.9	2.5	12.2
FARM WORKERS	383	100.0	4.0	5.1	10.7	20.7	41.6	11.0	4.3	2.6	12.2

¹ Includes persons reporting no school years completed.

² Percent and median not shown where base is less than 75,000.

TABLE 3 Women as Percent of Experienced Civilian Labor Force, 14 Years of Age and Over by Occupational Categories 1981, 1970, and 1960

Occupational Category	Percent of Experienced Labor Force		
	1981	1970	1960
Professional, Technical, and Kindred Workers	42.8	40.1	38.1
Managers and Administrators, Except Farm	27.5	16.7	19.5
Sales Workers	45.4	48.9	36.3
Clerical and Kindred Workers	80.5	73.8	67.4
Craftsmen and Kindred Workers	6.3	4.9	2.9
Operatives and Transport	33.4	31.9	28.1
Laborers, Except Farm	11.5	8.2	3.6
Farmers and Farm Managers	11.3	5.1	4.7
Farm Laborers and Farm Foremen	25.5	17.6	17.4
Service Workers, Except Private Household	59.2	55.8	52.5
Private Household Workers	96.5	97.0	96.5
Unemployed or Not Reporting			
Total Number	42,969,916	30,534,658	22,293,172
Percent of Total Experienced Labor Force	42.8	38.1	32.8

Source: Derived from figures presented in the following tables from the U.S. Bureau of the Census: 1960 Census Subject Reports, *Occupational Characteristics*, Table 1, pp. 1–9; 1970 Census, Subject Reports, *Occupational Characteristics,* Table 1, pp. 1–11. For 1979: U.S. Bureau of Labor Statistics.

205

TABLE 4 Median Earnings of the Experienced Labor Force by Occupation for 50–52 Weeks Worked by Sex, 1980, 1970, and 1960

Occupation	1980			1970			1960		
	M	F	F as % of M	M	F	F as % of M	M	F	F as % of M
Total	$18,612	$11,197	60.2	$ 8,633	$4,925	57.0	$5,307	$3,118	58.8
Professional	23,026	15,285	66.4	11,535	7,117	61.7	7,124	4,186	58.8
Managers	23,558	12,936	54.9	11,409	6,207	54.4	6,926	3,800	54.9
Sales Workers	19,910	9,748	49.0	9,634	3,819	39.6	5,639	2,370	42.0
Clerical Workers	18,247	10,997	60.2	8,087	5,260	65.0	5,206	3,546	68.1
Craftsmen	18,671	11,701	62.6	8,762	5,370	61.3	5,699	3,555	62.4
Operatives	15,702	9,440	60.1	7,489	4,386	58.6	4,897	2,911	59.4
Laborers	12,157	9,747	80.2	6,323	4,110	65.0	4,018	2,863	71.3
Farmers and Managers	7,482	*	—	5,328	2,759	51.8	2,458	916	37.3
Farm Laborers	8,402	*	—	3,833	2,651	69.2	1,919	821	42.8
Service Workers	13,097	7,982	60.9	6,582	3,695	56.1	4,012	2,102	52.4
Private Household Workers	*	4,562	—	3,534	1,635	46.3	2,075	922	44.4

Source: 1980, Bureau of Labor Statistics; U.S. Bureau of the Census 1970 Census, Subject Reports *Occupational Characteristics*, Table 15, pp. 280–3; 1960 Census, Subject Reports, *Occupational Characteristics*, Table 16, pp. 232–34.
*1980 figures not available for occupations with fewer than 75,000 workers.

Two Essays on Punishment of Crimes

The following two essays take opposite sides on one of the important issues of our time: the proper treatment of people convicted of crimes. In reading them, you are asked to consider the following questions:

1. How does each author define crime? How does he categorize the relationship between the convicted person, what that person has done, and what should be done to or for that person?
2. What parts of each argument seem most convincing? Why?
3. How would you paraphrase or summarize each argument? What roles do ''definition'' and ''cause-and-effect'' reasoning play in each?
4. Do you think one argument better than the other? Why?
5. Has either changed your mind? If so, how?

Karl Menninger, ''The Crime of Punishment''

Few words in our language arrest our attention as do ''crime,'' ''violence,'' ''revenge,'' and ''injustice.'' We abhor crime; we adore justice; we boast that we live by the rule of law. Violence and vengefulness we repudiate as unworthy of our civilization, and we assume this sentiment to be unanimous among all human beings. 1

Yet crime continues to be a national disgrace and a world-wide problem. It is threatening, alarming, wasteful, expensive, abundant, and apparently increasing! In actuality it is decreasing in frequency of occurrence, but it is certainly increasing in visibility and the reactions of the public to it. 2

Our system for controlling crime is ineffective, unjust, expensive. Prisons seem to operate with revolving doors—the same people going in and out and in and out. *Who cares?* 3

Our city jails and inhuman reformatories and wretched prisons are jammed. They are known to be unhealthy, dangerous, immoral, indecent, crime-breeding dens of iniquity. Not everyone has smelled them, as some of us have. Not many have heard the groans and the curses. Not everyone has seen the hate and despair in a thousand blank, hollow faces. But, in a way, we all know how miserable prisons are. *We want them to be that way.* And they are. *Who cares?* 4

Professional and big-time criminals prosper as never before. 5 **207**
Gambling syndicates flourish. White-collar crime may even exceed
all others, but goes undetected in the majority of cases. We are all
being robbed and we know who the robbers are. They live nearby.
Who cares?

The public filches millions of dollars worth of food and clothing 6
from stores, towels and sheets from hotels, jewelry and knick-knacks
from shops. The public steals, and the same public pays it back in
higher prices. *Who cares?*

Time and time again somebody shouts about this state of affairs, 7
just as I am shouting now. The magazines shout. The newspapers
shout. The television and radio commentators shout (or at least they
"deplore"). Psychologists, sociologists, leading jurists, wardens,
and intelligent police chiefs join the chorus. Governors and mayors
and Congressmen are sometimes heard. They shout that the situation is bad, bad, bad, and getting worse. Some suggested that we
immediately replace obsolete procedures with scientific methods. A
few shout contrary sentiments. Do the clear indications derived from
scientific discovery for appropriate changes continue to fall on deaf
ears? Why is the public so long-suffering, so apathetic, and thereby
so continuingly self-destructive? How many Presidents (and other
citizens) do we have to lose before we do something?

The public behaves as a sick patient does when a dreaded treat- 8
ment is proposed for his ailment. We all know how the aching tooth
may suddenly quiet down in the dentist's office, or the abdominal
pain disappear in the surgeon's examining room. Why should a sufferer seek relief and shun it? Is it merely the fear of the pain of the
treatment? Is it the fear of unknown complications? Is it distrust of
the doctor's ability? All of these, no doubt.

But, as Freud made so incontestably clear, the sufferer is always 9
somewhat deterred by a kind of subversive, internal opposition to
the work of cure. He suffers on the one hand from the pains of his
affliction and yearns to get well. But he suffers at the same time from
traitorous impulses that fight against the accomplishment of any
change in himself, even recovery! Like Hamlet, he wonders whether
it may be better after all to suffer the familiar pains and aches associated with the old method than to face the complications of a new and
strange, even though possibly better, way of handling things.

The inescapable conclusion is that society *wants* crime, *needs* 10
crime, and gains definite satisfactions from the present mishandling
of it! We condemn crime; we punish offenders for it; but we need it.
The crime and punishment ritual is a part of our lives. We need
crimes to wonder at, to enjoy vicariously, to discuss and speculate
about, and to publicly deplore. We need criminals to identify ourselves with, to envy secretly, and to punish stoutly. They do for us

the forbidden, illegal things we *wish* to do, and, like scapegoats of old, they bear the burdens of our displaced guilt and punishment—''the iniquities of us all.'' . . .

Fifty years ago, Winston Churchill declared that the mood and temper of the public in regard to crime and criminals is one of the unfailing tests of the civilization of any country. Judged by this standard, how civilized are we? 11

The chairman of the President's National Crime Commission . . . declared recently that organized crime flourishes in America because enough of the public wants its services, and most citizens are apathetic about its impact. It will continue uncurbed as long as Americans accept it as inevitable and, in some instances, desirable. 12

Are there steps that we can take which will reduce the aggressive stabs and self-destructive lurches of our less well-managing fellow men? Are there ways to prevent and control the grosser violations, other than the clumsy traditional maneuvers which we have inherited? These depend basically upon intimidation and slow-motion torture. We call it punishment, and justify it with our ''feeling.'' We know it doesn't work. 13

Yes, there *are* better ways. There are steps that could be taken; some *are* taken. But we move too slowly. Much better use, it seems to me, could be made of the members of my profession and other behavioral scientists than having them deliver courtroom pronunciamentos. The consistent use of a diagnostic clinic would enable trained workers to lay what they can learn about an offender before the judge who would know best how to implement the recommendation. 14

This would no doubt lead to a transformation of prisons, if not to their total disappearance in their present form and function. Temporary and permanent detention will perhaps always be necessary for a few, especially the professionals, but this could be more effectively and economically performed with new types of ''facility'' (that strange, awkward word for institution). 15

I assume it to be a matter of common and general agreement that our object in all this is to protect the community from a repetition of the offense by the most economical method consonant with our other purposes. Our ''other purposes'' include the desire to prevent these offenses from occurring, to reclaim offenders for social usefulness, if possible, and to detain them in protective custody, if reclamation is *not* possible. But how? 16

The treatment of human failure or dereliction by the infliction of pain is still used and believed in by many nonmedical people. ''Spare the rod and spoil the child'' is still considered wise counsel by many. 17

Whipping is still used by many secondary schoolmasters in England, I am informed, to stimulate study, attention, and the love of learning. Whipping was long a traditional treatment for the "crime" of disobedience on the part of children, pupils, servants, apprentices, employees. And slaves were treated for centuries by flogging for such offenses as weariness, confusion, stupidity, exhaustion, fear, grief, and even overcheerfulness. It was assumed and stoutly defended that these "treatments" cured conditions for which they were administered.

Meanwhile, scientific medicine was acquiring many new healing methods and devices. Doctors can now transplant organs and limbs; they can remove brain tumors and cure incipient cancers; they can halt pneumonia, meningitis, and other infections; they can correct deformities and repair breaks and tears and scars. But these wonderful achievements are accomplished on *willing* subjects, people who voluntarily ask for help by even heroic measures. And the reader will be wondering, no doubt, whether doctors can do anything with or for people who *do not want* to be treated at all, in any way! Can doctors cure willful aberrant behavior? Are we to believe that crime is a *disease* that can be reached by scientific measures? Isn't it merely "natural meanness" that makes all of us do wrong things at times even when we "know better"? And are not self-control, moral stamina, and will power the things needed? Surely there is no medical treatment for the lack of those!

Let me answer this carefully, for much misunderstanding accumulates here. I would say that according to the prevalent understanding of the words, crime is *not* a disease. Neither is it an illness, although I think it *should* be! It *should* be treated, and it could be; but it mostly isn't.

These enigmatic statements are simply explained. Diseases are undesired states of being which have been described and defined by doctors, usually given Greek or Latin appellations, and treated by long-established physical and pharmacological formulae. Illness, on the other hand, is best defined as a state of impaired functioning of such a nature that the public expects the sufferer to repair to the physician for help. The illness may prove to be a disease; more often it is only vague and nameless misery, but something which doctors, not lawyers, teachers, or preachers, are supposed to be able and willing to help.

When the community begins to look upon the expression of aggressive violence as the symptom of an illness or as indicative of illness, it will be because it believes doctors can do something to correct such a condition. At present, some better-informed individuals do believe and expect this. However angry at or sorry for the of-

19

20

21

22

fender, they want him "treated" in an effective way so that he will cease to be a danger to them. And they know that traditional punishment, "treatment-punishment," will not effect this.

What *will?* What effective treatment is there for such violence? It will surely have to begin with motivating or stimulating or arousing in a cornered individual the wish and hope and intention to change his methods of dealing with the realities of life. Can this be done by education, medication, counseling, training? I would answer *yes*. It can be done successfully in a majority of cases, if undertaken in time.

The present penal system and the existing legal philosophy do not stimulate or even expect such a change to take place in the criminal. Yet change is what medical science always aims for. The prisoner, like the doctor's other patients, should emerge from his treatment experience a different person, differently equipped, differently functioning, and headed in a different direction than when he began the treatment.

It is natural for the public to doubt that this can be accomplished with criminals. But remember that the public *used* to doubt that change could be effected in the mentally ill. No one a hundred years ago believed mental illness to be curable. Today *all* people know (or should know) that *mental illness is curable* in the great majority of instances and that the prospects and rapidity of cure are directly related to the availability and intensity of proper treatment.

The forms and techniques of psychiatric treatment used today number in the hundreds. No one patient requires or receives all forms, but each patient is studied with respect to his particular needs, his basic assets, his interests, and his special difficulties. A therapeutic team may embrace a dozen workers—as in a hospital setting—or it may narrow down to the doctor and the spouse. Clergymen, teachers, relatives, friends, and even fellow patients often participate informally but helpfully in the process of readaptation.

All of the participants in this effort to bring about a favorable change in the patient—i.e., in his vital balance and life program—are imbued with what we may call a *therapeutic attitude*. This is one in direct antithesis to attitudes of avoidance, ridicule, scorn, or punitiveness. Hostile feelings toward the subject, however justified by his unpleasant and even destructive behavior, are not in the curriculum of therapy or in the therapist. This does not mean that therapists approve of the offensive and obnoxious behavior of the patient; they distinctly disapprove of it. But they recognize it as symptomatic of continued imbalance and disorganization, which is what they are seeking to change. They distinguish between disapproval, penalty, price, and punishment.

Doctors charge fees; they impose certain "penalties" or prices, ₂₈ **211**
but they have long since put aside primitive attitudes of retaliation
toward offensive patients. A patient may cough in the doctor's face
or may vomit on the office rug; a patient may curse or scream or
even struggle in the extremity of his pain. But these acts are not
"punished." Doctors and nurses have no time or thought for inflicting unnecessary pain even upon patients who may be difficult, dis-
agreeable, provocative, and even dangerous. It is their duty to care
for them, to try to make them well, and to prevent them from doing
themselves or others harm. This requires love, not hate. This is the
deepest meaning of the therapeutic attitude. Every doctor knows
this; every worker in a hospital or clinic knows it (or should).

There is another element in the therapeutic attitude. It is the qual- 29
ity of hopefulness. If no one believes that the patient can get well, if
no one—not even the doctor—has any hope, there probably won't
be any recovery. Hope is just as important as love in the therapeutic
attitude.

"But you were talking about the mentally ill," readers may inter- 30
ject, "those poor, confused, bereft, frightened individuals who
yearn for help from you doctors and nurses. Do you mean to imply
that willfully perverse individuals, our criminals, can be similarly
reached and rehabilitated? Do you really believe that effective treatment of the sort you visualize can be applied to people *who do not
want any help*, who are so willfully vicious, so well aware of the
wrongs they are doing, so lacking in penitence or even common de-
cency that punishment seems to be the only thing left?"

Do I believe there is effective treatment for offenders, and that 31
they *can* be changed? *Most certainly and definitely I do.* Not all cases, to
be sure; there are also some physical afflictions which we cannot
cure at the moment. Some provision has to be made for incurables—
pending new knowledge—and these will include some offenders. But
I believe the majority of them would prove to be curable. The will-
fulness and the viciousness of offenders are part of the thing for
which they have to be treated. These must not thwart the therapeutic attitude.

It is simply not true that most of them are "fully aware" of what 32
they are doing, nor is it true that they want no help from anyone, although some of them say so. Prisoners are individuals: Some want
treatment, some do not. Some don't know what treatment is. Many
are utterly despairing and hopeless. Where treatment is made available in institutions, many prisoners seek it even with the full knowledge that doing so will not lessen their sentences. In some prisons,
seeking treatment by prisoners is frowned upon by the officials.

Various forms of treatment are even now being tried in some pro- 33 gressive courts and prisons over the country—eductional, social, industrial, religious, recreational, and psychological treatment. Socially acceptable behavior, new work-play opportunities, new identity and companion patterns all help toward community reacceptance. Some parole officers and some wardens have been extremely ingenious in developing these modalities of rehabilitation and reconstruction—more than I could list here even if I knew them all. But some are trying. The secret of success in all programs, however, is the replacement of the punitive attitude with a therapeutic attitude.

Offenders with propensities for impulsive and predatory aggression should not be permitted to live among us unrestrained by some kind of social control. *But the great majority of offenders, even "criminals," should never become prisoners if we want to "cure" them.* 34

There are now throughout the country many citizens' action groups and programs for the prevention and control of crime and delinquency. With such attitudes of inquiry and concern, the public could acquire information (and incentive) leading to a change of feeling about crime and criminals. It will discover how unjust is much so-called "justice," how baffled and frustrated many judges are by the ossified rigidity of old-fashioned, obsolete laws and state constitutions which effectively prevent the introduction of sensible procedures to replace useless, harmful ones. 35

I want to proclaim to the public that things are not what it wishes them to be, and will only become so if it will take an interest in the matter and assume some responsibility for its own self-protection. 36

Will the public listen? 37

If the public does become interested, it will realize that we must have more facts, more trial projects, more checked results. It will share the dismay of the President's Commission in finding that no one knows much about even the incidence of crime with any definiteness or statistical accuracy. 38

The average citizen finds it difficult to see how any research would in any way change his mind about a man who brutally murders his children. But just such inconceivably awful acts most dramatically point up the need for research. Why should—how can—a man become so dreadful as that in our culture? How is such a man made? Is it comprehensible that he can be born to become so depraved? 39

There are thousands of questions regarding crime and public protection which deserve scientific study. What makes some individuals maintain their interior equilibrium by one kind of disturbance of the social structure rather than by another kind, one that would have landed him in a hospital? Why do some individuals specialize in certain types of crime? Why do so many young people reared in areas 40 of delinquency and poverty and bad example never become habitual delinquents? (Perhaps this is a more important question than why some of them do.)

The public has a fascination for violence, and clings tenaciously to its yen for vengeance, blind and deaf to the expense, futility, and dangerousness of the resulting penal system. But we are bound to hope that this will yield in time to the persistent, penetrating light of intelligence and accumulating scientific knowledge. The public will grow increasingly ashamed of its cry for retaliation, its persistent demand to punish. This is its crime, *our* crime against criminals—and, incidentally, our crime against ourselves. For before we can diminish our sufferings from the ill-controlled aggressive assaults of fellow citizens, we must renounce the philosophy of punishment, the obsolete, vengeful penal attitude. In its place we would seek a comprehensive constructive social attitude—therapeutic in some instances, restraining in some instances, but preventive in its total social impact. 41

In the last analysis this becomes a question of personal morals and values. No matter how glorified or how piously disguised, vengeance as a human motive must be personally repudiated by each and every one of us. This is the message of old religions and new psychiatries. Unless this message is heard, unless we, the people—the man on the street, the housewife in the home—can give up our delicious satisfactions in opportunities for vengeful retaliation on scapegoats, we cannot expect to preserve our peace, our public safety, or our mental health. 42

C. S. Lewis, "The Humanitarian Theory of Punishment"

In England we have lately had a controversy about Capital Punishment. I do not know whether a murderer is more likely to repent and make a good end on the gallows a few weeks after his trial or in the prison infirmary thirty years later. I do not know whether the fear of death is an indispensable deterrent. I need not, for the purpose of this article, decide whether it is a morally permissible deterrent. Those are questions which I propose to leave untouched. My subject is not Capital Punishment in particular, but that theory of punishment in general which the controversy showed to be almost universal among my fellow-countrymen. It may be called the Humanitarian theory. Those who hold it think that it is mild and merciful. In this I believe that they are seriously mistaken. I believe that the "Humanity" which it claims is a dangerous illusion and disguises 1 the possibility of cruelty and injustice without end. I urge a return to the traditional or Retributive theory not solely, not even primarily, in the interests of society, but in the interests of the criminal.

According to the Humanitarian theory, to punish a man because he deserves it, and as much as he deserves, is mere revenge and, therefore, barbarous and immoral. It is maintained that the only legitimate motives for punishing are the desire to deter others by example or to mend the criminal. When this theory is combined, as frequently happens, with the belief that all crime is more or less pathological, the idea of mending tails off into that of healing or curing, and punishment becomes therapeutic. Thus it appears at first sight that we have passed from the harsh and self-righteous notion of giving the wicked their deserts to the charitable and enlightened one of tending the psychologically sick. What could be more amiable? One little point which is taken for granted in this theory needs, however, to be made explicit. The things done to the criminal, even if they are called cures, will be just as compulsory as they were in the old days when we called them punishments. If a tendency to steal can be cured by psychotherapy, the thief will no doubt be forced to undergo the treatment. Otherwise, society cannot continue.

My contention is that this doctrine, merciful though it appears, really means that each one of us, from the moment he breaks the law, is deprived of the rights of a human being.

The reason is this. The Humanitarian theory removes from Punishment the concept of Desert. But the concept of Desert is the only connecting link between punishment and justice. It is only as deserved or undeserved that a sentence can be just or unjust. I do not here contend that the question "Is it deserved?" is the only one we can reasonably ask about a punishment. We may very properly ask whether it is likely to deter others and to reform the criminal. But neither of these two last questions is a question about justice. There is no sense in talking about a "just deterrent" or a "just cure." We demand of a deterrent not whether it is just but whether it will deter. We demand of a cure not whether it is just but whether it succeeds. Thus when we cease to consider what the criminal deserves and consider only what will cure him or deter others, we have tacitly removed him from the sphere of justice altogether; instead of a person, a subject of rights, we now have a mere object, a patient, a "case."

The distinction will become clearer if we ask who will be qualified to determine sentences when sentences are no longer held to derive their propriety from the criminal's deservings. On the old view the problem of fixing the right sentence was a moral problem. Accordingly, the judge who did it was a person trained in jurisprudence; trained, that is, in a science which deals with rights and duties, and which, in origin at least, was consciously accepting guidance from the Law of Nature and from Scripture. We must admit that in the actual penal code of most countries at most times these high originals were so much modified by local custom, class interests, and utilitarian concessions as to be very imperfectly recognizable. But the code was never in principle, and not always in fact, beyond the control of the conscience of the society. And when (say, in eighteenth-century England) actual punishments conflicted too violently with the moral sense of the community, juries refused to convict and reform was finally brought about. This was possible because, so long as we are thinking in terms of Desert, the propriety of the penal code, being a moral question, is a question on which every man has the right to an opinion, not because he follows this or that profession, but because he is simply a man, a rational animal enjoying the Natural Light. But all this is changed when we drop the concept of Desert. The only two questions we may now ask about a punishment are whether it deters and whether it cures. But these are not questions on which anyone is entitled to have an opinion simply because he is a man. He is not entitled to an opinion even if, in addition to being a man, he should happen also to be a jurist, a Christian, and a moral theologian. For they are not questions about principle but about matter of fact; and for such *cuiquam in sua arte credendum.*[1] Only the expert ''penologist'' (let barbarous things have barbarous names), in the light of previous experiment, can tell us what is likely to deter: Only the psychotherapist can tell us what is likely to cure. It will be in vain for the rest of us, speaking simply as men, to say, ''But this punishment is hideously unjust, hideously disproportionate to the criminal's deserts.'' The experts with perfect logic will reply, ''But nobody was talking about deserts. No one was talking about *punishment* in your archaic, vindictive sense of the word. Here are the statistics proving that this treatment deters. Here are the statistics proving that this other treatment cures. What is your trouble?''

The Humanitarian theory, then, removes sentences from the hands of jurists whom the public conscience is entitled to criticize and places them in the hands of technical experts whose special sciences do not even employ such categories as rights or justice. It might be argued that since this transference results from an abandonment of the old idea of punishment, and, therefore, of all vindictive motives, it will be safe to leave our criminals in such hands. I will not pause to comment on the simple-minded view of fallen human nature which such a belief implies. Let us rather remember that

6

[1]''We must believe the expert in his own field.''

the "cure" of criminals is to be compulsory; and let us then watch how the theory actually works in the mind of the Humanitarian. The immediate starting point of this article was a letter I read in one of our Leftist weeklies. The author was pleading that a certain sin, now treated by our laws as a crime, should henceforward be treated as a disease. And he complained that under the present system the offender, after a term in jail, was simply let out to return to his original environment, where he would probably relapse. What he complained of was not the shutting up but the letting out. On his remedial view of punishment the offender should, of course, be detained until he was cured. And of course the official straighteners are the only people who can say when that is. The first result of the Humanitarian theory is, therefore, to substitute for a definite sentence (reflecting to some extent the community's moral judgment on the degree of ill-desert involved) an indefinite sentence terminable only by the word of those experts—and they are not experts in moral theology nor even in the Law of Nature—who inflict it. Which of us, if he stood in the dock, would not prefer to be tried by the old system?

It may be said that by the continued use of the word "punishment" and the use of the verb "inflict" I am misrepresenting Humanitarians. They are not punishing, not inflicting, only healing. But do not let us be deceived by a name. To be taken without consent from my home and friends; to lose my liberty; to undergo all those assaults on my personality which modern psychotherapy knows how to deliver; to be re-made after some pattern of "normality" hatched in a Viennese laboratory to which I never professed allegiance; to know that this process will never end until either my captors have succeeded or I have grown wise enough to cheat them with apparent success—who cares whether this is called Punishment or not? That it includes most of the elements for which any punishment is feared—shame, exile, bondage, and years eaten by the locust—is obvious. Only enormous ill-desert could justify it; but ill-desert is the very conception which the Humanitarian theory has thrown overboard. 7

If we turn from the curative to the deterrent justification of punishment we shall find the new theory even more alarming. When you punish a man *in terrorem*,[2] make of him an "example" to others, you are admittedly using him as a means to an end; someone else's end. This, in itself, would be a very wicked thing to do. On the classical theory of Punishment it was of course justified on the ground that the man deserved it. That was assumed to be established before any question of "making him an example" arose. You then, as the 8

---

[2] "To frighten."

saying is, killed two birds with one stone; in the process of giving him what he deserved you set an example to others. But take away desert and the whole morality of the punishment disappears. Why, in Heaven's name, am I to be sacrificed to the good of society in this way?—unless, of course, I deserve it.

But that is not the worst. If the justification of exemplary punish- 9 ment is not to be based on desert but solely on its efficacy as a deterrent, it is not absolutely necessary that the man we punish should even have committed the crime. The deterrent effect demands that the public should draw the moral, "If we do such an act we shall suffer like that man." The punishment of a man actually guilty whom the public think innocent will not have the desired effect; the punishment of a man actually innocent will, provided the public think him guilty. But every modern State has powers which make it easy to fake a trial. When a victim is urgently needed for exemplary purposes and a guilty victim cannot be found, all the purposes of deterrence will be equally served by the punishment (call it "cure" if you prefer) of an innocent victim, provided that the public can be cheated into thinking him guilty. It is no use to ask me why I assume that our rulers will be so wicked. The punishment of an innocent, that is, an undeserving, man is wicked only if we grant the traditional view that righteous punishment means deserved punishment. Once we have abandoned that criterion, all punishments have to be justified, if at all, on other grounds that have nothing to do with desert. Where the punishment of the innocent can be justified on those grounds (and it could in some cases be justified as a deterrent) it will be no less moral than any other punishment. Any distaste for it on the part of a Humanitarian will be merely a hang-over from the Retributive theory.

It is, indeed, important to notice that my argument so far sup- 10 poses no evil intentions on the part of the Humanitarian and considers only what is involved in the logic of his position. My contention is that good men (not bad men) consistently acting upon that position would act as cruelly and unjustly as the greatest tyrants. They might in some respects act even worse. Of all tyrannies a tyranny sincerely exercised for the good of its victims may be the most oppressive. It may be better to live under robber barons than under omnipotent moral busybodies. The robber baron's cruelty may sometimes sleep, his cupidity may at some point be satiated; but those who torment us for our own good will torment us without end, for they do so with the approval of their own conscience. They may be more likely to go to Heaven yet at the same time likelier to make a Hell of earth. Their very kindness stings with intolerable insult. To be "cured" against one's will and cured of states which we may not regard as disease is to be put on a level with those who have not yet reached the age of reason or those who never will; to be classed with infants, imbeciles, and domestic animals. But to be punished, however severely, because we have deserved it, because we "ought to have known better," is to be treated as a human person made in God's image.

In reality, however, we must face the possibility of bad rulers 11 armed with a Humanitarian theory of punishment. A great many popular blueprints for a Christian society are merely what the Elizabethans called "eggs in moonshine" because they assume that the whole society is Christian or that the Christians are in control. This is not so in most contemporary States. Even if it were, our rulers would still be fallen men and, therefore, neither very wise nor very good. As it is, they will usually be unbelievers. And since wisdom and virtue are not the only or the commonest qualifications for a place in the government, they will not often be even the best unbelievers.

The practical problem of Christian politics is not that of drawing 12 up schemes for a Christian society, but that of living as innocently as we can with unbelieving fellow-subjects under unbelieving rulers who will never be perfectly wise and good and who will sometimes be very wicked and very foolish. And when they are wicked the Humanitarian theory of punishment will put in their hands a finer instrument of tyranny than wickedness ever had before. For if crime and disease are to be regarded as the same thing, it follows that any state of mind which our masters choose to call disease can be treated as crime and compulsorily cured. It will be vain to plead that states of mind which displease government need not always involve moral turpitude and do not therefore always deserve forfeiture of liberty. For our masters will not be using the concepts of Desert and Punishment but those of disease and cure. We know that one school of psychology already regards religion as a neurosis. When this particular neurosis becomes inconvenient to government, what is to hinder government from proceeding to "cure" it? Such "cure" will, of course, be compulsory; but under the Humanitarian theory it will not be called by the shocking name of Persecution. No one will blame us for being Christians, no one will hate us, no one will revile us. The new Nero will approach us with the silky manners of a doctor, and though all will be in fact as compulsory as the *tunica molesta*[3] or Smithfield or Tyburn,[4] all will go on within the unemotional ther-

[3]An uncomfortable tunic worn as a punishment.
[4]Two places of execution in England.

apeutic sphere, where words like "right" and "wrong" or "freedom" and "slavery" are never heard. And thus when the command is given, every prominent Christian in the land may vanish overnight into Institutions for the Treatment of the Ideologically Unsound, and it will rest with the expert jailers to say when (if ever) they are to re-emerge. But it will not be persecution. Even if the treatment is painful, even if it is lifelong, even if it is fatal, that will be only a regrettable accident; the intention was purely therapeutic. In ordinary medicine there were painful operations and fatal operations; so in this. But because they are "treatment," not punishment, they can be criticized only by fellow-experts and on technical grounds, never by men as men and on grounds of justice.

This is why I think it essential to oppose the Humanitarian theory   13 of punishment, root and branch, wherever we encounter it. It carries on its front a semblance of mercy which is wholly false. That is how it can deceive men of good will. The error began, perhaps, with Shelley's statement that the distinction between mercy and justice was invented in the courts of tyrants. It sounds noble, and was indeed the error of a noble mind. But the distinction is essential. The older view was that mercy "tempered" justice, or (on the highest level of all) that mercy and justice had met and kissed. The essential act of mercy was to pardon; and pardon in its very essence involves the recognition of guilt and ill-desert in the recipient. If crime is only a disease which needs cure, not a sin which deserves punishment, it cannot be pardoned. How can you pardon a man for having a gumboil or a club foot? But the Humanitarian theory wants simply to abolish Justice and substitute Mercy for it. This means that you start being "kind" to people before you have considered their rights, and then force upon them supposed kindnesses which no one but you will recognize as kindnesses and which the recipient will feel as abominable cruelties. You have overshot the mark. Mercy, detached from Justice, grows unmerciful. That is the important paradox. As there are plants which will flourish only in mountain soil, so it appears that Mercy will flower only when it grows in the crannies of the rock of Justice: Transplanted to the marsh-lands of mere Humanitarianism, it becomes a man-eating weed, all the more dangerous because it is still called by the same name as the mountain variety. But we ought long ago to have learned our lesson. We should be too old now to be deceived by those humane pretensions which have served to usher in every cruelty of the revolutionary period in which we live. These are the "precious balms" which will "break our heads."[5]

[5]Psalm cxli. 6.

There is a fine sentence in Bunyan: "It came burning hot into my mind, whatever he said, and however he flattered, when he got me home to his House, he would sell me for a Slave."[6] There is a fine couplet, too, in John Ball:

> Be war or ye be wo;
> Knoweth your frend from your foo.[7]

PRACTICE

Arguing a Hypothetical Case of Punishment or Treatment for a Convicted Criminal

You have read what a social scientist and a theologian have to say about dealing properly with criminals. You may feel that one is right and the other wrong or that the truth is somewhere in between. In any case, here is a chance for you to argue for your own solution to the problem.

To make your argument sufficiently different from the other two so that you can avoid repeating what they have said, make your own argument in terms of a specific but hypothetical criminal. That is, invent a crime of some serious but not hideous sort, imagine the history of the criminal (especially age, family background, previous criminal record) and argue the case for proper treatment of this particular person, convicted of this particular crime.

Assume the availability of a full range of responses, ranging from what Menninger would approve to what Lewis would recommend. Take into account the probable result of your recommendation, both for the person who has been convicted and for society.

You may quote Lewis and Menninger if you wish, either for support or in order to dispute with them. However, this should

[6]*The Pilgrim's Progress*, ed. James Blanton Wharey, 2nd ed. (rev. Roger Sharrock), Oxford English Texts (Oxford, 1960), part 1, p. 70.
[7]"John Ball's Letter to the Peasants of Essex, 1381," lines 11–12, found in *Fourteenth Century Verse and Prose*, ed. Kenneth Sisam (Oxford, 1921), p. 161.

not be the main purpose of your argument. You should be trying to convince a group of reasonable people (us, your teacher, your classmates) that your recommendation is the proper one.

You must *not* deal with a case like a starving parent stealing food for a baby, or a serial killer of innocent youngsters who tortures and mutilates the victims. Stick to the middle range of crime, to deeds that are clearly wrong but not monstrous. Suppose, for instance, an idealistic young student decides to rob a grasping slumlord who squeezes riches out of poor tenants. The student intends to give the fruits of the robbery to some needy friends. In committing the crime, the student is surprised by the landlord and picks up a kitchen knife, stabs the landlord three times, and runs out of the apartment abandoning the goods.

There is no question about the student's guilt. He was seen entering and leaving the victim's home and has confessed to the attempted robbery and the stabbing that resulted in death. He has no previous criminal record except for traffic violations. Assume that he is a person like yourself, except that he has been transformed into a criminal by violent actions against life and property. Assume that the victim was not an entirely nice person, but had some friends and relatives who cared for him and have been hurt by his death. In other words, we have a real crime here, of an important sort, that society cannot ignore. Whatever crime you invent, the question for you to decide is essentially whether "punishment" or "treatment" is the better response, from the point of view of society; that is, whether Lewis or Menninger is right. You might consider how you would wish to be dealt with yourself if you were the criminal— or how you would wish the criminal treated if you were the child of the victim. But the real question cannot be solved on a personal level. You must try to formulate an argument for the proper response to serious crime *in general*, using your hypothetical case as your main example, and the arguments of Lewis and Menninger as your main source of positions on the issue at hand.

Remember, this is not a detective story, but an argument. Give yourself a problem that your argument will attempt to resolve, not a mystery that must be solved. Above all, try to be balanced, reasonable, and thoughtful, rather than getting carried away by emotion.

10 Analysis: Taking Things Apart

Analysis is a way of studying things by seeing how the parts that make up the whole thing are related to one another. We can analyze anything that works in a systematic and coherent way: an ecosystem, a living creature, a social group, or a written text. Writing analytically is a way of reporting on a completed analysis, but it can also help in the conduct of the analytic study.

You may, for instance, make an outline in which you indicate what you will be looking for in your analysis and what your order of study will be. As you feed observations into your outline, you may notice gaps that require filling, or complex units that should be broken down into smaller units. Analysis is a way of using writing to improve observation. It is not just a report on a finished set of observations; it is a *way* of observing.

One of the most important elements of analytic writing is classification, because classification connects things not by space or time but by qualities or categories: ''all these critters have wool; they are *sheep* and go over here; these other smelly rascals don't produce much wool; they are *goats* and go over there'' and so on. You can see, even from this trifling example, how classification is based on comparing like things (sheep and goats are closely related animals) and contrasting unlike things (sheep are very woolly; goats are only slightly woolly). Comparing and contrasting, connecting and distinguishing, searching for causes and effects—these are the ways that analysis leads toward synthesis. It was Charles Darwin's attempt to classify and explain the data he had collected on the voyage of the *Beagle* that led him, most reluctantly, to the synthesis we call the theory of evolution.

Analysis moves toward synthesis as we develop a *thesis* about the object of our analysis. Presenting a thesis always involves us in a structure of argument. Analysis that does not lead to a synthetic conclusion is always a bit unfinished; like classification, it is a tool of study and research rather than a final product. Still, within the framework of academic study we often undertake analytic projects. In particular, we devote a good deal of attention to the analysis of texts. Most of the practices in this section offer opportunities for this kind of analytic writing. The final practice, on images of women in advertising, encourages the development of analysis in the direction of synthesis.

READING

Comparison and Contrast

The following brief essay appeared in the New York *Tribune* in February of 1892. It was the work of Stephen Crane, a young man of twenty, who had recently left college to pursue a career as a writer. This was the first of a series of ''sketches'' of Sullivan County in New York's Catskill Mountains, which began Crane's career.

Stephen Crane, ''The Last of the Mohicans''

Few of the old, gnarled and weather-beaten inhabitants of the pines and boulders of Sullivan County are great readers of books or students of literature. On the contrary, the man who subscribes for the county's weekly newspaper is the man who has attained sufficient position to enable him to leave his farm labors for literary pursuits. The historical traditions of the region have been handed down from generation to generation, at the firesides in the old homesteads. The aged grandsire recites legends to his grandson; and when the grandson's head is silvered he takes his corncob pipe from his mouth and transfixes his children and his children's children with stirring tales of hunter's exploit and Indian battle. Historians are wary of this form of procedure. Insignificant facts, told from mouth to mouth down the years, have been known to become of positively appalling importance by the time they have passed from behind the last corncob in the last chimney corner. Nevertheless, most of these fireside stories are verified by books written by learned men, who have dived into piles of moldy documents and dusty chronicles to establish their facts.

This gives the great Sullivan County thunderbolt immense weight. And they hurl it at no less a head than that which once evolved from its inner recesses the famous Leatherstocking Tales. The old story-tellers of this district are continually shaking metaphorical fists at *The Last of the Mohicans* of J. Fenimore Cooper. Tell them that they are aiming their shafts at one of the standard novels of American literature and they scornfully sneer; endeavor to oppose them with the intricacies of Indian history and they shriek defiance. No consideration for the author, the literature or the readers can stay their hands, and they claim without reservation that the last of the Mohicans, the real and only authentic last of the Mohicans, was a demoralized, dilapidated inhabitant of Sullivan County.

The work in question is of course a visionary tale and the historical value of the plot is not a question of importance. But when the two heroes of Sullivan County and J. Fenimore Cooper, respectively, are compared, the pathos lies in the contrast, and the lover of the noble and fictional Uncas is overcome with great sadness. Even as Cooper claims that his Uncas was the last of the children of the Turtle, so do the sages of Sullivan County roar from out their rockbound fastnesses that their nondescript Indian was the last of the children of the Turtle. The pathos lies in the contrast between the noble savage of fiction and the sworn-to-claimant of Sullivan County.

All know well the character of Cooper's hero, Uncas, that bronze god in a North American wilderness, that warrior with the eye of the eagle, the ear of the fox, the tread of the catlike panther, and the tongue of the wise serpent of fable. Over his dead body a warrior cries:

"Why has thou left us, pride of the Wapanachki? Thy time has been like that of the sun when in the trees; thy glory brighter than his light at noonday. Thou art gone, youthful warrior, but a hundred Wyandots are clearing the briers from thy path to the world of spirits. Who that saw thee in battle would believe that thou couldst die? Who before thee has ever shown Uttawa the way into the fight? Thy feet were like the wings of eagles; thine arm heavier than falling branches from the pine; and thy voice like the Manitto when he speaks in the clouds. The tongue of Uttawa is weak and his heart exceedingly heavy. Pride of the Wapanachki, why hast thou left us?''

The last of the Mohicans supported by Sullivan County is a totally different character. They have forgotten his name. From their description of him he was no warrior who yearned after the blood of his enemies as the hart panteth for the water-brooks; on the contrary he developed a craving for the rum of the white men which rose superior to all other anxieties. He had the emblematic Turtle tattooed somewhere under his shirtfront. Arrayed in tattered, torn and ragged garments which some white man had thrown off, he wandered listlessly from village to village and from house to house, his only ambition being to beg, borrow or steal a drink. The settlers helped him because they knew his story. They knew of the long line of mighty sachems sleeping under the pines of the mountains. He was a veritable ''poor Indian.'' He dragged through his wretched life in helpless misery. No one could be more alone in the world than he and when he died there was no one to call him pride of anything nor to inquire why he had left them.

PRACTICE

Analysis of an Analysis

Crane's sketch, as you have no doubt noticed, is a classic comparison and contrast essay. Your assignment is to analyze Crane's sketch to illustrate how Crane has put it together. You should first produce an outline of the sketch, indicating what each paragraph accomplishes. Then you should consider in some detail the actual process of comparing and contrasting, which Crane begins in paragraph 3 with, ''But when the two heroes . . . are compared, the pathos lies in the contrast. . . .'' How is the language of the two closing paragraphs used to reinforce the contrast? How does this comparison *work*?

In developing your analysis, you might begin by writing down, in two columns, phrases from Crane's text that balance one another. For instance, the contrasting phrases that conclude the final two paragraphs could come at the bottom of your columns:

Noble Savage	*Real Indian*
● ● ● ●	● ● ● ●
● ● ● ●	● ● ● ●
why hast thou left us?	no one . . . to inquire why he had left them.

PRACTICE:

Myth and Reality

Write an essay in which you compare and contrast two versions of a contemporary figure that you know something about, such as the doctor, the professor, the farmer, the cop, the immigrant, the corporate executive, the computer whiz. How is this figure presented in popular culture (such as movies, television series, or novels)? And how does this fictional presentation compare with what you actually know about the real person? To achieve a balance in comparing and contrasting, start by listing the points to be compared for each version of your figure. Then arrange your points in some order of importance. Will your essay be more effective if you start with the most important points of similarity or difference, or if you end with them? In your conclusion you might consider why we, like James Fenimore Cooper, continue to construct myths about certain figures.

READING AND PRACTICE

Two Poets Look at a Painting

As we have said, one of the basic tools of analytic writing is the method of comparison and contrast. Our minds work in terms of relationships. It is very hard—perhaps impossible—for us to consider a thing by itself. Inevitably, we make analogies or invent metaphors whenever we are forced to discuss a single thing in isolation.

The method of comparison and contrast simply formalizes what we all do when thinking. In using this method, we look separately for points of resemblance (comparison) between two objects and for points of difference (contrast). If there are no points of resemblance, then there is no reason to discuss the two things together. On the other hand, if two things are too similar, there is not much to say about them. The method of comparison and contrast is of most use when we wish to distinguish the specific differences between two things that are both members of the same category: like humans and monkeys (same genus, different species), or men and women (same species, different sex), or this shortstop and that shortstop (same function, different performance).

In this assignment, you are to compare and contrast two modern poems by different poets that were inspired by the same painting, Pieter Brueghel's *The Fall of Icarus*. The painting is based on the Greek legend of Icarus and his father, Daedalus, who tried to escape from imprisonment on the island of Crete. A master craftsman, Daedalus made wings for himself and his son out of birds' feathers held together with wax. He warned the boy not to fly too low or the water would wet the wings and weigh him down, nor too high or the heat of the sun would melt the wax. But Icarus was a high-spirited lad and ignored his father's advice. He flew too high, his wings came apart, and he fell into the sea and drowned.

There is a moral here for the writer of comparison and contrast papers. Follow directions, and keep a good balance between finding resemblances and noting differences.

Your specific task is to discuss the similarities and differences between the two poems in terms of their ideas and the language in which the ideas are conveyed. You are not being asked to judge which is the better poem. The thesis of your paper should simply be a statement as to whether the *similarities* or *differences* seem to you most significant. For example, you might argue, "The most striking thing about these two poems is that they treat the same painting in such different ways," or "The interesting thing about these two poems is that, despite superficial differences in style, they treat the painting in essentially the same way."

Read the poems several times, take notes, and try to sort out your thoughts before you begin composing your essay. For inspiration, we present Jeff MacNelly's cartoon version of young Skyler Fishawk at work upon a similar project. Please do *not* follow his method of composition. He understands the theory of comparison and contrast very well, but he manages to avoid the practice completely. You may wish to analyze his practice so as to avoid this sort of padding in your own work.

Musée des Beaux Arts[1]

About suffering they were never wrong, 1
The Old Masters: how well they understood
Its human position; how it takes place
While someone else is eating or opening a window or just walking
  dully along;
How, when the aged are reverently, passionately waiting
For the miraculous birth, there always must be
Children who did not specially want it to happen, skating
On a pond at the edge of the wood:

[1]Museum of Fine Arts.

The Fall of Icarus by Pieter Brueghel.

ANALYSIS: TAKING THINGS APART

They never forgot
That even the dreadful martyrdom must run its course
Anyhow in a corner, some untidy spot
Where dogs go on with their doggy life and the torturer's horse
Scratches its innocent behind on a tree.

In Brueghel's *Icarus*, for instance: how everything turns away   2
Quite leisurely from the disaster; the ploughman may
Have heard the splash, the forsaken cry,
But for him it was not an important failure; the sun shone
As it had to on the white legs disappearing into the green
Water; and the expensive delicate ship that must have seen
Something amazing, a boy falling out of the sky,
Had somewhere to get to and sailed calmly on.

—W. H. AUDEN

Landscape With the Fall of Icarus

According to Brueghel   1
when Icarus fell
it was spring

a farmer was ploughing   2
his field
the whole pageantry

of the year was   3
awake tingling
near

the edge of the sea   4
concerned
with itself

sweating in the sun   5
that melted
the wings' wax

unsignificantly   6
off the coast
there was

a splash quite unnoticed   7
this was
Icarus drowning

—WILLIAM CARLOS WILLIAMS

Analyzing an Advertisement

Here is a reproduction of a full-page advertisement from a contemporary magazine, along with an analysis of the advertisement written for a graduate seminar at Brown University. Consider both the ad and the analysis before looking at the questions.

Manhattan shirts make the man.

Monica Weimersheimer, Analysis of a Manhattan Shirt Advertisement

A sepia-tint photograph of a room with dark wooden walls; a portrait of President Roosevelt, a Normal Rockwell depiction of a   1 happy family, and an American flag decorating those walls; a metal-barred cashier's cage. A public place: a post office? a bank? the waiting and ticket room of a train station? People: an anonymous man's back, a blur-face sleeping soldier, a young woman in vaguely forties' dress. And in the foreground, a fashionably dressed and otherwise attractive man smiles—half-conspiratorially? half-mockingly? certainly with confidence and an air of easy proprietorship—at the public. The headlined meaning of this photograph: "Manhattan shirts make the man." But this is publicity, and "the man" is not any man. The elements in the photograph, in both their content and their arrangement, promote and reinforce the Image of what a real man should be, and they promise that that status may be obtained by the purchase of the product. The question that the ad really asks is "What is *the man?*" and it answers that question in terms of sexual, cultural, material, and temporal values. The perceived scene itself is not as important as what its elements signify.

To take that headline one step further, the shirt makes the man, and the man makes (if he chooses) the woman. He does not look at her, nor she at him, yet the appreciative and proprietory smile of the man and the woman's own half-smile, her downcast eyes, her concentration on whatever she is doing mitigated by the angle of her face (turned ever so slightly towards the man in the foreground) would be unmistakable signs of mutual interest if they faced each other. The implications are made more subtle, but not lost, in this particular arrangement. The very technical devices of the photograph—the fact that the woman, of all the objects in the background, is in distinct focus and "matches" him in the tone of her dress and in her very animation—link the two. The shirt enhances his physical appearance, and the ease and perfection of its fit bespeak expensive—but more importantly, discriminating—taste, an aesthetic sensibility that is the outgrowth of an upper-class refinement. Taste, wealth, success, and physical "presence": all culturally determined qualities which attract the woman and boil down to the affirmation of man's sexual nature. Clothes literally make the man, by affirming it. 2

The man in the shirt also establishes dominance over another figure in the photograph—the man in the uniform. Clothes—or Manhattan shirts—make the man by making him unique or, as is more in keeping with the consumer/owner image being promoted by the advertisement, privileged—flatteringly distinguished from his fellow men. The soldier's dress is, of course, the extreme sign of the undifferentiated mass, both literally—one uniform is just like another—and in terms of human potentiality and action. The soldier under orders is denied originality, choice, or freedom. He is part of a hierarchy—a system based on unequality—who serves rather than shapes the society. Furthermore, the soldier is asleep, 3 waiting. Unconscious, he is incapable of action—*he* will never get that girl.

The dreaming soldier, the pictures and the flag in the background 4 are themselves part of a dream, a dream of the past, and a particularly American vision of that past. It connotes a time of idealism, most probably during the Second World War, when there was a clearer, more unified sense of the right and the wrong sides of the political situation—Democracy being very much in the right—and the romantic sense that is associated with any dream of the past. It anchors the man in a history that is shared by the reader or consumer and also reinforces the image of that "man." It was a man's time, a time of action and of girls waiting back home, but these connotations need not be realized fully to make the image of the past effective. The nostalgia evoked is persuasive; it is attractive, yet out of the reach of ordinary men. For while "the man" in the shirt is a part of the past, he also dominates the present. His implied interaction with the woman whose association with the past is suggested by her style of dress and her relegation to the middle, if not background, of the scene, suggests his association with the past. Yet his absolutely dominant position in the scene makes him a force of the present.

The force of the image is achieved by the fact that it relies on fa- 5 miliar, although deliberately manufactured, notions of what is desirable—the power and the freedom of being a man, and a man in a capitalist, democratic society—to create an impossible paradigm, but one that, more significantly, does not appear quite impossible precisely because of its familiarity. The stereotype has become a part of culture, as the belief that acquisition of shirts or of other material goods will achieve that stereotype. A mass image such as this one presents the curious paradox that assures democracy: *anyone* may become this man—one of the elite, the envied man—through this purchase.

QUESTIONS

1. How is the analysis organized? What is the topic of each paragraph? How are the paragraphs arranged and connected? How are they related to the ad and to one another?
2. Consider the organization within a single paragraph—the first, for instance. How are the elements of the visual image organized in the words of the analyst? Why does she use the order she does?
3. How does the analyst use comparison and contrast? Consider man versus woman and man versus soldier as examples.
4. What causes and effects are mentioned or suggested? How important are they to the analysis?
5. How would you restate the conclusions of the analysis in your own words? Do you agree with them?

PRACTICE

Analyzing a Full-Page Advertisement

Select a full-page ad from a current magazine and produce a brief analysis of it. Consider the purpose of the ad and the various means used to achieve it. You may wish to evaluate the purpose, but do not make this the focus of your essay. Concentrate on analysis.

READING

A Critic Looks at Advertising

The following selection by the British art critic John Berger is taken from *Ways of Seeing*, a book on the language of images. In this brief analysis Berger probes for the real message that underlies most advertising (or *publicity*, as he calls it, using the British term).

John Berger, from **Ways of Seeing**

Publicity is usually explained and justified as a competitive medium which ultimately benefits the public (the consumer) and the most efficient manufacturers—and thus the national economy. It is closely related to certain ideas about freedom: freedom of choice for the purchaser; freedom of enterprise for the manufacturer. The great hoardings and the publicity neons of the cities of capitalism are the immediate visible sign of ''The Free World.'' 1

For many in Eastern Europe such images in the West sum up what they in the East lack. Publicity, it is thought, offers a free choice. 2

It is true that in publicity one brand of manufacture, one firm, competes with another; but it is also true that every publicity image confirms and enhances every other. Publicity is not merely an assembly of competing messages: it is a language in itself which is always being used to make the same general proposal. Within publicity, choices are offered between this cream and that cream, that car and this car, but publicity as a system only makes a single proposal. 3

It proposes to each of us that we transform ourselves, or our lives, by buying something more. 4

This more, it proposes, will make us in some way richer—even though we will be poorer by having spent our money. 5

Publicity persuades us of such a transformation by showing us people who have apparently been transformed and are, as a result, enviable. The state of being envied is what constitutes glamor. And publicity is the process of manufacturing glamor.

It is important here not to confuse publicity with the pleasure or benefits to be enjoyed from the things it advertises. Publicity is effective precisely because it feeds upon the real. Clothes, food, cars, cosmetics, baths, sunshine are real things to be enjoyed in themselves. Publicity begins by working on a natural appetite for pleasure. But it cannot offer the real object of pleasure and there is no convincing substitute for a pleasure in that pleasure's own terms. The more convincingly publicity conveys the pleasure of bathing in a warm, distant sea, the more the spectator-buyer will become aware that he is hundreds of miles away from that sea and the more remote the chance of bathing in it will seem to him. This is why publicity can never really afford to be about the product or opportunity it is proposing to the buyer who is not yet enjoying it. Publicity is never a celebration of a pleasure-in-itself. Publicity is always about the future buyer. It offers him an image of himself made glamorous by the product or opportunity it is trying to sell. The image then makes him envious of himself as he might be. Yet what makes this self-which-he-might-be enviable? The envy of others. Publicity is about social relations, not objects. Its promise is not of pleasure, but of happiness: happiness as judged from the outside by others. The happiness of being envied is glamor.

Being envied is a solitary form of reassurance. It depends precisely upon not sharing your experience with those who envy you. You are observed with interest but you do not observe with interest—if you do, you will become less enviable. In this respect the envied are like bureaucrats; the more impersonal they are, the greater the illusion (for themselves and for others) of their power. The power of the glamorous resides in their supposed happiness: the power of the bureaucrat in his supposed authority. It is this which explains the absent, unfocused look of so many glamor images. They look out *over* the looks of envy which sustain them.

The spectator-buyer is meant to envy herself as she will become if she buys the product. She is meant to imagine herself transformed by the product into an object of envy for others, an envy which will then justify her loving herself. One could put this another way: the publicity image steals her love of herself as she is, and offers it back to her for the price of the product.

QUESTIONS

1. How does Berger qualify the idea that publicity is a sign of freedom of choice and freedom of enterprise?

2. Why does he call publicity a "language in itself"?
3. What does Berger mean when he says, "Publicity is about social relations, not objects"?
4. Cite an example of a new product being advertised that would illustrate Berger's statement that "The state of being envied is what constitutes glamor."

PRACTICE

Images of Women in Advertising

We present here a brief survey of the presentation of women in American advertising. Read each ad carefully, analyzing its visual and verbal text and considering how one complements the other (for an example of such analysis, see "Analysis of a Manhattan Shirt Advertisement," pp. 231–233). How is glamor being defined in each of these ads? Or, to put it in Berger's terms, what desirable transformations of self are being offered to the woman who reads these advertisements?

What similarities or differences do you find when you consider the ads as a group? If you read the ads as a sort of historical narrative of advertising, do you find any significant changes in the image of woman created by advertising over the years? While it's obvious that clothing and hair styles have changed during the twentieth century, has there been any change, for example, in advertising's concept of femininity? In developing your thesis, you may want to investigate a concept such as femininity or glamor, or you may want to test the validity of one of Berger's statements by using evidence provided by the advertisements. The more carefully you consider your evidence, the richer your essay will be.

If your instructor wishes to include some library research in this assignment so that you can consider the topic more thoroughly, you might concentrate on women's image in a particular decade, such as the 1950s, by looking at the advertising in a number of popular magazines of that period. Or, if you wish to enlarge your historical survey, concentrate on advertising over a period of several decades in one or more magazines with fairly long publishing histories, such as *Ladies' Home Journal, Redbook, Cosmopolitan,* or *Good Housekeeping.*

1913

Make that dream come true

WHAT woman lives who has not at some time enjoyed the vision of herself a bride. For many the dream has been fulfilled. Don't allow a bad complexion to place you among the others!

Your beauty of feature, becoming dress, graceful bearing, keen wit, can be completely overshadowed by a blotchy or otherwise unattractive skin. But there is no excuse for submission to such a condition, when to correct it is so easy.

Usually all that nature requires to make a clear pleasing complexion is right living—and—proper, regular cleansing of the skin. It is this knowledge that has made Resinol Soap a favorite in thousands of homes where it is now in daily use.

If you are neglected and humiliated because of a red, oily, or otherwise repellent skin, begin today the following treatment:

Gently work the profuse foamy lather of Resinol Soap well into the pores with the finger tips. It rinses easily and completely with a little clear warm water. A dash of cold water to close the pores completes the treatment. Now see how velvety your skin looks and feels—how invigorated it is—and what a delicate glow it has. These are only the first happy effects of this delightful toilet soap.

At all drug and toilet goods counters. May we send you a free trial? Write now. Dept. 5-A, Resinol, Baltimore, Md.

"Girls who know this secret always win out"

says Irene Dunne

1 YEARS AGO MY LOVELY SOUTHERN GRANDMOTHER FIRST TAUGHT ME THAT A GIRL WHO WANTS TO BREAK HEARTS SIMPLY MUST HAVE A TEA-ROSE COMPLEXION.

RKO-RADIO STAR

2 NOW THAT I'M ON THE SCREEN I REALIZE MORE THAN EVER THE FASCINATION THERE IS IN PEARLY-SMOOTH SKIN. I FOLLOW MY LUX TOILET SOAP BEAUTY TREATMENT REGULARLY EVERY DAY.

3 IT'S REALLY AMAZING HOW QUICKLY JUST THIS SIMPLE CARE BRINGS TEMPTING NEW BEAUTY TO THE SKIN. TRY IT-YOU GIRLS WHO WANT TO MAKE NEW CONQUESTS! YOU'RE SURE TO WIN OUT!

SO MANY GIRLS have asked Irene Dunne how to make themselves more attractive . . . how to win admiration . . . romance.

Here this lovely star tells you! And her beauty method is so simple . . . so easy to try . . . regular, everyday care with exquisitely gentle Lux Toilet Soap.

Do follow her advice! See how much clearer, softer *your* skin becomes . . . how that extra-lovely complexion wins hearts—and *holds* them!

9 out of 10 glamorous Hollywood stars . . . countless girls the country over . . . have *proved* what this fragrant, white soap does for the skin. Is yours just an "average" complexion? Don't be content—start today—have the *added beauty* Lux Toilet Soap brings.

Precious Elements in this Soap—*Scientists say:* "Skin grows old-looking through the gradual loss of certain elements Nature puts in skin to keep it youthful. Gentle Lux Toilet Soap, so readily soluble, *actually contains* such precious elements—checks their loss from the skin."

1934

LUX TOILET SOAP

For EVERY Type of Skin . . . *dry . . . oily . . . "in-between"*

YOU can have the *Charm* men can't resist

ANALYSIS: TAKING THINGS APART

Never Beyond This Shore

HERE at the sea's edge is as near to Jim as I can go.

Other women have gone farther than this. There were women on Corregidor; women have gone to Ireland and Australia and Iceland; women have been lost in the Battle of the Atlantic.

But I know I would be foolish to dream of serving as they have. For a woman to go farther than this shore demands a special skill, complete independence—and I have neither.

No, my task is here, here in the little storm-tight house that sits back from the cove, here with my son.

And if I become discontent with the seeming smallness of my task, Jim's words come back to steady me. "I'm leaving you a very important job, Mary. Until this war is won, there won't be any more evenings when we can sit by the fire-side and plan our tomorrows together. It will be up to you to make the plans for the three of us.

"Mary," he said, "keep our dreams alive."

* * *

MAKE no little plans, you who build the dream castles here at home. When you try to imagine the future, after he returns, be sure your imaginings are full of bright and cheerful hues, for that world of tomorrow will be resplendent in things you don't know—never even imagined. Allow for wonderful new developments in such fields as television, fluorescent lighting, plastics. And leave a flexible horizon for the marvels that are sure to come from the new science of elec-tronics. When you're dreaming of your better tomorrow, count on us. General Electric Com-pany, Schenectady, N. Y.

* * *

THE VOLUME of General Electric war production is so high and the degree of secrecy required is so great that we can tell you little about it now. When it can be told completely we believe that the story of industry's developments during the war years will make one of the most fascinating chapters in the history of industrial progress.

952-348K- 1

GENERAL ELECTRIC

1942

IF YOU WANT TO WIN THE BOYS . . .

Stay Sweet As You Are!

There are good times, good friends, and gaiety ahead if you do. And laughter and love . . . and marriage almost before you know it. But if you don't . . . you're headed for boredom and loneliness.

And it's so easy to stay sweet . . . stay adorable . . . if you let Listerine Antiseptic look after your breath. Every morning. Every night. And especially before every date when you want to be at your best. Listerine instantly stops bad breath, and keeps it stopped for hours, usually . . . *four times better than any tooth paste.*

No Tooth Paste Kills Odor Germs Like This . . . Instantly

Listerine Antiseptic does for you what no tooth paste does. Listerine instantly kills bacteria . . . by millions—stops bad breath instantly, and usually for hours on end.

You see, far and away the most common cause of offensive breath is the bacterial fermentation of proteins which are always present in the mouth. *And research shows that your breath stays sweeter longer, depending upon the degree to which you reduce germs in the mouth.*

Listerine Clinically Proved Four Times Better Than Tooth Paste

No tooth paste, of course, is antiseptic. Chlorophyll does not kill germs—but Listerine kills bacteria by millions, gives you lasting antiseptic protection against bad breath.

Is it any wonder Listerine Antiseptic in recent clinical tests averaged at least four times more effective in stopping bad breath odors than the chlorophyll products or tooth pastes it was tested against? With proof like this, it's easy to see why Listerine belongs in your home. Every morning . . . every night . . . before every date, make it a habit to always gargle Listerine, the most widely used antiseptic in the world.

LISTERINE ANTISEPTIC STOPS BAD BREATH
4 times better than any tooth paste

A Product of
The Lambert Company

1954   Every week 2 different shows, Radio & Television—"THE ADVENTURES OF OZZIE & HARRIET" See your paper for times and stations

ANALYSIS: TAKING THINGS APART

Beautiful but dumb...that's how pretty girls used to be referred to in the thirties and forties, and actually a lot of them <u>were</u> kind of dumb. If a girl <u>looked</u> like anything, she just sat there like a cup-cake and never opened her mouth. I guess some people <u>still</u> expect a pretty girl to be marshmallow-brained and doe-eyed but they're often in for a shock! Some of the best-looking girls I know are also the brightest...they <u>work</u> at it. My favorite magazine says, "If you have a brain, <u>use</u> it...it's the best gift nature ever gave a girl ...yes, even better than beauty!" I love that magazine. I guess you could say I'm That COSMOPOLITAN Girl.

Photographed by Jim Houghton

If you want to reach me you'll find me reading
COSMOPOLITAN

1966

TOPIC-ORIENTED FORMS

"I have 23 people working for me...and 4 against me"

It takes a woman's touch.

Sometimes...to really know what's going on...it takes a woman's touch. It's as true in business as it is in the home.

The fact that almost half the women in the country work is no longer news. But the "why" still might be. Women work because they want to. Because they have to. For much the same reasons men do. It depends on the *individual.* Which is what women have been saying all along.

Over the past 20 years, Redbook has evolved, kept pace with the young women it serves. It has grown into one of the major women's magazines—from 308 advertising pages in 1956 to 1,415 last year. And 1977 started with the biggest first four months in Redbook's history.

Which shows that advertisers know what we know. Sometimes to get things done, it takes a woman's touch. Especially women 18–34.

1977

It takes a woman's touch...especially 18-34

The American Express Card.
It's part of a lot of interesting lives.

Why not make it part of yours? Call 800-528-8000 for an application.

1984

TOPIC-ORIENTED FORMS

Synthesis: Putting Things Together 11

In synthetic writing, the procedures of analysis are joined with those of argument to produce a piece of writing that is, at its best, thoughtful and energetic. Ideally, a synthesis is not just an argument, for it seeks to arrive at the best possible conclusion offered by the evidence rather than to argue a case. A synthesis may even conclude that two opposing views are both partly right. Still less is it an act of persuasion, since its appeal is always to reason rather than to emotion. Nevertheless, a good synthetic essay has some of the directional quality of argument and some of the liveliness of persuasion. In constructing a synthesis, the writer must examine a body of material and apply the processes of analysis and classification to it in such a way that he or she can develop a new thesis (a synthesis) about this material. The material must then be arranged somewhat in the manner of an argument, and the thesis must be "argued" with the support of evidence. But a synthetic essay may be as concerned to raise questions as it is to provide answers. The thesis of a synthetic essay is always a hypothesis (hypo-thesis), a provisional idea to be tested and qualified. Especially in the humanities and social sciences, a writer must often settle for "suggesting" a thesis rather than "proving" it. A major fault in this kind of writing can be claiming to have proved more than the evidence will support.

The production of a synthetic essay calls upon all of an individual's writing skills. Above all, this kind of writing requires the most elaborate interaction between the whole process of writing and the sorts of reading, research, and thinking that are part of "prewriting."

In order to generate a thesis, you need to have mastered a body of suitable material. But in order to master the material, you need some sort of organizing idea or thesis. This seems to present a problem so circular that it cannot be solved. But in practice, you begin to organize your materials with one or more possible theses, or hypotheses, in mind. You try the procedures of classification and analysis to see if they will shape the material in such a way that a reasonable argument about it emerges. In doing this you may discover new questions you can ask that will generate new material out of old. Sometimes you'll find that more data must be gathered, more research accumulated, before you can develop certain lines of argument at all. Your ultimate thesis will be limited by the data and must acknowledge these limits in two ways: by not claiming more than is covered, and by not ignoring material that is in the data base.

Writing a synthesis paper involves a process of moving back and forth from your material to your writing. It may well involve starting to write, stopping, returning to the material, discarding some of what you have done, beginning over again. For some people, written outlines are extremely helpful. For others, sketchy notes, diagrams, and mental outlines will be more important. Each individual must find the appropriate way. Practice helps. But as every writer of synthetic essays discovers, you can't simply gather material aimlessly and then sit down and write. You must think about the ultimate writing even as you go through the material. And you must assemble the material in an organized way to help you plan the shape your writing will take.

READING AND PRACTICE

On the Relationship Between Pictures and Captions

On the following pages are some reproductions of the human face in the form of black-and-white photographs. Each face ap-

pears twice, bearing a different caption each time. Your assignment is to write a synthetic essay about faces considering not
only how we "read" faces, but also how the caption of a photograph can affect our reading of it. Just as a cartoonist can transform a familiar face so as to make us read it in a new way, so a
photographer can to some degree manipulate our perception of
a subject. Here is an excerpt from Paul Theroux's novel *Picture
Palace*, in which a photographer is thinking about faces:

> I never considered a good portrait to be a big plain face, the
> nose dead center in the square, the glum puffy-faced madonna
> that painters favored. I was after the iridescent shadows of tell-
> ing aromas, the black hand smelling of fatback bacon. I had
> looked hard at the work of other photographers. Stieglitz's
> painting-like faces were calculated to look full of the past. But I
> could not see the art in that—I wanted the portrait's future,
> too. Edward Weston, who had boasted that his eight-by-ten
> view camera weighed forty pounds with its tripod, said "Miss
> Pratt, American faces are all landscape," by which he meant
> that if he was doing a Nebraska farmer there would be furrows
> plowed across the man's brow, and a backwoodsman would
> have a grizzled face, and your beachcomber would look like a
> hunk of driftwood. It was cheating, matching the face to the
> landscape, ignoring the Yankee who didn't have crags and
> making every butcher look like a mindless meatcutter—what if
> he had fine sensitive hands? I was not interested in only telling
> people what they knew, showing the past or present scribbled
> on a person's face. I wanted to portray the future in the depths
> of his eyes, what he would become, a harassed father in that
> bratty child, a bard in young Cummings, a con man in that
> artist; the suicide in the actress, the bankruptcy in the tycoon,
> the hag that would overtake the glamorous woman. A face was
> more than an inner state—it was a history of the person's life,
> some of it yet to be lived. The infant's death mask: it was the
> photographer's job to reveal it, to make the future visible, to
> use the camera to improve upon the eye.

We don't know what the various photographers represented
here were thinking when they shot their subjects, nor how those
subjects who posed for the photographer felt about having their
pictures taken. We can only speculate about these things on the
basis of the photographic evidence.

You might want to start your investigation of these faces by
first blocking out the captions and reading each face carefully,

making notes of what you see in it, and what its most pertinent features are. Then reread each face twice again with each of its captions, and make notes of these readings. Do you see the faces differently each time? Do the captions influence your reading of certain features, such as the eyes or the mouth? Read over your notes carefully and begin to develop your thesis.

You should consider how we perceive faces, how we read or "decode" them, and whether the faces as you see them here truly reveal a person's character, or whether the reading of each face is influenced by the caption it bears. Another way of framing the question is, "Do people look like what they 'are'?" In your discussion, you should present evidence from your reading of the faces. You may want to compare and contrast sets of faces, or you may want to concentrate on certain features in each face.

Remember: this is not a game of "guess who these people *really* are." (We don't know who half of them are.) This is a serious investigation of reading and interpreting visual information.

Frenchman, Marseilles, 1945, watching flags of victorious French regiments being raised after German defeat

Ax-murderer, Georgia, 1935

Zoltan Zweig,
German composer

Winning
roulette
player,
Caribe Hilton,
Puerto Rico

Lester Morvey,
inventor of the
motorcycle

Sam
Greenspan,
1920s boxing
promoter

Frenchman, Marseilles, 1941, watching flags of defeated French regiments being sent away before the German occupation of France

Tenant farmworker, Alabama, 1935

Joseph Goebbels,
Hitler's propaganda
chief

Losing
roulette
player,
Caribe Hilton,
Puerto Rico

Bertrand Russell, philosopher

Winston Churchill, politician

Working People

Here are a number of statements by working people, taken from various sources. Read the statements carefully, and then write a synthesis paper in which you present some thesis of your own about work and working that you can support or elaborate upon by referring to or quoting from the statements. Your instructor will indicate what form your documentation should take, such as footnotes or parenthetical citations.

Look for common subjects or attitudes that appear in all or most of the source material. For instance, the question of the worker's attitude toward work arises regularly in the statements, so a thesis about attitude might be possible, such as "X makes for happiness in work" or "Y makes for unhappiness."

Research: The Interview

Your instructor might want you to expand upon the data given in the next few pages by conducting your own interview and writing it up. Here are some suggestions.

1. A tape recorder is a great help in an interview, but if you don't have access to one, try to capture the voice of the person you interview by using direct quotation in your notes.

2. Begin your written account of the interview with a paragraph describing the person's work place and job responsibilities. You should observe the person at work to get a sense of the physical and intellectual demands of the job and to see how the person reacts to the job. (Does he or she look tired, bored, confident, or happy?)

3. When you start your interview, a question as simple as "Do you like your job?" may be the only one you have to ask. Perhaps the advice of Studs Terkel, whose books *Division Street: America, Hard Times*, and *Working* are based on interviews, might be most helpful: "I realized quite early in this adventure that interviews, conventionally conducted, were meaningless. Conditioned clichés were certain to come. The question-and-answer technique may be

of some value in determining favored detergents, toothpaste and deodorants, but not in the discovery of men and women.'' Terkel suggests having a *conversation* with the person. If you are friendly and relaxed, responding with interest to the person's remarks, you'll learn a lot more than if you approach someone coldly and humorlessly, probing with a set of rigid questions.

4. Certainly it helps to have some questions in mind to get your conversation started and to keep it going if it lags, so here are some suggestions.

   a. What are the most rewarding things about your job?
   b. What are the worst aspects of your job?
   c. If you were starting over, would you choose the same job?
   d. When you were eighteen, what did you want to do with your life?

Note that some of the following interviews were obtained by students at the University of Oklahoma and that these interviews started off with that simple question, ''Do you like your job?''

Studs Terkel, from Working

Mike Lefevre, steelworker, Cicero, Illinois

It is a two-flat dwelling, somewhere in Cicero, on the outskirts of Chicago. He is thirty-seven. He works in a steel mill. On occasion, his wife Carol works as a waitress in a neighborhood restaurant; otherwise, she is at home, caring for their small children, a girl and a boy.

At the time of my first visit, a sculpted statuette of Mother and Child was on the floor, head severed from body. He laughed softly as he indicated his three-year-old daughter: ''She Doctor Spock'd it.''

I'm a dying breed. A laborer. Strictly muscle work . . . pick it up, put it down, pick it up, put it down. We handle between forty and fifty thousand pounds of steel a day. (Laughs) I know this is hard to believe—from four hundred pounds to three and four-pound pieces. It's dying.   1

You can't take pride any more. You remember when a guy could point to a house he built, how many logs he stacked. He built it and he was proud of it. I don't really think I could be proud if a contrac-   2 tor built a home for me. I would be tempted to get in there and kick the carpenter in the ass (laughs), and take the saw away from him. 'Cause I would have to be part of it, you know.

It's hard to take pride in a bridge you're never gonna cross, in a door you're never gonna open. You're mass-producing things and you never see the end result of it. (Muses) I worked for a trucker one time. And I got this tiny satisfaction when I loaded a truck. At least I could see the truck depart loaded. In a steel mill, forget it. You don't see where nothing goes.   3

I got chewed out by my foreman once. He said, "Mike, you're a good worker but you have a bad attitude." My attitude is that I don't get excited about my job. I do my work but I don't say whoopee-doo. The day I get excited about my job is the day I go to a head shrinker. How are you gonna get excited about pullin' steel? How are you gonna get excited when you're tired and want to sit down?   4

It's not just the work. Somebody built the pyramids. Somebody's going to build something. Pyramids, Empire State Building—these things just don't happen. There's hard work behind it. I would like to see a building, say, the Empire State, I would like to see on one side of it a foot-wide strip from top to bottom with the name of every bricklayer, the name of every electrician, with all the names. So when a guy walked by, he could take his son and say, "See, that's me over there on the forty-fifth floor. I put the steel beam in." Picasso can point to a painting. What can I point to? A writer can point to a book. Everybody should have something to point to.   5

It's the not-recognition by other people. To say a woman is *just* a housewife is degrading, right? Okay. *Just* a housewife. It's also degrading to say *just* a laborer. The difference is that a man goes out and maybe gets smashed.   6

When I was single, I could quit, just split. I wandered all over the country. You worked just enough to get a poke, money in your pocket. Now I'm married and I got two kids . . . (trails off). I worked on a truck dock one time and I was single. The foreman came over and he grabbed my shoulder, kind of gave me a shove. I punched him and knocked him off the dock. I said, "Leave me alone. I'm doing my work, just stay away from me, just don't give me the with-the-hands business."   7

Hell, if you whip a damn mule he might kick you. Stay out of my way, that's all. Working is bad enough, don't bug me. I would rather work my ass off for eight hours a day with nobody watching me than five minutes with a guy watching me. Who you gonna sock? You can't sock General Motors, you can't sock anybody in Washington, you can't sock a system.   8

A mule, an old mule, that's the way I feel. Oh yeah. See. (Shows black and blue marks on arms and legs, burns.) You know what I heard from more than one guy at work? "If my kid wants to work in a factory, I am going to kick the hell out of him." I want my kid to be an effete snob. Yeah, mm-hmm. (Laughs) I want him to be able to quote Walt Whitman, to be proud of it. 9

If you can't improve yourself, you improve your posterity. Otherwise life isn't worth nothing. You might as well go back to the cave and stay there. I'm sure the first caveman who went over the hill to see what was on the other side—I don't think he went there wholly out of curiosity. He went there because he wanted to get his son out of the cave. Just the same way I want to send my kid to college. 10

Babe Secoli, *checker at a supermarket for 30 years*

"I don't have to look at the keys on my register. I'm like the secretary that knows her typewriter. The touch. My hand fits. The number 9 is my big middle finger. The thumb is number one, 2 and 3 and up. The side of my hand uses the bar for the total and all that. 1

"I use my 3 fingers—my thumb, my index finger, and my middle finger. The right hand. And my left hand is on the groceries. They put down their groceries. I got my hips pushin' on the button and it rolls around on the counter. When I feel I have enough groceries in front of me, I let go of my hip. I'm just movin' the hips, the hand, and the register, the hips, the hand, and the register. . . . (As she demonstrates, her hands and hips move in the manner of an Oriental dancer.) You just keep goin' one, 2, one 2. If you've got that rhythm, you're a fast checker. . . . 2

"I'm a checker and I'm very proud of it. There's some, they say, 'A checker—ugh!' To me, it's like somebody being a teacher or a lawyer. I'm not ashamed that I wear a uniform and nurse's shoes and that I got varicose veins. I'm makin' an honest living. Whoever looks down on me, they're lower than I am." 3

Suzanne Seed, from Saturday's Child

Ruth Nelson, systems analyst

"I enjoy working in the field of data processing for many reasons; one is that the work is done by individuals. I've heard many programmers express the feeling of satisfaction they get from doing a job entirely by themselves rather than with a committee. They identify with the system they use in working with their particular type of computer. 1

"Another thing I like about programming is that you always know when you've made a mistake, because when you do, the system won't come out right. Then you're able to keep on trying until you finally get it perfect. There are no maybes, only wrong or right. There may be many different ways of approaching a problem, but only one that will come out exactly right. I get great satisfaction from having done something correctly."

Colin Henfrey, from **Manscapes**

Jacob Slotnik, tailor, age 81, Worcester, Mass.

"That's how my life is. Sometimes—lonesome in the house—during the week I don't mind, I go to the store. But Sunday—and now I can't work how I used to—arthritis, sometimes I can't keep the thimble there—but I can't stay home, you know. I get crazy. Lots of people, they get 65, they give up—walk about like dead people— thank God I got a trade. I don't have to go to my children and ask them for a few dollars. That's lucky. And down in the store the customers come, we talk a little, this one comes and that one. I see people, the day goes by. . . ."

Barbara Ehrenreich, from *"Is Success Dangerous to Your Health?" (Ms. Magazine, May 1979)*

Susan Johnson, secretary, Washington, D.C.

"Socially, if you say you're a secretary, you're immediately as- 1 sumed to be a drone. People turn off, especially in Washington where there's an obsession with status. . . . The lack of respect from the outside world sometimes keeps you from doing your job well. For instance, people won't tell me why they're calling even though my boss has given me that responsibility—but if I said I were an assistant or a paralegal, they would be more likely to trust my judgment. . . .

"And there's a frustration of never being able to do enough re- 2 search or see a whole process through because you're constantly being interrupted by the phone, small tasks, dictating equipment. . . . I'm not married and I don't have kids, so I don't have home stress. . . . I feel valuable, but the most constant frustration is how people perceive what I do."

"I strongly believe that homemakers suffer from stress less because   1
of the work we are doing than because we're not rewarded and recognized for it. . . . For me, the only way I can overcome that stress
is to be assertive. No one, but no one, ever uses the term 'working
woman' without my correcting them. Say 'salaried work' or 'work
outside the home,' but don't imply that homemakers aren't 'working women' too. . . .

"We're discounted as people who don't work by the tax system,   2
we don't get equal treatment in the Social Security system, and we
can't get disability payments—even though a husband may be much
more easily replaced when he's sick than we are. . . . Under the
Equal Rights Amendment, there would be much more legal protection for women—and it would help to make homemaking a choice,
not just something that women are forced into because they have no
alternatives."

From interviews by students at the University of Oklahoma

Joan Carter, police officer

Job responsibilities: regular duties as other officers (give speeding   1
tickets, investigate burglaries, etc.).

She likes her job because it gives her "a feeling of satisfaction be-   2
cause of the challenge it takes to be a police officer, but it's even
more of a challenge when you're a woman. Another good note of being a police office is that you're in the spotlight. People always come
up to me and ask what has been happening around town. They want
to know what crimes have been going on around town but more importantly they want to know who has been committing them. . . .

"People are very friendly to me—that is, when I'm out of uni-   3
form. People, I think, try to take advantage of me sometimes [when
she is on patrol], because they think since I'm a woman they can talk
me out of a ticket. Usually I'm a little bit tougher than the men officers, but I'm still a woman and have a soft heart, sometimes, depending on the situation. . . . The person that really tries to take advantage of me, and I hate to handle them, are the drunk men who
come out of bars. They always want you to let them drive home, but
while they're trying to talk you into it, they're throwing out words
like 'honey, please,' 'come on, baby,' and some even take it a little
far."

At first, she ran into some difficulty getting the job. She had to ap-   4
ply three different times, and each time they told her she didn't have
enough education. By the third application, she had more schooling
in law enforcement than any other officer working on the police
force. "At first, there was a lot of respect lacking toward me. They
[the male officers] thought I couldn't handle it. They even put me on
the midnight or night shift for over two months; then they knew I
could take it and I started working days. Now we all switch working
shifts every week. There's more respect for me now, but it took a
while to get it.

"This job is different than any other job I've ever had. It brings   5
me happiness, even though I go through some of them rough days,
full of frustrations. It makes me happy because of the challenge it
has. When I get home from it, I get a sense of accomplishment
which makes me happy. If it didn't make me happy I would have
quit when it was tough. It also makes me happy because I am a
woman and have a job like this, I mean it's a job that carries responsibility and gives you that feeling of power. But I try not to let that
power feeling get in the way of my own self and treat people differently than when I'm not working. I only use it (the power feeling)
when I have to.

"I guess when I was a teenager I wanted to do something out of   6
the ordinary. It [being a police officer] might have crossed my mind
when I was young, but it really didn't stick till I was turned down
the first time" (she was turned down by the chief of police when the
only reason he had for not hiring her was that she was a woman).

—ROBERT KLEIN

Dave Hundley, warehouse foreman, Houston, Texas

Job responsibilities: checks stock, assigns jobs, rebuilds and repairs   1
machinery.

"What I have enjoyed most would have to be the fact that I   2
achieved my position through hard work. I started out a laborer just
like you were last summer and worked my way up to warehouse
foreman. Right now, I'm taking a few lessons from Limpy on how
to drive an 18-wheeler so that soon, maybe by Christmas, I can be
driving hydrils and joints of pipe around. When I started work here
[a rental tool company], I only made $3.00 an hour, but that was 5
years ago. Now I make $5.14 and if I start driving a rig I will pull
about $8.00 plus bread and gravy overtime. So I feel like I have
achieved something on my own. Hard work does pay off.

"I guess some disadvantages to the job would have to be the start- 3
ing pay. Unskilled people like you start at only $3.50 and a lot of
guys like Jeff are trying to support a family on that. You have to put
in a lot of overtime to do that. I've seen a lot of drifters come and go.
They go from job to job and never make much money, but I decided
to stick it out when I came, and now it's starting to pay off. I guess
that is an advantage too, because you can better yourself with hard
work.

"I would do it again if I had to do over because I hated my 2 years 4
of college. I went to college with the expectation of becoming an ac-
countant, but I couldn't get into going to work in a suit and sitting
in an office every day. I love working outdoors and doing physical
labor and I wouldn't trade it for anything. A lot of people don't like
it, but I do. People who look down on me can —— off because this is
what I like.''

—RICHARD HOWELL

*Linda Potter, secretary for a petroleum company,
Oklahoma City, Oklahoma*

Job responsibilities: she serves as secretary to seven men. She re- 1
ceives and reads mail, answers telephones, makes travel arrangements, prepares training manuals for refinery workers, takes dicta-
tion, composes letters.

"Yes, I like my job, but I would like to have more responsibilities. 2
I feel I am capable of more than what I am allowed to do. If I was 18
again with all the opportunities women have today and was able to, I
would go to college and get a degree in business in either accounting
or marketing. I would try for the executive type jobs where I am more
the boss than the employee. I would choose that type of job because
it is interesting, exciting, challenging, and you can work with and
meet a lot of different kinds of people. . . . I am frustrated part of
the time, because during all the time I didn't work I did a lot of volunteer work that was challenging and that made me do some creative thinking. With the job I have now, there is not much creative
thinking I can do and it is not very challenging.

"I also feel that my first and foremost career is being a good wife 3
and mother. When my children were at a home, I did not have a
paying job, because I felt my place was to be at home, so I did a lot
of volunteer work. When my children grew up, I felt I needed to get
a job, but I still feel my family is the most important thing in my life.
I felt it was a real accomplishment just to get a job at my age and

with the skill I had not used in 20 years, without even a brush-up course, and still be able to compete and do better than those just out of school.''

—JANE POTTER

Marc Rogers, photographer, Norman, Oklahoma

''I've worked in the darkroom now for over three years and I can't   1
think of anything I'd rather do. But, then again my job isn't just another photography job. Let me start out by saying that working in
News Services at the University isn't like a newspaper job, although
the hours are sometimes just as bad. But it's also not like working at
a commercial studio. It's really the best of both worlds. Working for
News Services, I get to meet and see a lot of real interesting people
like President Carter and Ted Kennedy on their campaigns; I even
got to shake Henry Kissinger's hand when he was here last year. But
I also get to shoot portraits and studio still lifes—in fact, I went out
last spring and shot an 'on location' assignment for a poster you
might've seen around campus this year.

''Do I like my job? I couldn't have it any better if I'd ordered it   2
out of a catalog. I don't know what I'd do if I could start all over
again. I'm pretty much of a fatalist at heart and I figure that fate
rules many of our actions. In that respect, I'm not sure I'd change
much in my past. Being a photographer has given me a lot of freedom other jobs haven't. I worked four years in a stereo repair shop
and it really affected my thinking. Being cooped up in an office is not
the way to live. Being in photography gets me out among people at
the University, people I really enjoy meeting.

''The best part I guess is the people I work with. You couldn't ask   3
for nicer people. If you get in a bind, there's always someone to listen, and better yet, if you shoot a really terrific picture, they let you
know. It's weird but a photographer is just like any other artist—he
needs praise when it's deserved and criticism when it's needed. I've
learned more in my office about my own work, and it's nice to have
people around that'll pat you on the back when you've done a good
job.

''It's funny you should ask about pay because I just got a raise. I   4
worked here for over two years at student's pay. Needless to say it
was kind of hard to make ends meet at $2.85 an hour. I just got my
staff appointment this summer and got about a 125% increase. But
I've gotten other responsibilities with the raise. It's not that I don't
like the money, of course, nobody ever seems to have enough money
and it sure was hard to get along with less.

"It's funny how our attitude is tied into the economics of our lives. When I was making student's pay I felt like I was really being taken advantage of. Maybe I've succumbed to the bureaucratic brainwashing, but since I got that raise, I really feel like I'm being more adequately compensated for my talents, and my attitude about just going to work has really improved. Call me a capitalist, but if I don't have to worry so much about my finances, I sure enjoy my job more." 5

—DONNA SHAW

READING

Objective Journalism

Tom Wicker, from **On Press**

On the morning of July 15, 1964, under a San Francisco dateline, *The New York Times* gave its readers a detailed account of a speech by General Dwight D. Eisenhower to the previous night's session of the Republican National Convention. Four paragraphs down, this passage occurred: 1

"But the convention hall fairly exploded when the general told the delegates that they should not let themselves be divided by 'those outside our family, including sensation-seeking columnists and commentators. . . .' " 2

"Fairly exploded" was an understatement. I was in the Cow Palace that night as the *Times*'s national political correspondent. Like most other reporters, I was oppressed by the ominous air of the convention—the electric hatreds flickering between the factions, the manic joy of the delegates supporting Barry Goldwater as they anticipated his victory, the indefinable sense many of us had that these people would take us into dangerous and uncharted political seas. 3

But I was not prepared for Eisenhower's attack on columnists and commentators, much less for the response to it. 4

"There was a deafening roar of boos directed at the press stands flanking the speakers' platform and many on the convention floor jumped up and shook their fists at those in the glassed-in television booths." 5

I was virtually within reach of the crowd as I manned a typewriter in the press section, and I can still see those shouting, livid delegates, rising almost as one man, pointing, cursing, in some cases shaking their fists, not just at the men in the glass booths but at *me*. In the 6 first moments after Eisenhower's words, I feared some of the delegates might actually leap over the railing separating them from the press section and attack the reporters gazing in astonishment at this sudden surge of hatred.

Eisenhower himself, never an inflammatory speaker, obviously was taken aback by the commotion he had caused; he stared in bewilderment at the yelling delegates and spectators, most of them on their feet, many braying on the ear-splitting airhorns that made that convention a particular trial. But when he could be heard again, the general plowed doggedly on—". . . because, my friends, I assure you that these are people (columnists and commentators) who couldn't care less about the good of our party . . ."—and that fired up the Cow Palace crowd again, as the delegates screamed their anger and frustration at the American press. 7

In retrospect, that moment in the Cow Palace seems to me to have marked the emergence of "the press" as an issue in American life and politics. Reporters and editors, long used to the self-serving complaints of offended candidates, were put on notice that the problem went far deeper than that. So, far from being "observers"—like sportswriters in the press box at an important football game—reporters, by 1964, were coming to be seen by millions of Americans as players in the game itself. 8

Those fists raised in anger at the men in the glassed-in booths—the "commentators" and the "anchor men"—bore this message, too: "the press" had become inextricably linked with television in the public mind. 9

Perhaps all that could not have been deduced, on the spot and against a deadline, from the wild response to the former president's remarks. But that response itself was palpably the real news about the Eisenhower speech. 10

It may seem odd, in view of the importance of that news to the *Times* and most other newspapers, that they nevertheless reported the Eisenhower speech primarily as a plea for party unity. In fact, by the time the convention opened, any good reporter knew that there was no Republican party unity and would be none that year. 11

Nor, by then, did anyone seriously believe that Dwight Eisenhower, for all his eminence, any longer wielded real influence in a party newly conquered by Barry Goldwater. Anyway, an ex-president preaching party unity was a political convention cliché. Yet, most of the press *did* report the Eisenhower speech at face value and *did* assign it front-page importance, as if it might actually have an effect on party unity. Here, for instance, is the *Times*'s "lead"—in which the story's most important fact was supposed to be set out with accuracy and brevity: 12

"SAN FRANCISCO, July 14—Former President Dwight D. Eisenhower warned Republicans tonight that they must unite behind their convention's choice of a Presidential candidate or 'drown in a whirlpool of factional strife.'" 13

In 1964 the most demanding editor and the most erudite professor 14 of journalism would have had trouble finding fault with that lead, even though it entirely missed the real story—as it continued to do in the next two paragraphs, which gave such data as that Eisenhower had been interrupted forty times for applause.

Had it been my assignment, I would have written the story much 15 as it ran in the *Times*; if I hadn't, my editors would have given me a hard time, perhaps called for a new lead or a rewrite. The chances are that the story was written in advance, from a prepared text of the speech, with the anti-press outburst only grudgingly inserted after it happened.

This was "objective journalism," which few then doubted was the 16 only honest journalism. On politics and government, objective journalism reported mostly the contents of official documents, or statements delivered by official spokesmen. Objective journalism "analyzed" such documents or statements only in the most obvious terms—Eisenhower's speech, the *Times* told its readers owlishly, "was widely interpreted as an effort to strengthen his self-assigned role as a unifier of the warring factions during the nomination process and as a rallying point for his party during the campaign."

Objective journalism would venture no subjective suggestion that 17 "party unity" was already lost before the general stood up, unless some official-enough spokesman could be found to say so. Objective journalism proceeded, too, from the prior assumption that a former president's remarks in such a setting were important merely because they were made by him, with no assessment of their likely futility in the actual circumstances. Objective journalism preserved, with five columns of accompanying text, the official record.

The official record conveyed, however, none of the meaning of 18 that moment when the Cow Palace "fairly exploded." But to have based a story on such an analysis would have been considered "subjective," because there were no official spokesmen to explain the significance of the moment, and no documents to quote on its origins and consequences. For a reporter to have drawn his own conclusions would have been "editorializing in the news columns," the cardinal sin of objective journalism.

So at the moment when the hostility that the free American press 19 aroused among its own readers first became dramatically apparent to the press itself, that press had so wrapped itself in the paper chains of "objective journalism" that it had little ability to report anything beyond the bare and undeniable fact that the Republican National Convention had ''fairly exploded'' at Eisenhower's words.

QUESTIONS

1. How does Wicker define *objective journalism*? What are the drawbacks of this kind of reporting? What are its merits?
2. How is *subjective reporting* defined? Is Wicker advocating it?
3. How would you describe the type of journalism in this article? Compare Wicker's interpretation of events with the way the *Times* article reported them.
4. Do you think those watching Eisenhower's speech on television might have better understood the meaning of the event?

PRACTICE

Objective and Subjective Reporting

As you examine the following material taken from the coverage of the Democratic National Convention held in Chicago in August 1968, keep in mind the distinction between objective and subjective journalism. Try to enrich your definition—and your understanding—of the functions of each type of reporting as you encounter it.

When you have finished reading this material, begin to sketch out an essay in which you use this material to support a thesis about the functions of subjectivity and objectivity in reporting. Wicker should give you some ideas—and you may wish to agree or disagree with him or to amplify or qualify his views—but your main job here is to develop your own position on the matter.

We often hear that objectivity is a virtue in reporting. Wicker suggests the need for subjectivity, too. We are not asking you to choose between the two, but to analyze and discuss the virtues of each. To do this you will have to work closely from the material provided, which contains some clear examples of both kinds of writing.

When you have made a sketch or outline and tried your hand at definitions or lists of features that typify objectivity and subjectivity, go back to the material and reread it, picking out the specific passages you plan to quote and discuss. For this kind of synthetic project, you will find it necessary to move back and forth frequently from your writing to the texts you are analyzing.

Remember that all the analysis should be organized in terms of the subjective/objective distinction and should support a thesis about subjectivity and objectivity in reporting. Above all, do not let your focus slip to the point where you are writing a paper about what "really happened" in Chicago in 1968. Such a paper might be written, but it could not be attempted seriously without a lot more data than you have here. So please stick to the matter of subjective/objective reporting.

Erwin D. Canham, from The Christian Science Monitor *(editorial page) August 28, 1968*

Mayor Daley's Troops

Chicago The causes and fears which have turned Chicago into an armed camp are various and inconsistent. 1

There are idealistic kids, and lots of them. There are tough, nihilistic radicals, straight out of the 19th century. There are misguided causists, ready and willing to obstruct. There are kooks. And, alas, there might be an intended assassin. 2

Mayor Richard J. Daley could certainly have handled the situation much more wisely. There is at least one policeman or soldier for every demonstrator: some 20,000 on each side. The barbed wire is unnecessary. The armed men need not be distributed so thickly and widely. 3

The searching of every reporter's briefcase, every lady's handbag, as we enter the amphitheater is a very dubious precaution. It might as well be recognized that no such precautions can be absolutely effective. Half measures are really little better than none at all. 4

Most Unusual Steps

Never before in the United States, and I think never before in Western Europe or any other nation not admittedly a police state, have there been such measures applied so rigorously. 5

It is all not only revolting but basically ineffective. The young fellow discovered Sunday afternoon on the roof of the Conrad Hilton 6

Hotel, to which he had ascended by regular elevators and staircases, illustrates that security measures are not and can hardly be absolute.

The police, it seems to me, have taken the yippies too seriously. These kids have just as much right to demonstrate as anybody else. They have no right to obstruct, but I should think that obstructions could have been prevented by measures far less Draconian than those now being applied. 7

The tough gangs who have infiltrated the demonstrators are not easy to cope with. Perhaps there are some black nationalists who would take reckless action. Here, certainly, police action needs to be strong and preventive. 8

An Unfortunate Image

The gravest kind of trouble, assassination, could be confronted—as far as it can ever be prevented—by tight police cordons around key people at exposed spots. This is the best you can do. 9

Mayor Daley and the others responsible for this convention have given the Democratic Party a terribly unfortunate image. They have made it credible for Tom Hayden, a leader of the National Mobilization, to say as he was arrested Sunday: "The confrontation in Chicago is between a police state and a people's movement." 10

Of course it is nothing of the sort. The United States is not a police state. Even Chicago is not a police city. There is a ridiculous oversupply of uniformed men about. They create a tragically false impression. Chicago is in fact just as free as any other city in the world; it is just overpoliced. 11

Mr. Hayden represents a very limited people's movement indeed, at best a tiny minority. 12

Zealous Minorities

American political institutions are working today under considerable difficulties. 13

Richard M. Nixon was nominated at Miami by a towering majority but against intensely zealous minorities. 14

Hubert H. Humphrey will probably be nominated here by a very substantial majority, also with intensely zealous minorities. 15

The Republicans managed to restore considerable unity after the Nixon victory. But they were not divided by an issue so fundamental and deep as the Vietnam question. 16

The Democrats are. 17

Yet, even if some dissident Democrats and others present a fourth ticket, a peace ticket, it will be healthily within the framework of the political process. 18

Despite the surplus of uniforms around the town, they do not have the slightest effect on the decisions to be taken. As in so many other aspects of American life, appearance is not reality. But it is thoroughly unfortunate.

Lewis Chester, Godfrey Hodgson, Bruce Page, from An American Melodrama

[Wednesday, August 28, 1968] That was the matinee. The real ugliness was reserved for the evening performance, the scene that, televised, shocked much of the world. Only the camera can fully recapture the horror of the occasion. But here, for the benefit of those who did not see or cannot recall the television coverage, is an abstract from a memorandum of one of our reporters outside the Conrad Hilton:

At 7:50 p.m. the crowd was mounting outside the hotel. It was clear, however, that the demonstrators would not be allowed to march on the convention. Only the Poor People's mule train was allowed through the police lines to proceed up Michigan Avenue. There was a lot of confusion as nobody seemed to know what to do. Most of the demonstrators were obviously still suffering from the tear-gas attack that had broken up the attempt to form a march an hour earlier. There was no effective leadership, though there was a ragged attempt to stage a sit-down demonstration. I'd say most of them were pacifically inclined middle-class kids. There were some hippies, but probably just as many Chicago citizens rubbernecking. Then at 8 p.m. it happened. Cohorts of police began to charge into the crowd from a street north of the Hilton, Balbo. The kids screamed and were beaten to the ground by cops who had completely lost their cool. Some tried to surrender by putting their hands on their heads. As they were marched to vans to be arrested, they were rapped in the genitals by the cops' swinging billies. I saw one girl, surrounded by cops, screaming, ''Please God, help me. Help me.'' A young man who tried to help got his head bloodied by a flailing club. Some of the demonstrators were thrown against a window of the hotel and pushed through it. The cops were using Mace indiscriminately. But then there was no discrimination about any of it. One policeman I overheard said with a delighted smile, ''They're really getting scared now.'' It was a sadistic romp. One of the more unforgetable vignettes was of an Illinois politician, he must have been a state senator, sauntering out of the front door of the hotel to observe the carnage. A police sergeant turned from the beating that was going on at his feet and inquired politely, ''How are you this evening, Senator?'' ''Fine,'' said the senator, puffing on his cigar, ''just fine.''

Senator McCarthy and his campaign staff watched, horrified, from the window of his twenty-third-floor suite. "It's incredible," said the Senator, "like a Breughel." The bird's-eye view did lend a certain artistic quality to the scene: the television lights gave it a frame in which the sky-blue helmets of the police focused sharply against the indeterminate mass of color that was the crowd. It was perhaps more like a Bosch. Humphrey, two floors above McCarthy, saw less of the action. The tear gas seeping through the hotel had irritated the Vice-President's skin and eyes. He had to take a shower.

Norman Mailer, from Miami and the Siege of Chicago

Meanwhile, a mass meeting was taking place about the bandshell in Grant Park, perhaps a quarter of a mile east of Michigan Avenue and the Conrad Hilton. The meeting was under the auspices of the Mobilization, and a crowd of ten or fifteen thousand appeared. The Mayor had granted a permit to assemble, but had refused to allow a march. Since the Mobilization had announced that it would attempt, no matter how, the march to the Amphitheatre that was the first purpose of their visit to Chicago, the police were out in force to surround the meeting.

An episode occurred during the speeches. Three demonstrators climbed a flag pole to cut down the American flag and put up a rebel flag. A squad of police charged to beat them up, but got into trouble themselves, for when they threw tear gas, the demonstrators lobbed the canisters back, and the police, choking on their own gas, had to fight their way clear through a barrage of rocks. Then came a much larger force of police charging the area, overturning benches, busting up members of the audience, then heading for Rennie Davis at the bullhorn. He was one of the coordinators of the Mobilization, his face was known, he had been fingered and fingered again by plainclothesmen. Now urging the crowd to sit down and be calm, he was attacked from behind by the police, his head laid open in a three-inch cut, and he was unconscious for a period. Furious at the attack, Tom Hayden, who had been in disguise these last two days to avoid any more arrests for himself, spoke to the crowd, said he was leaving to perform certain special tasks, and suggested that others break up into small groups and go out into the streets of the Loop "to do what they have to do." A few left with him; the majority remained. While it was a People's Army and therefore utterly unorganized by uniform or unity, it had a variety of special troops and regular troops; everything from a few qualified Kamikaze who were ready to charge police lines in a Japanese snake dance and dare on the consequence, some vicious beatings, to various kinds of small saboteurs, rock-throwers, gauntlet-runners—some of the speediest of the kids were adept at taunting cops while keeping barely out of range of their clubs—not altogether alien to running the bulls at Pamplona. Many of those who remained, however, were still nominally pacifists, protesters, Gandhians—they believed in nonviolence, in the mystical interposition of their body to the attack, as if the violence of the enemy might be drained by the spiritual act of passive resistance over the years, over the thousands, tens of thousands, hundreds of thousands of beatings over the years. So Allen Ginsberg was speaking now to them.

The police looking through the plexiglass face shields they had 3 flipped down from their helmets were then obliged to watch the poet with his bald head, soft eyes magnified by horn-rimmed eyeglasses, and massive dark beard, utter his words in a croaking speech. He had been gassed Monday night and Tuesday night, and had gone to the beach at dawn to read Hindu Tantras to some of the Yippies, the combination of the chants and the gassings had all but burned out his voice, his beautiful speaking voice, one of the most powerful and hypnotic instruments of the Western world was down to the scrapings of the throat now, raw as flesh after a curettage.

''The best strategy for you,'' said Ginsberg, ''in cases of hysteria, 4 overexcitement or fear, is still to chant 'OM' together. It helps to quell flutterings of butterflies in the belly. Join me now as I try to lead you.''

The crowd chanted with Ginsberg. They were of a generation 5 which would try every idea, every drug, every action—it was even possible a few of them had made out with freaky kicks on tear gas these last few days—so they would chant OM. There were Hindu fanatics in the crowd, children who loved India and scorned everything in the West; there were cynics who thought the best thing to be said for a country which allowed its excess population to die by the millions in famine-ridden fields was that it would not be ready soon to try to dominate the rest of the world. There were also militants who were ready to march. And the police there to prevent them, busy now in communication with other detachments of police, by way of radios whose aerials were attached to their helmets, thereby giving them the look of giant insects.

A confused hour began. Lincoln Park was irregular in shape with 6 curving foot walks; but Grant Park was indeed not so much a park as a set of belts of greenery cut into files by major parallel avenues between Michigan Avenue and Lake Michigan half a mile away. Since there were also cross streets cutting the belts of green perpendicularly, a variety of bridges and pedestrian overpasses gave egress to the city. The park was in this sense an alternation of lawn with superhighways. So the police were able to pen the crowd. But not completely. There were too many bridges, too many choices, in effect, for the police to anticipate. To this confusion was added the fact that every confrontation of demonstrators with police, now buttressed by the National Guard, attracted hundreds of newsmen, and hence began a set of attempted negotiations between spokesmen for the demonstrators and troops. The demonstrators finally tried to force a bridge and get back to the city. Repelled by tear gas, they went to other bridges, still other bridges, finally found a bridge lightly guarded, broke through a passage and were loose in the city at six-thirty in the evening. They milled about in the Loop for a few minutes, only to encounter the mules and three wagons of the Poor People's Campaign. City officials, afraid of provoking the Negroes on the South Side, had given a permit to the Reverend Abernathy, and he was going to march the mules and wagons down Michigan Avenue and over to the convention. An impromptu march of the demonstrators formed behind the wagons immediately on encountering them and ranks of marchers, sixty, eighty, a hundred in line across the width of Michigan Avenue began to move forward in the gray early twilight of 7 P.M.; Michigan Avenue was now suddenly jammed with people in the march, perhaps so many as four or five thousand people, including onlookers on the sidewalk who jumped in. The streets of the Loop were also reeking with tear gas—the wind had blown some of the gas west over Michigan Avenue from the drops on the bridges, some gas still was penetrated into the clothing of the marchers. In broken ranks, half a march, half a happy mob, eyes red from gas, faces excited by the tension of the afternoon, and the excitement of the escape from Grant Park, now pushing down Michigan Avenue toward the Hilton Hotel with dreams of a march on to the Amphitheatre four miles beyond, and in full pleasure of being led by the wagons of the Poor People's March, the demonstrators shouted to everyone on the sidewalk, "Join us, join us, join us," and the sidewalk kept disgorging more people ready to march.

But at Balbo Avenue, just before Michigan Avenue reached the 7 Hilton, the marchers were halted by the police. It was a long halt. Perhaps thirty minutes. Time for people who had been walking on the sidewalk to join the march, proceed for a few steps, halt with the others, wait, get bored, and leave. It was time for someone in command of the hundreds of police in the neighborhood to communicate with his headquarters, explain the problem, time for the dilemma to be relayed, alternatives examined, and orders conceivably sent back to attack and disperse the crowd. If so, a trap was first set. The mules were allowed to cross Balbo Avenue, then were separated by a line of police from the marchers, who now, several thousand compressed in this one place, filled the intersection of Michigan Avenue and Balbo. There, dammed by police on three sides, and cut off from the wagons of the Poor People's March, there, right beneath the windows of the Hilton which looked down on Grant Park and Michigan Avenue, the stationary march was abruptly attacked. The police attacked with tear gas, with Mace, and with clubs, they attacked like a chain saw cutting into wood, the teeth of the saw the edge of their clubs, they attacked like a scythe through grass, lines of twenty and thirty policemen striking out in an arc, their clubs beating, demonstrators fleeing. Seen from overhead, from the nineteenth floor, it was like a wind blowing dust, or the edge of waves riding foam on the shore.

The police cut through the crowd one way, then cut through them another. They chased people into the park, ran them down, beat them up; they cut through the intersection at Michigan and Balbo like a razor cutting a channel through a head of hair, and then drove columns of new police into the channel who in turn pushed out, clubs flailing, on each side, to cut new channels, and new ones again. As demonstrators ran, they reformed in new groups only to be chased by the police again. The action went on for ten minutes, fifteen minutes, with the absolute ferocity of a tropical storm, and watching it from a window on the nineteenth floor, there was something of the detachment of studying a storm at evening through a glass, the light was a lovely gray-blue, the police had uniforms of sky-blue, even the ferocity had an abstract elemental play of forces of nature at battle with other forces, as if sheets of tropical rain were driving across the street in patterns, in curving patterns which curved upon each other again. Police cars rolled up, prisoners were beaten, shoved into wagons, driven away. The rain of police, maddened by the uncoiling of their own storm, pushed against their own barricades of tourists pressed on the street against the Hilton Hotel, then pressed them so hard—but here is a quotation from J. Anthony Lukas in *The New York Times*:

> Even elderly bystanders were caught in the police onslaught. At one point, the police turned on several dozen persons standing quietly behind police barriers in front of the Conrad Hilton Hotel watching the demonstrators across the street.
>
> For no reason that could be immediately determined, the blue-helmeted policemen charged the barriers, crushing the spectators against the windows of the Haymarket Inn, a restaurant in the hotel. Finally the window gave way, sending screaming middle-aged women and children backward through the broken shards of glass.

The police then ran into the restaurant and beat some of the victims who had fallen through the windows and arrested them.

Now another quote from Steve Lerner in *The Village Voice*:   9

When the charge came, there was a stampede toward the sidelines. People piled into each other, humped over each other's bodies like coupling dogs. To fall down in the crush was just as terrifying as facing the police. Suddenly I realized my feet weren't touching the ground as the crowd pushed up onto the sidewalk. I was grabbing at the army jacket of the boy in front of me; the girl behind me had a stranglehold on my neck and was screaming incoherently in my ear.

Now, a longer quotation from Jack Newfield in *The Village Voice*.   10
(The accounts in *The Voice* of September 5 were superior to any others encountered that week.)

At the southwest entrance to the Hilton, a skinny, long-haired kid of about seventeen skidded down on the sidewalk, and four overweight cops leaped on him, chopping strokes on his head. His hair flew from the force of the blows. A dozen small rivulets of blood began to cascade down the kid's temple and onto the sidewalk. He was not crying or screaming, but crawling in a stupor toward the gutter. When he saw a photographer take a picture, he made a V sign with his fingers.

A doctor in a white uniform and Red Cross arm band began to run toward the kid, but two other cops caught him from behind and knocked him down. One of them jammed his knee into the doctor's throat and began clubbing his rib cage. The doctor squirmed away, but the cops followed him, swinging hard, sometimes missing.

A few feet away a phalanx of police charged into a group of women, reporters, and young McCarthy activists standing idly against the window of the Hilton Hotel's Haymarket Inn. The terrified people began to go down under the unexpected police charge when the plate glass window shattered, and the people tumbled backward through the glass. The police then climbed through the broken window and began to beat people, some of whom had been drinking quietly in the hotel bar.

At the side entrance of the Hilton Hotel four cops were chasing one frightened kid of about seventeen. Suddenly, Fred Dutton, a former aide to Robert Kennedy, moved out from under the marquee and interposed his body between the kid and the police.

"He's my guest in this hotel," Dutton told the cops.

The police started to club the kid.

Dutton screamed for the first cop's name and badge number. The cop grabbed Dutton and began to arrest him, until a Washington *Post* reporter identified Dutton as a former RFK aide.

Demonstrators, reporters, McCarthy workers, doctors, all began to stagger into the Hilton lobby, blood streaming from face and head wounds. The lobby smelled from tear gas, and stink bombs dropped by the Yippies. A few people began to direct the wounded to a makeshift hospital on the fifteenth floor, the McCarthy staff headquarters.

Fred Dutton was screaming at the police, and at the journalists to report all the "sadism and brutality." Richard Goodwin, the ashen nub of a cigar sticking out of his fatigued face, mumbled, "This is just the beginning. There'll be four years of this."

The defiant kids began a slow, orderly retreat back up Michigan Avenue. They did not run. They did not panic. They did not fight back. As they fell back they helped pick up fallen comrades who were beaten or gassed. Suddenly, a plainclothesman dressed as a soldier moved out of the shadows and knocked one kid down with an overhand punch. The kid squatted on the pavement of Michigan Avenue, trying to cover his face, while the Chicago plainclothesman punched him with savage accuracy. Thud, thud, thud. Blotches of blood spread over the kid's face. Two photographers moved in. Several police formed a closed circle around the beating to prevent pictures. One of the policemen then squirted Chemical Mace at the photographers, who dispersed. The plainclothesman melted into the line of police.

Let us escape to the street. The reporter, watching in safety from the nineteenth floor, could understand now how Mussolini's son-in-law had once been able to find the bombs he dropped from his airplane beautiful as they burst, yes, children, and youths, and middle-aged men and women were being pounded and clubbed and gassed and beaten, hunted and driven, sent scattering in all directions by teams of policemen who had exploded out of their restraints like the bursting of a boil, and nonetheless he felt a sense of calm and beauty, void even of the desire to be down there, as if in years to come there would be beatings enough, some chosen, some from nowhere, but it was as if the war had finally begun, and this was therefore a great and solemn moment, as if indeed even the gods of history had come together from each side to choose the very front of the Hilton Hotel before the television cameras of the world and the eyes of the campaign workers and the delegates' wives, yes, there before the eyes of half the principals at the convention was this drama

11

played, as if the military spine of a great liberal party had finally separated itself from the skin, as if, no metaphor large enough to suf-
fice, the Democratic Party had here broken in two before the eyes of
a nation like Melville's whale charging right out of the sea.

A great stillness rose up from the street through all the small noise   12
of clubbing and cries, small sirens, sigh of loaded arrest vans as off
they pulled, shouts of police as they wheeled in larger circles, the intersection clearing further, then further, a stillness rose through the
steel and stone of the hotel, congregating in the shocked centers of
every room where delegates and wives and Press and campaign
workers innocent until now of the intimate working of social force,
looked down now into the murderous paradigm of Vietnam there
beneath them at this huge intersection of this great city. Look—a
boy was running through the park, and a cop was chasing. There he
caught him on the back of the neck with his club! There! The cop is
returning to his own! And the boy stumbling to his feet is helped off
the ground by a girl who has come running up.

Yes, it could only have happened in a meeting of the Gods, that   13
history for once should take place not on some back street, or some
inaccessible grand room, not in some laboratory indistinguishable
from others, or in the sly undiscoverable hypocrisies of a committee
of experts, but rather on the center of the stage, as if each side had
said, "Here we will have our battle. Here we will win."

The demonstrators were afterward delighted to have been man-   14
handled before the public eye, delighted to have pushed and prod-
ded, antagonized and provoked the cops over these days with rocks
and bottles and cries of "Pig" to the point where police had charged
in a blind rage and made a stage at the one place in the city (besides
the Amphitheatre) where audience, actors, and cameras could all
convene, yes, the rebels thought they had had a great victory, and
perhaps they did; but the reporter wondered, even as he saw it, if the
police in that half hour of waiting had not had time to receive instructions from the power of the city, perhaps the power of the land,
and the power had decided, "No, do not let them march another ten
blocks and there disperse them on some quiet street, no, let it happen before all the land, let everybody see that their dissent will soon
be equal to their own blood; let them realize that the power is im-
placable, and will beat and crush and imprison and yet kill before it
will ever relinquish the power. So let them see before their own eyes
what it will cost to continue to mock us, defy us, and resist. There
are more millions behind us than behind them, more millions who
wish to weed out, poison, gas, and obliterate every flower whose
power they do not comprehend than heroes for their side who will
view our brute determination and still be ready to resist. There are

more cowards alive than the brave. Otherwise we would not be where we are,'' said the Prince of Greed.

Who knew. One could thank the city of Chicago where drama was 15 still a property of the open stage. It was quiet now, there was nothing to stare down on but the mules, and the police guarding them. The mules had not moved through the entire fray. Isolated from the battle, they had stood there in harness waiting to be told to go on. Only once in a while did they turn their heads. Their role as actors in the Poor People's March was to wait and to serve. Finally they moved on. The night had come. It was dark. The intersection was now empty. Shoes, ladies' handbags and pieces of clothing lay on the street outside the hotel.

J. Anthony Lukas, from **The New York Times,** *Thursday, August 29, 1968*

HUMPHREY NOMINATED ON THE FIRST BALLOT AFTER HIS PLANK ON VIETNAM IS APPROVED; POLICE BATTLE DEMONSTRATORS IN STREETS

HUNDRED INJURED

---

178 Are Arrested as Guardsmen Join in Using Tear Gas

CHICAGO, Thursday, Aug. 29—The police and National Guards- 1 men battled young protestors in downtown Chicago last night as the week-long demonstrations against the Democratic National Convention reached a violent and tumultuous climax.

About 100 persons, including 25 policemen, were injured and at 2 least 178 were arrested as the security forces chased down the demonstrators. The protesting young people had broken out of Grant Park on the shore of Lake Michigan in an attempt to reach the International Amphitheater where the Democrats were meeting, four miles away.

The police and Guardsmen used clubs, rifle butts, tear gas and 3 Chemical Mace on virtually anything moving along Michigan Avenue and the narrow streets of the Loop area.

Shortly after midnight, an uneasy calm ruled the city. However, 4
1,000 National Guardsmen were moved back in front of the Conrad
Hilton Hotel to guard it against more than 5,000 demonstrators who
had drifted back into Grant Park.

The crowd in front of the hotel was growing, booing vociferously 5
every time new votes for Vice President Humphrey were broadcast
from the convention hall.

The events in the streets stirred anger among some delegates at 6
the convention. In a nominating speech Senator Abraham A. Ribicoff of Connecticut told the delegates that if Senator George
McGovern were President ''we would not have these Gestapo tactics
in the streets of Chicago.''

When Mayor Richard J. Daley of Chicago and other Illinois dele- 7
gates rose shouting angrily, Mr. Ribicoff said, ''How hard it is to
accept the truth.''

Crushed Against Windows

Even elderly bystanders were caught in the police onslaught. At 8
one point, the police turned on several dozen persons standing quietly behind police barricades in front of the Conrad Hilton Hotel
watching the demonstrators across the street.

For no reason that could be immediately determined, the blue- 9
helmeted policemen charged the barriers, crushing the spectators
against the windows of the Haymarket Inn, a restaurant in the hotel.
Finally the window gave way, sending screaming middle-aged
women and children backward through the broken shards of glass.

The police then ran into the restaurant and beat some of the vic- 10
tims who had fallen through the windows and arrested them.

At the same time, other policemen outside on the broad, tree-lined 11
avenue were clubbing the young demonstrators repeatedly under
television lights and in full view of delegates' wives looking out of the
hotel's windows.

Afterward, newsmen saw 30 shoes, women's purses and torn 12
pieces of clothing lying with shattered glass on the sidewalk and
street outside the hotel and for two blocks in each direction.

It was difficult for newsmen to estimate how many demonstrators 13
were in the streets of midtown Chicago last night. Although 10,000
to 15,000 young people gathered in Grant Park for a rally in the
afternoon, some of them had apparently drifted home before the violence broke out in the evening.

Estimates of those involved in the action in the night ranged be- 14
tween 2,000 and 5,000.

Although some youths threw bottles, rocks, stones and even loaves 15
of bread at the police, most of them simply marched and counter-
marched, trying to avoid the flying police squads.

Some of them carried flags—the black anarchist flag, the red flag, 16
the Vietcong flag and the red and blue flags with a yellow peace
symbol.

Stayed Defiant

Although clearly outnumbered and outclassed by the well armed 17
security forces, the thousands of antiwar demonstrators, supporters
of Senator Eugene J. McCarthy and Yippies maintained an air of
defiance throughout the evening.

They shouted "The streets belong to the people," "This land is 18
our land," and "Hell no, we won't go," as they skirmished along
the avenue and among the side streets.

When arrested youths raised their hands in the V for victory sign 19
that has become a symbol of the peace movement, other demonstrators shouted "Sieg heil" or "Pigs" at the policemen making the arrests.

Frank Sullivan, the Police Department's public information direc- 20
tor, said the police had reacted only after "50 hard-core leaders"
had staged a charge into a police line across Michigan Avenue.

Mr. Sullivan said that among those in charge were Prof. Sidney 21
Peck, cochairman of the Mobilization Committee to End the War in
Vietnam, the group that is spearheading the demonstration. He said
Professor Peck had struck James M. Rochford, Deputy Superin-
tendent of Police, with his fist. Mr. Peck was arrested and charged
with aggravated assault.

As the night wore on, the police dragnet spread from Michigan 22
Avenue and the area around the Hilton throughout downtown Chicago.

On the corner of Monroe Street and Michigan Avenue, policemen 23
chased demonstrators up the steps of the Chicago Art Institute, a
neoclassical Greek temple, and arrested one of them.

As in the previous nights of unrest here, newsmen found them- 24
selves special targets of the police action. At Michigan Avenue and
Van Buren Street, a young photographer ran into the street, terrified, his hands clasped over his head and shrieking "Press, press."

As the police arrested him, he shouted, "What did I do? What did 25
I do?"

The policeman said, "If you don't know you shouldn't be a pho- 26
tographer."

Barton Silverman, a photographer for the New York Times, was 27
briefly arrested near the Hilton Hotel.

Bob Kieckhefer, a reporter for United Press International, was hit 28 in the head by a policeman during the melee in front of the Hilton. He staggered into the UPI office on Michigan Avenue and was taken for treatment to Wesley Memorial Hospital.

Reporters Hampered

Reporters and photographers were repeatedly hampered by the police last night while trying to cover the violence. They were herded into small areas where they could not see the action. On Jackson Street, police forced a mobile television truck to turn off its lights.   29

Among those arrested was the Rev. John Boyles, Presbyterian chaplain at Yale and a McCarthy staff worker, who was charged with breach of the peace.   30

"It's an unfounded charge," Mr. Boyles said. "I was protesting the clubbing of a girl I knew from the McCarthy staff. They were beating her on the head with clubs and I yelled at them 'Don't hit a woman.' At that point I was slugged in the stomach and grabbed by a cop who arrested me."   31

Last night's violence broke out when hundreds of demonstrators tried to leave Grant Park after a rally and enter the Loop area.   32

At the Congress Street bridge leading from the park onto Michigan Avenue, National Guardsmen fired and sprayed tear gas at the demonstrators five or six times around 7 P.M. to hold them inside the park.   33

However, one group moved north inside the park and managed to find a way out over another bridge. There they met a contingent of the Poor People's Campaign march led by their symbol, three mule wagons.   34

Chase Youths

The march was headed south along Michigan Avenue and the police did not disrupt it, apparently because it had a permit. But they began chasing the youths along Michigan Avenue and into side streets.   35

The demonstrators were then joined by several thousand others who had originally set out from the park in a "non-violent" march to the amphitheatre led by David Dellinger, national chairman of the Mobilization Committee to End the War in Vietnam, and Allen Ginsberg, the poet.   36

The climactic day of protests began with a mass rally sponsored by the mobilization committee in the band shell in Grant Park.   37

The rally was intended both as a mass expression of anger at the proceedings across town in the convention and as a "staging ground" for the smaller, more militant march on the amphitheatre.   38

However, before the rally was an hour old, it, too, was interrupted 39 by violence. Fighting broke out when three demonstrators started hauling down the American flag from a pole by the park's band shell where speakers were denouncing the Chicago authorities, the Johnson administration and the war in Vietnam.

Four blue-helmeted policemen moved in to stop them and were 40 met by an angry group of demonstrators who pushed them back against a cluster of trees by the side of the band shell. Then the demonstrators, shouting "pig, pig," pelted the isolated group of 4 policemen with stones, bricks and sticks.

Grenade Hurled Back

Snapping their plexiglass shields over their faces, the police moved 41 toward the crowd. One policeman threw or fired a tear-gas grenade into the throng. But a demonstrator picked up the smoking grenade and heaved it back among the police. The crowd cheered with surprise and delight.

But then, from the Inner Drive west of the park, a phalanx of po 42 licemen moved into the crowd, using their billy clubs as prods and then swinging them. The demonstrators, who replied with more stones and sticks were pushed back against the rows of flaking green benches and trapped there.

Among those injured was Rennie Davis, one of the coordinators 43 for the Mobilization to End the War in Vietnam, which has been spearheading the demonstrations in Chicago.

As the police and the demonstrators skirmished on the huge grassy 44 field, mobilization committee leaders on the stage of the baby-blue band shell urged the crowd to sit down and remain calm.

The worst of the fighting was over in 10 minutes, but the two sides 45 were still jostling each other all over the field when Mr. Ginsberg approached the microphone.

Speaking in a cracked and choking voice, Mr. Ginsberg said: "I 46 lost my voice chanting in the park the last few nights. The best strategy for you in cases of hysteria, overexcitement or fear is still to chant 'Om' together. It helps to quell flutterings of butterflies in the belly. Join me now as I try to lead you."

So, as the policemen looked on in astonishment through their 47 plexiglass face shields, the huge throng chanted the Hindu "Om, om," sending deep mystic vibrations off the glass office towers along Michigan Avenue.

Following Mr. Ginsberg to the microphone was Jean Genet, the 48 French author. His bald head glistening in the glare of television lights, Mr. Genet said through a translator:

"It took an awful lot of deaths in Hanoi for a happening such as 49 this is taking place here to occur."

Next on the platform was William Burroughs, author of "The Naked Lunch." A gray fedora on his head, Mr. Burroughs said in a dry, almost distant voice:

"I've just returned from London, England, where there is no effective resistance at all. It's really amazing to see people willing to do something about an unworkable system. It's not evil or immoral, just unworkable. And they're trying to make it work by force. But they can't do it."

Mailer Apologizes

Mr. Burroughs was followed by Norman Mailer, the author who is here to write an article on the convention. Mr. Mailer, who was arrested during the march on the Pentagon last October, apologized to the crowd for not marching in Chicago.

Thrusting his jaw into the microphone, he said: "I'm a little sick about all this and also a little mad, but I've got a deadline on a long piece and I'm not going to go out and get arrested. I just came here to salute all of you."

Then Dick Gregory, the comedian and Negro militant leader, took the platform. Dressed in a tan sport shirt and matching trousers with a Khaki rain hat on his head, Mr. Gregory said: "You just have to look around you at all the police and soldiers to know you must be doing something right."

Many of the demonstrators in Grant Park had drifted down in small groups from Lincoln Park, where 300 policemen had moved in at 12:15 A.M. yesterday and laid down a barrage of tear gas to clear the area. About 2,000 young protestors had attempted to stay in the park despite the 11 P.M. curfew.

Saville R. Davis, from The Christian Science Monitor, *August 30, 1968*

A Night of Raging Protest

This is the story of a night in which protest raged and the establishment of the Democratic Party grimly held its lines.

The confrontation rolled up out of Michigan Avenue where young demonstrators and the Chicago police collided and the National Guard joined the police. The wave crashed in the convention hall itself, whither the struggle in the streets was carried by television.

It spent its force in both places and receded. When it was over the police and the Johnson-Humphrey political machine held the field. The youthful protesters and their mentors at the convention, the forces of candidates McCarthy and McGovern, had been overrun by superior voice and superior physical force.

The outcome, in terms of outrage and impotence on the Democratic Left, victory and chagrin on the side of the party elders, is yet to be appraised. Its effect on the voting television audience will have to be measured by the polls.   4

Two Points of Opposite View

What was certain was that the country was treated to a perplexing and highly controversial case study in the problems of law and order, political protest, and the implacably conflicting attitudes that may make them the chief issue of the coming election campaign.   5

The events as they unrolled can be presented with a reasonable degree of honesty only from two points of view. Those who worked hard for the Humphrey nomination looked at the iron control of the convention process, which beat back repeated protests that broke out on the convention floor during the day as a calm by men who had the votes.   6

For them it was like the old days of Sam Rayburn gaveling down the opposition, or of the cool convention control of the Kennedys in 1960.   7

The minority saw a party machine driving a steamroller relentlessly over the various terms of protest and maneuver that they relied on to make their case before the public, if not on the convention itself.   8

Out on the downtown avenue, it can be said with some objectivity that the police overreacted, in many cases grossly. The forces of protest were denied any legitimate outlet. They were struck with massive and sometimes brutal force by overwhelming battalions of police backed by the Army. The casualties are yet to be measured accurately.   9

But the news media were heavily involved in a protest of their own, with a large number of their own ranks clubbed and manhandled on the night before. They came ready to play up every instance of abuse and all through the evening the worst cases of arrest, manhandling, and girlhandling were given maximum play. The police-state atmosphere was bad enough to those of us who watched. Its impact on the convention brought dramatic defections from the Humphrey ranks and its effect on the watching and reading public is yet incalculable.   10

Youngsters Filled With Dreams

On the streets quiet and nonviolent youngsters, whose aim was the kind of dissent that the American tradition honors, were filled with wrath and dismay and tended to support the violent element that infiltrated its ranks and caused Sen. Eugene J. McCarthy to plead in vain that his supporters stay away.   11

Many of them had never seen battles like this that experienced re-   12 porters knew from the terrible days of the suppression of the labor movement or the hot summers in Mississippi or the recent big-city riots. The effect on them was consequently more unnerving and devastating.

But from this point on, reporting has to encompass two points of 13 view and leave judgment to public opinion.

As the evening began this correspondent and a colleague arrived 14 at the battleground, the corner of south Michigan Avenue and Balbo by the Conrad Hilton Hotel, as the confrontation was shaping up. A medium-sized crowd of youngsters was pressing in tight ranks from across the avenue into no-man's-land, denied any time and place to march and determined to make their protest. More police were forming up.

Stage Set for Action

Everyone knew it was coming and everyone was ready. Above the 15 Hilton marquee were television cameras of CBS and NBC with their festoons of power cables sweeping back into the hotel and their red eyes unblinking. Out in the middle of no-man's-land was an NBC television truck and ABC mobile units were all around. The stage was set.

Down Balbo Avenue and into Michigan swept large company- 16 sized units of blue-helmeted police at a dog trot and tore into the crowds to force them back. A number of resisters were seized with lightning speed, separated from the crowd, dragged back on the run to a Blue Maria—one of four blue and white police vans—and forced in at panic speed.

At that point we saw several clubbed on the head, not with full 17 force but enough to cause substantial injury and very likely worse in the rush to subdue them quickly and set an example to the crowd. One boy had blood on the back of his head, another had a club wound on the side of his face. We inspected two casualties taken to the curb and given first aid by the Red Cross unit of the demonstrators. They ultimately got up and were led away and the extent of their wounds could not be easily estimated. Two girls got in without police aid, apparently determined to be arrested.

Crowd Shocked

It was the shock of the attack on a tightly massed crowd that could 18 not give way easily that caused the more serious casualties that were then followed in a number of cases by dragging at high speed and clubbing. The crowd lurched back at several points and the police began to form up again. More units arrived at quick step.

All this was recorded at the perfect distance of 20 to 30 feet by the 19 television cameras above us on the marquee. They had unimpeded vision of the clubbing and manhandling.

The van backed past us and was replaced by another. A boy was [20] shouting through the wire window, "Don't fight the police. I was arrested but I still say this. Don't use violence on them. Be calm."

By then there must have been a thousand police in the immediate [21] vicinity. And from then on, began a series of maneuvers that are familiar to reporters. Cordons of police systematically blocked off sections of sidewalk and street, and a long, thick attack line began to push the main crowd of protesters back up Michigan Avenue.

Two Lines in Confrontation

Before they advanced there was a long period of confrontation, the [22] two lines facing each other across a 20-foot space. Suddenly a company or so of regular United States Army troops appeared. The young GIs in battle dress, holding their guns slanted upward, formed up behind the police.

Intermittent canisters of tear gas were lobbed into the demonstra- [23] tors and a policeman sprayed the noxious Mace liquid into the crowd from time to time, and it reeled backward only to return. There seemed to be as many girls as boys in the front line. Cans were thrown intermittently and we were told there were some rocks but didn't see them.

The order was given to advance. Another vanload of resisters was [24] filled not with clubs this time. Others knelt or stood with their hands in an attitude of prayer. When seized, they went readily into arrest. The crowd again lurched back. We walked behind their front ranks and a student loudspeaker called out, "Keep cool. Stand together. Don't fight. We know we don't have the facilities to battle the police.

"We are here to have this city see what it means to have some- [25] body who disagreed. We are here because of the American liberty we were brought up to believe in."

From then on, the pattern was the same. Slow pushing back by the [26] police with the soldiers not directly taking part but always in the rear. Occasional scuffles but clubs not directly used at that point. A camera was torn off its strap.

"People bound to get hurt"

"We have generally been treated all right," said an ABC newsman. [27] "But one reporter was messed up." An obviously subdued policeman nearby pleaded with bystanders, "Will you please move back." Another argued, "You just try to move a crowd like that. People are bound to get hurt."

"Fascists, Nazis," a girl quietly cried. "I never thought I'd see a [28] police state." A student Red Cross worker said he thought there were about 40 serious injuries. The police crunched on but with less resistance after the loudspeaker called out the message.

We left for the convention hall.

The vast auditorium was trembling with suppressed excitement 30
and concern. Everywhere delegates and reporters were watching television screens of the battle downtown and no one knew when the
volcano would erupt.

Prof. John Kenneth Galbraith made his elegant but punchy as- 31
sault on the party old guard. Mayor Joseph L. Alioto of San Francisco, billed as one of the "new men" of the party, was making an
old-style nominating speech for the Vice-President. Instead of "the
man who," he repeatedly ended a list of the Humphrey achievements with the refrain, "He did it."

Just as earlier in the day, the left-wing Democrats boiled with 32
cheers and boos centered on the New York and California delega-
tions, the former with a cheerleader out front and a lot of nondele-
gates in its seats. They shouted "Stop the War" in unison. The gal-
lery was mostly for the minority too. The majority sat impassively
on its votes and only applauded to drown out too many boos or when
noise was indicated.

Floor Erupts

The "new-type demonstration" without the paid frolic from non- 33
delegates was a comparatively dignified holding of placards by
standing, immobile, cheering delegates and galleries, a great im-
provement over the boring circuses of the past.

Then at 10 p.m. Chicago time it happened. 34

The leader of the Colorado delegation demanded of the chair 35
through his microphone: "Is there any way Mayor Daley can be
compelled to end the police terror that is taking place in this city at
this moment?" And the floor erupted.

It was a wild moment with everyone doing his own thing. Chair- 36
man Albert swiftly shouted through the microphone against the ca-
cophony that the request was against the rules: nothing according to
the rules could stop a roll call of the states. Boos shook the house and
Mayor Daley sat there with a half-grin on his ruddy face.

Speech Torn Up

Five minutes later as this steamroller tried to pour off steam, Sen. 37
Abraham A. Ribicoff came to the microphone to place in nomination the name of George McGovern. He put his prepared speech
down and looked away from it and said, "I cannot find it in my
heart to deliver what I intended to say, in view of the events taking
place downtown. . . . With George McGovern as President of the
United States we wouldn't have to have Gestapo tactics on the
streets of Chicago."

Five Illinois delegates around Mayor Daley, and the Mayor him- 38
self, were on their feet angrily shouting "no" and gesturing as if to

288

force Senator Ribicoff off the platform. The Senator looked away from them and continued.

"How hard it is to accept the truth," he said and repeated, "How hard it is to accept the truth." And again the convention blew. Noise that must have been just a mass of decibels in television loud-speakers was a wild, reverberating torrent of sound in the big hall, explosive in its force. Senator Ribicoff tore up his unused manu-script and walked away.

There were more such references in speeches that the chairman could not stop, because they were legitimate nominating and sec-onding speeches. Frank Mankiewicz, former press secretary to Rob-ert F. Kennedy, denouncing "the nightsticks and tear gas and the mindless brutality we have seen on our television screens tonight and on this convention floor." Philip Stern, nominating a Negro pastor, the Rev. Channing Philips, for president: "When you re-turn downtown tonight look about you at the barbed wire and the helmets and the boots. . . ."

Mayor Quoted

Mayor Daley, said an Associated Press reporter, told him, "The se-curity is needed to prevent violence. The same forces creating disor-der outside the convention hall are creating it inside." ·

"Who is creating the disorder, Mr. Mayor?" asked the reporter.

"You are," the Mayor was quoted as replying.

In this superheated context, with both sides yammering at each other whenever they could break through the chairman's correct but tough rulings, the nomination of Mr. Humphrey came almost like an anti-climax. Various efforts by the minority forces to adjourn or recess the convention, played to the full on the television networks but barely breaking into the formal proceedings on the floor, were gaveled down and declared out of order.

The chair allowed nothing but roll calls during the last two hours, and these were technically inviolate.

Parallel on Voting

The voting for the Humphrey nomination generally followed the same lines as during the vote on the platform and its foreign-policy plank earlier in the day: California and New York massively against him, the South and Illinois and Texas massively for, and the other states generally following expectable patterns. The chair ignored the last boos and protests and abruptly adjourned the session at the stroke of high midnight.

These are a sampling of the happenings of that turbulent day.

Account Incomplete

Toward the end, former Postmaster General Lawrence F. O'Brien, in charge of the Humphrey campaign, made an eloquent plea to a

39

40

41

42

43

44

45

46

47

48

television reporter that this was an open convention in the best Democratic and democratic American tradition. The party could now turn to reunifying itself. An observer made the inevitable counter: The only openness, he said, was forced on a reluctant chairman who did everything he could to railroad the majority actions through.

This account is necessarily incomplete and in the heat of events is 49 compelled to be partial. One reporter's observations of the downtown debacle has in the nature of things to be checked against the reports of many others.

At this writing, there is so deep a conflict of political outlook and 50 conviction between the ''law-and-order'' legions here and those who believe in the validity of protest even if it involves risks, that talk of reunifying the party has to be left to tomorrow and to be judged by events.

The same is true of the argument over an ''open'' convention, especially where the issues of war and peace, and of civil disorder at 51 home when it bursts so palpably into the convention itself, have so high an emotional and ideological content.

Dawn on Michigan Avenue

Outrage at police repression is vying with concern that radicals 52 would subvert the convention. The collision is especially poignant because the earlier ghetto riots, which were much more violent physically on both sides, did not touch the political process of the country. The Chicago repression, by contrast, and the protest which it routed, were carried directly into the nomination of a candidate for President of the United States with the whole nation looking on.

The effect seems likely, at this point in time, to be felt far down the 53 campaign trail that lies just ahead.

As dawn rose over Michigan Avenue the police had withdrawn. 54 Some protesters remained on the opposite side. The three blocks of earlier battleground were filled with a convoy and masses of troops. The United States Army had taken over.

Jack Gould, from The New York Times, *August 29, 1968*

TV: A CHILLING SPECTACLE IN CHICAGO

Delegates See Tapes of Clashes in the Streets

Television's influence in covering the Democratic National Convention is likely to be a subject of study for years. Last night, untold millions of viewers, as well as the delegates in the hall, saw chilling TV 1 tape recordings of Chicago policemen clearing the streets in front of the Conrad Hilton Hotel.

The tapes, relayed by motorcycle couriers to the headquarters of the networks in the International Amphitheater, showed girls being dragged across streets and young men being clubbed. How complete the visual accounts of the disturbance may have been could not be ascertained from only looking at the screen, but the pictures alone were enough to send a shudder down a viewer's spine.

R. W. Apple, Jr., from The New York Times, *August 30, 1968*
Daley Defends His Police; Humphrey Scores Clashes

CHICAGO, Aug. 29—Infuriated by attacks upon himself, his city and his police force, Mayor Richard J. Daley defended today the manner in which antiwar, anti-Humphrey demonstrations were suppressed in downtown Chicago last night. 1

Mr. Daley described the demonstrators as "terrorists" and said they had come here determined to "assault, harass and taunt the police into reacting before television cameras." 2

The Mayor flushed deeply as he denounced the reports of newspapers, radio and television last night. He asserted that "the whole purpose of the city and the law enforcement agencies" had been "distorted and twisted." 3

"In the heat of emotion and riot," Mr. Daley said, "some policemen may have overreacted, but to judge the entire police force by the alleged action of a few would be just as unfair as to judge our entire younger generation by the actions of the mob." 4

In an interview tonight on the Columbia Broadcasting System television network, the Mayor said he had "intelligence reports" indicating that persons whom he did not identify had planned to assassinate him, the three leading Presidential contenders and others. He gave no further details. 5

Mr. Daley also commented bitterly on the program about remarks made by young men and women in the demonstrations. He said they had used "the foulest of language that you wouldn't hear in a brothel hall." 6

Mayor Daley appeared in the conference room adjacent to his office to read a two-minute statement at 1:20 P.M. He was cheered by members of his staff who gathered at the rear of the room minutes before. 7

When he finished his toughly worded, combative remarks, the 65- 8 year-old Mayor said, ''This is my statement, gentlemen it speaks for itself.'' Then stalked off the podium without giving newsmen an opportunity to ask questions.

Mr. Daley and his aides appeared to be aware that the Mayor had been singled out, both by the demonstrators and anti-Administration delegates on the floor of the Democratic National Convention, as a symbol of repression and old-line party leadership. 9

But they were prepared to concede almost nothing. Earl Bush, the Mayor's press secretary, volunteered the information that Mr. Daley was ''determined to continue to do the right thing.'' And he said that telephone calls to City Hall were running 100-to-1 in support of Mr. Daley. 10

Mayor Daley met this morning with Vice President Humphrey, who has condemned what he called ''storm trooper tactics,'' but no account of their conversation was available. It was also reliably reported that before Mr. Daley left the convention hall last night he was urged in telephone calls from party leaders to do what he could to restrain the police in the Loop district. 11

Cites Policemen's Injuries

The Mayor reported that 51 policemen had been injured, but he did not mention that from 100 to 200 demonstrators had been hurt. He also said that ''60 per cent of those arrested did not live in Illinois.'' 12

''This administration and the people of Chicago,'' Mr. Daley went on, ''have never condoned brutality at any time, but they will never permit a lawless, violent group of terrorists to menace the lives of millions of people, destroy the purpose of a national political convention, and take over the streets.'' 13

Reflecting his resentment at news coverage of the demonstrations, the Mayor began by saying that he expected his statement to ''be given the same kind of distribution on press, radio and television as the mob of rioters was given yesterday.'' 14

''In every instance,'' he said, the recommendation of the National Advisory Commission on Civil Disorders—''to use manpower instead of firepower''—had been followed. 15

Hard Line Is Taken

Attached to a copy of his statement that was handed to newsmen were copies of articles, favorable to the Mayor, from The Christian Science Monitor, The Chicago Tribune, Chicago's American and Barron's magazine, a weekly Wall Street publication. 16

Sources acquainted with Mr. Daley's thinking said that he was particularly angry at what he considered unfair aspersions cast upon the name of Chicago, a place he loves deeply and has often described as ''the greatest city in the world.'' 17

Frank J. Sullivan, the police department's director of public infor- 18
mation, took a similarly hard line at a news conference this morning.

Mr. Sullivan described the demonstrators as "revolutionaries" 19
and called some of their leaders, including Tom Hayden and Rennie
Davis, "Communists who are the allies of the men who are killing
American soldiers."

"The intellectuals of America hate Richard J. Daley," Mr. Sul- 20
livan declared, "because he was elected by the people—unlike Walter Cronkite."

Besides Mr. Cronkite, the anchor man for the Columbia Broad- 21
casting System's convention coverage, Mr. Sullivan denounced in
general terms both C.B.S. and the National Broadcasting Company. He contended that they had conducted a "colossal propaganda campaign" against Chicago and the Chicago police.

The public relations officer insisted that there had been no "pat- 22
tern of excessive force" in the clashes last night. His chief, Police Su-
perintendent James B. Conlisk Jr., said, "The force used was the
force necessary to repel the mob."

Mr. Sullivan made a point of denying published reports that the 23
police had smashed a window in the Haymarket Lounge at the Conrad Hilton Hotel by pushing people, including bystanders, through
the plate glass. He said that the window had been smashed by the
protesters.

The New York Times was among the newspapers that published 24
accounts criticized by Mr. Sullivan. Its article was based on an eye-
witness account by Earl Caldwell, one of its reporters.

Richard F. Salant, president of C.B.S. News, replied to Mr. Sul- 25
livan in a statement that said, "The pictures and sound of the Chicago police department in action speak for themselves—louder than
any words of ours or any attempt by them to find any scapegoats."

"If Mr. Sullivan feels that the unedited pictorial record showed 26
excessive force," said Reuven Frank, president of N.B.C. News,
"and therefore that the rules of his own department were being broken, that must be his conclusion. Anyone else in the country who
watched and came to the same conclusion also did so on his own."

READING

The Western: Theory and Practice

The material presented here is designed to support a serious
piece of synthetic writing without additional research. The first

selection is taken from the scholar John Cawelti's book, *Six-Gun Mystique*. In the parts of his book reprinted here, Cawelti tries to define the elements that came to constitute the formula used in hundreds of Western stories, novels, plays, and movies. We suggest that you use Cawelti's discussion as a kind of working hypothesis, to be tested against the two stories by Stephen Crane that follow, which were written while the formula described by Cawelti was still being developed. You may wish to look over the essay and the stories before turning to the two Practice assignments at the end of the second story, but you should probably turn to the Practices before you begin a careful study of this material.

John Cawelti, from The Six-Gun Mystique

The Western was created in the early nineteenth century by James 1
Fenimore Cooper. Cooper's initial invention of the Leatherstocking (*The Pioneers*, 1823) paved the way for many fictional treatments of the West which strongly resembled his patterns of plot, character, and theme (e.g. R.M. Bird's *Nick of the Woods* and W. G. Simms, *The Yemassee*). By 1860 these patterns had become sufficiently stereotyped that they could serve Edward Ellis as the basis of his *Seth Jones; or The Captives of the Frontier*, one of the most successful early dime novels. In the later nineteenth century, the Western formula continued to flourish in the dime novel and in popular drama. Even the autobiographical narratives of Western experiences and popular biographies of Western heroes like Kit Carson, Buffalo Bill, and General Custer, increasingly reflected the main elements of the formula, which was finally enshrined in the great spectacle of the Wild West Show. Gradually the cowboy replaced the frontier scout as the archetypal Western hero. Finally, in a number of works published around the turn of the century, the most important of which was Owen Wister's best-seller *The Virginian*, the western formula arrived at most of the characteristics it has held through innumerable novels, stories, films and TV shows in the twentieth century.

In one sense the Western formula is far easier to define that that of 2
the detective story, for when we see a couple of characters dressed in ten-gallon hats and riding horses, we know we are in a Western. On the other hand, the Western formula contains a greater variety of plot patterns than the detective story with its single line of criminal investigation. Frank Gruber, a veteran writer of pulp Westerns, suggests that there are seven basic Western plots which he lists as: (1) The Union Pacific Story centering around the construction of a railroad, telegraph or stagecoach line or around the adventures of a

wagon train; (2) The Ranch Story with its focus on conflicts between ranchers and rustlers or cattlemen and sheepmen; (3) The Empire Story, which is an epic version of the Ranch Story; (4) The Revenge Story; (5) Custer's Last Stand, or the Cavalry and Indian Story; (6) the Outlaw Story; and (7) The Marshal Story. One could doubtless construct other lists of plots that have been used in Westerns, though Gruber's seems quite adequate. Later, I will suggest that there is a kind of action pattern that the Western tends to follow whether it be about ranchers, cavalrymen, outlaws, or marshals, but the possibility of such diversity of plot patterns suggests that we know a Western primarily by the presence of ten-gallon hats and horses. In other words, the Western formula is initially defined by its setting. Therefore in analyzing the components of the Western formula I will deal initially with the setting.

Setting

Tentatively, we might say that the western setting is a matter of geography and costume; that is, a Western is a story that takes place somewhere in the western United States in which the characters wear certain distinctive styles of clothing. However, this formulation is clearly inadequate since there are many stories set in the American West which we would not call Westerns under any circumstances, for example the novels and stories of Hamlin Garland, or Ole Rolvaag. Moreover, there are novels set in the eastern United States which are really Westerns, for example, the Leatherstocking Tales of James Fenimore Cooper. Our geographical definition must immediately be qualified by a social and historical definition of setting: the Western is a story which takes place on or near a frontier, and consequently, the Western is generally set at a particular moment in the past.

The portrayal of the frontier in the Western formula differs significantly from Frederick Jackson Turner's frontier thesis. For Turner, the frontier was less important as "the meeting point between savagery and civilization" than as a social and economic factor in American history. His well-known frontier thesis consisted of two central propositions: first, because the American frontier lay "at the hither edge of free land" it had maintained the democratic mobility and fluidity of American life; and second, there tended to grow up in frontier settlements a distinctively individualistic way of life which continually revitalized the democratic spirit in America. Though a view of the frontier resembling Turner's sometimes plays a role in the structure of more complex and serious Westerns, the central purport of the frontier in most Westerns has simply been its potential as a setting for exciting, epic conflicts. The Western formula tends to portray the frontier as "meeting point between civilization and savagery" because the clash of civilization ("law and order") with savagery, whether represented by Indians or lawless outlaws, generates dramatic excitement and striking antitheses without raising basic questions about American society or about life in general. In the Western formula savagery is implicitly understood to be on the way out. It made no difference whether the creator of the Western viewed savagery as a diabolical or criminal force (as in most of the dime novels) or as a meaningful way of life for which he felt a certain degree of elegaic nostalgia (an attitude in many Westerns from Cooper to the movies of John Ford), there was never a question that savagery might prevail, just as in the detective story there is never really a doubt that the criminal will ultimately be caught. While one might seriously seek to espouse certain "natural" values and to reject those of society (e.g. as in Thoreau's *Walden* or the poetry of Whitman) and while an American character in a novel by Henry James might be deeply torn between the European and American ways of life, the Western hero never has to make a basic choice like this, for, insofar as he is a hero it must be in relation to the victory of civilization over savagery, even if this victory, as it often does, puts him out of a job. Edwin Fussell suggests that in the first half of the nineteenth century, the frontier retained enough of an air of mystery that it could represent a fundamental confrontation between human history and the possibility of a society transcending it. However, Fussell believes that as actual settlement progressed, the frontier lost its power as a fundamental moral antithesis to society. By 1850, according to Fussell, the frontier had ceased to be a major theme for the greatest American writers. Fussell's discussion supplements Henry Nash Smith's definition of the mythical West as the potential locus of a new and more natural human society. Like Fussell, Smith defines the early American conception of the frontier as a serious antithesis to existing society. However, Smith believes that the romanticization of nature implicit in this conception of the frontier could never support a serious literature. Thus, after Cooper, the Western story declined to a point where "devoid alike of ethical and social meaning, [it] could develop in no direction save that of a straining and exaggeration of its formulas."

Smith's treatment of the Western story is a bit harsh, ignoring as it does the rich flourishing of the Western in literature and on film in the twentieth century. However, Smith is essentially correct in pointing out that the Western formula has been an artistic device for resolving problems rather than confronting their irreconcilable ambiguities. Therefore the frontier setting and the role of the savage have invariably been defined in the formula as occasions for action rather than as the focus of the analysis. In other words, the Indian rarely stands for a possible alternative way of life which implies a serious criticism of American society. Instead he poses a problem for the hero. Leslie Fiedler points out how often the complex relationship between a young white boy and an Indian or Negro is the central theme of major American novels. In his recent study, *The Return of the Vanishing American*, Fiedler argues that the Indian way of life has become an important counter-cultural symbol for many young radicals. But the Indian never plays such a role in the formula Western, because he is always in the process of vanishing. In fact, the treatment of the Indian in the formula Western bears out Roy Harvey Pearce's analysis of the American idea of savagism. Pearce shows how the various seventeenth and eighteenth century views of the Indian with their complex dialectic between the Indian as devil and as noble savage quickly gave way in the nineteenth century to a definition of the Indian way of life as an inferior and earlier stage in the development of civilization. This redefinition of the Indian justified his assimilation or extermination and therefore served the need of nineteenth century American society for a philosophical rationale to justify its brutal elimination of the native Indian cultures. Even in Westerns quite sympathetic to the Indian, such as John Ford's version of Mari Sandoz' *Cheyenne Autumn*, the focus of the action usually shifts from the Indians themselves to the dilemmas their situation poses for the white hero and heroine. In short, the Western formula seems to prescribe that the Indian be a part of the setting to a greater extent than he is ever a character in his own right. The reason for this is twofold: to give the Indian a more complex role would increase the moral ambiguity of the story and thereby blur the sharp dramatic conflicts; and second, if the Indian represented a significant way of life rather than a declining savagery, it would be far more difficult to resolve the story with a reaffirmation of the values of modern society.

Taken together, the work of Smith, Fussell, and Pearce suggest 6 that the Western formula emerged as American attitudes toward the frontier gradually underwent significant change around the middle of the nineteenth century. It was possible for Americans in the early nineteenth century to treat the frontier as a symbol of fundamental moral antitheses between man and nature, and, consequently, to use a frontier setting in fiction that engaged itself with a profound exploration of the nature and limitations of man and society. However, the redefinition of the frontier as a place where advancing civilization met a declining savagery changed the frontier setting into a locus of conflicts which were always qualified and contained by the knowledge that the advance of civilization would largely eliminate them. Or, to put it another way, the frontier setting now provided a fictional justification for enjoying violent conflicts and the expression of lawless force without feeling that they threatened the values or the fabric of society.

Thus, the social and historical aspects of setting are perhaps even more important in defining the Western formula than geography. The Western story is set at a certain moment in the development of American civilization, namely at that point when savagery and lawlessness are in decline before the advancing wave of law and order, but are still strong enough to pose a local and momentarily significant challenge. In the actual history of the West, this moment was probably a relatively brief one in any particular area. In any case, the complex clashes of different interest groups over the use of Western resources and the pattern of settlement surely involved more people in a more fundamental way than the struggle with Indians or outlaws. Nonetheless, it is the latter which has become central to the Western formula. The relatively brief stage in the social evolution of the West when outlaws or Indians posed a threat to the community's stability has been erected into a timeless epic past in which heroic individual defenders of law and order without the vast social resources of police and courts stand poised against the threat of lawlessness or savagery. But it is also the nature of this epic moment that the larger forces of civilized society are just waiting in the wings for their cue. However threatening he may appear at the moment, the Indian is vanishing and the outlaw about to be superseded. It is because they too represent this epic moment that we are likely to think of such novels as Cooper's *Last of the Mohicans*, Bird's *Nick of the Woods*, or more recent historical novels like Walter Edmonds' *Drums Along the Mohawk* as Westerns, though they are not set in what we have come to know as the West.

Why then has this epic moment been primarily associated in fiction with a particular West, that of the Great Plains and the mountains and deserts of the "Far West" and with a particular historical moment, that of the heyday of the open range cattle industry of the later nineteenth century? Westerns can be set at a later time—some of Zane Grey's stories take place in the twenties and some, like those of Gene Autry, Roy Rogers, or "Sky King" in the present—but even at those later dates the costumes and the way of life represented tend to be that of the later nineteenth century. Several factors probably contributed to this particular fixation of the epic moment. Included among these would be the ideological tendency of Americans to see the Far West as the last stronghold of certain traditional values, as well as the peculiar attractiveness of the cowboy hero. But more important than these factors, the Western requires a means of isolating and intensifying the drama of the frontier encounter between social order and lawlessness. For this purpose, the geographic setting of the Great Plains and adjacent areas has proved particularly appropriate, especially since the advent of film and television have placed a primary emphasis on visual articulation. Four characteristics of the Great Plains topography have been especially important: its openness, its aridity and general inhospitability to human life, its great extremes of light and climate, and, paradoxically, its grandeur and beauty. These topographic features create an effective backdrop for the action of the Western because they exemplify in visual images the thematic conflict between civilization and savagery and its resolution. In particular, the Western has come to center about the image of the isolated town or ranch or fort surrounded by the vast open grandeur of prairie or desert and connected to the rest of the civilized world by a railroad, a stagecoach, or simply a trail. This tenuous link can still be broken by the forces of lawlessness, but never permanently. We can conceive it as a possibility that the town will be swept back into the desert—the rickety wooden buildings with their tottering false fronts help express the tenuousness of the town's position against the surrounding prairie—nonetheless we do not see the town solely as an isolated fort in hostile country—like an outpost of the French foreign legion in *Beau Geste*—but as the advance guard of an oncoming civilization. Moreover, while the prairie or desert may be inhospitable, it is not hostile. Its openness, freshness, and grandeur also play an important role in the Western. Thus, the open prairie around the town serves not only as a haven of lawlessness and savagery, but as a backdrop of epic magnitude and even, at times, as a source of regenerating power.

This characteristic setting reflects and helps dramatize the tripartite division of characters that dominates the Western pattern of action. The townspeople hover defensively in their settlement, threatened by the outlaws or Indians who are associated with the inhospitable and uncontrollable elements of the surrounding landscape. The townspeople are static and largely incapable of movement beyond their little settlement. The outlaws or savages can move freely across the landscape. The hero, though a friend of the townspeople, has the lawless power of movement in that he, like the savages, is a horseman and possesses skills of wilderness existence. The moral character of the hero also appears symbolically in the Western setting. In its rocky aridity and climatic extremes the Great Plains landscape embodies the hostile savagery of Indians and outlaws, while its vast openness, its vistas of snow-covered peaks in the distance, and its great sunrises and sunsets (in the purple prose of Zane Grey, for example) suggest the epic courage and regenerative power of the hero. Thus, in every respect, Western topography

9

helps dramatize more intensely the clash of characters and the thematic conflicts of the story. These dramatic resources of setting can of course be used more or less skillfully by the Western writer or film director, but even at their flattest they have a tendency to elevate rather commonplace plots into epic spectacles. When employed with conscious and skillful intent, as in the Western films of John Ford, the lyrical and epic power of landscape can sometimes transcend even the inherent limitations of popular culture and raise escapist adventure to a level of high artistry.

The special qualities of the Western setting emerge still more clearly from a comparison with the treatment of setting in the colonial adventure novels of English writers like H. Rider Haggard. Since it too involved adventures on the periphery of what its readers defined as civilization, the colonial adventure is the closest European analogue to the American Western. Like the Western setting, the tropical jungles of the colonial adventure have both hostile and attractive qualities. Haggard's African veldts, like the Western plains, contain savagery and raw nature which threaten the representatives of civilization. They are also full of exotic animals, beautiful natural spectacles, glamorous and mysterious cults, hidden treasures, and other exciting secrets. But, in contrast to the fresh and open grandeur of the Western landscape, these double qualities of the colonial jungle are superficially attractive, but essentially subversive and dangerous. They are associated not with a redeeming hero who saves civilization from the threat of lawlessness and savagery, but with temptations which undermine the hero's commitment to civilization. The Western landscape can become the setting for a regenerated social order once the threat of lawlessness has been overcome, but the colonial landscape remains alien. Its doubleness simply reflects the difference between the overt threat of savage hostility and the more insidious danger of the attractiveness of alien cults and exotic ways of life. Perhaps because it contains an unresolved antithesis between man and the jungle, the colonial adventure has inspired truly profound works of literature, as instanced by such examples as Joseph Conrad's "Heart of Darkness," while the Western formula has at best produced good novels like Wister's *The Virginian* or Clark's *The Ox-Bow Incident*.

The first major writer who brought together the tripartite division of townsmen, savages, and intermediate hero with a vision of the landscape was James Fenimore Cooper, who thereby became the creator of the Western. Even though Cooper's novels are set in the Eastern forests and many of his thematic emphases are quite different from the later Western, his landscapes show the same basic pattern. The new settlement (*The Pioneers*) or fort (*The Last of the Mohi-*

cans, The Pathfinder) or "ranch" (Hutter's "castle" in *The Deerslayer*) is surrounded by miles of forested wilderness. It is clear, however, that civilization has irreversibly begun its advance. Like many later Western writers, Cooper liked frequently to call his reader's attention to the difference between the peaceful settlements of "today" and the dark mysterious forests of the earlier period of the story, thus insuring that the reader knew he was dealing with a stage of historical development which was definitely in the past. It is implicit in such a setting that the conflict between settlement and wilderness will soon be resolved. Cooper's wilderness also exemplifies the doubleness of the Western formula landscape. The forest is dark and frightening, but also the place where one gets the strongest feeling of the divine presence; it is the locus of the bloodthirsty and savage "Mingos" but also of the noble and heroic Delawares.

I have now discussed the effectiveness of the Western setting as   12
both background and source of dramatic conflicts and have indicated its potentiality both as a means of exploring certain historical themes and as a way of evoking a sense of epic grandeur. But we must not forget that one reason for the success of the Western as a popular form in the twentieth century has been its unique adaptability to film. Two major characteristics of the western setting turned out to have an enormous potential for cinematic expression: its great openness of space and its powerful visual contrasts.

The special openness of the topography of the Great Plains and   13
western desert has made it particularly expressive for the portrayal of movement. Against the background of this terrain, a skillful director can create infinite variations of space ranging from long panoramas to close-ups and he can clearly articulate movement across these various spaces. No matter how often one sees it, there is something inescapably effective about that scene, beloved of Western directors, in which a rider appears like an infinitely small dot at the far end of a great empty horizon and then rides toward us across the intervening space, just as there is a different thrill about the vision of a group of horses and men plunging pell-mell from the foreground into the empty distance. Nor is there anything which quite matches the feeling of suspense when the camera picks up a little group of wagons threading their way across the middle distance and then pans across the arid rocks and up the slopes of a canyon until it suddenly comes upon a group of Indians waiting in ambush. Moreover, the western landscape is uniquely adaptable to certain kinds of strong visual effects because of the sharp contrasts of light and shadow characteristic of an arid climate together with the topographical contrasts of plain and mountain, rocky outcrops and flat

deserts, steep bare canyons and forested plateaus. The characteristic
openness and aridity of the topography also makes the contrast between man and nature and between wilderness and society visually
strong.

Perhaps no film exploits the visual resources of the western land- 14
scape more brilliantly than John Ford's 1939 *Stagecoach*. The film
opens on a street in one of those western shantytowns characterized
by rickety false fronts. By the rushing motion of horses and wagons
along the street and by the long vista down the street and out into the
desert we are immediately made aware of the surrounding wilderness and of the central theme of movement across it which will
dominate the film. This opening introduction of the visual theme of
fragile town contrasted with epic wilderness will be developed
throughout the film in the contrast between the flimsy stagecoach
and the magnificent landscape through which it moves. Similarly,
the restless motion of the opening scene will be projected into the
thrust of the stagecoach across the landscape. This opening is followed by several brief scenes leading up to the departure of the
stagecoach. These scenes are cut at a rather breathless pace so that
they do not slow down the sense of motion and flight generated by
the opening. Visually, they dwell on two aspects of the town, its
dark, narrow, and crowded interiors and its ramshackle sidewalks
and storefronts, thus establishing in visual terms the restrictive and
artificial character of town life. Then the stagecoach departs on its
voyage and we are plunged into the vast openness and grandeur of
the wilderness with the crowded wooden stagecoach serving as a visual reminder of the narrow town life it has left behind. Ford chose
to shoot the major portion of the stagecoach's journey in Monument
Valley, a brilliant choice because the visual characteristics of that topography perfectly embody the complex mixture of epic grandeur
and savage hostility that the film requires. The valley itself is a large,
flat desert between steep hills. Thrusting up out of the valley floor gigantic monoliths of bare rock dwarf the stagecoach as it winds across
this vast panorama. This combination of large open desert broken
by majestic upthrusts of rock and surrounded by threatening hills
creates an enormously effective visual environment for the story,
which centers around the way in which the artificial social roles and
attitudes of the travellers break down under the impact of the wilderness. Those travellers who are able to transcend their former roles
are regenerated by the experience: the drunken doctor delivers a
baby, the meek salesman shows courage, the whore becomes the
heroine of a romance, and the outlaw becomes a lover. By stunning
photographic representation of the visual contrasts of desert, hills

and moving stagecoach, Ford transforms the journey of the stage-coach into an epic voyage that transcends the film's rather limited romantic plot.

Costume—another feature of the Western setting—has also con-   15
tributed greatly to the Western's success in film. Like topography, western costume gains effectiveness both from intrinsic interest and from the way writers and filmmakers have learned how to make it reflect character and theme. In simplest form, as in the B Westerns, costumes symbolized moral opposition. The good guy wears clean, well-pressed clothes and a white hat. The villain dresses sloppily in black. The importance of this convention, simple-minded as it was, became apparent when, to create a more sophisticated "adult" Western, directors frequently chose to dress their heroes in black. However, the tradition of western costume also contains more complex meanings. An important distinction marks off both hero and villain from the townspeople. The townspeople usually wear the ordinary street clothing associated with the later nineteenth century, suits for men and long dresses for women. On the whole this clothing is simple as compared to the more elaborate fashions of the period and this simplicity is one way of expressing the Westernness of the costume. However, in the midst of the desert, the townspeople's clothing has an air of non-utilitarian artificiality somewhat like the ubiquitous false fronts of the town itself. It is perhaps significant that even in Westerns purportedly set at a later date, the women tend to wear the full-length dresses of an earlier period.

The costumes associated with heroes and outlaws or savages are   16
more striking. Paradoxically, they are both more utilitarian and more artificial than those of the townspeople. The cowboy's boots, tight-fitting pants or chaps, his heavy shirt and bandanna, his gun, and finally his large ten-gallon hat all symbolize his adaptation to the wilderness. But utility is only one of the principles of the hero-outlaw's dress. The other is dandyism, that highly artificial love of elegance for its own sake. In the Western, dandyism sometimes takes the overt and obvious form of elaborate costumes laid over with fringes, tassels and scrollwork like a rococo drawing room. But it is more powerfully exemplified in the elegance of those beautifully tailored cowboy uniforms which John Wayne so magnificently fills out in the Westerns of John Ford and Howard Hawks.

The enormous attraction of this combination of naturalness and   17
artifice has played a significant role in both popular and avant-garde art since the middle of the nineteenth century. Baudelaire's fascination with the dandyism of the savage which he described as "the supreme incarnation of the idea of Beauty transported into the material world," is just one indication of the nineteenth century's fasci-

nation with the mixture of savagery and elegance which has been implicit in the costume of the Western hero from the beginning. Cooper's Leatherstocking even gained his name from his costume, suggesting the extent to which this particular kind of dress excited Cooper's imagination. Like later cowboys, Leatherstocking's costume combined nature and artifice. His dress was largely made of the skins of animals and it was particularly adapted to the needs of wilderness life. Yet at the same time it was subtly ornamented with buckskin fringes and porcupine quills "after the manner of the Indians." Still, it is important to note that Leatherstocking's costume is not that of the Indians, but rather a more utilitarian wilderness version of the settler's dress. Thus, costume exemplified the mediating role of the hero between civilization and savagery. Later the formula cowboy's costume developed along the same lines. In its basic outlines it resembled town dress more than that of the Indian, yet it was more functional for movement across the plains than that of the townspeople. At the same time, the cowboy dress had a dandyish splendor and elegance lacking in the drab fashions of the town and based on Indian or Mexican models. In later Westerns, the hero shared many of these qualities with the villain, just as Leatherstocking had a touch of the Indian, despite his repeated assurances that he was "a man without a cross," i.e. actual Indian kinship. But the hero's costume still differentiated him from the savage, whether Indian or outlaw, both by its basic resemblance to civilized dress and by its greater restraint and decorum. Thus costume, like setting, expressed the transcendent and intermediate quality of the hero. By lying between two ways of life, he transcended the restrictions and limitations of both. Or, to put it another way, the Western setting and costume embody the basic escapist principle of having your cake and eating it too. . . .

The Hero

The hero is a man with a horse and the horse is his direct tie to the freedom of the wilderness, for it embodies his ability to move freely across it and to dominate and control its spirit. Through the intensity of his relationship to his horse, the cowboy excites that human fantasy of unity with natural creatures—the same fantasy seen in such figures as the centaurs of Greek mythology, in Siegfried's ability to understand the language of birds, and in a hero whose popularity was contemporaneous with the flourishing of the Western: Tarzan of the Apes.   18

The Western hero is also a man with a gun. The interaction of American attitudes toward violence and the image of the Western   19 hero as gunfighter is so complex that it seems impossible to determine which causes the other. Critics of violence in the mass media believe that the heroic romanticized violence of the Western hero is a dangerous model for young people and stimulates them to imitation of the man with the gun. Defenders of the mass media argue that Westerns and other violent adventure dramas simply reflect the culture's fascination with guns. There have been many investigations of violence in the mass media and a large-scale government inquiry has recently been undertaken. Insofar as it seeks to determine the causal role of the Western hero in fostering violence among those who follow his adventures, this inquiry will probably be as inconclusive as the rest, for in my opinion both the tendency to admire gunfighter heroes and the actual social incidence of violence with guns are both symptoms of a more complex cultural force: the sense of decaying masculine potency which has long afflicted American culture. The American obsession with masculinity so often observed by Europeans and so evident in every aspect of our culture from serious artists like Ernest Hemingway to the immense range of gutsy men's magazines, *Playboy* images, and mass sports reflect a number of major social trends which undercut the sense of male security. Among the most important of these developments is the tendency of industrial work to depend increasingly on the superior potency of machines, the increasing importance of women in the industrial economy, the nationalizing trend of American life which has eroded local communities and the individual's sense of control over his life and finally, the decline of parental authority in the family which has undercut the basic source of masculine supremacy. Yet, at the same time, the American tradition has always emphasized individual masculine force; Americans love to think of themselves as pioneers, men who have conquered a continent and sired on it a new society. This radical discrepancy between the sense of eroding masculinity and the view of America as a great history of men against the wilderness has created the need for a means of symbolic expression of masculine potency in an unmistakable way. This means is the gun, particularly the six-gun.

Walter Prescott Webb suggests that the development of Colt's revolver was the critical invention that made possible the American assault on the Great Plains. As Webb sees it, the Plains Indians with their horses and their extraordinary skill with the bow and arrow had a mobility and firepower unequalled until the adoption of the six-gun by the Texas Rangers. From that point on the Americans had a military advantage over the Plains Indians and the rapid development of the "Cattle Kingdom" followed. The historical and cultural significance of the gun as the means by which the cowboy

20

drove out the Indian inhabitants of the plains and shaped a new culture happened to coincide with a long-standing tradition of heroism and masculine honor, that of the medieval knight, and its later off-shoot, the code of the duel. For the westerner's six-gun and his way of using it in individual combat was the closest thing in the armory of modern violence to the knight's sword and the duellist's pistol. Thus in a period when violence in war was becoming increasingly anonymous and incomprehensible with massed attacks and artillery duels accounting for most of the casualties, the cowboy hero in his isolated combat with Indian or outlaw seemed to reaffirm the traditional image of masculine strength, honor, and moral violence. The cowboy hero with his six-gun standing between the uncontrolled violence of the savages and the evolving collective forces of the legal process played out in new terms the older image of chivalrous adventure. Not surprisingly an age which so enjoyed the historical romances of Sir Walter Scott would color the cowboy with tints freely borrowed from *Ivanhoe* and *Rob Roy*.

Many critics of the Western have commented upon the gun as a 21 phallic symbol, suggesting that the firing of the gun symbolizes the moment of ejaculation in a sexual act. Insofar as this is the case it bears out the emphasis on masculine potency already noted. However, this kind of phallic symbolism is an almost universal property of adventure heroes. The knight has his sword, the hard-boiled detective his automatic pistol, Buck Rogers his ray gun. The distinctive characteristic of the cowboy hero is not his possession of a symbolic weapon, but the way in which he uses it.

Where the knight encountered his adversary in bloody hand-to- 22 hand combat, the cowboy invariably meets his at a substantial distance and goes through the complex and rigid ritual of the ''draw'' before finally consummating the fatal deed. The most important implication of this killing procedure seems to be the qualities of reluctance, control, and elegance which it associates with the hero. Unlike the knight, the cowboy hero does not seek out combat for its own sake and he typically shows an aversion to the wanton shedding of blood. Killing is an act forced upon him and he carries it out with the precision and skill of a surgeon and the careful proportions of an artist. We might say that the six-gun is that weapon which enables the hero to show the largest measure of objectivity and detachment while yet engaging in individual combat. This controlled and aesthetic mode of killing is particularly important as the supreme mark of differentiation between the hero and the savage. The Indian or outlaw as savage delights in slaughter, entering into combat with a kind of manic glee to fulfill an uncontrolled lust for blood. The hero never engages in violence until the last moment and he never kills until the savage's gun has already cleared his holster. Suddenly it is there and the villain crumples.

This peculiar emphasis on the hero's skilled and detached killing from a distance has been a part of the Western since its inception. One thinks, for example, of that climactic scene in *The Last of the Mohicans* where Leatherstocking picks the villainous Magua off the cliff top with a single shot from his unerring long rifle. The cowboy hero fights in a little closer within the smaller range of the six-gun, but the same basic pattern of individual combat at a distance with the hero's last minute precision and control defeating the villain's undisciplined and savage aggression is the same. Careful staging of the final duel with all its elaborate protocol became a high point of the film Western, another example of an element of the literary Western which turned out to have even greater potential for the film. 23

The hero often fights with his fists, but he never kills in this kind of direct hand-to-hand combat. Moreover, he rarely uses any weapon other than his fists, since knives and clubs suggest a more aggressive uncontrolled kind of violence which seems instinctively wrong for the character of the cowboy hero. Thus, the hero's special skill at gunfighting not only symbolizes his masculine potency, but indicates that his violence is disciplined and pure. Something like the old ideal of knightly purity and chastity survives in the cowboy hero's basic aversion to the grosser and dirtier forms of violence. In addition, the hero's reluctant but aesthetic approach to killing seems to reflect the ambiguity about violence which pervades modern society. Twentieth century America is perhaps the most ideologically pacifistic nation in history. Its political and social values are anti-militaristic, its legal ideals reject personal violence and it sees itself as a nation dedicated to world peace and domestic harmony through law and order. Yet this same nation supports one of the largest military establishments in history, its rate of violent crimes is enormously high, and it possesses the technological capacity to destroy the world. Perhaps one source of the cowboy hero's appeal is the way in which he resolves this ambiguity by giving a sense of moral significance and order to violence. His reluctance and detachment, the way in which he kills only when he forced to do so, the aesthetic order he imposes upon his acts of violence through the abstract ritual of the showdown, and finally, his mode of killing cleanly and purely at a distance through the magic of his six-gun cover the nakedness of violence and aggression beneath a skin of aesthetic grace and moral propriety. 24

Certain other characteristics are connected with the hero's role as middleman between the pacifistic townspeople and the violent savages. There is his oft-noted laconic style, for example. Not all 25

Western heroes are tight-lipped strong, silent types. Some, like Leatherstocking, are downright garrulous. But the laconic style is commonly associated with the Western hero, particularly in the twentieth century when movie stars like Gary Cooper, John Wayne, James Stewart, and Henry Fonda have vied for the prize as the Western hero who can say the fewest words with the least expression. Actually, tight lips are far more appropriate to the formula hero than the torrent of didacticism which flows from the lips of Natty Bumppo, and which most readers of Cooper resolutely ignore. Like his gun, language is a weapon the hero rarely uses, but when he does it is with precise and powerful effectiveness. In addition, the hero's reluctance with language reflects his social isolation and his reluctance to commit himself to the action which he knows will invariably lead to another violent confrontation.

Reluctance with words often matches the hero's reluctance toward women. Cooper's Leatherstocking marked out one basic course that the Western hero would take with respect to the fair sex. The one girl Natty falls in love with, Mabel Dunham, in *The Pathfinder*, is too young and civilized to return his love and he gives her up to the younger, less wilderness-loving Jasper Western. On the other hand, the girl who falls in love with Natty, Judith Hutter in *The Deerslayer*, is too wild and too passionate to capture the affection of the chaste and pure Leatherstocking. This romantic situation reflects Natty's position as a man who mediates between civilization and wildness. Cooper found it increasingly difficult to resolve this antithesis and Natty remained caught in the middle between his beloved forest and the oncoming civilization which he had served. At other periods, writers have tried to make a romantic hero out of the cowboy, as in Wister's *The Virginian* and the many novels of Zane Grey. However, even when the hero does get the girl, the clash between the hero's adherence to the "code of the West" and the heroine's commitment to domesticity, social success, or other genteel values usually plays a role in the story. Heroes such as the Lone Ranger tend to avoid romance altogether. They are occasionally pursued by women, but generally manage to evade their clutches. . . .

26

Stephen Crane, "The Bride Comes to Yellow Sky"
I

The great Pullman was whirling onward with such dignity of motion that a glance from the window seemed simply to prove that the plains of Texas were pouring eastward. Vast flats of green grass, dull-hued spaces of mesquite and cactus, little groups of frame

1

houses, woods of light and tender trees, all were sweeping into the east, sweeping over the horizon, a precipice.

A newly married pair had boarded this coach at San Antonio. The man's face was reddened from many days in the wind and sun, and a direct result of his new black clothes was that his brick-colored hands were constantly performing in a most conscious fashion. From time to time he looked down respectfully at his attire. He sat with a hand on each knee, like a man waiting in a barber's shop. The glances he devoted to other passengers were furtive and shy. ₂

The bride was not pretty, nor was she very young. She wore a dress of blue cashmere, with small reservations of velvet here and there, and with steel buttons abounding. She continually twisted her head to regard her puff sleeves, very stiff, straight, and high. They embarrassed her. It was quite apparent that she had cooked, and that she expected to cook, dutifully. The blushes caused by the careless scrutiny of some passengers as she had entered the car were strange to see upon this plain, under-class countenance, which was drawn in placid, almost emotionless lines. ₃

They were evidently very happy. "Ever been in a parlor-car before?" he asked, smiling with delight. ₄

"No," she answered; "I never was. It's fine, ain't it?" ₅

"Great! And then after a while we'll go forward to the diner, and get a big lay-out. Finest meal in the world. Charge a dollar." ₆

"Oh, do they?" cried the bride. "Charge a dollar? Why, that's too much—for us—ain't it, Jack?" ₇

"Not this trip, anyhow," he answered bravely. "We're going to go the whole thing." ₈

Later he explained to her about the trains. "You see, it's a thousand miles from one end of Texas to the other; and this train runs right across it, and never stops but four times." He had the pride of an owner. He pointed out to her the dazzling fittings of the coach; and in truth her eyes opened wider as she contemplated the sea-green figured velvet, the shining brass, silver, and glass, the wood that gleamed as darkly brilliant as the surface of a pool of oil. At one end a bronze figure sturdily held a support for a separated chamber, and at convenient places on the ceiling were frescos in olive and silver. ₉

To the minds of the pair, their surroundings reflected the glory of their marriage that morning in San Antonio; this was the environment of their new estate; and the man's face in particular beamed with an elation that made him appear ridiculous to the negro porter. This individual at times surveyed them from afar with an amused and superior grin. On other occasions he bullied them with skill in ways that did not make it exactly plain to them that they were being ₁₀

bullied. He subtly used all the manners of the most unconquerable
kind of snobbery. He oppressed them; but of this oppression they
had small knowledge, and they speedily forgot that infrequently a
number of travellers covered them with stares of derisive enjoyment.
Historically there was supposed to be something infinitely humorous
in their situation.

"We are due in Yellow Sky at 3:42," he said, looking tenderly   11
into her eyes.

"Oh, are we?" she said, as if she had not been aware of it. To   12
evince surprise at her husband's statement was part of her wifely
amiability. She took from a pocket a little silver watch; and as she
held it before her, and stared at it with a frown of attention, the new
husband's face shone.

"I bought it in San Anton' from a friend of mine," he told her   13
gleefully.

"It's seventeen minutes past twelve," she said, looking up at him   14
with a kind of shy and clumsy coquetry. A passenger, noting this
play, grew excessively sardonic, and winked at himself in one of the
numerous mirrors.

At last they went to the dining-car. Two rows of negro waiters, in   15
glowing white suits, surveyed their entrance with the interest, and
also the equanimity, of men who had been forewarned. The pair fell
to the lot of a waiter who happened to feel pleasure in steering them
through their meal. He viewed them with the manner of a fatherly
pilot, his countenance radiant with benevolence. The patronage, en-
twined with the ordinary deference, was not plain to them. And yet,
as they returned to their coach, they showed in their faces a sense of
escape.

To the left, miles down a long purple slope, was a little ribbon of   16
mist where moved the keening Rio Grande. The train was approaching it at an angle, and the apex was Yellow Sky. Presently it
was apparent that, as the distance from Yellow Sky grew shorter, the
husband became commensurately restless. His brick-red hands were
more insistent in their prominence. Occasionally he was even rather
absent-minded and far-away when the bride leaned forward and addressed him.

As a matter of truth, Jack Potter was beginning to find the shadow   17
of a deed weigh upon him like a leaden slab. He, the town marshal
of Yellow Sky, a man known, liked, and feared in his corner, a
prominent person, had gone to San Antonio to meet a girl he believed he loved, and there, after the usual prayers, had actually induced her to marry him, without consulting Yellow Sky for any part
of the transaction. He was now bringing his bride before an innocent
and unsuspecting community.

310

Of course people in Yellow Sky married as it pleased them, in accordance with a general custom; but such was Potter's thought of his duty to his friends, or of their idea of his duty, or of an unspoken form which does not control men in these matters, that he felt he was heinous. He had committed an extraordinary crime. Face to face with this girl in San Antonio, and spurred by his sharp impulse, he had gone headlong over all the social hedges. At San Antonio he was like a man hidden in the dark. A knife to sever any friendly duty, any form, was easy to his hand in that remote city. But the hour of Yellow Sky—the hour of daylight—was approaching. 18

He knew full well that his marriage was an important thing to his town. It could only be exceeded by the burning of the new hotel. His friends could not forgive him. Frequently he had reflected on the advisability of telling them by telegraph, but a new cowardice had been upon him. He feared to do it. And now the train was hurrying him toward a scene of amazement, glee, and reproach. He glanced out of the window at the line of haze swinging slowly in toward the train. 19

Yellow Sky had a kind of brass band, which played painfully, to the delight of the populace. He laughed without heart as he thought of it. If the citizens could dream of his prospective arrival with his bride, they would parade the band at the station and escort them, amid cheers and laughing congratulations, to his adobe home. 20

He resolved that he would use all the devices of speed and plainscraft in making the journey from the station to his house. Once within that safe citadel, he could issue some sort of vocal bulletin, and then not go among the citizens until they had time to wear off a little of their enthusiasm. 21

The bride looked anxiously at him. ''What's worrying you, Jack?'' 22

He laughed again. ''I'm not worrying, girl; I'm only thinking of Yellow Sky.'' 23

She flushed in comprehension. 24

A sense of mutual guilt invaded their minds and developed a finer tenderness. They looked at each other with eyes softly aglow. But Potter often laughed the same nervous laugh; the flush upon the bride's face seemed quite permanent. 25

The traitor to the feelings of Yellow Sky narrowly watched the speeding landscape. ''We're nearly there,'' he said. 26

Presently the porter came and announced the proximity of Potter's home. He held a brush in his hand, and, with all his airy superiority gone, he brushed Potter's new clothes as the latter slowly turned this way and that way. Potter fumbled out a coin and gave it to the porter, as he had seen others do. It was a heavy and musclebound business, as that of a man shoeing his first horse. 27

The porter took their bag, and as the train began to slow they moved forward to the hooded platform of the car. Presently the two engines and their long string of coaches rushed into the station of Yellow Sky.

"They have to take water here," said Potter, from a constricted throat and in mournful cadence, as one announcing death. Before the train stopped his eye had swept the length of the platform, and he was glad and astonished to see there was none upon it but the station-agent, who, with a slightly hurried and anxious air, was walking toward the water-tanks. When the train had halted, the porter alighted first, and placed in position a little temporary step.

"Come on, girl," said Potter, hoarsely. As he helped her down they each laughed on a false note. He took the bag from the negro, and bade his wife cling to his arm. As they slunk rapidly away, his hang-dog glance perceived that they were unloading the two trunks, and also that the station-agent, far ahead near the baggage-car, had turned and was running toward him, making gestures. He laughed, and groaned as he laughed, when he noted the first effect of his marital bliss upon Yellow Sky. He gripped his wife's arm firmly to his side, and they fled. Behind them the porter stood, chuckling fatuously.

II

The California express on the Southern Railway was due at Yellow Sky in twenty-one minutes. There were six men at the bar of the Weary Gentleman saloon. One was a drummer who talked a great deal and rapidly; three were Texans who did not care to talk at that time; and two were Mexican sheepherders, who did not talk as a general practice in the Weary Gentleman saloon. The barkeeper's dog lay on the boardwalk that crossed in front of the door. His head was on his paws, and he glanced drowsily here and there with the constant vigilance of a dog that is kicked on occasion. Across the sandy street were some vivid green grass-plots, so wonderful in appearance, amid the sands that burned near them in a blazing sun, that they caused a doubt in the mind. They exactly resembled the grass mats used to represent lawns on the stage. At the cooler end of the railway station, a man without a coat sat in a tilted chair and smoked his pipe. The fresh-cut bank of the Rio Grande circled near the town, and there could be seen beyond it a great plum-colored plain of mesquite.

Save for the busy drummer and his companions in the saloon, Yellow Sky was dozing. The newcomer leaned gracefully upon the bar, and recited many tales with the confidence of a bard who has come upon a new field.

"—and at the moment that the old man fell downstairs with the   33
bureau in his arms, the old woman was coming up with two scuttles
of coal, and of course—"

The drummer's tale was interrupted by a young man who sud-   34
denly appeared in the open door. He cried: "Scratchy Wilson's
drunk, and has turned loose with both hands." The two Mexicans
at once set down their glasses and faded out of the rear entrance of
the saloon.

The drummer, innocent and jocular, answered: "All right, old   35
man. S'pose he has? Come in and have a drink, anyhow."

But the information had made such an obvious cleft in every skull   36
in the room that the drummer was obliged to see its importance. All
had become instantly solemn. "Say," said he, mystified, "what is
this?" His three companions made the introductory gesture of eloquent speech; but the young man at the door forestalled them.

"It means, my friend," he answered, as he came into the saloon,   37
"that for the next two hours this town won't be a health resort."

The barkeeper went to the door, and locked and barred it; reach-   38
ing out of the window, he pulled in heavy wooden shutters, and
barred them. Immediately a solemn, chapel-like gloom was upon
the place. The drummer was looking from one to another.

"But say," he cried, "what is this, anyhow? You don't mean   39
there is going to be a gunfight?"

"Don't know whether there'll be a fight or not," answered one   40
man, grimly; "but there'll be some shootin'—some good shootin'."

The young man who had warned them waved his hand. "Oh,   41
there'll be a fight fast enough, if anyone wants it. Anybody can get a
fight out there in the street. There's a fight just waiting."

The drummer seemed to be swayed between the interest of a for-   42
eigner and a perception of personal danger.

"What did you say his name was?" he asked.   43

"Scratchy Wilson," they answered in chorus.   44

"And will he kill anybody? What are you going to do? Does this   45
happen often? Does he rampage around like this once a week or so?
Can he break in that door?"

"No; he can't break down that door," replied the barkeeper.   46
"He's tried it three times. But when he comes you'd better lay down
on the floor, stranger. He's dead sure to shoot at it, and a bullet may
come through."

Thereafter the drummer kept a strict eye upon the door. The time   47
had not yet been called for him to hug the floor, but, as a minor precaution, he sidled near to the wall. "Will he kill anybody?" he said
again.

The men laughed low and scornfully at the question.   48

"He's out to shoot, and he's out for trouble. Don't see any good   49
in experimentin' with him.''

"But what do you do in a case like this? What do you do?''   50

A man responded: "Why, he and Jack Potter—''   51

"But," in chorus the other men interrupted, "Jack Potter's in   52
San Anton'.''

"Well, who is he? What's he got to do with it?''   53

"Oh, he's the town marshal. He goes out and fights Scratchy   54
when he gets on one of these tears.''

"Wow!'' said the drummer, mopping his brow. "Nice job he's   55
got.''

The voices had toned away to mere whisperings. The drummer   56
wished to ask further questions, which were born of an increasing
anxiety and bewilderment; but when he attempted them, the men
merely looked at him in irritation and motioned him to remain silent. A tense waiting hush was upon them. In the deep shadows of
the room their eyes shone as they listened for sounds from the street.
One man made three gestures at the barkeeper; and the latter, moving like a ghost, handed him a glass and a bottle. The man poured a
full glass of whisky, and set down the bottle noiselessly. He gulped
the whisky in a swallow, and turned again toward the door in immovable silence. The drummer saw that the barkeeper, without a
sound, had taken a Winchester from beneath the bar. Later he saw
this individual beckoning to him, so he tiptoed across the room.

"You better come with me back of the bar.''   57

"No, thanks," said the drummer, perspiring; "I'd rather be   58
where I can make a break for the back door.''

Whereupon the man of bottles made a kindly but peremptory ges-   59
ture. The drummer obeyed it, and, finding himself seated on a box
with his head below the level of the bar, balm was laid upon his soul
at sight of various zinc and copper fittings that bore a resemblance to
armorplate. The barkeeper took a seat comfortably upon an adjacent box.

"You see," he whispered, "this here Scratchy Wilson is a wonder   60
with a gun—a perfect wonder; and when he goes on the war-trail,
we hunt our holes—naturally. He's about the last one of the old
gang that used to hang out along the river here. He's a terror when
he's drunk. When he's sober he's all right—kind of simple—
wouldn't hurt a fly—nicest fellow in town. But when he's drunk—
whoo!''

There were periods of stillness. "I wish Jack Potter was back from   61
San Anton'," said the barkeeper. "He shot Wilson up once—in the
leg—and he would sail in and pull out the kinks in this thing.''

Presently they heard from a distance the sound of a shot, followed   62 by three wild yowls. It instantly removed a bond from the men in the darkened saloon. There was a shuffling of feet. They looked at each other. ''Here he comes,'' they said.

III

A man in a maroon-colored flannel shirt, which had been purchased   63
for purposes of decoration, and made principally by some Jewish women on the East Side of New York, rounded a corner and walked into the middle of the main street of Yellow Sky. In either hand the man held a long, heavy, blue-black revolver. Often he yelled, and these cries rang through a semblance of a deserted village, shrilly flying over the roofs in a volume that seemed to have no relation to the ordinary vocal strength of a man. It was as if the surrounding stillness formed the arch of a tomb over him. These cries of ferocious challenge rang against walls of silence. And his boots had red tops with gilded imprints, of the kind beloved in winter by little sledding boys on the hillsides of New England.

The man's face flamed in a rage begot of whisky. His eyes, roll-   64
ing, and yet keen for ambush, hunted the still doorways and windows. He walked with the creeping movement of the midnight cat. As it occurred to him, he roared menacing information. The long revolvers in his hands were as easy as straws; they were moved with an electric swiftness. The little fingers of each hand played sometimes in a musician's way. Plain from the low collar of the shirt, the cords of his neck straightened and sank, straightened and sank, as passion moved him. The only sounds were his terrible invitations. The calm adobes preserved their demeanor at the passing of this small thing in the middle of the street.

There was no offer of fight—no offer of fight. The man called to   65
the sky. There were no attractions. He bellowed and fumed and swayed his revolvers here and everywhere.

The dog of the barkeeper of the Weary Gentleman saloon had not   66
appreciated the advance of events. He yet lay dozing in front of his master's door. At sight of the dog, the man paused and raised his revolver humorously. At sight of the man, the dog sprang up and walked diagonally away, with a sullen head, and growling. The man yelled, and the dog broke into a gallop. As it was about to enter an alley, there was a loud noise, a whistling, and something spat the ground directly before it. The dog screamed, and, wheeling in terror, galloped headlong in a new direction. Again there was a noise, a whistling, and sand was kicked viciously before it. Fear-stricken, the dog turned and flurried like an animal in a pen. The man stood laughing, his weapons at his hips.

Ultimately the man was attracted by the closed door of the Weary   67
Gentleman saloon. He went to it and, hammering with a revolver,
demanded drink.

The door remaining imperturbable, he picked a bit of paper from   68
the walk, and nailed it to the framework with a knife. He then
turned his back contemptuously upon this popular resort and, walking to the opposite side of the street and spinning there on his heel
quickly and lithely, fired at the bit of paper. He missed it by a half-
inch. He swore at himself, and went away. Later he comfortably fu-
silladed the windows of his most intimate friend. The man was playing with this town; it was a toy for him.

But still there was no offer of fight. The name of Jack Potter, his   69
ancient antagonist, entered his mind, and he concluded that it would
be a glad thing if he should go to Potter's house, and by bombard-
ment induce him to come out and fight. He moved in the direction
of his desire, chanting Apache scalp-music.

When he arrived at it, Potter's house presented the same still front   70
as had the other adobes. Taking up a strategic position, the man
howled a challenge. But this house regarded him as might a great
stone god. It gave no sign. After a decent wait, the man howled further challenges, mingling with them wonderful epithets.

Presently there came the spectacle of a man churning himself into   71
deepest rage over the immobility of a house. He fumed at it as the
winter wind attacks a prairie cabin in the North. To the distance
there should have gone the sound of a tumult like the fighting of two
hundred Mexicans. As necessity bade him, he paused for breath or
to reload his revolvers.

IV

Potter and his bride walked sheepishly and with speed. Sometimes   72
they laughed together shamefacedly and low.

"Next corner, dear," he said finally.   73

They put forth the efforts of a pair walking bowed against a strong   74
wind. Potter was about to raise a finger to point the first appearance
of the new home when, as they circled the corner, they came face to
face with a man in a maroon-colored shirt, who was feverishly pushing cartridges into a large revolver. Upon the instant the man
dropped his revolver to the ground and, like lightning, whipped another from its holster. The second weapon was aimed at the bride-
groom's chest.

There was a silence. Potter's mouth seemed to be merely a grave   75
for his tongue. He exhibited an instinct to at once loosen his arm
from the woman's grip, and he dropped the bag to the sand. As for

316 the bride, her face had gone as yellow as old cloth. She was a slave to hideous rites, gazing at the apparitional snake.

The two men faced each other at a distance of three paces. He of 76 the revolver smiled with a new and quiet ferocity.

"Tried to sneak up on me," he said. "Tried to sneak up on me!" 77 His eyes grew more baleful. As Potter made a slight movement, the man thrust his revolver venomously forward "No; don't you do it, Jack Potter. Don't you move a finger toward a gun just yet. Don't you move an eyelash. The time has come for me to settle with you, and I'm goin' to do it my own way, and loaf along with no inter- ferin'. So if you don't want a gun bent on you, just mind what I tell you."

Potter looked at his enemy. "I ain't got a gun on me Scratchy," 78 he said. "Honest, I ain't." He was stiffening and steadying, but yet somewhere at the back of his mind a vision of the Pullman floated: the sea-green figured velvet, the shining brass, silver, and glass, the wood that gleamed as darkly brilliant as the surface of a pool of oil— all the glory of the marriage, the environment of the new estate. "You know I fight when it comes to fighting, Scratchy Wilson; but I ain't got a gun on me. You'll have to do all the shootin' yourself."

His enemy's face went livid. He stepped forward, and lashed his 79 weapon to and fro before Potter's chest. "Don't you tell me you ain't got no gun on you, you whelp. Don't tell me no lie like that. There ain't a man in Texas ever seen you without no gun. Don't take me for no kid." His eyes blazed with light, and his throat worked like a pump.

"I ain't takin' you for no kid," answered Potter. His heels had 80 not moved an inch backward. "I'm takin' you for a damn fool. I tell you I ain't got a gun, and I ain't. If you're goin' to shoot me up, you better begin now; you'll never get a chance like this again."

So much enforced reasoning had told on Wilson's rage; he was 81 calmer. "If you ain't got a gun, why ain't you got a gun?" he sneered. "Been to Sunday-school?"

"I ain't got a gun because I've just come from San Anton' with 82 my wife. I'm married," said Potter. "And if I'd thought there was going to be any galoots like you prowling around when I brought my wife home, I'd had a gun, and don't you forget it."

"Married!" said Scratchy, not at all comprehending. 83

"Yes, married. I'm married," said Potter, distinctly. 84

"Married?" said Scratchy. Seemingly for the first time, he saw 85 the drooping, drowning woman at the other man's side. "No!" he said. He was like a creature allowed a glimpse of another world. He moved a pace backward, and his arm, with the revolver, dropped to his side. "Is this the lady?" he asked.

"Yes; this is the lady," answered Potter.

There was another period of silence.

"Well," said Wilson at last, slowly, "I s'pose it's all off now."

"It's all off if you say so, Scratchy. You know I didn't make the trouble." Potter lifted his valise.

"Well, I 'low it's off, Jack," said Wilson. He was looking at the ground. "Married!" He was not a student of chivalry; it was merely that in the presence of this foreign condition he was a simple child of the earlier plains. He picked up his starboard revolver, and, placing both weapons in their holsters, he went away. His feet made funnel-shaped tracks in the heavy sand.

Stephen Crane, "The Blue Hotel"

I

The Palace Hotel at Fort Romper was painted a light blue, a shade that is on the legs of a kind of heron, causing the bird to declare its position against any background. The Palace Hotel, then, was always screaming and howling in a way that made the dazzling winter landscape of Nebraska seem only a grey swampish hush. It stood alone on the prairie, and when the snow was falling the town two hundred yards away was not visible. But when the traveller alighted at the railway station he was obliged to pass the Palace Hotel before he could come upon the company of low clapboard houses which composed Fort Romper, and it was not to be thought that any traveller could pass the Palace Hotel without looking at it. Pat Scully, the proprietor, had proved himself a master of strategy when he chose his paints. It is true that on clear days, when the great transcontinental expresses, long lines of swaying Pullmans, swept through Fort Romper, passengers were overcome at the sight, and the cult that knows the brown-reds and the subdivisions of the dark greens of the East expressed shame, pity, horror, in a laugh. But to the citizens of this prairie town and to the people who would naturally stop there, Pat Scully had performed a feat. With this opulence and splendor, these creeds, classes, egotisms, that streamed through Romper on the rails day after day, they had no color in common.

As if the displayed delights of such a blue hotel were not sufficiently enticing, it was Scully's habit to go every morning and evening to meet the leisurely trains that stopped at Romper and work his seductions upon any man that he might see wavering, gripsack in hand.

One morning, when a snow-crusted engine dragged its long string of freight cars and its one passenger coach to the station, Scully performed the marvel of catching three men. One was a shaky and quick-eyed Swede, with a great shining cheap valise; one was a tall bronzed cowboy, who was on his way to a ranch near the Dakota line; one was a little silent man from the East, who didn't look it, and didn't announce it. Scully practically made them prisoners. He was so nimble and merry and kindly that each probably felt it would be the height of brutality to try to escape. They trudged off over the creaking board sidewalks in the wake of the eager little Irishman. He wore a heavy fur cap squeezed tightly down on his head. It caused his two red ears to stick out stiffly, as if they were made of tin.

At last, Scully, elaborately, with boisterous hospitality, conducted them through the portals of the blue hotel. The room which they entered was small. It seemed to be merely a proper temple for an enormous stove, which, in the center, was humming with godlike violence. At various points on its surface the iron had become luminous and glowed yellow from the heat. Beside the stove Scully's son Johnnie was playing High-Five with an old farmer who had whiskers both grey and sandy. They were quarrelling. Frequently the old farmer turned his face toward a box of sawdust—colored brown from tobacco juice—that was behind the stove, and spat with an air of great impatience and irritation. With a loud flourish of words Scully destroyed the game of cards, and bustled his son upstairs with part of the baggage of the new guests. He himself conducted them to three basins of the coldest water in the world. The cowboy and the Easterner burnished themselves fiery red with this water, until it seemed to be some kind of metal-polish. The Swede, however, merely dipped his fingers gingerly and with trepidation. It was notable that throughout this series of small ceremonies the three travellers were made to feel that Scully was very benevolent. He was conferring great favors upon them. He handed the towel from one to another with an air of philanthropic impulse. 4

Afterward they went to the first room, and, sitting about the stove, listened to Scully's officious clamor at his daughters, who were preparing the midday meal. They reflected in the silence of experienced men who tread carefully amid new people. Nevertheless, the old farmer, stationary, invincible in his chair near the warmest part of the stove, turned his face from the sawdust-box frequently and addressed a glowing commonplace to the strangers. Usually he was answered in short but adequate sentences by either the cowboy or the Easterner. The Swede said nothing. He seemed to be occupied in making furtive estimates of each man in the room. One might have thought that he had the sense of silly suspicion which comes to guilt. He resembled a badly frightened man. 5

Later, at dinner, he spoke a little, addressing his conversation entirely to Scully. He volunteered that he had come from New York, 6 where for ten years he had worked as a tailor. These facts seemed to strike Scully as fascinating, and afterward he volunteered that he had lived at Romper for fourteen years. The Swede asked about the crops and the price of labor. He seemed barely to listen to Scully's extended replies. His eyes continued to rove from man to man.

Finally, with a laugh and a wink, he said that some of these West- 7 ern communities were very dangerous; and after his statement he straightened his legs under the table, tilted his head, and laughed again, loudly. It was plain that the demonstration had no meaning to the others. They looked at him wondering and in silence.

II

As the men trooped heavily back into the front room, the two little 8 windows presented views of a turmoiling sea of snow. The huge arms of the wind were making attempts—mighty, circular, futile— to embrace the flakes as they sped. A gate-post like a still man with a blanched face stood aghast amid this profligate fury. In a hearty voice Scully announced the presence of a blizzard. The guests of the blue hotel, lighting their pipes, assented with grunts of lazy masculine contentment. No island of the sea could be exempt in the degree of this little room with its humming stove. Johnnie, son of Scully, in a tone which defined his opinion of his ability as a card-player, challenged the old farmer of both grey and sandy whiskers to a game of High-Five. The farmer agreed with a contemptuous and bitter scoff. They sat close to the stove, and squared their knees under a wide board. The cowboy and the Easterner watched the game with interest. The Swede remained near the window, aloof, but with a countenance that showed signs of an inexplicable excitement.

The play of Johnnie and the grey-beard was suddenly ended by 9 another quarrel. The old man arose while casting a look of heated scorn at his adversary. He slowly buttoned his coat, and then stalked with fabulous dignity from the room. In the discreet silence of all the other men the Swede laughed. His laughter rang somehow childish. Men by this time had begun to look at him askance, as if they wished to inquire what ailed him.

A new game was formed jocosely. The cowboy volunteered to be- 10 come the partner of Johnnie, and they all then turned to ask the Swede to throw in his lot with the little Easterner. He asked some questions about the game, and, learning that it wore many names, and that he had played it when it was under an alias, he accepted the invitation. He strode toward the men nervously, as if he expected to be assaulted. Finally, seated, he gazed from face to face and laughed shrilly. This laugh was so strange that the Easterner looked up quickly, the cowboy sat intent and with his mouth open, and Johnnie paused, holding the cards with still fingers.

Afterward there was a short silence. Then Johnnie said, "Well, let's get at it. Come on now!" They pulled their chairs forward until their knees were punched under the board. They began to play, and their interest in the game caused the others to forget the manner of the Swede. 11

The cowboy was a board-whacker. Each time that he held superior cards he whanged them, one by one, with exceeding force, down upon the improvised table, and took the tricks with a glowing air of prowess and pride that sent thrills of indignation into the hearts of his opponents. A game with a board-whacker in it is sure to become intense. The countenances of the Easterner and the Swede were miserable whenever the cowboy thundered down his aces and kings, while Johnnie, his eyes gleaming with joy, chuckled and chuckled. 12

Because of the absorbing play none considered the strange ways of the Swede. They paid strict heed to the game. Finally, during a lull caused by a new deal, the Swede suddenly addressed Johnnie: "I suppose there have been a good many men killed in this room." The jaws of the others dropped and they looked at him. 13

"What in hell are you talking about?" said Johnnie. 14

The Swede laughed again his blatant laugh, full of a kind of false courage and defiance. "Oh, you know what I mean all right," he answered. 15

"I'm a liar if I do!" Johnnie protested. The card was halted, and the men stared at the Swede. Johnnie evidently felt that as the son of the proprietor he should make a direct inquiry. "Now, what might you be drivin' at, mister?" he asked. The Swede winked at him. It was a wink full of cunning. His fingers shook on the edge of the board. "Oh, maybe you think I have been to nowheres. Maybe you think I'm a tenderfoot?" 16

"I don't know nothin' about you," answered Johnnie, "and I don't give a damn where you've been. All I got to say is that I don't know what you're driving at. There hain't never been nobody killed in this room." 17

The cowboy, who had been steadily gazing at the Swede, then spoke: "What's wrong with you, mister?" 18

Apparently it seemed to the Swede that he was formidably menaced. He shivered and turned white near the corners of his mouth. He sent an appealing glance in the direction of the little Easterner. During these moments he did not forget to wear his air of advanced pot-valor. "They say they don't know what I mean," he remarked mockingly to the Easterner. 19

The latter answered after prolonged and cautious reflection. "I 20 don't understand you," he said, impassively.

The Swede made a movement then which announced that he 21 thought he had encountered treachery from the only quarter where he had expected sympathy, if not help. "Oh, I see you are all against me. I see—"

The cowboy was in a state of deep stupefaction. "Say," he cried, 22 as he tumbled the deck violently down upon the board, "say, what are you gittin' at, hey?"

The Swede sprang up with the celerity of a man escaping from a 23 snake on the floor. "I don't want to fight!" he shouted, "I don't want to fight!"

The cowboy stretched his long legs indolently and deliberately. 24 His hands were in his pockets. He spat into the sawdust-box. "Well, who the hell thought you did?" he inquired.

The Swede backed rapidly toward a corner of the room. His hands 25 were out protectingly in front of his chest, but he was making an obvious struggle to control his fright. "Gentlemen," he quavered, "I suppose I am going to be killed before I can leave this house! I suppose I am going to be killed before I can leave this house!" In his eyes was the dying-swan look. Through the windows could be seen the snow turning blue in the shadow of dusk. The wind tore at the house, and some loose thing beat regularly against the clapboards like a spirit tapping.

A door opened, and Scully himself entered. He paused in surprise 26 as he noted the tragic attitude of the Swede. Then he said, "What's the matter here?"

The Swede answered him swiftly and eagerly: "These men are 27 going to kill me."

"Kill you!" ejaculated Scully. "Kill you! What are you talkin'?" 28

The Swede made the gesture of a martyr. 29

Scully wheeled sternly upon his son. "What is this, Johnnie?" 30

The lad had grown sullen. "Damned if I know," he answered. "I 31 can't make no sense to it." He began to shuffle the cards, fluttering them together with an angry snap. "He says a good many men have been killed in this room, or something like that. And he says he's goin' to be killed here too. I don't know what ails him. He's crazy, I shouldn't wonder."

Scully then looked for explanation to the cowboy, but the cowboy 32 simply shrugged his shoulders.

"Kill you?" said Scully again to the Swede. "Kill you? Man, 33 you're off your nut."

"Oh, I know," burst out the Swede. "I know what will happen. 34 Yes, I'm crazy—yes. Yes, of course, I'm crazy—yes. But I know one thing—'' There was a sort of sweat of misery and terror upon his face. "I know I won't get out of here alive."

The cowboy drew a deep breath, as if his mind was passing into the last stages of dissolution. "Well, I'm doggoned," he whispered to himself.

Scully wheeled suddenly and faced his son. "You've been troublin' this man!"

Johnnie's voice was loud with its burden of grievance. "Why, good Gawd, I ain't done nothin' to 'im."

The Swede broke in. "Gentlemen, do not disturb yourselves. I will leave this house. I will go away, because"—he accused them dramatically with his glance—"because I do not want to be killed."

Scully was furious with his son. "Will you tell me what is the matter, you young divil? What's the matter, anyhow? Speak out!"

"Blame it!" cried Johnnie in despair, "don't I tell you I don't know? He—he says we want to kill him, and that's all I know. I can't tell what ails him."

The Swede continued to repeat: "Never mind, Mr. Scully; never mind. I will leave this house. I will go away, because I do not wish to be killed. Yes, of course, I am crazy—yes. But I know one thing! I will go away. I will leave this house. Never mind, Mr. Scully; never mind. I will go away."

"You will not go 'way," said Scully. "You will not go 'way until I hear the reason of this business. If anybody has troubled you I will take care of him. This is my house. You are under my roof, and I will not allow any peaceable man to be troubled here." He cast a terrible eye upon Johnnie, the cowboy, and the Easterner.

"Never mind, Mr. Scully; never mind. I will go away. I do not wish to be killed." The Swede moved toward the door which opened upon the stairs. It was evidently his intention to go at once for his baggage.

"No, no," shouted Scully peremptorily; but the white-faced man slid by him and disappeared. "Now," said Scully severely, "what does this mane?"

Johnnie and the cowboy cried together: "Why, we didn't do nothin' to 'im!"

Scully's eyes were cold. "No," he said "you didn't?"

Johnnie swore a deep oath. "Why, this is the wildest loon I ever see. We didn't do nothing' at all. We were jest sittin' here playin' cards, and he—"

The father suddenly spoke to the Easterner. "Mr. Blanc," he asked, "what has these boys been doin'?"

The Easterner reflected again. "I didn't see anything wrong at all," he said at last, slowly.

Scully began to howl. "But what does it mane?" He stared fero- 50 **323**
ciously at his son. "I have a mind to lather you for this, me boy."

Johnnie was frantic. "Well, what have I done?" he bawled at his 51
father.

III

"I think you are tongue-tied," said Scully finally to his son, the 52
cowboy, and the Easterner; and at the end of this scornful sentence
he left the room.

Upstairs the Swede was swiftly fastening the straps of his great va- 53
lise. Once his back happened to be half turned toward the door, and,
hearing a noise there, he wheeled and sprang up, uttering a loud
cry. Scully's wrinkled visage showed grimly in the light of the small
lamp he carried. This yellow effulgence, streaming upward, colored
only his prominent features, and left his eyes, for instance, in mysterious shadow. He resembled a murderer.

"Man! man!" he exclaimed, "have you gone daffy?" 54

"Oh, no! Oh, no!" rejoined the other. "There are people in this 55
world who know pretty nearly as much as you do—understand?"

For a moment they stood gazing at each other. Upon the Swede's 56
deathly pale cheeks were two spots brightly crimson and sharply
edged, as if they had been carefully painted. Scully placed the light
on the table and sat himself on the edge of the bed. He spoke rumi-
natively. "By cracky, I never heard of such a thing in my life. It's a
complete muddle. I can't, for the soul of me, think how you ever got
this idea into your head." Presently he lifted his eyes and asked:
"And did you sure think they were going to kill you?"

The Swede scanned the old man as if he wished to see into his 57
mind. "I did," he said at last. He obviously suspected that this answer might precipitate an outbreak. As he pulled on a strap his
whole arm shook, the elbow wavering like a bit of paper.

Scully banged his hand impressively on the footboard of the bed. 58
"Why, man, we're goin' to have a line of ilictric streetcars in this
town next spring."

"'A line of electric streetcars,'" repeated the Swede, stupidly. 59

"And," said Scully, "there's a new railroad goin' to be built 60
down from Broken Arm to here. Not to mintion the four churches
and the smashin' big brick schoolhouse. Then there's the big factory, too. Why, in two years Romper'll be a met-tro-*pol*-is."

Having finished the preparation of his baggage, the Swede 61
straightened himself. "Mr. Scully," he said, with sudden hardi-
hood, "how much do I owe you?"

"You don't owe me anythin'," said the old man, angrily. 62

"Yes, I do," retorted the Swede. He took seventy-five cents from his pocket and tendered it to Scully; but the latter snapped his fingers in disdainful refusal. However, it happened that they both stood gazing in a strange fashion at three silver pieces on the Swede's open palm. 63

"I'll not take your money," said Scully at last. "Not after what's been goin' on here." Then a plan seemed to strike him. "Here," he cried, picking up his lamp and moving toward the door. "Here! Come with me a minute." 64

"No," said the Swede, in overwhelming alarm. 65

"Yes," urged the old man. "Come on! I want you to come and see a picter—just across the hall—in my room." 66

The Swede must have concluded that his hour was come. His jaw dropped and his teeth showed like a dead man's. He ultimately followed Scully across the corridor, but he had the step of one hung in chains. 67

Scully flashed the light high on the wall of his own chamber. There was revealed a ridiculous photograph of a little girl. She was leaning against a balustrade of gorgeous decoration, and the formidable bang to her hair was prominent. The figure was as graceful as an upright sled-stake, and, withal, it was of the hue of lead. "There," said Scully, tenderly, "that's the picter of my little girl that died. Her name was Carrie. She had the purtiest hair you ever saw! I was that fond of her, she—" 68

Turning then, he saw that the Swede was not contemplating the picture at all, but, instead, was keeping keen watch on the gloom in the rear. 69

"Look, man!" cried Scully, heartily. "That's the picter of my little gal that died. Her name was Carrie. And then here's the picter of my oldest boy, Michael. He's a lawyer in Lincoln, an' doin' well. I gave that boy a grand eddication, and I'm glad for it now. He's a fine boy. Look at 'im now. Ain't he bold as blazes, him there in Lincoln, an honored an' respicted gintleman! An honored and respicted gintleman," concluded Scully with a flourish. And, so saying, he smote the Swede jovially on the back. 70

The Swede faintly smiled. 71

"Now," said the old man, "there's only one more thing." He dropped suddenly to the floor and thrust his head beneath the bed. The Swede could hear his muffled voice. "I'd keep it under me piller if it wasn't for that boy Johnnie. Then there's the old woman—Where is it now? I never put it twice in the same place. Ah, now come out with you!" 72

Presently he backed clumsily from under the bed, dragging with 73

him an old coat rolled into a bundle. "I've fetched him," he muttered. Kneeling on the floor, he unrolled the coat and extracted from
its heart a large yellow-brown whisky bottle.

His first maneuver was to hold the bottle up to the light. Reas-   74
sured, apparently, that nobody had been tampering with it, he
thrust it with a generous movement toward the Swede.

The weak-kneed Swede was about to eagerly clutch this element of   75
strength, but he suddenly jerked his hand away and cast a look of
horror upon Scully.

"Drink," said the old man affectionately. He had risen to his feet,   76
and now stood facing the Swede.

There was a silence. Then again Scully said: "Drink!"   77

The Swede laughed wildly. He grabbed the bottle, put it to his   78
mouth; and as his lips curled absurdly around the opening and his
throat worked, he kept his glance, burning with hatred, upon the old
man's face.

IV

After the departure of Scully the three men, with the card-board still   79
upon their knees, preserved for a long time an astounded silence.
Then Johnnie said: "That's the doddangedest Swede I ever see."

"He ain't no Swede," said the cowboy, scornfully.   80

"Well, what is he then?" cried Johnnie. "What is he then?"   81

"It's my opinion," replied the cowboy deliberately, "he's some   82
kind of a Dutchman." It was a venerable custom of the country to
entitle as Swedes all light-haired men who spoke with a heavy
tongue. In consequence the idea of the cowboy was not without its
daring. "Yes, sir," he repeated. "It's my opinion this feller is some
kind of a Dutchman."

"Well, he says he's a Swede, anyhow," muttered Johnnie, sulk-   83
ily. He turned to the Easterner: "What do you think, Mr. Blanc?"

"Oh, I don't know," replied the Easterner.   84

"Well, what do you think makes him act that way?" asked the   85
cowboy.

"Why, he's frightened." The Easterner knocked his pipe against   86
a rim of the stove. "He's clear frightened out of his boots."

"What at?" cried Johnnie and the cowboy together.   87

The Easterner reflected over his answer.   88

"What at?" cried the others again.   89

"Oh, I don't know, but it seems to me this man has been reading   90
dime novels, and he thinks he's right out in the middle of it—the
shootin' and stabbin' and all."

"But," said the cowboy, deeply scandalized, "this ain't Wyoming, ner none of them places. This is Nebrasker." 91

"Yes," added Johnnie, "an' why don't he wait till he gits *out West*?" 92

The travelled Easterner laughed. "It isn't different there even—not in these days. But he thinks he's right in the middle of hell." 93

Johnnie and the cowboy mused long. 94

"It's awful funny," remarked Johnnie at last. 95

"Yes," said the cowboy. "This is a queer game. I hope we don't git snowed in, because then we'd have to stand this here man bein' around with us all the time. That wouldn't be no good." 96

"I wish pop would throw him out," said Johnnie. 97

Presently they heard a loud stamping on the stairs, accompanied by ringing jokes in the voice of old Scully, and laughter, evidently from the Swede. The men around the stove stared vacantly at each other. "Gosh!" said the cowboy. The door flew open, and old Scully, flushed and anecdotal, came into the room. He was jabbering at the Swede, who followed him, laughing bravely. It was the entry of two roisterers from a banquet hall. 98

"Come now," said Scully sharply to the three seated men, "move up and give us a chance at the stove." The cowboy and the Easterner obediently sidled their chairs to make room for the newcomers. Johnnie, however, simply arranged himself in a more indolent attitude, and then remained motionless. 99

"Come! Git over, there," said Scully. 100

"Plenty of room on the other side of the stove," said Johnnie. 101

"Do you think we want to sit in the draft?" roared the father. 102

But the Swede here interposed with a grandeur of confidence. "No, no. Let the boy sit where he likes," he cried in a bullying voice to the father. 103

"All right! All right!" said Scully, deferentially. The cowboy and the Easterner exchanged glances of wonder. 104

The five chairs were formed in a crescent about one side of the stove. The Swede began to talk; he talked arrogantly, profanely, angrily. Johnnie, the cowboy, and the Easterner maintained a morose silence, while old Scully appeared to be receptive and eager, breaking in constantly with sympathetic ejaculations. 105

Finally the Swede announced that he was thirsty. He moved in his chair, and said that he would go for a drink of water. 106

"I'll git it for you," cried Scully at once. 107

"No," said the Swede, contemptuously. "I'll get it for myself." He arose and stalked with the air of an owner off into the executive parts of the hotel. 108

As soon as the Swede was out of hearing Scully sprang to his feet and whispered intensely to the others: "Upstairs he thought I was tryin' to poison 'im." 109

"Say," said Johnnie, "this makes me sick. Why don't you throw 'im out in the snow?" 110

"Why, he's all right now," declared Scully. "It was only that he was from the East, and he thought this was a tough place. That's all. He's all right now." 111

The cowboy looked with admiration upon the Easterner. "You were straight," he said. "You were on to that there Dutchman." 112

"Well," said Johnnie to his father, "he may be all right now, but I don't see it. Other time he was scared, but now he's too fresh." 113

Scully's speech was always a combination of Irish brogue and idiom, Western twang and idiom, and scraps of curiously formal diction taken from the storybooks and newspapers. He now hurled a strange mass of language at the head of his son. "What do I keep? What do I keep? What do I keep?" he demanded, in a voice of thunder. He slapped his knee impressively, to indicate that he himself was going to make reply, and that all should heed. "I keep a hotel," he shouted. "A hotel, do you mind? A guest under my roof has sacred privileges. He is to be intimidated by none. Not one word shall he hear that would prijudice him in favor of goin' away. I'll not have it. There's no place in this here town where they can say they iver took in a guest of mine because he was afraid to stay here." He wheeled suddenly upon the cowboy and the Easterner. "Am I right?" 114

"Yes, Mr. Scully," said the cowboy, "I think you're right." 115

"Yes, Mr. Scully," said the Easterner, "I think you're right." 116

V

At six-o'clock supper, the Swede fizzed like a fire-wheel. He sometimes seemed on the point of bursting into riotous song, and in all his madness he was encouraged by old Scully. The Easterner was encased in reserve; the cowboy sat in wide-mouthed amazement, forgetting to eat, while Johnnie wrathily demolished great plates of food. The daughters of the house, when they were obliged to replenish the biscuits, approached as warily as Indians, and, having succeeded in their purpose, fled with ill-concealed trepidation. The Swede domineered the whole feast, and he gave it the appearance of a cruel bacchanal. He seemed to have grown suddenly taller; he gazed, brutally disdainful, into every face. His voice rang through the room. Once when he jabbed out harpoon-fashion with his fork to 117

328

pinion a biscuit, the weapon nearly impaled the hand of the Easterner, which had been stretched quietly out for the same biscuit.

After supper, as the men filed toward the other room, the Swede   118
smote Scully ruthlessly on the shoulder. "Well, old boy, that was a
good, square meal." Johnnie looked hopefully at his father; he knew
that shoulder was tender from an old fall; and, indeed, it appeared
for a moment as if Scully was going to flame out over the matter, but
in the end he smiled a sickly smile and remained silent. The others
understood from his manner that he was admitting his responsibility
for the Swede's new viewpoint.

Johnnie, however, addressed his parent in an aside. "Why don't   119
you license somebody to kick you downstairs?" Scully scowled
darkly by way of reply.

When they were gathered about the stove, the Swede insisted on   120
another game of High-Five. Scully gently deprecated the plan at
first, but the Swede turned a wolfish glare upon him. The old man
subsided, and the Swede canvassed the others. In his tone there was
always a great threat. The cowboy and the Easterner both remarked
indifferently that they would play. Scully said that he would presently have to go to meet the 6:58 train, and so the Swede turned
menacingly upon Johnnie. For a moment their glances crossed like
blades, and then Johnnie smiled and said, "Yes, I'll play."

They formed a square, with the little board on their knees. The   121
Easterner and the Swede were again partners. As the play went on,
it was noticeable that the cowboy was not board-whacking as usual.
Meanwhile, Scully, near the lamp, had put on his spectacles and,
with an appearance curiously like an old priest, was reading a newspaper. In time he went out to meet the 6:58 train, and, despite his
precautions, a gust of polar wind whirled into the room as he opened
the door. Besides scattering the cards, it chilled the players to the
marrow. The Swede cursed frightfully. When Scully returned, his
entrance disturbed a cosy and friendly scene. The Swede again
cursed. But presently they were once more intent, their heads bent
forward and their hands moving swiftly. The Swede had adopted the
fashion of board-whacking.

Scully took up his paper and for a long time remained immersed   122
in matters which were extraordinarily remote from him. The lamp
burned badly, and once he stopped to adjust the wick. The newspaper, as he turned from page to page, rustled with a slow and com-
fortable sound. Then suddenly he heard three terrible words: "You
are cheatin'!"

Such scenes often prove that there can be little of dramatic import   123
in environment. Any room can present a tragic front; any room can
be comic. This little den was now hideous as a torture-chamber. The

new faces of the men themselves had changed it upon the instant. The Swede held a huge fist in front of Johnnie's face, while the latter looked steadily over it into the blazing orbs of his accuser. The Easterner had grown pallid; the cowboy's jaw had dropped in that expression of bovine amazement which was one of his important mannerisms. After the three words, the first sound in the room was made by Scully's paper as it floated forgotten to his feet. His spectacles had also fallen from his nose, but by a clutch he had saved them in air. His hand, grasping the spectacles, now remained poised awkwardly and near his shoulder. He stared at the card-players.

Probably the silence was while a second elapsed. Then, if the floor 124 had been suddenly twitched out from under the men they could not have moved quicker. The five had projected themselves headlong toward a common point. It happened that Johnnie, in rising to hurl himself upon the Swede, had stumbled slightly because of his curiously instinctive care for the cards and the board. The loss of the moment allowed time for the arrival of Scully, and also allowed the cowboy time to give the Swede a great push which sent him staggering back. The men found tongue together, and hoarse shouts of rage, appeal, or fear burst from every throat. The cowboy pushed and jostled feverishly at the Swede, and the Easterner and Scully clung wildly to Johnnie; but through the smoky air, above the swaying bodies of the peace-compellers, the eyes of the two warriors ever sought each other in glances of challenge that were at once hot and steely.

Of course the board had been overturned, and now the whole 125 company of cards was scattered over the floor, where the boots of the men trampled the fat and painted kings and queens as they gazed with their silly eyes at the war that was waging above them.

Scully's voice was dominating the yells. ''Stop now! Stop, I say! 126 Stop, now—''

Johnnie, as he struggled to burst through the rank formed by 127 Scully and the Easterner, was crying, ''Well, he says I cheated! He says I cheated! I won't allow no man to say I cheated! If he says I cheated, he's a — —!''

The cowboy was telling the Swede, ''Quit, now! Quit, d'ye 128 hear—''

The screams of the Swede never ceased: ''He did cheat! I saw 129 him! I saw him—''

As for the Easterner, he was importuning in a voice that was not 130 heeded: ''Wait a moment, can't you? Oh, wait a moment. What's the good of a fight over a game of cards? Wait a moment—''

In this tumult no complete sentences were clear. ''Cheat''— 131 ''Quit''—''He says''—these fragments pierced the uproar and rang out sharply. It was remarkable that, whereas Scully undoubtedly made the most noise, he was the least heard of any of the riotous band.

Then suddenly there was a great cessation. It was as if each man 132 had paused for breath; and although the room was still lighted with the anger of men, it could be seen that there was no danger of immediate conflict, and at once Johnnie, shouldering his way forward, almost succeeded in confronting the Swede. "What did you say I cheated for? What did you say I cheated for? I don't cheat, and I won't let no man say I do!"

The Swede said, "I saw you! I saw you!" 133

"Well," cried Johnnie, "I'll fight any man what says I cheat!" 134

"No, you won't," said the cowboy. "Not here." 135

"Ah, be still, can't you?" said Scully, coming between them. 136

The quiet was sufficient to allow the Easterner's voice to be heard. 137 He was repeating, "Oh, wait a moment, can't you? What's the good of a fight over a game of cards? Wait a moment!"

Johnnie, his red face appearing above his father's shoulder, hailed 138 the Swede again. "Did you say I cheated?"

The Swede showed his teeth. "Yes." 139

"Then," said Johnnie, "we must fight." 140

"Yes, fight," roared the Swede. He was like a demoniac. "Yes, 141 fight! I'll show you what kind of a man I am! I'll show you who you want to fight! Maybe you think I can't fight! Maybe you think I can't! I'll show you, you skin, you card-sharp! Yes, you cheated! You cheated! You cheated!"

"Well, let's go at it, then, mister," said Johnnie, coolly. 142

The cowboy's brow was beaded with sweat from his efforts in in- 143 tercepting all sorts of raids. He turned in despair to Scully. "What are you goin' to do now?"

A change had come over the Celtic visage of the old man. He now 144 seemed all eagerness; his eyes glowed.

"We'll let them fight," he answered, stalwartly. "I can't put up 145 with it any longer. I've stood this damned Swede till I'm sick. We'll let them fight."

VI

The men prepared to go out of doors. The Easterner was so nervous 146 that he had great difficulty in getting his arms into the sleeves of his new leather coat. As the cowboy drew his fur cap down over his ears his hands trembled. In fact, Johnnie and old Scully were the only ones who displayed no agitation. These preliminaries were conducted without words.

Scully threw open the door. "Well, come on," he said. Instantly a
terrific wind caused the flame of the lamp to struggle at its wick,
while a puff of black smoke sprang from the chimney-top. The stove
was in mid-current of the blast, and its voice swelled to equal the
roar of the storm. Some of the scarred and bedabbled cards were
caught up from the floor and dashed helplessly against the farther
wall. The men lowered their heads and plunged into the tempest as
into a sea.

No snow was falling, but great whirls and clouds of flakes, swept 148
up from the ground by the frantic winds, were streaming southward
with the speed of bullets. The covered land was blue with the sheen
of an unearthly satin, and there was no other hue save where, at the
low, black railway station—which seemed incredibly distant—one
light gleamed like a tiny jewel. As the men floundered into a thigh-
deep drift, it was known that the Swede was bawling out something.
Scully went to him, put a hand on his shoulder, and projected an
ear. "What's that you say?" he shouted.

"I say," bawled the Swede again, "I won't stand much show 149
against this gang. I know you'll all pitch on me."

Scully smote him reproachfully on the arm. "Tut, man!" he 150
yelled. The wind tore the words from Scully's lips and scattered
them far alee.

"You are all a gang of—" boomed the Swede, but the storm also 151
seized the remainder of this sentence.

Immediately turning their backs upon the wind, the men had 152
swung around a corner to the sheltered side of the hotel. It was the
function of the little house to preserve here, amid this great devasta-
tion of snow, an irregular V-shape of heavily encrusted grass, which
crackled beneath the feet. One could imagine the great drifts piled
against the windward side. When the party reached the comparative
peace of this spot it was found that the Swede was still bellowing.

"Oh, I know what kind of a thing this is! I know you'll all pitch on 153
me. I can't lick you all!"

Scully turned upon him panther-fashion. "You'll not have to 154
whip all of us. You'll have to whip my son Johnnie. An' the man
what troubles you durin' that time will have me to dale with."

The arrangements were swiftly made. The two men faced each 155
other, obedient to the harsh commands of Scully, whose face, in the
subtly luminous gloom, could be seen set in the austere impersonal
lines that are pictured on the countenances of the Roman veterans.
The Easterner's teeth were chattering, and he was hopping up and
down like a mechanical toy. The cowboy stood rock-like.

The contestants had not stripped off any clothing. Each was in his 156
ordinary attire. Their fists were up, and they eyed each other in a
calm that had the elements of leonine cruelty in it.

During this pause, the Easterner's mind, like a film, took lasting   157
impressions of three men—the iron-nerved master of the ceremony;
the Swede, pale, motionless, terrible; and Johnnie, serene yet ferocious, brutish yet heroic. The entire prelude had in it a tragedy
greater than the tragedy of action, and this aspect was accentuated
by the long, mellow cry of the blizzard, as it sped the tumbling and
wailing flakes into the black abyss of the south.

"Now!" said Scully.   158

The two combatants leaped forward and crashed together like   159
bullocks. There was heard the cushioned sound of blows, and of a
curse squeezing out from between the tight teeth of one.

As for the spectators, the Easterner's pent-up breath exploded   160
from him with a pop of relief, absolute relief from the tension of the
preliminaries. The cowboy bounded into the air with a yowl. Scully
was immovable as from supreme amazement and fear at the fury of
the fight which he himself had permitted and arranged.

For a time the encounter in the darkness was such a perplexity of   161
flying arms that it presented no more detail than would a swiftly revolving wheel. Occasionally a face, as if illumined by a flash of light,
would shine out, ghastly and marked with pink spots. A moment
later, the men might have been known as shadows, if it were not for
the involuntary utterance of oaths that came from them in whispers.

Suddenly a holocaust of warlike desire caught the cowboy, and he   162
bolted forward with the speed of a bronco. "Go it, Johnnie! Go it!
Kill him! Kill him!"

Scully confronted him. "Kape back," he said; and by his glance   163
the cowboy could tell that this man was Johnnie's father.

To the Easterner there was a monotony of unchangeable fighting   164
that was an abomination. This confused mingling was eternal to his
sense, which was concentrated in a longing for the end, the priceless
end. Once the fighters lurched near him, and as he scrambled hastily
backward he heard them breathe like men on the rack.

"Kill him, Johnnie! Kill him! Kill him! Kill him!" The cowboy's   165
face was contorted like one of those agony masks in museums.

"Keep still," said Scully, icily.   166

Then there was a sudden loud grunt, incomplete, cut short, and   167
Johnnie's body swung away from the Swede and fell with sickening
heaviness to the grass. The cowboy was barely in time to prevent the
mad Swede from flinging himself upon his prone adversary. "No,
you don't," said the cowboy, interposing an arm. "Wait a second."

Scully was at his son's side. "Johnnie! Johnnie, me boy!" His   168
voice had a quality of melancholy tenderness. "Johnnie! Can you go
on with it?" He looked anxiously down into the bloody, pulpy face
of his son.

There was a moment of silence, and then Johnnie answered in his ordinary voice, "Yes, I—it—yes." 169

Assisted by his father he struggled to his feet. "Wait a bit now till you git your wind," said the old man. 170

A few paces away the cowboy was lecturing the Swede. "No, you don't! Wait a second!" 171

The Easterner was plucking at Scully's sleeve. "Oh, this is enough," he pleaded. "This is enough! Let it go as it stands. This is enough!" 172

"Bill," said Scully, "git out of the road." The cowboy stepped aside. "Now." The combatants were actuated by a new caution as they advanced toward collision. They glared at each other, and then the Swede aimed a lightning blow that carried with it his entire weight. Johnnie was evidently half stupid from weakness, but he miraculously dodged, and his fist sent the overbalanced Swede sprawling. 173

The cowboy, Scully, and the Easterner burst into a cheer that was like a chorus of triumphant soldiery, but before its conclusion the Swede had scuffled agilely to his feet and come in berserk abandon at his foe. There was another perplexity of flying arms, and Johnnie's body again swung away and fell, even as a bundle might fall from a roof. The Swede instantly staggered to a little wind-waved tree and leaned upon it, breathing like an engine, while his savage and flame-lit eyes roamed from face to face as the men bent over Johnnie. There was a splendor of isolation in his situation at this time which the Easterner felt once when, lifting his eyes from the man on the ground, he beheld that mysterious and lonely figure, waiting. 174

"Are you any good yet, Johnnie?" asked Scully in a broken voice. 175

The son gasped and opened his eyes languidly. After a moment he answered, "No—I ain't—any good—any—more." Then, from shame and bodily ill, he began to weep, the tears furrowing down through the blood stains on his face. "He was too—too—too heavy for me." 176

Scully straightened and addressed the waiting figure. "Stranger," he said, evenly, "it's all up with our side." Then his voice changed into that vibrant huskiness which is commonly the tone of the most simple and deadly announcements. "Johnnie is whipped." 177

Without replying, the victor moved off on the route to the front door of the hotel. 178

The cowboy was formulating new and unspellable blasphemies. The Easterner was startled to find that they were out in a wind that seemed to come direct from the shadowed arctic floes. He heard again the wail of the snow as it was flung to its grave in the south. He 179 knew now that all this time the cold had been sinking into him deeper and deeper, and he wondered that he had not perished. He felt indifferent to the condition of the vanquished man.

"Johnnie, can you walk?" asked Scully.   180

"Did I hurt—hurt him any?" asked the son.   181

"Can you walk, boy? Can you walk?"   182

Johnnie's voice was suddenly strong. There was a robust impa-   183
tience in it. "I asked you whether I hurt him any!"

"Yes, yes, Johnnie," answered the cowboy, consolingly; "he's   184
hurt a good deal."

They raised him from the ground, and as soon as he was on his   185
feet he went tottering off, rebuffing all attempts at assistance. When
the party rounded the corner they were fairly blinded by the pelting
of the snow. It burned their faces like fire. The cowboy carried Johnnie through the drift to the door. As they entered, some cards again
rose from the floor and beat against the wall.

The Easterner rushed to the stove. He was so profoundly chilled   186
that he almost dared to embrace the glowing iron. The Swede was
not in the room. Johnnie sank into a chair and, folding his arms on
his knees, buried his face in them. Scully, warming one foot and
then the other at a rim of the stove, muttered to himself with Celtic
mournfulness. The cowboy had removed his fur cap, and with a
dazed and rueful air he was running one hand through his tousled
locks. From overhead they could hear the creaking of boards, as the
Swede tramped here and there in his room.

The sad quiet was broken by the sudden flinging open of a door   187
that led toward the kitchen. It was instantly followed by an inrush of
women. They precipitated themselves upon Johnnie amid a chorus
of lamentation. Before they carried their prey off to the kitchen,
there to be bathed and harangued with that mixture of sympathy
and abuse which is a feat of their sex, the mother straightened herself
and fixed old Scully with an eye of stern reproach. "Shame be upon
you, Patrick Scully!" she cried. "Your own son, too. Shame be
upon you!"

"There, now! Be quiet, now!" said the old man, weakly.   188

"Shame be upon you, Patrick Scully!" The girls, rallying to this   189
slogan, sniffled disdainfully in the direction of those trembling ac-
complices, the cowboy and the Easterner. Presently they bore Johnnie away, and left the three men to dismal reflection.

VII

"I'd like to fight this here Dutchman myself," said the cowboy,   190
breaking a long silence.

Scully wagged his head sadly. "No, that wouldn't do. It wouldn't 191
be right. It wouldn't be right."

"Well, why wouldn't it?" argued the cowboy. "I don't see no 192
harm in it."

"No," answered Scully, with mournful heroism. "It wouldn't be 193
right. It was Johnnie's fight, and now we mustn't whip the man just
because he whipped Johnnie."

"Yes, that's true enough," said the cowboy; "but—he better not 194
get fresh with me, because I couldn't stand no more of it."

"You'll not say a word to him," commanded Scully, and even 195
then they heard the tread of the Swede on the stairs. His entrance
was made theatric. He swept the door back with a bang and swag-
gered to the middle of the room. No one looked at him. "Well," he
cried, insolently, at Scully, "I s'pose you'll tell me now how much I
owe you?"

The old man remained stolid. "You don't owe me nothin'." 196

"Huh!" said the Swede, "huh! Don't owe 'im nothin'." 197

The cowboy addressed the Swede. "Stranger, I don't see how you 198
come to be so gay around here."

Old Scully was instantly alert. "Stop!" he shouted, holding his 199
hand forth, fingers upward. "Bill, you shut up!"

The cowboy spat carelessly into the sawdust-box. "I didn't say a 200
word, did I?" he asked.

"Mr. Scully," called the Swede, "how much do I owe you?" It 201
was seen that he was attired for departure, and that he had his valise
in his hand.

"You don't owe me nothin'," repeated Scully in the same imper- 202
turbable way.

"Huh!" said the Swede. "I guess you're right. I guess if it was 203
any way at all, you'd owe me somethin'. That's what I guess." He
turned to the cowboy. "'Kill him! Kill him! Kill him!'" he mim-
icked, and then guffawed victoriously. "'Kill him!'" He was con-
vulsed with ironical humor.

But he might have been jeering the dead. The three men were im- 204
movable and silent, staring with glassy eyes at the stove.

The Swede opened the door and passed into the storm, giving one 205
derisive glance backward at the still group.

As soon as the door was closed, Scully and the cowboy leaped to 206
their feet and began to curse. They trampled to and fro, waving
their arms and smashing into the air with their fists. "Oh, but that
was a hard minute!" wailed Scully. "That was a hard minute! Him
there leerin' and scoffin'! One bang at his nose was worth forty dollars to me that minute! How did you stand it, Bill?"

"How did I stand it?" cried the cowboy in a quivering voice. 207
"How did I stand it? Oh!"

The old man burst into sudden brogue. "I'd loike to take that 208
Swade," he wailed, "and hould 'im down on a shtone flure and bate
'im to a jelly wid a shtick!"

The cowboy groaned in sympathy. "I'd like to git him by the neck 209
and ha-ammer him"—he brought his hand down on a chair with a
noise like a pistol-shot—"hammer that there Dutchman until he
couldn't tell himself from a dead coyote!"

"I'd bate 'im until he—" 210

"I'd show *him* some things—" 211

And then together they raised a yearning, fanatic cry—"Oh-o-oh! 212
if we only could—"

"Yes!" 213

"Yes!" 214

"And then I'd—" 215

"O-o-oh!" 216

VIII

The Swede, tightly gripping his valise, tacked across the face of the 217
storm as if he carried sails. He was following a line of little naked,
grasping trees which, he knew, must mark the way of the road. His
face, fresh from the pounding of Johnnie's fists, felt more pleasure
than pain in the wind and the driving snow. A number of square
shapes loomed upon him finally, and he knew them as the houses of
the main body of the town. He found a street and made travel along
it, leaning heavily upon the wind whenever, at a corner, a terrific
blast caught him.

He might have been in a deserted village. We picture the world as 218
thick with conquering and elate humanity, but here, with the bugles
of the tempest pealing, it was hard to imagine a peopled earth. One
viewed the existence of man then as a marvel, and conceded a
glamor of wonder to these lice which were caused to cling to a whirling, fire-smitten, ice-locked, disease-stricken, space-lost bulb. The
conceit of man was explained by this storm to be the very engine of
life. One was a coxcomb not to die in it. However, the Swede found
a saloon.

In front of it an indomitable red light was burning, and the snow- 219
flakes were made blood-color as they flew through the circumscribed
territory of the lamp's shining. The Swede pushed open the door of
the saloon and entered. A sanded expanse was before him, and at
the end of it four men sat about a table drinking. Down one side of
the room extended a radiant bar, and its guardian was leaning upon
his elbows listening to the talk of the men at the table. The Swede

dropped his valise upon the floor and, smiling fraternally upon the barkeeper, said, "Gimme some whisky, will you?" The man placed a bottle, a whisky-glass, and a glass of ice-thick water upon the bar. The Swede poured himself an abnormal portion of whisky and drank it in three gulps. "Pretty bad night," remarked the bartender, indifferently. He was making the pretension of blindness which is usually a distinction of his class; but it could have been seen that he was furtively studying the half-erased blood stains on the face of the Swede. "Bad night," he said again.

"Oh, it's good enough for me," replied the Swede, hardily, as he   220
poured himself some more whisky. The barkeeper took his coin and maneuvered it through its reception by the highly nickelled cash-machine. A bell rang; a card labelled "20 cts." had appeared.

"No," continued the Swede, "this isn't too bad weather. It's   221
good enough for me."

"So?" murmured the barkeeper, languidly.   222

The copious drams made the Swede's eyes swim, and he breathed   223
a trifle heavier. "Yes, I like this weather. I like it. It suits me." It was apparently his design to impart a deep significance to these words.

"So?" murmured the bartender again. He turned to gaze dreamily at the scroll-like birds and bird-like scrolls which had been drawn   224
with soap upon the mirrors in back of the bar.

"Well, I guess I'll take another drink," said the Swede, presently.   225
"Have something?"

"No, thanks; I'm not drinkin'," answered the bartender. After-   226
ward he asked, "How did you hurt your face?"

The Swede immediately began to boast loudly. "Why, in a fight.   227
I thumped the soul out of a man down here at Scully's hotel."

The interest of the four men at the table was at last aroused.   228

"Who was it?" said one.   229

"Johnnie Scully," blustered the Swede. "Son of the man what   230
runs it. He will be pretty near dead for some weeks, I can tell you. I made a nice thing of him, I did. He couldn't get up. They carried him in the house. Have a drink?"

Instantly the men in some subtle way encased themselves in re-   231
serve. "No, thanks," said one. The group was of curious formation. Two were prominent local businessmen; one was the district attorney; and one was a professional gambler of the kind known as "square." But a scrutiny of the group would not have enabled an observer to pick the gambler from the men of more reputable pursuits. He was, in fact, a man so delicate in manner, when among people of fair class, and so judicious in his choice of victims, that in the strictly masculine part of the town's life he had come to be ex-

plicitly trusted and admired. People called him a thoroughbred. The fear and contempt with which his craft was regarded were undoubtedly the reason why his quiet dignity shone conspicuous above the quiet dignity of men who might be merely hatters, billiard-markers, or grocery clerks. Beyond an occasional unwary traveller who came by rail, this gambler was supposed to prey solely upon reckless and senile farmers, who, when flush with good crops, drove into town in all the pride and confidence of an absolutely invulnerable stupidity. Hearing at times in circuitous fashion of the despoilment of such a farmer, the important men of Romper invariably laughed in contempt of the victim, and if they thought of the wolf at all, it was with a kind of pride at the knowledge that he would never dare think of attacking their wisdom and courage. Besides, it was popular that this gambler had a real wife and two real children in a neat cottage in a suburb, where he led an exemplary home life; and when anyone even suggested a discrepancy in his character, the crowd immediately vociferated descriptions of this virtuous family circle. Then men who led exemplary home lives, and men who did not lead exemplary home lives, all subsided in a bunch, remarking that there was nothing more to be said.

However, when a restriction was placed upon him—as, for instance, when a strong clique of members of the new Pollywog Club refused to permit him, even as a spectator, to appear in the rooms of the organization—the candor and gentleness with which he accepted the judgment disarmed many of his foes and made his friends more desperately partisan. He invariably distinguished between himself and a respectable Romper man so quickly and frankly that his manner actually appeared to be a continual broadcast compliment. 232

And one must not forget to declare the fundamental fact of his entire position in Romper. It is irrefutable that in all affairs outside his business, in all matters that occur eternally and commonly between man and man, this thieving card-player was so generous, so just, so moral, that, in a contest, he could have put to flight the consciences of nine tenths of the citizens of Romper. 233

And so it happened that he was seated in this saloon with the two prominent local merchants and the district attorney. 234

The Swede continued to drink raw whisky, meanwhile babbling at the barkeeper and trying to induce him to indulge in potations. "Come on. Have a drink. Come on. What—no? Well, have a little one, then. By gawd, I've whipped a man tonight, and I want to celebrate. I whipped him good, too. Gentlemen," the Swede cried to the men at the table, "have a drink?" 235

"Ssh!" said the barkeeper. 236

The group at the table, although furtively attentive, had been pre- 237 **339**
tending to be deep in talk, but now a man lifted his eyes toward the
Swede and said, shortly, "Thanks. We don't want any more."

At this reply the Swede ruffled out his chest like a rooster. 238
"Well," he exploded, "it seems I can't get anybody to drink with
me in this town. Seems so, don't it? Well!"

"Ssh!" said the barkeeper. 239

"Say," snarled the Swede, "don't you try to shut me up. I won't 240
have it. I'm a gentleman, and I want people to drink with me. And I
want 'em to drink with me now. *Now*—do you understand?" He
rapped the bar with his knuckles.

Years of experience had calloused the bartender. He merely grew 241
sulky. "I hear you," he answered.

"Well," cried the Swede, "listen hard then. See those men over 242
there? Well, they're going to drink with me, and don't you forget it.
Now you watch."

"Hi!" yelled the barkeeper, "this won't do!" 243

"Why won't it?" demanded the Swede. He stalked over to the ta- 244
ble, and by chance laid his hand upon the shoulder of the gambler.
"How about this?" he asked wrathfully. "I asked you to drink with
me."

The gambler simply twisted his head and spoke over his shoulder. 245
"My friend, I don't know you."

"Oh, hell!" answered the Swede, "come and have a drink." 246

"Now, my boy," advised the gambler, kindly, "take your hand 247
off my shoulder and go 'way and mind your own business." He was
a little, slim man, and it seemed strange to hear him use this tone of
heroic patronage to the burly Swede. The other men at the table said
nothing.

"What! You won't drink with me, you little dude? I'll make you, 248
then! I'll make you!" The Swede had grasped the gambler fren-
ziedly at the throat, and was dragging him from his chair. The other
men sprang up. The barkeeper dashed around the corner of his bar.
There was a great tumult, and then was seen a long blade in the
hand of the gambler. It shot forward, and a human body, this citadel
of virtue, wisdom, power, was pierced as easily as if it had been a
melon. The Swede fell with a cry of supreme astonishment.

The prominent merchants and the district attorney must have at 249
once tumbled out of the place backward. The bartender found himself hanging limply to the arm of a chair and gazing into the eyes of a
murderer.

"Henry," said the latter, as he wiped his knife on one of the tow- 250
els that hung beneath the bar rail, "you tell 'em where to find me.

I'll be home, waiting for 'em.'' Then he vanished. A moment afterward the barkeeper was in the street dinning through the storm for help and, moreover, companionship.

The corpse of the Swede, alone in the saloon, had its eyes fixed upon a dreadful legend that dwelt atop of the cash-machine: ''This registers the amount of your purchase.'' 251

IX

Months later, the cowboy was frying pork over the stove of a little ranch near the Dakota line, when there was a quick thud of hoofs outside, and presently the Easterner entered with the letters and the papers. 252

''Well,'' said the Easterner at once, ''the chap that killed the Swede has got three years. Wasn't much, was it?'' 253

''He has? Three years?'' The cowboy poised his pan of pork, while he ruminated upon the news. ''Three years. That ain't much.'' 254

''No. It was a light sentence,'' replied Easterner as he unbuckled his spurs. ''Seems there was a good deal of sympathy for him in Romper.'' 255

''If the bartender had been any good,'' observed the cowboy, thoughtfully, ''he would have gone in and cracked that there Dutchman on the head with a bottle in the beginnin' of it and stopped all this here murderin'.'' 256

''Yes, a thousand things might have happened,'' said the Easterner, tartly. 257

The cowboy returned his pan of pork to the fire, but his philosophy continued. ''It's funny, ain't it? If he hadn't said Johnnie was cheatin' he'd be alive this minute. He was an awful fool. Game played for fun, too. Not for money. I believe he was crazy.'' 258

''I feel sorry for that gambler,'' said the Easterner. 259

''Oh, so do I,'' said the cowboy. ''He don't deserve none of it for killin' who he did.'' 260

''The Swede might not have been killed if everything had been square.'' 261

''Might not have been killed?'' exclaimed the cowboy. ''Everythin' square? Why, when he said that Johnnie was cheatin' and acted like such a jackass? And then in the saloon he fairly walked up to git hurt?'' With these arguments the cowboy browbeat the Easterner and reduced him to rage. 262

''You're a fool!'' cried the Easterner, viciously. ''You're a bigger jackass than the Swede by a million majority. Now let me tell you one thing. Let me tell you something. Listen! Johnnie *was* cheating!'' 263

" 'Johnnie,' " said the cowboy, blankly. There was a minute of silence, and then he said, robustly, "Why, no. The game was only for fun."

"Fun or not," said the Easterner, "Johnnie was cheating. I saw 265 him. I know it. I saw him. And I refused to stand up and be a man. I let the Swede fight it out alone. And you—you were simply puffing around the place and wanting to fight. And then old Scully himself! We are all in it! This poor gambler isn't even a noun. He is kind of an adverb. Every sin is the result of a collaboration. We, five of us, have collaborated in the murder of this Swede. Usually there are from a dozen to forty women really involved in every murder, but in this case it seems to be only five men—you, I, Johnnie, old Scully; and that fool of an unfortunate gambler came merely as a culmination, the apex of a human movement, and gets all the punishment."

The cowboy, injured and rebellious, cried out blindly into this fog 266 of mysterious theory: "Well, I didn't do anythin', did I?"

PRACTICE

Stephen Crane and the Western Formula

Your assignment here is to use the Western formula discussed in John Cawelti's essay to analyze the two stories by Stephen Crane, and to arrive at a thesis for your essay.

First, you should read through the material carefully, and you should make notes of what you consider to be Cawelti's main points about setting and heroes in the Western. In reading Crane's stories, you should also make notes of passages you consider important, of your responses to the stories, and of connections or contrasts you find between the stories and Cawelti's essay.

A general approach to the Crane stories might consider one of the following:

1. In what ways do Crane's stories exemplify Cawelti's formula?
2. In what ways do these stories deviate from the formula of the traditional Western?
3. In what ways do the stories comment on the traditional Western code?

From such general considerations you can narrow your approach to an analysis of setting or of heroes (or the lack of them) in the stories. You might compare and contrast aspects of setting or of characters in the stories to illustrate a thesis about the traditional or nontraditional treatment of character or setting. You might want to investigate the clash of civilization and wilderness, or consider the stories as commentaries on masculine rituals or mythic ideas about the West.

But remember: while Cawelti's essay will provide a frame through which to read the stories as well as a number of possible theses to investigate, your choice of a thesis and your effective development of it will depend on your own careful reading and gathering of evidence from the stories.

PRACTICE

Crane: The Man and the Stories

What relation has Stephen Crane's life to the fiction he wrote? To investigate this question, you should look at the biographical material on Crane in Chapter 6, pp. 117–123.[1] Consider what sort of man Crane was, and why the American West would have interested him as a topic for his fiction. In reading the two stories reprinted in this chapter, consider what attitude toward the West is expressed. Given what you know of Crane's life, is it possible to say that any of the characters in the stories reflect his point of view?

Your instructor can decide whether further research into Crane's trip to the West in 1895 is necessary, or whether you might read Crane's Western nonfiction to see whether any of his own experiences were transformed into such fiction as ''The Bride Comes to Yellow Sky'' or ''The Blue Hotel.''

READING AND PRACTICE

The Elegy

The material provided for synthesis here consists of eight poems. All are elegies, or poems for the dead, and each one was written about the death of a young person. In finding a topic for a synthesis paper, consider the features that mark these elegies

[1]Also relevant is Crane's ''The Last of the Mohicans,'' pp. 223–225.

as poetic texts, distinguishable from prose, and also those features that make them similar to or different from one another in both form and content.

First you should read them all for prose sense. Make sure you understand each sentence. You may wish to employ analytic techniques learned earlier. Then you should begin to generate a thesis that asserts a view about the relationship of the poems. In presenting your thesis, you will need to note the similar features of form and subject matter as well as those features that are unique to each poem. Here are some tentative theses for your consideration:

1. One of these poems is the most effective elegy because of X, Y, and Z.
2. An elegy need not be a purely sad or mournful poem.
3. Elegiac poets tend to use a certain kind of image in a certain way.
4. In elegiac poetry, the poet's own situation is often a hidden subject.
5. Difficulties in the interpretation of poetry tend to arise from the following problems in syntax and semantics.

You may choose to follow none of these sample theses. They are certainly not intended to cramp your style. The main point is to use the poems for discussion of some thesis that is relevant to them and supported by evidence drawn from the poems. This is *not* a research paper, and you are not expected to consult outside sources.

On My First Son

Farewell, thou child of my right hand, and joy; 1
My sin was too much hope of thee, loved boy:
Seven years thou'wert lent to me, and I thee pay,
Exacted by thy fate, on the just day.
O could I lose all father now! for why
Will man lament the state he could envý,
To have so soon 'scaped world's and flesh's rage,
And, if no other misery, yet age?
Rest in soft peace, and asked, say, "Here doth lie
Ben Johnson his best piece of poetry."
For whose sake henceforth all his vows be such
As what he loves may never like too much.   *1616*

—BEN JONSON

In Memory of My Dear Grandchild Elizabeth Bradstreet, Who Deceased August, 1665, Being A Year and Half Old

Farewell dear babe, my heart's too much content,   1
Farewell sweet babe, the pleasure of mine eye,
Farewell fair flower that for a space was lent,
Then ta'en away unto eternity.
Blest babe, why should I once bewail thy fate,
Or sigh thy days so soon were terminate,
Sith thou art settled in an everlasting state.

By nature trees do rot when they are grown,   2
And plums and apples thoroughly ripe do fall,
And corn and grass are in their season mown,
And time brings down what is both strong and tall.
But plants new set to be eradicate,
And buds new blown to have so short a date,
Is by His hand alone that guides nature and fate.

—ANNE BRADSTREET

From *In Memoriam* A. H. H.

XIX

The Danube to the Severn gave   1
  The darkened heart that beat no more;
  They laid him by the pleasant shore,
And in the hearing of the wave.

There twice a day the Severn fills;   2
  The salt sea-water rushes by,
  And hushes half the babbling Wye,
And makes a silence in the hills.

The Wye is hushed nor moved along,   3
  And hushed my deepest grief of all,
  When filled with tears that cannot fall,
I brim with sorrow drowning song.

The tide flows down, the wave again   4
  Is vocal in its wooded walls;
  My deeper anguish also falls,
And I can speak a little then.   *1834*

—ALFRED, LORD TENNYSON

To an Athlete Dying Young

The time you won your town the race   1
We chaired you through the market-place;
Man and boy stood cheering by,
And home we brought you shoulder-high.

To-day, the road all runners come,   2
Shoulder-high we bring you home,
And set you at your threshold down,
Townsman of a stiller town.

Smart lad, to slip betimes away   3
From fields where glory does not stay
And early though the laurel grows
It withers quicker than the rose.

Eyes the shady night has shut   4
Cannot see the record cut,
And silence sounds no worse than cheers
After earth has stopped the ears:

Now you will not swell the rout   5
Of lads that wore their honors out,
Runners whom renown outran
And the name died before the man.

So set, before its echoes fade,   6
The fleet foot on the sill of shade,
And hold to the low lintel up
The still-defended challenge-cup.

And round that early-laurelled head   7
Will flock to gaze the strengthless dead,
And find unwithered on its curls
The garland briefer than a girl's.   *1896*

—A. E. HOUSMAN

Bells for John Whiteside's Daughter

There was such speed in her little body,   1
And such lightness in her footfall,
It is no wonder her brown study
Astonishes us all.

Her wars were bruited in our high window.   2
We looked among orchard trees and beyond
Where she took arms against her shadow,
Or harried unto the pond

The lazy geese, like a snow cloud   3
Dripping their snow on the green grass,
Tricking and stopping, sleepy and proud,
Who cried in goose, Alas,

For the tireless heart within the little   4
Lady with rod that made them rise
From their noon apple-dreams and scuttle
Goose-fashion under the skies!

But now go the bells, and we are ready,   5
In one house we are sternly stopped
To say we are vexed at her brown study,
Lying so primly propped.   *1924*

                      —JOHN CROWE RANSOM

A Refusal to Mourn the Death, by Fire, of a Child in London

Never until the mankind making   1
Bird beast and flower
Fathering and all humbling darkness
Tells with silence the last light breaking
And the still hour
Is come of the sea tumbling in harness

And I must enter again the round   2
Zion[1] of the water bead
And the synagogue[2] of the ear of corn
Shall I let pray the shadow of a sound
Or sow my salt seed
In the least valley of sackcloth[3] to mourn

The majesty and burning of the child's death.   3
I shall not murder
The mankind of her going with a grave truth
Nor blaspheme down the stations of the breath[4]
With any further
Elegy of innocence and youth.

Deep with the first dead[5] lies London's daughter,   4
Robed in the long friends,
The grains beyond age, the dark veins of her mother,[6]
Secret by the unmourning water
Of the riding Thames.
After the first death,[7] there is no other.   *1945*

                    —DYLAN THOMAS

[1] *Zion:* The name of one of the hills of Jerusalem, on which the city of David was built; also, the house or household of God, the Christian church, heaven as final home for believers, a place of worship.

[2] *synagogue:* (Greek: to bring together) The regular assembly or congregation of Jews for religious instruction and worship apart from the service of the temple; a building or meeting place for worship and instruction.

[3] *sackcloth:* The coarsest possible clothing as the material of mourning; clothed in sackcloth and having ashes sprinkled on the head as a sign of lamentation.

[4] *stations of the breath:* suggesting stations of the cross, a traditional series of representations in painting or sculpture (generally 14 in number) of Christ's passion, to be visited in order for meditation and prayer.

[5] *the first dead:* Adam, Eve, and those who died in the first bombings of London by the Germans in World War II.

[6] *mother:* as in "Mother Earth."

[7] *the first death:* the death of Christ on the cross.

Elegy for Jane

My Student, Thrown by a Horse

I remember the neckcurls, limp and damp as tendrils;   1
And her quick look, a sidelong pickerel smile;
And how, once startled into talk, the light syllables leaped for her,
And she balanced in the delight of her thought,
A wren, happy, tail into the wind,
Her song trembling the twigs and small branches.
The shade sang with her;
The leaves, their whispers turned to kissing;
And the mold sang in the bleached valleys under the rose.

Oh, when she was sad, she cast herself down into such
    a pure depth,   2
Even a father could not find her:
Scraping her cheek against straw;
Stirring the clearest water.

My sparrow, you are not here,   3
Waiting like a fern, making a spiny shadow.
The sides of wet stones cannot console me,
Nor the moss, wound with the last light.

If only I could nudge you from this sleep,   4
My maimed darling, my skittery pigeon.
Over this damp grave I speak the words of my love:
I, with no rights in this matter,
Neither father nor lover.   *1953*

—THEODORE ROETHKE

Ricky

I go into the back yard   1
and arrange some twigs
and a few flowers. I go alone
and speak to you as I never could
when you lived, when you
smiled back at me shyly.
Now I can talk to you as I talked
to a star when I was a boy,
expecting no answer, as I talked
to my father who had become
the wind, particles of rain
and fire, these few twigs
and flowers that have no name.

Last night they said a rosary
and my boys went, awkward
in slacks and sport shirts,
and later sitting under the hidden
stars they were attacked and beaten.
You are dead, and a nameless rage
is loose. It is 105,
the young and the old burn
in the fields, and though they cry
enough the sun hangs on
bloodying the dust above the aisles
of cotton and grape.

3

This morning they will say a mass
and then the mile-long line of cars.
Teddy and John, their faces swollen,
and four others will let you
slowly down into the fresh earth
where you go on. Scared now,
they will understand some of it.
Not the mass or the rosary
or the funeral, but the rage.
Not you falling through the dark
moving underwater like a flower
no one could find until
it was too late and you had gone out,
your breath passing through dark water
never to return to the young man,
pigeon-breasted, who rode
his brother's Harley up the driveway.

4

Wet grass sticks to my feet, bright
marigold and daisy burst in the new day.
The bees move at the clumps
of clover, the carrots—
almost as tall as I—
have flowered, pale lacework.
Hard dark buds
of next year's oranges, new green
of slick leaves, yellow grass
tall and blowing by the fence. The grapes
are slow, climbing the arbor,
but some day there will be shade
here where the morning sun whitens
everything and punishes my eyes.

SYNTHESIS: PUTTING THINGS TOGETHER

Your people worked so hard   5
for some small piece of earth,
for a home, adding a room
a boy might want. Butchie said
you could have the Harley
if only you would come back,
anything that was his.

A dog barks down the block   6
and it is another day. I hear
the soft call of the dove,
screech of mockingbird and jay.
A small dog picks up the tune,
and then *tow-weet tow-weet*
of hidden birds, and two finches
darting over the low trees—
there is no end.

What can I say to this mound   7
of twigs and dry flowers, what
can I say now that I would speak
to you? Ask the wind, ask
the absence or the rose burned
at the edges and still blood red.
And the answer is you
falling through black water
into the stillness that fathers
the moon, the bees ramming into
the soft cups, the eucalyptus
swaying like grass under water.
My John told me your cousin
punched holes in the wall
the night you died and was afraid
to be alone. Your brother
walks staring at the earth.
I am afraid of water.

And the earth goes on   8
in blinding sunlight.
I hold your image
a moment, the long
Indian face
the brown almond eyes
your dark skin full

and glowing as you grew
into the hard body
of a young man.

And now it is bird screech   9
and a tree rat suddenly
parting the tall grass
by the fence, lumbering
off, and in the distance
the crashing of waves
against some shore
maybe only in memory.

We lived by the sea.   10
Remember, my boys wrote
postcards and missed you
and your brother. I slept
and wakened to the sea,
I remember in my dreams
water pounded the windows
and walls, it seeped
through everything,
and like your spirit,
Ricky, like your breath,
nothing could contain it.   *1963*

                        —PHILIP LEVINE

Elegy for Samuel Herrera, My Student, Killed in a Tactical Squad Stakeout

You were a spidery thing;   1
Dark and skinny-limbed,
You always moved in sudden bursts.
Even sitting down
Your body seemed to dance,
As though the web of your nerves
Had been woven too tightly.
The strands are loosening,
One by one,
Taut muscles are falling slack,
As you make this last
Fluid move
Toward a quiet you must have wanted.

If I could, Samuel,
I'd take you in my arms
And do my best to ease your way
Into the next world.
I know it wouldn't be easy:
I'd have to face
The desperation inside of you
That spun you around
To fire two shots at the cops;
Shotgunned to the floor,
Still you fought them
To get to your gun
Until they put the cuffs on you.

3

I think I could face it,
But there's no way past the guard
To the room where you lie,
In even light and filtered air,
And feel the hand
That has come to point the way
To the dark door
That opens on darkness.
I don't know if there's anything
To wish for you now,
But I do hope someone is there
To hold the door for you.   *1982*

C. G. HANZLICEK

Russell Baker, exerpt from GROWING UP, © 1982 by Russell Baker. By **353** permission of Congdon & Weed, Inc.

Theodore Roethke, "Elegy for Jane" © 1950 by Theodore Roethke. From *The Collected Poems of Theodore Roethke*. Reprinted by permission of Doubleday & Company, Inc.

Excerpt from *Camera Lucida* by Roland Barthes, translated by Richard Howard. Translation copyright © 1981 by Farrar, Straus & Giroux, Inc. Originally published in French as *La Chamore Claire* © Editions due Seuil 1980. Reprinted by permission of Hill & Wang, a division of Farrar, Straus & Giroux, Inc.

Thomas Gullason, "Stephen Crane—A Chronology," from *The Complete Short Stories*, by Thomas A. Gullason. Reprinted by permission of the author.

Excerpt from MIDDLETOWN by Robert S. and Helen M. Lynd, copyright 1929 by Harcourt Brace Jovanovich, Inc.; copyright renewed by Robert S. & Helen M. Lynd. Reprinted by permission of the publisher.

"We Real Cool," "The Pool Players," "Seven at the Golden Shovel," from *The World of Gwendolyn Brooks*. Copyright © 1959 by Gwendolyn Brooks.

"Basic Pie Pastry" from *The New York Times Cookbook* by Craig Claiborne. Copyright © 1961 by Craig Claiborne. Both selections reprinted by permission of Harper & Row, Publishers, Inc.

Dylan Thomas, "A Refusal to Mourn the Death by Fire of a Child in London." From THE POEMS OF DYLAN THOMAS. Copyright 1946 by Dylan Thomas. By permission of New Directions Publishing Company and by permission of J. M. Dent & Sons, and the Trustees for the copyrights of the late Dylan Thomas.

From "Two Tramps in Mud Time" from THE POETRY OF ROBERT FROST, edited by Edward Connery Latham. Copyright © 1964 by Lesley Frost Ballantine. Copyright © 1969 by Holt, Rinehart and Winston. Reprinted by permission of Holt, Rinehart and Winston, Publishers.

A. E. Houseman, "To an Athlete Dying Young." From "A Shropshire Lad," authorized edition from THE COLLECTED POEMS OF A. E. HOUSEMAN. Copyright 1939, 1940, and 1965 by Holt, Rinehart and Winston. Copyright © 1967, 1968 by Robert E. Symons. Reprinted by permission of Holt, Rinehart and Winston, Publishers.

Philip Levine, "Ricky." Copyright Philip Levine. First published in THE IOWA REVIEW. Reprinted by permission of the author.

"A Day in Samoa" from COMING OF AGE IN SAMOA by Margaret Mead. Copyright 1938, 1955 by Margaret Mead. By permission of William Morrow & Company.

Excerpt from MIAMI AND THE SIEGE OF CHICAGO, by Norman Mailer, reprinted by permission of The New American Library.

From Gary Snyder, "Looking at Pictures To Be Put Away." From Gary Snyder, THE BACK COUNTRY. Copyright © 1968 by Gary Snyder. Reprinted by permission of New Directions Publishing Corporation.

From William Carlos Williams "Landscape with the Fall of Icarus." From

INDEX

"Abandoned City, The" (Stewart), 106–107
Advertising
    analysis of, 231–244
    and argumentation, 168–169
    images of women in, 236–244
    persuasion in, 72–75, 76–81, 163
Agee, James, 138–139, 140
"American Melodrama, An" (Chester, Hodgson, Page), 270–271
Analysis, 12, 222–244
    of advertisements, 231–244
    of analysis, 225–226
    and classification, 222
    and comparison/contrast, 222–230
    meaning of, 12, 222
    of paintings and poems, 226–230
    practice in analytical writing, 225–230, 234, 236–244
    and study, 223
    and synthesis, 222–223, 245, 246
    as a tool, 223
"Analysis of a Manhattan Shirt Advertisement" (Weimersheimer), 231–233, 236
Apple, R. W., Jr., 290–292
Argument, in description, 125
Argumentation, 12, 17, 162–221
    and advertising, 165–169

complexity of, 164
about creation science, 169–177
development of, 184
elements of, 165, 201
emotion in, 178
about feminism, 178–183
goal of, 163
logic and, 165
about persuasion, 165–168
vs. persuasion, 12, 162, 163
practice of, 164–165
presenting a thesis, 166–221
about punishment of crimes, 206–221
reflection and, 163
about the sexes, 183
about slavery, 184–190
statistics and, 190–205
and synthesis, 245, 246
theory of, 164–165
about women, 200–205
writing, 168–169, 177, 183, 190–191, 191–203, 220–221
Aristotle, 144
Auden, W. H., 230
Audience, for writing, see Reader

Baker, Russell, 45–47, 64
Ballantine Ale, 79–81
Barthes, Roland, 35–36, 50–51, 52
Baseball statistics, 191–199
"Basic Pastry Pie," 58–59

Bell Jar, The (Plath), 33
"Bells for John Whiteside's
    Daughter" (Ransom), 346
Berger, John, 234–236
"Blackberry Winter" (Mead),
    43–45
Bierce, Ambrose, 103–104
Biography, as narration, 117–123,
    124
"Blue Hotel, The" (Crane), 317–
    341, 342
Booth, George, 101–102
Bradstreet, Anne, 344
"Bride Comes to Yellow Sky,
    The" (Crane), 307–317,
    342
Brooks, Gwendolyn, 48–49
Brueghel, Pieter, 227, 229
"Buster Keaton" (Agee), 138–
    139

Canham, Erwin D., 268–270
Cartoons, 101–103
"Cat in the Rain" (Hemingway),
    37–40
Category, in classification, 144,
    145
Cather, Willa, 132–133
Cause and effect, 12
Cawelti, John, 292–307, 341, 342
Chester, Lewis, 270–271
Christian Science Monitor, 283–289
Churchill, Winston, 254
Classification, 11, 17, 144–161
    and analysis, 144–145, 222, 223
    and argument, 144–145
    categories and, 144, 145
    of commercials, 148–153
    comparison/contrast and, 144
    definition of, 144
    examples of, 143–144
    organization by logic, 11
    organization of data, 144–161
    of power forms, 158–160
    practice in writing, 148, 153–
        154, 158, 160, 161
    and prewriting, 144
    and research, 144

and revising, 145
    of social groups, 146–147
    of students, 154–157
    and synthesis, 246
    as a tool, 223
Communication, 2–4, 6–8, 27
Comparison and contrast, 12,
    144, 145, 223–230
Concept of Mind, The (Ryle), 164
Cooper, James Fenimore, 226
Cortázar, Julio, 112–115, 116
Crane, Stephen, 223–225, 293,
    307–342
    life of, 117–123, 124, 342
"Crime of Punishment, The"
    (Menninger), 206–213
Critic, The (Feyerabend), 163

"Daley Defends His Police . . ."
    (Apple), 290–292
Davis, Saville, R., 283–289
Darwin, Charles, 223
"Day in Samoa, A" (Mead), 103,
    108–111, 112
Description, 11, 125–143
    from, to symbolism, 140–142
    of a face, 138–143
    vs. narration, 101, 125
    organization of space in, 125–
        126, 129, 133–134
    perception and writing of, 125,
        126, 129
    of a place with history, 134
    point of view in, 125–126, 129,
        131
    practice in writing, 129, 133–
        134, 137, 140, 142–143
    problems of writing, 125–126
    purpose and, 126
Dickens, Charles, 132
Dinesen, Isak, 53–54, 55
Directions, 10, 58–70
    examples of, 58–62, 67–70
    vs. persuasion, 58
    practice in writing, 63–67
    pseudodirection, 67–70
    rules for writing, 60
    writing, 101

See also Reader-oriented forms
of writing
Douglas, Stephen A., 190–191
Drafting, 18–19

Earth Abides (Stewart), 106–107
Ehrenreich, Barbara, 259–260
Elbow, Peter, 27–28, 32
"Elegy for Jane" (Roethke), 348
"Elegy for Samuel Herrera . . ."
(Hanzlicek), 351–352
"Empty Park, The" (Stewart),
106–107
"Evolution as Fact and Theory"
(Gould), 170–177
Ewing, J. R., 142–143
Expression, 9, 26–40
through association, 30
of ideas, 34–40
of mood, 32–34
purpose of, 27
through role-playing, 40
as transformation, 28–30
See also Writer-oriented forms of
writing

Fall of Icarus, The, 227–229
"Farewell, My Lovely" (White),
105
Fellini, Federico, 34–35
Fellini on Fellini (Fellini), 34–35
Feyerabend, Paul, 163
"Fields" (Cather), 132–133
"First Inaugural Address"
(Roosevelt), 82–86
Fly-Tox advertisement, 72–75
Focus, 16, 28
Forms of writing, 7, 8–12
reader-oriented, 10, 57–97
topic-oriented, 10–12, 99–352
writer-oriented, 8–9, 25–55
Franklin, Benjamin, 61
Frenchmen, photos of, 249, 252
Freud, Sigmund, 4

Gass, W. H., 30–31, 42
Goebbels, Joseph, 253
"Gorgias" (Plato), 165–168

Gould, Jack, 289–290
Gould, Stephen Jay, 169, 170–177
Greenspan, Sam, 251
"Growing Up" (Baker), 45–47

Hagman, Larry, 142
Handke, Peter, 28–29, 31
Hanzlicek, C. G., 352
Hard Times (Dickens), 121
Hemingway, Ernest, 37–40, 79, 81
Henfrey, Colin, 259
Hodgson, Godfrey, 270–271
Hogan, Candace Lyle, 61–62
Hogarth, William, 126–129
Housman, A. E., 345
"How I Write" (Moonstone), 65
"How to Make a Lightning Rod"
(Franklin), 61
Howell, Richard, 262
"Humanitarian Theory of Pun-
ishment, The" (Lewis),
213–220
"Humphrey Nominated . . ."
(Lukas), 278–283
Hypothesis, and synthesis, 235–
246, 293

Ibsen, Henrik, 82
"Iguana, The" (Dinesen), 53–54
In Memoriam A. H. H. (Tenny-
son), 344
"In Memory of My Dear Grand-
child Elizabeth Bradstreet"
(Bradstreet), 344
Interviews, 255–264
examples of, 256–264
suggestions for, 255–256
by students at the University of
Oklahoma, 260–264
"Ip Gissa Gul" (Booth), 101–102,
103
"Is Success Dangerous to Your
Health?" (Ehrenreich),
259

Jonson, Ben, 343
Journalism, objective and subjective, 264–292

Joyce, James, 131–132

Keaton, Buster, 138
Kinneavy, James L., 86
Klein, Robert, 261

"La Gioconda" (Pater), 140–142
"Landscape with the Fall of
    Icarus" (Williams), 230
Language, 2–4, 53
"Last of the Mohicans, The"
    (Crane), 223–225
Leonardo da Vinci, 141
Letters
  of application, writing, 89, 91,
    93
  writing, 21–23
Levine, Philip, 351
Lewis, C. S., 213–220, 221
Lincoln, Abraham, 145, 184–191
London street scene, 129, 130
"Looking at Pictures To Be Put
    Away" (Snyder), 50
"Looking for My Mother"
    (Barthes), 50
Lover's Discourse, A (Barthes),
    35–36
Lukas, J. Anthony, 278–283
Lynd, Helen, 103, 154–157
Lynd, Robert, 103, 154–157

MacNelly, Jeff, 228
Mad magazine, 142
Mailer, Norman, 271–278
Man Made Language (Spender),
    178–182
Manscape (Henfrey), 259
Marlboro Man, 77–79
Martineau, Pierre, 77, 79
"Mayor Daley's Troops"
    (Canham), 268–270
Mead, Margaret, 43–45, 47, 103,
    108–111
Menninger, Karl, 206–213, 220,
    221
Merwin, W. S., 67–70
"Miami and the Siege of Chi-
    cago" (Mailer), 271–278

"Mid-August at Sourdough
    Mountain Lookout" (Sny-
    der), 32
Middletown (Lynd), 103, 153–154
Mingo, Norman, 142
"Mona Lisa," 140, 141
Moonstone, Ashley, 65–66
Morvey, Lester, 251
Motivation in Advertising (Marti-
    neau), 77
Ms. Magazine, 259–260
Murderer, photo of a, 249
"Musée des Beaux Arts"
    (Auden), 228, 230
My Philosophical Development Rus-
    sell), 162

Narration, 11, 17, 100–124
  in biography, 117–124
  in cartoons, 101–103
  vs. description, 101, 125
  and directive writing, 101
  of an event, 112–116
  in fiction, 100
  order in, 100
  organization by time, 11, 17,
    100–124
  process, 101, 104–108, 108–112
  in speech, 100
  technical, 100–101
  tense, 101, 103–104
  in thought, 100
  types of, 100–101
  writing, 102–103, 104, 105–
    106, 107–108, 112, 116,
    124
"Natchez Trace, The" (Welty),
    134–137
Nation of Strangers, A (Packard), 147
Neuman, Alfred E., 142
New York Times, The, 278–283,
    289–292
New York Times Cook Book, The,
    58–60
"Night of Raging Protest, A"
    (Davis), 283–289
"Ninety Second Test, The"
    (Nyad and Hogan), 61–62

"Noon" (Hogarth), 126, 127
  description of, 126, 128–129
Nyad, Diana, 61–62

O Pioneers! (Cather), 132–133
"Occurrence at Owl Creek
    Bridge, An" (Bierce), 103–
    104
"On Being Blue" (Gass), 30–31
"On Carving Crystal" (Theophi-
    lus), 60–61
"On My First Son" (Jonson), 343
On Press (Wicker), 264–267
Order, 100
Organization, in writing, 11, 53,
    246
  of data, 144–161
  by logic, 11
  by space, 11
  of space, 125–143
  by time, 11, 17, 53
Orwell, George, 129, 131
Out of Africa (Dinesen), 53–54
Outlines, 18, 177, 190, 222, 246

Packard, Vance, 147, 148
Page, Bruce, 270–271
Pater, Walter, 140–142, 143
Perception, 125, 126, 129
Persuasion, 10, 68, 71–97
  in advertising, 72–75, 76–81,
    163
  vs. argumentation, 12, 162, 163
  political, 81–87
  and synthesis, 245
  See also Reader-oriented forms
    of writing
Picture Palace (Theroux), 247
Plath, Sylvia, 33
Plato, 144, 165–168
Point of view, 125–126, 129, 131
Potter, Jane, 263
Power (Russell), 158, 159–160
Prewriting, 16–18, 144, 246
Process narration
  of a day, 108–112
  familiar, 104–106
  natural, 106–108

Proofreading, 20
Pseudodirection, 67–70
Purpose, and description, 126

Ransom, John Crowe, 346
Reader, 6, 17–18
Reader-oriented forms of writing,
    10, 57–97
  direction, 10, 58–70
  persuasion, 10, 68, 71–97
  practice in writing, 63–68,
    75–77, 79, 81, 87–89, 93,
    96–97
Receiver, in communication, 6
Reflection, 9, 41–55
  on experience, 53–55
  on photographs, 49–52
  on previous writing, 42
  on school days, 43–48
  as revision, 43
  See also Writer-oriented forms of
    writing
"Refusal to Mourn the Death, by
    Fire, of a Child in London,
    A" (Thomas), 346–347
Renaissance, The (Pater), 141–142
Research, 144, 246, 342
  and classification, 223
  play and, 145
  and synthesis, 246, 255–256
"Restaurant, A" (Joyce), 131–132
Résumé, writing a, 89, 93
Revising, 19–20, 42–43, 64
"Ricky" (Levine), 348–351
Road to Wigan Pier, The (Orwell),
    131
Roethke, Theodore, 348
"Room, A" (Orwell), 131
Roosevelt, Franklin D., 81–87
Roulette players, photos of, 250,
    253
Russell, Bertrand, 158–160, 161,
    162–163, 254
Ryle, Gilbert, 164

Sartre, Jean-Paul, 20
Saturday's Child (Seed), 258–259
Seed, Suzanne, 258–259

Selection, in description, 125
Self, the
    as object, 41–55
    as subject, 26–40
"Self-Accusation" (Handke), 29
Sender, in communication, 6
Sentence structure, and writing, 7
Shaw, Donna, 264
"Simulacra" (Cortázar), 112–
    115, 116
Six-Gun Mystique, The (Cawelti),
    293–307
Snyder, Gary, 32, 50, 51
Socrates, 165, 168–169
"Some Notes on River Country"
    (Welty), 134–137
Space, organization of, in descrip-
    tion, 125–126, 129, 133–
    134
Speaking, writing and, 3–4
"Speech at Cooper Union, New
    York" (Lincoln), 184–189
Spender, Dale, 178–182, 183
Statistics, in argumentation, 190–
    205
Stewart, George, 106–107
Symbolism, from description to,
    140–142
Synthesis, 12, 245–352
    and analysis, 222–223, 245, 246
    and argumentation, 245, 246
    and the elegy, 342–352
    meaning of, 12, 245–246
    of objective and subjective jour-
        nalism, 264–292
    and persuasion, 245
    of pictures and captions, 246–
        254
    practice in writing, 245–246,
        246–254, 255–264, 267–
        292, 292–342, 342–352
    and research, 246, 255–256
    and thesis, 245–246, 343
    and the Western, 292–342
    of work and writing, 255–264

Tenant farmworker, photo of, 252
Tennyson, Alfred, Lord, 344

Terkel, Studs, 255–258
Text, 7, 8
Theophilus, 60–61
Theory of Discourse, A (Kin-
    neavy), 86
Theroux, Paul, 247
Thesis
    and analysis, 223
    in argumentation, 12, 17, 162–
        163, 164, 184, 223
    and synthesis, 245–246, 343
Thomas, Dylan, 347
Time
    management of, 53
    organization of, 11, 17, 100–
        124
"To an Athlete Dying Young"
    (Housman), 345
Topic, 7, 16–17, 43, 76
Topic-oriented forms of writing,
    10–12, 99–352
    analysis, 12, 222–244
    argumentation, 12, 17, 162–221
    classification, 11, 144–161
    description, 11, 125–143
    narration, 11, 110–124
    synthesis, 12, 245–352
    See also Analysis; Argumenta-
        tion; Classification; De-
        scription; Narration; Syn-
        thesis
"Town, A" (Dickens), 132
"TV: A Chilling Spectacle in Chi-
    cago" (Gould), pp. 289–
    290
"TV Commercials That Move
    Merchandise" (Wright),
    148–152

Ulysses (Joyce), 131–132
"Unchopping a Tree" (Merwin),
    68–70

"Vacation in Aruba . . .," 76–77

Ways of Seeing (Berger), 234–236
"We Real Cool" (Brooks), 48–49
Welty, Eudora, 134–137, 137–138

Weimersheimer, Monica, 231–233

White, E. B., 104–105

Wicker, Tom, 264–265

Williams, William Carlos, 230

Women, census data on, 201–205

Words, 2, 3, 7

Working (Terkel), 255–258

Wright, John W., 148–152

Writer, 6, 17–18, 20–21, 27

Writer-oriented forms of writing, 8–9, 25–55

   expression, 9, 26–40

   practice in writing, 28, 29–30, 31, 34, 36, 40, 43, 47–48, 49, 51–52, 54–55

   reflection, 9, 41–55

Writing

   act of, 15–20

     drafting, 18–19

     prewriting, 16–18

     revising, 19–20

   as communication, 3–4, 6–7

   directive, 101

   as expression, 26–27

   forms of, 7, 8–12

   as a human act, 1–23

   reading as an aid to, 13–14

   situation, 6–8

   speaking and, 3–6

   See also Reader-oriented forms of writing; Topic-oriented forms of writing; Writer-oriented forms of writing; Writing situation

Writing process, the open-ended, 27–28

Writing situation, 6–8

   diagram of the 6, 8

   reader, 6

   text and, 7, 8

   topic and, 7

   words and, 7

   writer, 6

"Writing with Power" (Elbow), 27–28

Zweig, Zoltan, 250